HUMAN RELATIONS
FOR CAREER
AND PERSONAL SUCCESS

FIFTH EDITION

HUMAN RELATIONS
FOR CAREER
AND PERSONAL SUCCESS

FIFTH EDITION

Andrew J. DuBrin
Rochester Institute of Technology

Prentice Hall
Upper Saddle River, New Jersey 07458

Library of Congress Cataloging-in-Publication Data

DuBrin, Andrew J.
    Human relations for career and personal success / Andrew J.
DuBrin.—5th ed.
        p.   cm.
    Includes bibliographical references and indexes.
    ISBN 0-13-924663-0
        1. Success in business.   2. Organizational behavior.
    3. Psychology, Industrial.   4. Interpersonal relations.   I. Title.
    HF5386.D768   1999
    650.1'3—dc20

                                                                CIP

Acquisitions editor: *Elizabeth Sugg*
Editorial Assistant: *Maria Kirk*
Manufacturing manager: *Ed O'Dougherty*
Director of Production and Manufacturing: *Bruce Johnson*
Production management/Composition: *North Market Street Graphics*
Editorial/production supervision: *Mary Carnis*
Interior Design: *Miguel Ortiz*
Creative Director: *Marianne Fraseo*
Cover Design: *Miguel Ortiz*
Cover Art: *Celia Johnson*

 © 1999, 1996 by Prentice-Hall, Inc.
Simon & Schuster/A Viacom Company
Upper Saddle River, New Jersey 07458

ISBN 0-13-924663-0

Printed in the United States of America
10 9 8 7 6 5 4 3 2 1

Prentice-Hall International (UK) Limited, *London*
Prentice-Hall of Australia Pty. Limited, *Sydney*
Prentice-Hall Canada Inc., *Toronto*
Prentice-Hall Hispanoamericana, S.A., *Mexico*
Prentice-Hall of India Private Limited, *New Delhi*
Prentice-Hall of Japan, Inc., *Tokyo*
Simon & Schuster Asia Pte. Ltd., *Singapore*
Editora Prentice-Hall do Brasil, Ltda., *Rio de Janeiro*

CONTENTS

PART 2: DEALING EFFECTIVELY WITH PEOPLE

PART 3: DEVELOPING CAREER THRUST

PART 4: MANAGING YOUR PERSONAL LIFE

PREFACE

Welcome to the fifth edition of *Human Relations for Career and Personal Success*. The purpose of this book is to show you how you can become more effective in your work and personal life through knowledge of and skill in human relations. A major theme of this text is that career and personal success are related. Success on the job often enhances personal success, and success in personal life can enhance job success. Dealing effectively with people is an enormous asset in both work and personal life.

One major audience for this book is students who will meet human relations problems on the job and in personal life. The text is designed for human relations courses taught in colleges, career schools, vocational-technical schools, and other postsecondary schools. Another major audience for this book is managerial, professional, and technical workers who are forging ahead in their careers.

 ## ORGANIZATION OF THE BOOK

The text is divided into four parts, reflecting the major issues in human relations. Part I covers four aspects of understanding and managing yourself: Chapter 1 focuses on self-understanding and the interrelationship of career and personal success; Chapter 2 explains how to use goal setting and other methods of self-motivation to improve your chances for success; Chapter 3 explains the basics of solving problems and making decisions with an emphasis on creativity; Chapter 4 deals with achieving wellness and managing stress; and Chapter 5 focuses on dealing with personal problems such as substance abuse, counterproductive habits, and other forms of self-defeating behavior.

Part II examines the heart of human relations—dealing effectively with other people. The topics in Chapters 6 through 9 are, respectively, communicating with people, handling conflict with others and being assertive, getting along with your manager, and getting along with your coworkers and customers.

Part III provides information to help career-minded people capitalize on their educations, experiences, talents, and ambitions. The topics of Chapters 10 through 13 are: choosing a career and developing a portfolio career; finding a suitable job, developing good work habits, and getting ahead in your career. Chapter 14 is about the related topics of developing self-confidence and becoming a leader.

Part IV, "Managing Your Personal Life," is divided into two chapters. Chapter 15 offers realistic advice on managing personal finances. Chapter 16 describes how to enhance social and family life, including how to find happiness, new friends, and keep a personal relationship vibrant.

Human Relations for Career and Personal Success is both a text and workbook of experiential exercises, including role plays and self-assessment exercises. (An experiential exercise allows for learning by doing, along with guided instruction.) Each chapter contains one or more exercises and ends with a human relations case problem. The experiential exercises can all be completed during a class session. In addition, they emphasize human interaction and thinking and minimize paperwork.

CHANGES IN THE FIFTH EDITION

The fifth edition reflects several significant changes along with an updating and selective pruning of previous editions, and expansion of others. The text has a more explicit skill-building emphasis, with each chapter containing at least one human relations skill-building exercise. Each chapter now begins with a lead-in case illustrating a major point in the chapter.

Chapter 1 contains more information on the development of self-esteem. Chapter 2 describes how to develop the self-discipline necessary to achieve goals and stay motivated. Chapter 16 now has a much stronger emphasis on achieving happiness, including the five principles of psychological functioning. New or expanded computer-related topics in the text are job finding through the Internet and using an electronic résumé, repetitive-motion disorders, on-line addictions, and information technology and communication. Other new topics include gender differences in communication style, managing conflict through cognitive restructuring, the portfolio career, the T-form cover letter, downshifting, dealing with a micromanaging supervisor, and a biochemical explanation for mutual attraction.

Several more complex cases have been added, many self-assessment exercises have been revised and many new ones added. Over 50 percent of the cases and examples are new.

INSTRUCTOR'S MANUAL AND TEST BANK

The instructor's manual for this text contains over 750 test questions, chapter outline and lecture notes, answers to discussion questions and case problems, and comments about the exercises. Computerized test banks, known as the Prentice Hall Test Manager, also accompany the text.

In addition, the manual includes step-by-step instruction for the use of Computer-Assisted Scenario Analysis (CASA).

CASA is a user-friendly way of using any word processing program with any computer to assist in analyzing cases. The student enters an existing case into the computer, and then analyzes it by answering the case questions in the text. Next, the student makes up a new scenario or adds a new twist to the case, and enters this scenario in **bold** into the case. The case questions are reanalyzed in light of this new scenario. Any changes in the answers are **printed in bold.** CASA gives the student experience in a creative application of word processing. Equally important, it helps students develop a "what-if" point of view in solving human relations problems.

INFORMATION ON SCANS REQUIREMENTS

In 1990, the Secretary's Commission on Achieving Necessary Skills (SCANS) was formed to encourage a high-performance economy characterized by high-skills, high-wage employment. To help achieve this goal, the Commission recommended that postsecondary schools teach five competencies and a three-part foundation of skills and personal qualities needed for job performance.

The competencies state that effective workers can productively use resources, interpersonal skills, information, systems, and technology. In addition, the foundation competence requires basic skills (such as reading, writing, and arithmetic), thinking skills (such as thinking creatively), and personal qualities (such as self-management and integrity)

Human Relations for Career and Personal Success provides information and exercises directly aimed at satisfying components of five of the above eight requirements (information, systems, and technology are ordinarily taught outside of a human relations curriculum). A guide to meeting the SCANS requirement is presented next.

COMPETENCIES: EFFECTIVE WORKERS CAN PRODUCTIVELY USE

- *Resources: allocating time, money, materials, space, and staff.* Chapter 12, about developing good work habits, deals directly with allocating time.

- *Interpersonal Skills: working on teams, teaching others, serving customers, leading, negotiating, and working well with people from culturally diverse backgrounds.* Chapter 9, about getting along with coworkers and customers, contains information about working on teams, helping teammates, and getting along well with people from culturally diverse backgrounds. Chapter 14, about developing self-confidence and becoming a leader, deals directly with leading. Chapter 7, about handling conflict and being assertive, deals directly with negotiation.

- *Basic Skills: reading, writing, arithmetic and mathematics, speaking and listening.*   Chapter 6, about communicating with people, provides suggestions for improved speaking and listening.

- *Thinking Skills: thinking creatively, making decisions, solving problems, seeing things in the mind's eye, knowing how to learn, and reasoning.*   Chapter 3, about solving problems and making decisions, deals directly with creative thinking, decision making, and problem solving. "Seeing things in the mind's eye" comes under the topic of visualization, which is described in several contexts: stress reduction, overcoming self-defeating behavior, and developing self-confidence.

- *Personal Qualities: individual responsibility, self-esteem, sociability, self-management and integrity.*   Chapter 1, about human relations and yourself, deals extensively with the development of self-esteem. Chapter 9, about getting along with coworkers and customers, deals directly with sociability. Chapter 2 is about self-motivation and goal setting, and thus deals directly with self-management.

ACKNOWLEDGMENTS

A book of this nature cannot be written and published without the cooperation of many people. My thanks go first to my editorial and production team at Prentice Hall Business Studies—Elizabeth Sugg, Maria Kirk, Mary Carnis, and Judy Casillo, along with Christine Ducker of North Market Street Graphics. My outside reviewers of this and the previous editions provided many constructive suggestions for improving the book. By name they are:

Mary D. Aun, DeVry Technical Institute

Donna Ana Branch and H. Ralph Todd, Jr., American River College

Hollis Chaleau Brown, Oakton Community College

Sheri Bryant, DeKalb Technical Institute

Win Chesney, St. Louis Community College

Ruth Keller, Indiana Vo-Tech College

Robert F. Pearse, Rochester Institute of Technology

Bernice Rose, Computer Learning Center

Pamela Simon, Baker College

Thanks also to my family members, friends, and acquaintances whose emotional support and encouragement assist my writing.

Andrew J. DuBrin
Rochester, New York

ABOUT THE AUTHOR

An accomplished author, Andrew J. DuBrin, Ph.D., brings to his work years of research experience in business psychology. His research has been reported in *Psychology Today, The Wall Street Journal*, and over 100 national magazines and local newspapers. An active speaker, Dr. DuBrin has appeared as a guest on over 350 radio and television shows. He has published numerous articles, textbooks, and well-publicized professional books. Dr. DuBrin received his Ph.D. from Michigan State University and is currently teaching leadership and organizational behavior at the Rochester Institute of Technology.

To Rosie,
the first of the new generation

HUMAN RELATIONS AND YOURSELF

Learning Objectives

After studying the information and doing the exercises in this chapter, you should be able to:

▼ Explain the meaning of human relations

▼ Pinpoint how work and personal life influence each other

▼ Explain how the self-concept influences behavior

▼ Summarize the nature and consequences of self-esteem

▼ Describe how to enhance self-esteem

▼ Recognize the dangers of preoccupation with the self

*L*inda, a restaurant manager, is a likable person who interacts well with people both on and off the job. She is only twenty-two years old, while several of the people who report to her are in their mid-twenties. As one of them puts it, "Who cares if Linda is young? The woman is a natural leader." Despite Linda's nontraditional working hours, she has many friends with whom she shares her free time. Her friends include those who

work during the day and those who work at night. They are particularly impressed with her smooth and confident manner and her ability to be a good listener at the same time.

The person just described tells us something about the meaning of human relations. Linda is effective with people in both work and personal settings. In the context used here, **human relations** is the art of using systematic knowledge about human behavior to improve personal, job, and career effectiveness. In other words, you can accomplish more in dealing with people in both personal and work life. You can do so by relying on guidelines developed by psychologists, counselors, and other human relations specialists.

This book presents a wide variety of suggestions and guidelines for improving your personal relationships both on and off the job. Most of them are based on systematic knowledge about human behavior. Our main concern, however, will be with the suggestions and guidelines themselves, not the methods by which these ideas were discovered.

HOW WORK AND PERSONAL LIFE INFLUENCE EACH OTHER

Most people reading this book will be doing so to improve their careers. Therefore, the book centers around relationships with people in a job setting. Keep in mind that human relationships in work and personal life have much in common. A study based on a nationwide sample supports the close relationship between job satisfaction and life satisfaction. The study also found that both job satisfaction and life satisfaction influence each other. Life satisfaction significantly influenced job satisfaction, and job satisfaction significantly influenced life satisfaction. The relationship between job and life satisfaction is particularly strong at a given time in a person's life. However, being satisfied with your job today has a smaller effect on future life satisfaction.[1]

Work and personal life influence each other in a number of specific ways. First, the satisfactions you achieve on the job contribute to your general life satisfactions. Conversely, if you suffer from chronic job dissatisfaction, your life satisfaction will begin to decline. Career disappointments have been shown to cause marital relationships to suffer. Frustrated on the job, many people start feuding with their partners and other family members.

Second, an unsatisfying job can also affect physical health, primarily by creating stress and burnout. Intense job dissatisfaction may even lead to heart disease, ulcers, intestinal disorders, and skin problems. People who have high job satisfaction even tend to live longer than those who suffer from prolonged job dissatisfaction. Finding the right type of job may thus add years to a person's life.

Third, the quality of your relationships with people in work and personal life influence each other. If you experience intense conflict in your family, you might be so upset that you will be unable to form good relationships with coworkers. Conversely, if you have a healthy, rewarding personal life, it will be easier for you to form good relationships on the job. People you meet on the job will find it pleasant to relate to a seemingly positive and untroubled person.

Personal relationships on the job also influence personal relationships off the job. Interacting harmoniously with coworkers can put one in a better mood for dealing with family and friends after hours. Crossing swords with employees and customers during working hours can make it difficult for you to feel comfortable and relaxed with people off the job.

Fourth, certain skills contribute to success in both work and personal life. For example, people who know how to deal effectively with others and get things accomplished on the job can use the same skills to enhance their personal lives. Similarly, people who are effective in dealing with friends and family members, and who can organize things, are likely to be effective supervisors.

Can you think of any other ways in which success in work and personal life are related to each other?

Another way of understanding how work life and personal life influence each other is to be aware of what employers are doing to help workers balance work and family demands. During the last decade, companies have established a variety of programs that make it easier for employees to meet the demands of career and personal life. A major rationale for these programs is that workers who have their personal lives under control can concentrate better at work. As a result, they will be more productive. In addition, workers who have family obligations running smoothly, will attend work more regularly. The challenge of balancing work and family demands is particularly intense for employees who are part of a two-wage-earner family, a group that includes 80 percent of the workforce in the United States and Canada.

Eddie Bauer, the casual-lifestyle retailer, is an example of a company that recognizes the close connection between work and personal life. Balance between home and work is a strong corporate value at Eddie Bauer. The company uses its work/life programs to help its associates (the company term for employee) lead more productive and balanced lives. Management at Eddie Bauer believes that physical and mental fitness contribute to a productive and satisfied workforce. The various programs help associates be more focused at work because they know resources are available to help them manage the demands of their personal lives. Over the past several years, the company has introduced more than 20 programs to help associates run their personal lives more smoothly. Among these programs are the following:

- Balance Day—a free day intended for associates to schedule a "call in well" absence, once a year

- Paid parental leave—allows mothers and fathers to take care of newborn children, or sick children of any age

- Customized Work Environment program—offers associates such options as job sharing (two people share one job), a compressed work week (such as working 40 hours in 4 days), and working at home[2]

Many other companies offer similar programs on a more modest scale. All of these programs are a way of recognizing that workers with personal lives under control can be happier and work more productively. The company cannot eliminate all personal strife, but it can offer assistance in a few important areas.

 ## HUMAN RELATIONS BEGINS WITH SELF-UNDERSTANDING

Before you can understand other people very well, you must understand yourself. All readers of this book already know something about themselves. An important starting point in learning more about yourself is self-examination. Suppose that instead of being about human relations, this book were about dancing. The reader would obviously need to know what other dancers do right and wrong. But the basic principles of dancing cannot be fully grasped unless they are seen in relation to your own style of dancing. Watching a videotape of your dancing, for example, would be helpful. You might also ask other people for comments and suggestions about your dance movements.

Similarly, to achieve **self-understanding,** you must gather valid information about yourself. (Self-understanding refers to knowledge about yourself, particularly with respect to mental and emotional aspects.) Every time you read a self-help book, take a personality quiz, or receive an evaluation of your work from a manager or instructor, you are gaining some self-knowledge.

In achieving self-understanding, it is helpful to recognize that the **self** is a complex idea. It generally refers to a person's total being or individuality. However, a distinction is sometimes made between the self a person projects to the outside world, and the inner self. The **public self** is what the person is communicating about himself or herself, and what others actually perceive about the person. The **private self** is the actual person that you may be.[3] A similar distinction is made between the real and the ideal self. Many people think of themselves in terms of an ideal version of what they are really like. To avoid making continuous distinctions between the various selves throughout this text, we will use the term *self* to refer to an accurate representation of the individual.

Because an entire chapter is devoted to the self, it does not imply that the other chapters do not deal with the self. Most of this text is geared toward using human relations knowledge for self-development and self-improvement. Throughout the text you will find questionnaires designed to improve insight. The self-knowledge emphasized here deals with psychological (such as personality traits and thinking style) rather than physical characteristics (such as height and blood pressure).

Here we discuss six types of information that contribute to self-understanding.

1. General information about human behavior

2. Informal feedback from people

3. Feedback from superiors

4. Feedback from coworkers

5. Feedback from self-examination exercises

6. Insights gathered in psychotherapy and counseling

General Information about Human Behavior

As you learn about people in general, you should also be gaining knowledge about yourself. Therefore, most of the information in this text is presented in a form that should be useful to you personally. Whenever general information is presented, it is your responsibility to relate such information to your particular situation. Chapter 7, for example, discusses some causes of conflicts in personal relationships. One such general cause is limited resources; that is, not everyone can have what he or she wants. See how this general principle applies to you. An example involving others is, "That's why I've been so angry with Melissa lately. She was the one given the promotion, while I'm stuck in the same old job."

In relating facts and observations about people in general to yourself, be careful not to misapply the information. Feedback from other people will help you avoid the pitfalls of introspection (looking into yourself).

Informal Feedback from People

As just implied, **feedback** is information that tells you how well you have performed. You can sometimes obtain feedback from the spontaneous comments of others, or by asking them for feedback. A materials-handling specialist grew one notch in self-confidence when coworkers began to call him, "Lightning." He was given this name because of the rapidity with which he processes orders. His experience illustrates that a valuable source of information for self-understanding is what the significant people in your life think of you. Although feedback of this type might make you feel uncomfortable, when it is consistent, it accurately reflects how you are perceived by others.

With some ingenuity you can create informal feedback. (In this sense, the term *formal* refers to not being part of a company-sponsored program.) A student enrolled in a human relations course obtained valuable information about himself from a questionnaire he sent to 15 people. His directions were:

> I am hoping that you can help me with one of the most important assignments of my life. I want to obtain a candid picture of how I am seen by others—what they think are my strengths, areas for improvement, good points, and bad points. Any other observations about me as an individual would also be welcome.
>
> Write down your thoughts on the enclosed sheet of paper. The information that you provide me will help me develop a plan for personal improvement that I am writing for a course in human relations. Mail the form back to me in the enclosed envelope. It is not necessary for you to sign the form.

A few skeptics will argue that friends never give you a true picture of yourself but, rather, say flattering things about you because they value your friendship. Experience has shown, however, that if you emphasize the importance of their opinions, most people will give you a few constructive suggestions. You also have to appear and be sincere. Since not everyone's comments will be helpful, you may have to sample many people.

FEEDBACK FROM SUPERIORS

Virtually all employers provide employees with formal and/or informal feedback on their performances. A formal method of feedback is called a *performance appraisal*. During a performance appraisal your superior will convey to you what he or she thinks you are doing well and not so well. These observations become a permanent part of your personnel record. Informal feedback occurs when a superior discusses your job performance with you but does not record these observations.

The feedback obtained from superiors in this way can help you learn about yourself. For instance, if two different bosses say that you are a creative problem solver, you might conclude that you are creative. If several bosses told you that you are too impatient with other people, you might conclude that you are impatient.

Given that work life consumes so much of a working adult's time, it becomes a valuable source of information about the self. Many people, in fact, establish much of their identity from their occupations. Next time you are at a social gathering, ask a person "What do you do?" Most likely, the person will respond in terms of an occupation or a company affiliation. It is a rare person in our culture who responds, "I sleep, I eat, I watch television, and I talk to friends."

FEEDBACK FROM COWORKERS

A growing practice in organizations is **peer evaluations,** a system in which coworkers contribute to an evaluation of a person's job performance. Although coworkers under this system do not have total responsibility for evaluating each other, their input is taken seriously. The amount of a worker's salary increase could thus be affected by peer judgments about his or her performance. The results of peer evaluations can also be used as feedback for learning about yourself. Assume that coworkers agree on several of your strengths and needs for improvement. You can conclude that you are generally perceived that way by others who work closely with you.

Customer service technicians (people who service and repair photocopying machines) at Xerox Corporation use an elaborate system of peer evaluations. A group of peers indicates whether a particular aspect of job performance or behavior is a strength or a **developmental opportunity.** A developmental opportunity is a positive way of stating that a person has a weakness. The five factors rated by peers are shown in Exhibit 1-1. The initials under "Peer Evaluations" are those of the coworkers who are doing the evaluations. The person being rated thus knows who to thank (or kick) for the feedback.

In addition to indicating whether a job factor is a strength or an opportunity, raters can supply comments and developmental suggestions. For example, CJ made the following written comment about Leslie Fantasia: "Missed 50 percent of our work group meetings. Attend work group member training and review our work group meeting ground rules."

FEEDBACK FROM SELF-ASSESSMENT EXERCISES

Many self-help books, including this one, contain questionnaires that you fill out by yourself, for yourself. The information that you pick up from these questionnaires often provides valuable clues to your preferences, values, and personal traits. Such self-examination questionnaires should not be confused with the scientifically researched test you might take in a counseling center or guidance department, or when applying for a job.

The amount of useful information gained from self-examination questionnaires depends on your candor. Since no outside judge is involved in these self-help quizzes, candor is usually not a problem. An exception is that we all have certain blind spots. Most people, for example, believe that they have considerably above-average skills in dealing with people.

As a starting point in conducting self-examination exercises, do Human Relations Self-Assessment Exercise 1-1. The exercise will help get you into the self-examination mode.

INSIGHTS GATHERED IN PSYCHOTHERAPY AND COUNSELING

Many people seek self-understanding through discussions with a psychotherapist or other mental health counselor. **Psychotherapy** is a

---

EXHIBIT 1-1

PEER EVALUATION OF CUSTOMER SERVICE TECHNICIAN

PERSON EVALUATED: Leslie Fantasia

Skill Categories and Expected Behaviors	Peer Evaluations for Each Category and Behavior					
	TR	JP	CK	JT	CJ	ML
Customer Care						
Takes ownership for customer problems	O	S	S	S	S	S
Follows through on customer commitments	S	S	S	S	S	S
Technical Knowledge and Skill						
Engages in continuous learning to update technical skills	O	S	S	S	S	O
Corrects problems on the first visit	O	O	S	S	S	S
Work Group Support						
Actively participates in work group meetings	S	S	S	S	O	S
Backs up other work group members by taking calls in other areas	S	O	O	S	S	S
Minimal absence	S	O	S	S	O	S
Finance Management						
Adhere to work group parts expense process	S	S	S	O	S	S
Pass truck audits	S	S	S	O	S	S

NOTE: S refers to a strength, O refers to developmental opportunity.

---

method of overcoming emotional problems through discussion with a mental health professional. However, many people enter into psychotherapy with the primary intention of gaining insight into themselves. A representative area of insight would be for the therapist to help the client detect patterns of self-defeating behavior. For example, some people unconsciously do something to ruin a personal relationship or perform poorly on the job just when things are going well. The therapist might point out this self-defeating pattern of behavior. Self-insight of this kind often—but not always—leads to useful changes in behavior.

HUMAN RELATIONS SELF-ASSESSMENT EXERCISE 1-1

The Written Self-Portrait

A good starting point in acquiring serious self-knowledge is to prepare a written self-portrait in the major life spheres (or aspects). In each of the spheres listed below, describe yourself in about 25–50 words. For example, under the social and interpersonal sphere, a person might write: "I'm a little timid on the surface. But those people who get to know me well understand that I'm filled with enthusiasm and joy. My relationships with people last a long time. I'm on excellent terms with all members of my family. And my significant other and I have been together for five years. We are very close emotionally, and should be together for a lifetime.

A. *Occupational and School:*

_____

_____

_____

_____

B. *Social and Interpersonal:*

_____

_____

_____

_____

C. *Beliefs, Values, and Attitudes:*

_____

_____

_____

_____

D. *Physical Description (body type, appearance, grooming):*

_____

_____

_____

_____

YOUR SELF-CONCEPT: WHAT YOU THINK OF YOU

Another aspect of self-understanding is the **self-concept,** or the way a person thinks about himself or herself in an overall sense. You might also look on the self-concept as what you think of you and who you think you are. The self-concept is an important part of personality development, including a person's key self-feelings and self-attitudes.[4] A successful person—one who is achieving his or her goals in work or personal life—usually has a positive self-concept. In contrast, an unsuccessful person often has a negative self-concept. Such differences in self-concept can have a profound influence on your career. If you see yourself as a successful person, you will tend to engage in activities that will help you prove yourself right. Similarly, if you have a limited view of yourself, you will tend to engage in activities that prove yourself right. For example, you may often look for convenient ways to prevent yourself from succeeding.

Self-concepts are based largely on what others have said about us. If enough people tell you that you are "terrific," after a while you will have the self-concept of a terrific person. When people tell you that you are not a worthwhile person, after a while your self-concept will become that of a not worthwhile person. People who say "I'm OK" are expressing a positive self-concept. People who say "I'm not OK" have a negative self-concept.

Another important fact about the self-concept is that it usually has several components. Many people, for example, have an academic self-concept and a nonacademic self-concept.[5] One person might feel proud and confident in a classroom yet quite humble and shaky on the job. Another person might feel unsure and uneasy in the classroom yet proud and con-

MANY PEOPLE HAVE AN ACADEMIC SELF-CONCEPT
AND A NONACADEMIC SELF-CONCEPT

fident on the job. Following the same logic, a person's self-concept with respect to personal life may differ from his or her career self-concept.

THE SELF-CONCEPT AND SELF-CONFIDENCE

A strong self-concept leads to self-confidence, which has many important implications for job performance. People who are confident in themselves are more effective in leadership and sales positions. Self-confident workers are also more likely to set higher goals for themselves, and persist in trying to reach their goals.[6]

Why some people develop strong self-concepts and self-confidence while others have weak self-concepts and self-confidence is not entirely known. One contributing factor may be inherited talents and abilities. Assume that a person quickly learns how to perform key tasks in life such as walking, talking, swimming, running, reading, writing, computing, and driving a car. This person is likely to be more self-confident than a person who struggled to learn these skills.

Another contributing factor to a positive self-concept and self-confidence is lifelong feedback from others (as previously mentioned). If, as a youngster, your parents, siblings, and playmates consistently told you that you were competent, you would probably develop a strong self-concept. However, some people might find you to be conceited.

Self-confidence also contributes heavily to leadership ability. How to build self-confidence will therefore be described in Chapter 14, which deals with becoming a leader.

YOUR BODY IMAGE AS PART OF YOUR SELF-CONCEPT

Our discussion of the self-concept so far has emphasized mental traits and characteristics. Your **body image,** or your perception of your body, also contributes to your self-concept. The current emphasis on physical fitness stems largely from a desire on the part of people to be physically fit and healthy. It is also apparent that being physically fit contributes to a positive self-concept, and being physically unfit can contribute to a negative self-concept. The relationship between the self-concept and physical fitness also works the other way: If your self-concept is positive, it may push you toward physical fitness. Conversely, if you have a negative self-concept, you may allow yourself to become physically unfit.

A distorted body image can result in such severe problems as anorexia nervosa. Anorexic people have such an intense fear of obesity that they undereat to the point of malnutrition and illness. About 5 percent of these people die from their disorder. Having a positive body image is obviously important for personal life. Some people, for example, who are dissatisfied with their bodies will not engage in sports or attend activities where too much of their bodies is revealed. Also, having a positive body image helps you be more confident in making new friends.

A positive body image can also be important on the job. Workers who have a positive body image are likely to feel confident performing jobs that require customer contact, such as sales work. Many firms expect their managers and customer-contact workers to appear physically fit and present a vigorous, healthy appearance. Managers and customer-contact workers with these qualities would generally have positive body images.

GROUP IDENTIFICATION AND THE SELF-CONCEPT

Another important source of the self-concept is the groups people join. According to research by social psychologist Marilynn Brewer, people join small groups to achieve some degree of individuality and identity.[7] People develop much of their self-concepts by comparing their own group to others. The group you identify with becomes part of your psychological self. Joining the group satisfies two conflicting needs. A person wants to retain some individuality, so being a member of a mega-group like students or a General Motors employee does not quite do the job. Yet people also yearn to have some group affiliation. So joining a small group that is distinctive from others is a happy compromise.

The smaller group the person joins becomes part of the self-image and self-concept for many people. A sampling of the groups that could become part of a person's self-concept include athletic teams, church groups, street gangs, motorcycle gangs, a musical band, and an Internet chat room. What group membership do you have that has become part of your self-concept?

THE NATURE AND CONSEQUENCES OF SELF-ESTEEM

Although the various approaches to discussing the self may seem confusing and overlapping, all of them strongly influence your life. A particularly important role is played by **self-esteem,** which refers to appreciating self-worth and importance, being accountable for your own behavior, and acting responsibly toward others.[8] People with positive self-esteem have a deep-down, inside-the-self feeling of their own worth. Consequently, they develop a positive self-concept. Before reading further, you are invited to measure your current level of self-esteem by doing Human Relations Self-Assessment Exercise 1-2. We look next at the nature of self-esteem and many of its consequences.

THE NATURE OF SELF-ESTEEM

The definition just presented tells a lot about self-esteem, yet there is much more to know about its nature. According to Nathaniel Brandon, self-esteem has two interrelated components: self-efficacy and self-respect.[9] **Self-efficacy** is confidence in your ability to carry out a specific task in contrast to generalized self-confidence. When self-efficacy is high, you believe you have the ability to do what is necessary to complete a task suc-

HUMAN RELATIONS SELF-ASSESSMENT EXERCISE 1-2

The Self-Esteem Checklist

Indicate whether each of the following statements is Mostly True or Mostly False, as it applies to you.

	Mostly True	Mostly False
1. I am excited about starting each day.	____	____
2. Most of any progress I have made in my work or school can be attributed to luck.	____	____
3. I often ask myself, "Why can't I be more successful?"	____	____
4. When I'm given a challenging assignment by my manager or team leader, I usually dive in with confidence.	____	____
5. I believe that I am working up to my potential	____	____
6. I am able to set limits to what I will do for others without feeling anxious.	____	____
7. I regularly make excuses for my mistakes.	____	____
8. Someone else's bad mood will affect my good mood.	____	____
9. I care very much how much money other people make, especially when they are working in my field.	____	____
10. I feel like a failure when I do not achieve my goals.	____	____
11. Hard work gives me an emotional lift.	____	____
12. When others compliment me, I doubt their sincerity.	____	____
13. Complimenting others makes me feel uncomfortable.	____	____
14. I find it comfortable to say, "I'm sorry."	____	____
15. It is difficult for me to face up to my mistakes.	____	____
16. My coworkers think I should not be promoted.	____	____
17. People who want to become my friends usually do not have much to offer.	____	____
18. If my manager praised me, I would have a difficult time believing it was deserved.	____	____
19. I'm just an ordinary person.	____	____
20. Having to face change really disturbs me.	____	____

(Continued)

Scoring and Interpretation: The answers in the high self-esteem direction are as follows:

1.	Mostly True	11.	Mostly True
2.	Mostly False	12.	Mostly False
3.	Mostly False	13.	Mostly False
4.	Mostly True	14.	Mostly True
5.	Mostly True	15.	Mostly False
6.	Mostly True	16.	Mostly False
7.	Mostly False	17.	Mostly False
8.	Mostly False	18.	Mostly False
9.	Mostly False	19.	Mostly False
10.	Mostly False	20.	Mostly False

17–20   You have very high self-esteem. Yet if your score is 20, it could be that you are denying any self-doubts.

11–16   Your self-esteem is in the average range. It would probably be worthwhile for you to implement strategies to boost your self-esteem (described in this chapter) so that you can develop a greater feeling of well-being.

0–10   Your self-esteem needs bolstering. Talk over your feelings about yourself with a trusted friend or with a mental health professional. At the same time attempt to implement several of the tactics for boosting self-esteem described in this chapter.

cessfully. Being confident that you can perform a particular task well contributes to self-esteem.

Self-respect, the second component of self-esteem, refers to how you think and feel about yourself. Self-respect fits the everyday meaning of self-esteem. Many street beggars are intelligent, able-bodied, and have a good physical appearance. You could argue that their low self-esteem enables them to beg. Also, people with low self-respect and self-esteem allow themselves to stay in relationships where they are frequently verbally and physically abused. These abused people have such low self-worth they think they deserve punishment.

Part of understanding the nature of self-esteem is knowing how it develops. As with the self-concept, self-esteem comes about from a variety of early-life experiences. People who were encouraged to feel good about themselves and their accomplishments by family members, friends, and teachers are more likely to enjoy high self-esteem. A widespread explanation of self-esteem development is that compliments, praise, and hugs alone build self-esteem. Yet many developmental psychologists seriously question this perspective. Instead, they believe that self-esteem results from accomplishing worthwhile activities, and then feeling proud of these accomplishments. Receiving encouragement, however, can help the person accomplish activities that build self-esteem.

Psychologist Martin Seligman argues that self-esteem is caused by a variety of successes and failures. To develop self-esteem people need to improve their skills for dealing with the world.[10] Self-esteem therefore comes about by genuine accomplishments, followed by praise and recognition. Heaping undeserved praise and recognition on people may lead to a temporary high, but it does not produce genuine self-esteem. The child develops self-esteem not from being told he or she can score a goal in soccer, but from scoring that goal.

THE CONSEQUENCES OF SELF-ESTEEM

One of the major consequences of high self-esteem is good mental health. People with high self-esteem feel good about themselves and have a positive outlook on life. One of the links between good mental health and self-esteem is that high self-esteem helps prevent many situations from being stressful. Few negative comments from others are likely to bother you when your self-esteem is high. A person with low self-esteem might crumble if somebody insulted his or her appearance. A person with high self-esteem might shrug off the insult as simply being the other person's point of view. If faced with an everyday setback such as losing keys, the high self-esteem person might think, "I have so much going for me, why fall apart over this incident?"

Although people with high self-esteem can readily shrug off undeserved insults, they still profit well from negative feedback. Because they are secure, they can profit from the developmental opportunities suggested by negative feedback.

Workers with high self-esteem develop and maintain favorable work attitudes and perform at a high level. These positive consequences take place because such attitudes and behavior are consistent with the personal belief that they are competent individuals. Mary Kay Ash, the legendary founder of a beauty-products company, put it this way, "It never occurred to me I couldn't do it. I always knew that if I worked hard enough, I could." Furthermore, research has shown that high self-esteem individuals value reaching work goals more than do low self-esteem individuals.[11]

A major consequence of low self-esteem is poor mental health. People with low self-esteem are often depressed, and many people who appear to have "paranoid personalities" are suffering from low self-esteem. A store manager who continually accused store associates of talking behind his back finally said to a mental health counselor, "Face it, I think I'm almost worthless, so I think people have negative things to say about me."

School children with low self-esteem are more likely to be delinquents. These same students generally have a poor relationship with teachers and parents.[12] Workers with low self-esteem often develop and maintain unfavorable work attitudes and perform below average. These negative behaviors are consistent with the self-belief that they are people of low competence.[13]

HOW TO ENHANCE SELF-ESTEEM

Improving self-esteem is a lifelong process because self-esteem is related to the success of your activities and interactions with people. Following are five approaches to enhancing self-esteem that are related to how self-esteem develops.

Legitimate Accomplishment and Self-Esteem

To emphasize again, accomplishing worthwhile activities is a major contributor to self-esteem in both children and adults. The comments of columnist Mona Charen support years of psychological research: "Self-esteem does not come in a jar. To be real, self-esteem must be based on something true. A child doesn't get a sense of accomplishment and pride by being told, 'You can ride a bicycle.' She gets it by riding the bike."[14] Similarly, giving people large trophies for mundane accomplishments is unlikely to raise self-esteem. More likely, the person will see through the transparent attempt to build his or her self-esteem and develop negative feelings about the self. What about you? Would your self-esteem receive a bigger boost by (1) receiving an A in a course in which 10 percent of the class received an A, or (2) receiving an A in a class in which everybody received the same grade?

Self-Disclosure and Self-Esteem

One method of increasing your self-esteem is to engage in the right amount of **self-disclosure,** the process of revealing your inner self to others. A person with a high degree of self-disclosure is open, while a person with a low degree of self-disclosure is closed. Self-disclosure assists self-acceptance because revealing more of yourself allows more for others to accept. As acceptance by others increases, so does self-esteem. Conversely, if you keep yourself hidden from others, there is little opportunity to be accepted by them. Keep this sequence of activities in mind: Self-disclosure→self-acceptance→self-esteem.

Nevertheless, you must be careful of excessive self-disclosure. Many people feel uneasy if another person is too self-revealing. The overly candid person thus risks rejection. For instance, if you communicate all your negative feelings and doubts to another person, that person may become annoyed and pull away from you.

Human Relations Self-Assessment Quiz 1-1 presents a questionnaire designed to assist you in assessing your level of self-disclosure. After taking the quiz, do Human Relations Skill-Building Exercise 1-1. It will help you develop skills in self-disclosure.

Awareness of Strengths and Self-Esteem

Another method of improving your self-esteem is to develop an appreciation of your strengths and accomplishments. Research with over 60 executives has shown that their self-concepts become more positive after one month of practicing this exercise for a few minutes every day.[15] A good starting point is to list your strengths and accomplishments on paper. This list is likely to be more impressive than you expected. The list of strengths and accomplishments requested in the Self-Knowledge Questionnaire presented later can be used for building self-esteem.

You can sometimes develop an appreciation of your strengths by participating in a group exercise designed for such purposes. A group of about seven people meet to form a support group. All group members first spend about ten minutes answering the question, "What are my three strongest points, attributes, or skills?" After each group member has recorded his or

HUMAN RELATIONS SELF-ASSESSMENT QUIZ 1-1

The Self-Disclosure Questionnaire

Directions

The following quiz may indicate how much of yourself you reveal to others. Think about the person closest to you, whether he or she is a spouse, parent, or close friend. Using the list of responses provided, review the questions and select the number of the response that best describes you.

1. I have not mentioned anything about this.
2. I have talked about this to some degree.
3. I have confided this to a large degree.
4. I have disclosed practically all there is to know about this.

Quiz

_____ 1. Traits I am ashamed of, such as jealousy, daydreaming, and procrastination

_____ 2. Pet peeves or prejudices about others

_____ 3. Facts about my love life, including details about flirting, dating, and sexual activity

_____ 4. Things I have done or said to others that I feel guilty about

_____ 5. What it takes to make me extremely angry

_____ 6. My feelings about my attractiveness and sex appeal, and my insecurities about how my romantic interests perceive me

_____ 7. Aspects of myself I wish I could improve, such as my physique, mental abilities, and shyness

_____ 8. What I worry about most, such as illness, job loss, and death

_____ 9. Impulses I fear will get out of control if I "let go," such as drinking, gambling, sex, and anger

_____ 10. My very deepest sensitivities, dreams, and goals

Scoring and Interpretation: To tally your score, add the numbers that correspond with the answers you gave to the quiz questions.

10 to 17 points: You are a closed person. You may feel satisfied with the level of intimacy you have established with others, but it's likely you would benefit from sharing your feelings more openly. Doing so allows others to give you feedback on your feelings and goals, helping you to get a clearer picture of yourself. Begin to change your style by making small disclosures at first. Perhaps it will be easier to start by talking about your goals.

18 to 28 points: You are average on self-disclosure and have a good balance between your private self and your openness.

(Continued)

her three strengths, that person discusses them with the other group members.

Each group member then comments on the list. Other group members sometimes add to your list of strengths or reinforce what you have to say. Sometimes you may find disagreement. One member told the group: "I'm handsome, intelligent, reliable, athletic, self-confident, and very moral. I also have a good sense of humor." Another group member retorted, "And I might add that you're unbearably conceited."

Minimize Settings and Interactions That Detract from Your Feelings of Competence

Most of us have situations in work and personal life that make us feel less than our best. If you can minimize exposure to those situations, you will have fewer feelings of incompetence. The problem with feeling incompetent is that it lowers your self-esteem. An office supervisor said she detested company picnics, most of all because she was forced into playing softball. At her own admission, she had less aptitude for athletics than any

HUMAN RELATIONS SKILL-BUILDING EXERCISE 1-1

Self-Disclosure Role Play

In a role play, you assume the role of the person described in a scenario. In this and other role plays presented in this book, it may be your responsibility to add details to the brief sketches provided. Unlike an actor or actress, you will have to improvise beyond the bare essentials of the script presented by the author. Or your instructor may modify the role play to provide you with additional details.

In this role play, two coworkers are having lunch together. One student plays the role of an employee who is eager to disclose as much as possible about his or her inner self. Similarly, this employee would like the luncheon partner to be self-disclosing.

Another student plays the role of the second employee. This person is much more closed than open but nevertheless does not necessarily dislike allowing the luncheon companion to open up to him or her.

Those students not in the role play should make observations of the role players, and later use these observations as a basis for class discussion. The class discussion may include comments about the effectiveness of the role players.

able-bodied person she knew. In addition, she felt uncomfortable with the small-talk characteristic of picnics. To minimize discomfort the woman attended only those picnics she thought were absolutely necessary. Instead of playing on the softball team, she volunteered to be the equipment manager.

A problem with avoiding all situations in which you feel lowly competent is that it might prevent you from acquiring needed skills. Also, it boosts your self-confidence and self-esteem to become comfortable in a previously uncomfortable situation.

Talk and Socialize Frequently with People Who Boost Your Self-Esteem

Psychologist Barbara Ilardie says that the people who can raise your self-esteem are usually those with high self-esteem themselves. They are the people who give honest feedback because they respect others and themselves. Such high self-esteem individuals should not be confused with yes-people who agree with others just to be liked. The point is that you typically receive more from strong people than weak ones. Weak people will flatter you but will not give you the honest feedback you need to build self-esteem.[16]

POTENTIAL DISADVANTAGES OF PREOCCUPATION WITH THE SELF

We have emphasized the importance of understanding the self as a starting point in developing good human relations skills. Much of this chapter was also devoted to the importance of developing self-esteem. Despite the soundness of this advice, a person must also guard against becoming too caught up in the self. A study of the self proposes that the modern individual is burdened with a too-weighty self. For many people, the self has too many components, aspiration levels, and hard-to-meet expectations.[17]

Too much attention to the self can lead a person to be self-centered, self-conscious, and uninterested in other people and the outside world. You have met people who include in almost every conversation a statement about their health, and whether they feel hot or cold. The same people are likely to inform others when they are fatigued, even when nobody asked.

Preoccupation with the self can lead to unattainable aspirations. As a consequence of not attaining these aspirations, the person develops a negative self-evaluation. According to one theory, these negative self-evaluations prompt the person to escape the self. The path chosen to escape the self is often alcoholism, drug abuse, and craze eating (bulimia).[18] More will be said about personal problems in Chapter 5. The right balance is to be concerned about yourself, your self-esteem, and your personal growth yet still focus on the world outside of you.

Focusing on the outside world can ultimately strengthen the self, because you develop skills and interests that will enhance your self-esteem. Kenny, a supervisor of electronics technicians, explains how his outside interests helped him achieve high self-esteem:

> I used to worry a lot about myself. I used to obsess over the fact that many people my age earned more money and owned better cars. I also used to worry too much about my appearance. Sometimes I would weigh myself several times a day, always hoping that I had shed a pound or two.
>
> It hit me one day that I had the most fun when I could get outside myself and not think so much about me. I then plunged myself further into my hobby of producing home videos. After shooting a scene, such as a trip to New York, I would edit the tape to make the production smooth. I showed my edited tapes to a few friends. Before long, many friends and acquaintances were calling me for help in editing their tapes. My reputation as a video expert spread. I felt great about myself because my hobby enabled me to help others.

HOW STUDYING HUMAN RELATIONS CAN HELP YOU

A person who carefully studies human relations and incorporates its suggestions into his or her work and personal life should derive the five benefits discussed next. Knowledge itself, however, is not a guarantee of success. Since people differ greatly in learning ability, personality, and life circumstances, some will get more out of studying human relations than will others.

You may, for example, be getting along well with coworkers or customers so that studying this topic seems unnecessary from your viewpoint. Or you may be so shy at this stage of your life that you are unable to capitalize on some of the suggestions for being assertive with people. You might have to work doubly hard to benefit from studying that topic.

The major benefits from studying human relations are:

1. *Acquiring valid information about human behavior.*   To feel comfortable with people and to make a favorable impression both on and off the job, you need to understand how people think and act. Studying human relations will provide you with some basic knowledge about interpersonal relationships such as the meaning of self-esteem, why goal setting works, and win-win conflict resolution. You will even learn about such things as mimicking another person's body movement to improve rapport with that person.

2. *Developing skills in dealing with people.*   People who aspire toward high-level positions or an enriched social life need to be able to communicate with others, manage stress, and behave confidently. Relating well to diverse cultural groups is also an asset. Studying information about such topics, coupled with practicing what you learn, should help you develop such interpersonal skills.

3. *Coping with job problems.*   Almost everyone who holds a job inevitably runs into human relations problems. Reading about these problems and suggestions for coping with them could save you considerable inner turmoil. Among the job survival skills that you will learn about in

the study of human relations are how to deal with difficult people and how to overcome what seems to be an overwhelming workload.

4. *Coping with personal problems.* We all have problems. An important difference between the effective and ineffective person is that the effective person knows how to manage them. Among the problems studying human relations will help you cope with are self-defeating behavior, finding a job when you're unemployed, overcoming low self-confidence, and working your way out of debt.

5. *Capitalizing on opportunities.* Many readers of this book will someday spend part of their working time taking advantage of opportunities rather than solving daily problems. Every career-minded person needs a few breakthrough experiences to make life more rewarding. Toward this end, studying human relations gives you ideas for developing your career and becoming a leader.

SUMMARY

Human relations is the art and practice of using systematic knowledge about human behavior to improve personal, job, and career effectiveness.

Work and personal life often influence each other in several ways. A high level of job satisfaction tends to spill over to your personal life. Conversely, an unsatisfactory personal life could lead to negative job attitudes. Another close tie between work and personal life is that your job can affect physical and mental health. Severely negative job conditions may lead to a serious stress disorder, such as heart disease.

The quality of relationships with people in work and personal life influence each other. Also, certain skills (such as the ability to listen) contribute to success in work and personal life. In recognition of the link between work and personal life, many employers conduct work/life programs, including a customized work environment. A major rationale for these program is that workers who have their personal lives under control can concentrate better at work. The challenge of balancing work and family demands is particularly intense for employees who are part of a two-wage-earner family.

To be effective in human relationships, you must first understand yourself. Six methods for gaining self-understanding are: (1) Acquire general information about human behavior and apply it to yourself; (2) obtain informal feedback from people; (3) obtain feedback from superiors; (4) obtain feedback from coworkers; (5) obtain feedback from self-examination exercises; (6) gather insights in psychotherapy and counseling.

An important aspect of self-understanding is the self-concept, or the way a person thinks about him- or herself in an overall sense. The self-concept is based largely on what others have said about us. A strong self-concept leads to self-confidence, which is a basic requirement for being successful as a leader or in sales.

Natural abilities contribute to a person's self-concept and level of self-confidence. Your body image, or your perception of your body, also contributes to your self-concept. A positive body image can help you in both your work and personal life because it enhances your self-concept. The relatively small-size groups to which a person belongs (such as a team or club) are other contributors to the self-concept.

Self-esteem refers to appreciating self-worth and importance, being accountable for your own behaviors, and acting responsibly toward others. People with high self-esteem develop a positive self-concept. Self-esteem has two interrelated components: self-efficacy (a task-related feeling of competence) and self-respect. Self-esteem develops from a variety of early-life experiences. People who were encouraged to feel good about themselves and their accomplishments by key people in their lives are more likely to enjoy high self-esteem. Of major significance, self-esteem also results from accomplishing worthwhile activities, and then feeling proud of these accomplishments. Praise and recognition for accomplishments also help develop self-esteem.

Good mental health is one of the major consequences of high self-esteem. One of the links between good mental health and self-esteem is that high self-esteem helps prevent many situations from being stressful. Workers with high self-esteem develop and maintain favorable work attitudes and perform at a high level.

A major consequence of low self-esteem is poor mental health. School children with low self-esteem are more likely to be delinquents. Workers with low self-esteem often develop and maintain unfavorable work attitudes and perform below expectations.

Self-esteem can be enhanced in many ways. Accomplishing worthwhile activities is a major contributor to self-esteem in both children and adults. The right amount of self-disclosure enhances self-esteem because it may lead to self-acceptance. Developing an appreciation of your strengths and accomplishments is another self-esteem builder. It is also important to minimize settings and interactions that detract from your feelings of competence. In addition, talk and socialize frequently with people who boost your self-esteem.

Despite the importance of self-understanding, guard against becoming too caught up in the self. Too much attention to the self can lead a person to be self-centered, self-conscious, and uninterested in other people and the outside world. Another problem is that failure to attain aspirations can lead to negative self-evaluation. The negative evaluation may lead to escapist behavior such as alcoholism.

Questions and Activities

1. To succeed in business, why is it important for people with good technical skills to also develop good human relations skills?

2. From what you have studied so far, is the term *human relations skills* just another way of saying "be nice to people"?

3. Give an example from your own experience of how work life influences personal life and vice versa.

4. Employers are supposed to be making a profit so that they can pay dividends and interest to people who have invested in the company. So why should employers be concerned about workers achieving a balance between work and personal life?

5. If you worked for Eddie Bauer (or do), explain why you would or would not use your "call in well" absence.

6. Of the six sources of information about the self described in this chapter, which one do you think is likely to be the most accurate? Why?

7. How can your self-concept affect your career?

8. What might a manager do to boost the self-esteem of a worker who appeared to be suffering from low self-esteem?

9. How can a partner (such as a spouse) lower the self-esteem of the other partner?

10. Interview a person whom you perceive to have a successful career. Ask that person to describe how he or she developed high self-esteem. Be prepared to discuss your findings in class.

REFERENCES

[1] Timothy A. Judge and Schinichiro Watanabe, "Another Look at the Job Satisfaction–Life Satisfaction Relationship," *Journal of Applied Psychology,* December 1933, pp. 939–948.

[2] Leslie Fraught, "At Eddie Bauer You Can Work and Have a Life," *Workforce,* April 1997, p. 84.

[3] C. R. Snyder, "So Many Selves," *Contemporary Psychology,* January 1988, p. 77.

[4] Dodge Fernald, *Psychology* (Upper Saddle River, NJ: Prentice Hall, 1977), p. 654.

[5] John Hattie, *Self-Concept* (Hillsdale, NJ: Erlbaum, 1992).

[6] Marilyn E. Gist, "Self-Efficacy: Implications for Organizational Behavior and Human Resource Management," *Academy of Management Review,* July 1987, pp. 472–485.

[7] Cited in Scott Sleek, "People Craft Their Self-Image from Groups," *The APA Monitor,* November 1993, p. 22.

[8] California State Department of Education, *Toward a State of Esteem,* Sacramento Department of Education, January 1990, p. 19.

[9] Wayne Weiten and Margaret Lloyd, *Psychology Applied to Modern Life* (Pacific Grove, CA: Brooks/Cole Publishing, 1994), p. 51.

[10] Randall Edwards, "Is Self-Esteem Really All that Important?" *The APA Monitor,* May 1995, p. 43.

[11] Jon L. Pierce, Donald G. Gardner, Larry L. Cummings, and Randall B. Dunham, "Organization-Based Self-Esteem: Construct Definition, Measurement, and Validation," *Academy of Management Journal,* September 1989, p. 623.

A HUMAN RELATIONS CASE PROBLEM

Self-Esteem Building at Pyramid Remanufacturing

Pyramid Remanufacturing opened for business ten years ago in a cinder block building with four employees. Today Pyramid is housed in an old factory building in a low-rent district. The company has 100 full-time employees and about 50 part-timers. The nature of the company's business is to salvage parts from used or broken equipment sent to them by other companies. One of Pyramid's remanufacturing projects is to salvage the workable parts from single-use cameras, and recycle the balance of the plastic parts. Another large company contract is to salvage parts from children's toys that are returned to retailers because they do not function properly. Both contracts also call for making new single-use cameras and toys, incorporating the salvaged parts.

The basic remanufacturing jobs can be learned in several hours. The work is not complex, but it is tedious. For example, a remanufacturing technician would be expected to tear down and salvage, and assemble about 100 single-use cameras per day. The jobs pay about twice the minimum wage, and full-time workers receive standard benefits.

Derrick Lockett, the president and founder of Pyramid, believes that his company plays an important role in society. As he explains, "First of all, note that we are *remanufacturers.* We are helping save the planet. Think of the thousands and thousands of single-use cameras that do not wind up in landfills because of our recycling efforts. The same goes for plastic toys. Consider also, that we hire a lot of people who would not be working if it were not for Pyramid. A lot of our employees would be on welfare if they were not working here. We hire a lot of people from the welfare roles. We also hire a lot of troubled teenagers, and seniors who can't find employment elsewhere.

"Some of our other employees have a variety of disabilities which make job-finding difficult for them. Two of our highest producers are blind. They have a wonderful sense of touch, and they can visualize the parts that have to be separated and assembled. Another source of good employees for us are recently released prisoners."

Lockett was asked if all Pyramid manufacturing employees were performing up to standard. He explained that about one-fourth of the workforce were either working so slowly, or doing such sloppy work, that they were a poor investment for the company. "Face it," said Lockett, "some of our employees are dragging us down. After awhile we have to weed out the workers who just don't earn their salary."

Next, Lockett gave his analysis of why some remanufacturing technicians are unable to perform properly. "Lots of reasons," said Lockett. "Some can't read; some have a poor work ethic; some have attention deficit disorders. But the big problem is that many of the poor performers have such rotten self-esteem. They don't believe in themselves. They think nobody wants them, and that they are incapable of being valuable employees."

Lucy Winters, the director of human resources and administration, explained what Pyramid was attempting to do about the self-esteem problem. "You have to realize," she said, "that it's not easy for a company to build the self-esteem of entry-level employees. Derrick and I would both like to save the world, but we can't do everything. But we are taking a few initiatives to build the self-esteem of our employees.

(Continued)

"One approach is that our supervisors give out brightly colored badges, imprinted with the words, 'I'm a real remanufacturer.' The supervisors are supposed to give out the badges when a technician looks to be down in the dumps. We also have a newsletter that features stories about our remanufacturing technicians. Each month we choose somebody to be the "Remanufacturer of the month." Usually it's an employee whose self-esteem appears to be hurting.

"Another approach is more informal. We ask our supervisors to remember to be cheerleaders. They're supposed to lift the spirits of employees who don't think much of themselves by saying things like, 'I know you can do it,' or 'I believe in you.'"

When asked how the self-esteem-building program was working, Winters and Lockett both said it was too early to tell with certainty. Winters did comment, however, "I see a few bright smiles out there among our technicians. And the turnover rate is down about five percent. So the program might be working."

Question

1. What is your evaluation of Lockett's analysis that low self-esteem could hurt the work performance of entry-level remanufacturing technicians?

2. What is your evaluation of the self-esteem building program at Pyramid?

3. What other suggestions can you offer for building the self-esteem of the Pyramid employees who appear to be having a self-esteem problem?

HUMAN RELATIONS SELF-ASSESSMENT EXERCISE 1-3

The Self-Knowledge Questionnaire

Directions: Complete the following questionnaire for your personal use. You might wish to create a computer file for this document, enabling you to readily edit and update your answers. The answers to these questions will serve as a source document for such purposes as self-understanding, career planning, and résumé preparation.

I. Education

1. How far have I gone in school?

2. What is my major field of interest?

3. Which are, or have been, my best subjects?

4. Which are, or have been, my poorest subjects?

5. Which extracurricular activities have I participated in?

6. Which ones did I enjoy? Why?

II. Work and Career

7. What jobs have I held since age 16?

8. What aspects of these jobs did I enjoy? Why?

(Continued)

9. What aspects of these jobs did I dislike? Why?

10. What have been my three biggest job accomplishments?

11. What compliments did I receive from managers, coworkers, or customers?

12. What criticisms or suggestions did I receive?

13. What would be an ideal job for me? (Give the job title and major responsibilities.)

III. Attitudes Toward People

14. What kind of people do I get along with best?

15. What kind of people do I get along with the least?

16. How much time do I prefer to be in contact with people versus working alone?

17. What are my arguments with people mostly about?

18. What characteristics of a boss would be best for me?

IV. Attitudes Toward and Perceptions about Myself

19. What are my strengths and good points?

20. What are my areas for improvement?

21. What is my biggest problem?

22. What aspects of my life do I enjoy the most?

23. What aspect of my life do I enjoy the least?

24. What has been the happiest period of my life? What made it so happy?

25. What are the biggest motivational forces in my life?

26. What do I do to defeat my own purposes?

V. How People Outside of Work See Me

27. What is the best compliment a loved-one has paid me?

28. In what ways would any of my loved-ones want me to change?

29. What do my friends like the most about me?

30. What do my friends like the least about me?

VI. Hobbies, Interests, Sports

31. What hobbies, interests, sports, or other pastimes do I pursue?

32. Which of these do I really get excited about, and why?

VII. My Future

33. What are my plans for further education and training?

34. What positions would I like to hold, or type of work would I like to perform, in the future?

(Continued)

35. What type of work would I like to be doing at the peak of my career?

36. What hobbies, interests, and sports would I like to pursue in the future?

37. What goals and plans do I have relating to friends, family, and marriage or partnership?

Additional Thoughts

1. What topics not covered in this questionnaire would contribute to my self-understanding?

2. To what uses can I put all this information, aside from those mentioned in the directions?

3. How did answering these questions contribute to my self-understanding?

[12]Lila L. Prigge and Charles M. Ray, "Social and Personality Development," in *The Hidden Curriculum* (*National Business Education Yearbook, No. 30*), 1992, p. 145.

[13]Pierce, Gardner, Cummings, and Dunham, "Organization-Based Self-Esteem," p. 623.

[14]Mona Charen, " 'Teaching' Self-Esteem a Costly Failure," syndicated column, May 16, 1994.

[15]Daniel L. Aroz, "The Manager's Self-Concept," *Human Resources Forum,* July 1989, p. 4.

[16]"Self-Esteem: You'll Need It to Succeed," *Executive Strategies,* September 1993, p. 12.

[17]Roy F. Baumeister, *Escaping the Self: Alcoholism, Spirituality, Masochism, and Other Flights from the Burden of Selfhood* (New York: Basic Books, 1991).

[18]Ibid.

ADDITIONAL READING

Branden, Nathaniel. *The Six Pillars of Self-Esteem.* New York: Bantam, 1994.

Brockner, Joel. *Self-Esteem at Work: Research, Theory, and Practice.* Lexington, MA: Lexington Books, 1986.

Byrne, Barbara M. *Measuring Self-Concept across the Life Span: Issues and Implementation.* Washington. D.C.: American Psychological Association, 1996.

Hillman, Carolynn. " 'Carress' Yourself: The 6 Keys to Self-Esteem." *New Woman,* June 1992, pp. 54–57.

Jourard, Sidney N. *The Transparent Self* (2d ed.). New York: Van Nostrand Reinhold, 1971.

Miller, Barbara E. "Rescue Your Work/Life Program." *Workforce,* June 1997, pp. 84–90.

Mruk, Chris. *Self-Esteem: Research, Theory, and Practice.* New York: Springer, 1995.

Neisser, Ulric, ed. *The Perceived Self: Ecological and Interpersonal Sources of Self-Knowledge.* New York: Cambridge University Press, 1993.

Palladino, Connie. *Developing Self-Esteem.* Los Altos, CA: Crisp Publications, 1996.

Stevens, Richard, ed. *Understanding the Self.* London: Sage, 1996.

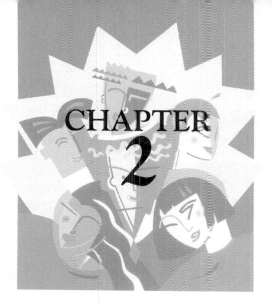

CHAPTER 2

SELF-MOTIVATION AND GOAL SETTING

Learning Objectives

After studying the information and doing the exercises in this chapter, you should be able to:

▼ Explain how needs and motives influence motivation

▼ Identify several needs and motives that could be propelling you into action

▼ Pinpoint how the hierarchy of needs could explain your behavior

▼ Explain why and how goals contribute to self-motivation

▼ Describe how to set effective goals

▼ Specify the problems sometimes created by goals

▼ Apply the self-discipline model to achieving your goals

Gary Rogers is the president of Jasco Tools, a company that employees 300 people. He thinks that the employee work ethic is a big problem. According to Rogers, job applicants come to the firm asking what's in the job for them, not what they can do to make the company a success. "It used to be that you would find job applicants dressed up for an interview. They would wear a suit and tie, or dress, and try to make a good impression. Now they come in jeans and hats turned around backwards." Rogers said that Jasco tries to teach virtues such as punctuality and teamwork. But basic attitudes won't change until schools and parents start to instill a work ethic.[1]

Whether you agree with Gary Rogers that the work ethic (belief in the dignity of work) is declining, his comments emphasize an important truth. You have to be motivated to achieve success in work. Strong motivation is also important for personal life. Unless you direct your energies toward specific goals, such as improving your productivity or meeting a new friend, you will accomplish very little. Knowledge of motivation and goal setting as applied to yourself can therefore pay substantial dividends in improving the quality of your life. Knowledge about motivation and goal setting is also important when attempting to influence others to get things accomplished. Motivating others, for example, is a major requirement of the manager's job.

Being well motivated is also necessary for career survival. Today most organizations insist on high productivity and quality from workers at all levels. Assuming you have the necessary skills, training, and equipment, being well motivated will enable you to achieve high productivity and quality. The general purpose of this chapter is to present information that can help you sustain a high level of motivation, centering around the importance of needs and goals.

HOW NEEDS AND MOTIVES INFLUENCE MOTIVATION

According to a widely accepted explanation of human behavior, people have needs and motives that propel them toward achieving certain goals. Needs and motives are closely related. A **need** is an internal striving or urge to do something, such as a need to drink when thirsty. It can be regarded as a biological or psychological requirement. Because the person is deprived in some way (such as not having enough fluid in the body), the person is motivated to take action toward a goal. In this case the goal might be simply getting something to drink.

A **motive** is an inner drive that moves a person to do something. The motive is usually based on a need or desire, and results in the intention to attain an appropriate goal. Because needs and motives are so closely related, the two terms are often used interchangeably. For example, "recognition need" and "recognition motive" refer to the same thing.

THE NEED THEORY OF MOTIVATION

The central idea behind need theory is that unsatisfied needs motivate us until they become satisfied. When people are dissatisfied or anxious about their present status or performance, they will try to reduce this anxiety. This need cycle is shown in Figure 2-1. Assume that you have a strong need or motive to achieve recognition. As a result, you experience tension that drives you to find some way of being recognized on the job. The action you take is to apply for a position as the team leader of your group. You reason that being appointed as team leader would provide ample recognition, particularly if the team performs well.

You are appointed to the position, and for now your need for recognition is at least partially satisfied as you receive compliments from your coworkers and friends. Once you receive this partial satisfaction, two things typically happen. Either you will soon require a stronger dose of recognition, or you will begin to concentrate on another need or motive, such as achievement.

In either case, the need cycle will repeat itself. You might seek another form of recognition or satisfaction of your need for power. For example, you might apply for a position as department manager or open your own business. Ideally, in this situation your boss would give you more responsibility. This could lead to more satisfaction of your recognition need and to some satisfaction of your need for achievement. (The needs mentioned so far, and others, are defined next.)

Figure 2-1   The Need Cycle

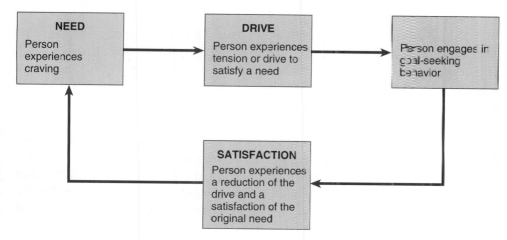

Important Needs and Motives People Attempt to Satisfy

Work and personal life offer the opportunity to satisfy dozens of needs and motives. In this and the following section, we describe important needs that propel people into action. As you read these needs and motives, relate them to yourself. For example, ask yourself, "Am I a power-seeking person?"

Achievement.   People with a strong achievement need find joy in accomplishment for its own sake. The achievement motive or need is especially important for self-employed people and employees occupying high-level managerial positions.[2] The achievement need can be satisfied by such activities as building things from the ground up or by completing a major project.

Power.   People with a high power need feel compelled to control resources, such as other people and money. Successful executives typically have a high power motive and exhibit three dominant characteristics: (1) They act with vigor and determination to exert their power; (2) they invest much time in thinking about ways to alter the behavior and thinking of others; and (3) they care about their personal standing with those around them.[3] The power need can be satisfied through occupying a high-level position or by becoming a highly influential person. Or you can name skyscrapers and hotels after yourself, following the lead of Donald Trump.

Affiliation.   People with a strong affiliation need seek out close relationships with others and tend to be loyal as friends or employees. The affiliation motive is met directly through belonging to the "office gang," a term of endearment implying that your coworkers are an important part of your life. Many people prefer working in groups to individual effort because of the opportunity the former provides for socializing with others.

Recognition.   People with a strong need for recognition want to be acknowledged for their contribution and efforts. The need for recognition is so pervasive that many companies have formal recognition programs in which outstanding or longtime employees receive gifts, plaques, and jewelry inscribed with the company logo. The recognition motive can be satisfied through means such as winning contests, receiving awards, and seeing your name in print.

Dominance.   People with a strong need for dominance want to influence others toward their way of thinking, often by forceful methods. People driven by a dominance motive often take over in meetings, volunteer to be leaders, and are good at the hard sell. A need for dominance could therefore be satisfied by taking control over any situation in which you are placed.

Order.   People with a strong need for order have the urge to put things in order. They also want to achieve arrangement, balance, neatness, and precision. The order motive can be quickly satisfied by cleaning and organizing your work or living space. Occupations offering the opportunity to satisfy the order motive almost every day include accountant, computer programmer, and paralegal assistant.

Thrill Seeking.   People with a strong thrill-seeking motive crave constant excitement and are driven to a life of stimulation and risk taking.[4] The thrill-seeking motive can be satisfied through performing such dangerous feats as setting explosives, capping an oil well, and controlling a radiation leak. Introducing a new product in a highly competitive environment is another way of satisfying the thrill-seeking motive. How might a person satisfy a need for thrill seeking off the job?

MASLOW'S NEED HIERARCHY

The best-known categorization of needs is **Maslow's need hierarchy.** At the same time, it is the most widely used explanation of human motivation. According to psychologist Abraham H. Maslow, people strive to satisfy the following groups of needs in step-by-step order:

1. *Physiological needs* refer to bodily needs, such as the requirements for food, water, shelter, and sleep.

2. *Safety needs* refer to actual physical safety and to a feeling of being safe from both physical and emotional injury.

3. *Social needs* are essentially love or belonging needs. Unlike the two previous levels of needs, they center around a person's interaction with other people.

4. *Esteem needs* represent an individual's demand to be seen as a person of worth by others—and to him- or herself.

5. *Self-actualizing needs* are the highest level of needs, including the needs for self-fulfillment and personal development.[5]

A diagram of the need hierarchy is presented in Figure 2-2. Notice the distinction between higher-level and lower-level needs. With few exceptions, higher-level needs are more difficult to satisfy. A person's needs for affiliation might be satisfied by being a member of a friendly work group. Yet to satisfy self-actualization needs, such as self-fulfillment, a person might have to develop an outstanding reputation in his or her company.

The need hierarchy implies that most people think of finding a job as a way of obtaining the necessities of life. Once these are obtained, a person may think of achieving friendship, self-esteem, and self-fulfillment on the job. When a person is generally satisfied at one level, he or she looks for satisfaction at a higher level. As Maslow describes it, a person is a "perpetually wanting animal." Very few people are totally satisfied with their lot in life, even the rich and famous.

The Extent of Need Satisfaction.   Not everybody can have as much need satisfaction as he or she wishes. Maslow estimated that the typical adult satisfies about 85 percent of physiological needs; 70 percent of safety and security needs; 50 percent of belongingness, social, and love needs; 40 percent of esteem needs; and 10 percent of self-actualization needs.[6]

Figure 2-2   Maslow's Need Hierarchy

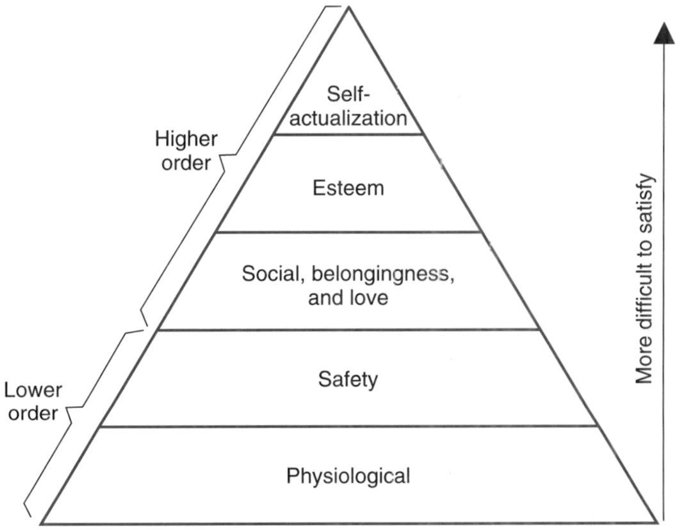

The extent of need satisfaction is influenced by a person's job. Some construction jobs, for example, involve dangerous work in severe climates, thus frustrating both physiological and safety needs. Ordinarily there is much more opportunity for approaching self-actualization when a person occupies a prominent position, such as a top executive or famous performer. However, a person with low potential could approach self-actualization by occupying a lesser position.

Need Theory and Self-Motivation.   How do Maslow's needs and the other needs described in this chapter relate to self-motivation? First you have to ask yourself, "Which needs do I really want to satisfy?" After answering the question honestly, concentrate your efforts on an activity that will most likely satisfy that need. For instance, if you are hungry for power, strive to become a high-level manager or a business owner. If you crave self-esteem, focus your efforts on work and social activities that are well regarded by others. The point is that you will put forth substantial effort if you think the goal you attain will satisfy an important need.

Many business people still use the Maslow's need hierarchy to guide their thinking about motivation in the workplace. Exhibit 2-1 illustrates one such application of the need hierarchy.

 GOALS AND MOTIVATION

A writer about success says, "All truly successful men or women I have met or read about have one thing in common. At some point in their lives, they sat down and wrote out their goals. The first great key to success begins with you, a piece of paper, and a pencil."[7] This statement indicates why goal setting is so important. A **goal** is an event, circumstance, object,

---

EXHIBIT 2-1

A BUSINESS OWNER APPLIES MASLOW'S NEED HIERARCHY

"I relate everything back to Maslow's theory," says Joseph J. Raymond, a Red Bank, New Jersey, entrepreneur. He has used the need hierarchy to guide the growth of the company he founded, Transworld Home HealthCare Inc. Placing employees in the right job is a specific area in which Raymond applies Maslow's ideas about motivation.

Raymond routinely places new employees in key positions based on extensive posthiring interviews in which he asks questions about the kind of house and neighborhood they live in and their tastes in movies, food, recreation, reading, and more. Newcomers to the firm are often confused and uneasy about the unusual questions, Raymond admits. But he asks them anyway because he feels it's important to know where each worker is on Maslow's hierarchy. "Once you get a good inkling as to where they're at, you try to apply the Maslow theory to motivate them," Raymond explains.

He typically finds that his management-level hires are somewhere between the social- or belonging-need level and the esteem level. For these people, money is frequently a less important motivator than symbols of status or membership." The yuppies are in that category," says Raymond. "That's why they want to have the keys to the executive washroom, the window office, or the country club membership.

"If I know an employee is operating at the esteem-need level, then this is the person I want to give the more challenging jobs to. They feel the need for self-esteem, to be able to pat themselves on the back."

SOURCE: Adapted with permission from Mark Hendricks, "Motivating Force," *Entrepreneur,* December 1995, pp. 70–71.

---

or condition a person strives to attain. A goal thus reflects your desire or intention to regulate your actions. Here we look at three topics to help you understand the nature of goals: (1) the advantages of goals, (2) the underlying reasons why they are motivational, and (3) different goal orientations.

ADVANTAGES OF GOALS

Goal setting is well accepted as a motivational tool. Substantial research indicates that setting specific, reasonably difficult goals improves performance.[8] Goals are useful for several reasons. First, when we guide our lives with goals, we tend to focus our efforts in a consistent direction. Without goals, our efforts may become scattered in many directions. We may keep trying, but we will go nowhere unless we happen to receive more than our share of luck.

Second, goal setting increases our chances for success, particularly because success can be defined as the achievement of a goal. The goals we set for accomplishing a task can serve as a standard to indicate when we have done a satisfactory job. A sales representative might set a goal of selling $300,000 worth of merchandise for the year. By November she might close a deal that places her total sales at $310,000. With a sigh of relief she can then say, "I've done well this year."

Third, goals serve as self-motivators and energizers. People who set goals tend to be motivated because they are confident that their energy is being invested in something worthwhile. Aside from helping you become more motivated and productive, setting goals can help you achieve personal satisfaction. Most people derive a sense of satisfaction from attaining a goal that is meaningful to them. The sales representative mentioned above probably achieved this sense of satisfaction when she surpassed her quota.

COGNITIVE AND NEUROLOGICAL REASONS WHY GOALS ARE EFFECTIVE

The advantages of goals just described provide some explanation of why goals help motivate people. Yet to fully understand the contribution of goals, it is important to dig further. Digging further refers here to uncovering the cognitive (or mental) and neurological reasons for the contribution of goals to motivation.

One cognitive explanation of the effectiveness of goals states they are not motivational by themselves. Rather, the discrepancy between what individuals have and what they aspire to achieve creates dissatisfaction. (The need cycle described earlier also deals with such discrepancies between a person's ideal and actual state.) The self-dissatisfaction serves as an incentive. People respond to reduce the discrepancy. A positive self-evaluation results from achieving the goal.[9]

An example will help clarify this cognitive explanation of why goals are motivational. Bob might be working as a telemarketer (a person who sells over the phone). He sets a goal of being promoted to an outside sales position where he can call on customers and earn a bigger commission. Having set this goal, he is now dissatisfied with the discrepancy between his present job and being an outside sales representative. Bob's dissatisfaction prompts him to work extra hard to perform well as a telemarketer. Because of this, his manager might offer him a promotion.

The motivational effects of goal setting also have a neurological (nervous system) explanation. A building block for this explanation is that many of our actions are influenced by an arousal mechanism. The strength of the arousal moves along a continuum from a low point during sleep to a high point of frantic effort or excitement. (Have you ever observed a sports fan watch his or her team win the "big game" at the buzzer?) The state of being aroused is associated with activity in the sympathetic nervous system. The sympathetic nervous system readies the body for action. It also governs the amount of energy and effort available for performing a task.[10]

Arousal is linked to goals because setting a goal often arouses the sympathetic nervous system to action. Assume that on Monday, paralegal Carla establishes the goal of preparing the paperwork for 15 house closings. The goal is a stretch for Carla, but not impossible. Her nervous system will be activated to gear up for the task. By having extra energy to meet these demands, Carla will in essence be well motivated. A problem, however, is that if the task is too demanding, the goal may produce over-arousal. As a result, the person may be too "hyper" to perform well and will back away from getting the task accomplished.

THE LEARNING AND PERFORMANCE ORIENTATIONS TOWARD GOALS

Another useful perspective on understanding how goals influence motivation, is that goals can be aimed at either learning or performing.[11] A learning-goal orientation means that an individual is focused on acquiring new skills and mastering new situations. For example, you might establish the goal of learning how to develop skill in making a computerized-presentation package. You say to yourself, "My goal is to learn how to use PowerPoint (or similar software)."

A performance-goal orientation is different. It is aimed at wanting to demonstrate and validate the adequacy of your competence by seeking favorable judgments about your competence. At the same time, the person wants to avoid seeking negative judgments. For example, your goal might be to make PowerPoint presentations that would highly impress whoever watched them. Your focus is on looking good and avoiding negative evaluations of your presentations.

A person's goal orientation usually affects his or her desire for feedback. People with a learning-goal orientation are more likely to seek feedback on how well they are performing. In contrast, people with a performance-goal orientation are less likely to seek feedback. If you focus too much on setting performance goals, you might have a tendency to overlook the value of feedback. Yet the feedback could help you improve your performance in the long run. It is also important to recognize that if you, the goal setter, seeks feedback, you will create a good impression.

Before studying more about goals, do Human Relations Self-Assessment Exercise 2-1. It gives you an opportunity to think through your readiness to accept goals as part of your life.

GOAL SETTING ON THE JOB

If you are already well into your career, you have probably been asked to set goals or objectives on the job. Virtually all modern organizations have come to accept the value of goal setting in producing the results they want to achieve.

In most goal-setting programs, executives at the top of the organization are supposed to plan for the future by setting goals such as "Improve profits 10 percent this year." Employees at the bottom of the organization are supposed to go along with such broad goals by setting more specific goals. An example is "I will decrease damaged merchandise by 10 percent this

HUMAN RELATIONS SELF-ASSESSMENT EXERCISE 2-1

Are You Ready for Goal Setting?

Answer each of the following questions spontaneously and candidly. As with all self-help quizzes, if you try to answer the question in a way that will put you in a favorable light, you will miss some potentially valuable diagnostic information. For each question answer 1 for strongly disagree, 2 for disagree, 3 for a neutral attitude, 4 for agree, and 5 for strongly agree.

1. I almost always know what day of the month it is.   _____

2. I regularly prepare "to do" lists.   _____

3. I make good use of my "to do" lists.   _____

4. I can tell you almost precisely how many times I engaged in my favorite sport or hobby this year.   _____

5. I keep close tabs on the win and lose record of my favorite athletic team.   _____

6. I have a reasonably accurate idea of the different income tax brackets.   _____

7. I use a budget to control my personal expenses.   _____

8. I know how much money I want to be making in five years.   _____

9. I know what position I want to hold in five years.   _____

10. Careful planning is required to accomplish anything of value.   _____

Total _____

Scoring and Interpretation: Add up your point score. If your score is 40 points or higher, you are probably already convinced of the value of goal setting. If your score is between 20 and 39 points, you are in the middle range of readiness to incorporate goal setting into your life. You probably need to study more about goal setting to capitalize on its value. If your score is between 10 and 19 points, you are far from ready to accept goal setting. Carefully review the information about the advantages of goal setting mentioned previously. Until you change your attitudes about the contribution of goals to your life, you will not become an active goal setter and planner.

year. I will accomplish this by making sure that our shelving is adequate for our needs."

An interesting aspect of goal-setting programs on the job is that they lead you to pursue goals set by both your employer and yourself. The firm or company establishes certain goals that are absolutely essential to staying in business. A bank, for example, might impose the following goal on the tellers: "Shortages and overages of cash must be kept within 2 percent of transactions each week." The tellers will thus work extra hard to be sure that they do not give customers too much or too little money. Similarly, the top management of a hospital might impose the following goal (or objective) on all ward personnel: "All prescription drugs must be accounted for with 100 percent accuracy."

You participate in the goal-setting process by designing goals to fit into the overall mission of the firm. As a teller in the bank mentioned previously, you might set a personal goal of this nature: "During rush periods and when I feel fatigued, I will double-count all the money that I handle." In some goal-setting programs, employees are requested to set goals that will lead to their personal improvement. An auditor for the state set this goal for herself: "Within the next 12 months, I will enroll in and complete a supervisory training course in a local college." This woman aspired toward becoming a supervisor.

An important part of goal setting, both on and off the job, is priority setting. You pursue with more diligence those goals that can have the biggest impact on performance or are most important to top management. Suppose that one of a purchasing associate's goals for the month is to trim the number e-mail messages, letter files, and data files stored in his computer. He rightfully assumes that if he cleans up his computer files, he will be able to think more clearly. Yet he is also working on a goal of much more interest to top management—finding new sources of supply of a precious metal used in manufacturing a key product. The purchasing associate should set aside his need for order for a while, and work on the precious metal goal.

To increase the motivational impact of goals, some managers encourage workers to track their own performances. One approach is to use a bar chart as a data-collecting tool. In this way, as employees fill in the boxes, they can see their progress immediately. The "fill-in-the-bar-chart" approach shows workers at a glance where to concentrate more effort as well as areas in which they are not performing well.[12] A portion of the bar chart for the purchasing associate might look like that shown in Figure 2-3.

Figure 2-3   Bar Graph Showing Progress Against Goal

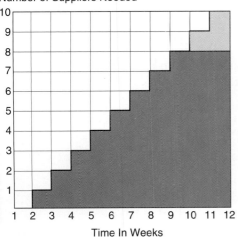

Number of Suppliers Needed

Time In Weeks

A sample set of work goals is shown in Figure 2-4. The service and repair shop supervisor who set these objectives took into account the requirements of his boss and the automobile dealership. Even if you set goals by yourself, they must still take into account the needs of your employer. As you read through the goals listed in Figure 2-4, see if they conform to the suggestions made in the section "Guidelines for Goal Setting."

 ## PERSONAL GOAL SETTING

Personal goals are important in their own right. If you want to lead a rewarding personal life, your chances of doing so increase if you plan it. Personal goals heavily influence the formulation of career goals as well. For this reason it is worthwhile to set personal goals in conjunction with career goals. Ideally they should be integrated to help achieve a balance between the demands of work and personal life. Two examples follow:

A man might have a strong interest in watching major league professional sports, shopping at a wide variety of retail stores, visiting

Figure 2-4 Memo Form Used in Automobile Dealership for Statement of Goals

---

JOB TITLE AND BRIEF JOB DESCRIPTION

Manager, Service Department:
Responsible for supervision of service department of automobile dealership. Responsible for staffing service department with appropriate personnel and for quality of service to customers. Work closely with owner of dealership to discuss unusual customer problems. Handle customer complaints about mechanical problems of cars purchased at dealership.

Objectives for Scott Gilley

1. By December 31 of this year, decrease by 10 percent customer demands for rework.

2. Hire two general mechanics within 45 days.

3. Hire two body specialists within 45 days.

4. Decrease by 30 percent the number of repairs returned by customers for rework.

5. Reduce by 10 percent the discrepancy between estimates and actual bills to customers.

comedy clubs, and dining at a variety of restaurants. He might establish the personal goals of having enough money for this lifestyle and living in an area where it would be available. His career goals should then include developing skills demanded by employers in large cities. Among the general fields that he might enter would be insurance, banking, financial services, and health services—all of which are in ample supply in large metropolitan areas.

- A woman might develop a preference early in life for the outdoors, particularly for hunting, fishing, and camping. She might also be interested in raising a large family. Part of her career goal setting should include developing skills that are in demand in rural areas where her preferences are easier to satisfy than in a large city. When she learns that many manufacturing facilities exist in rural and semirural areas, her career planning might then include the goal of developing job skills demanded in a factory or mill. She might, for example, take courses in manufacturing technology and supervision to qualify for a position as a manufacturing technician. Or she might simply seek employment in a variety of office positions found in a factory environment such as computer analyst or administrative assistant. Following this track, her career preparation would focus on office occupations.

TYPES OF PERSONAL GOALS

Personal goals can be subdivided into those relating to social and family life, hobbies and interests, physical and mental health, and finances. An example or two of each type follows:

Social and family: "By age 30 I would like to have a spouse and two children"; "have my own apartment by age 23."

Hobbies and interests: "Become a black belt in karate by age 28"; "qualify as a downhill ski instructor by age 21."

Physical and mental health: "Be able to run four miles without stopping or panting for breath by April 15 of next year"; "get my dermatitis under control within six months from now"; "maintain normal blood pressure for the indefinite future."

Financial: "Within the next four years be earning $40,000 per year, adjusted for inflation"; "build my money market fund account into a total value of at least $20,000 within five years."

Human Relations Skill-Building Exercise 2-1 will give you an opportunity to set both work and personal goals. Ideally, reading this chapter and doing the exercises in it will start you on a lifelong process of using goals to help you plan your life. But before you can capitalize on the benefits of goal setting, you need a method for translating goals into action.

HUMAN RELATIONS SKILL-BUILDING EXERCISE 2-1

Goal-Setting and Action Plan Worksheet

Before writing down your goals, consult the section, "Guidelines for Goal Setting." If you are not currently employed, set up hypothetical goals and action plans for a future job.

Long-Range Goals (beyond five years)

Work: _____

    Action plan: _____

Personal: _____

    Action plan: _____

Medium-Range Goals (two to five years)

Work: _____

    Action plan: _____

Personal: _____

    Action plan: _____

Short-Range Goals (within two years)

Work: _____

    Action plan: _____

Personal: _____

    Action plan: _____

ACTION PLANS TO SUPPORT GOALS

An **action plan** describes how you are going to reach your goal. The major reason you need an action plan for most goals is that without a method for achieving what you want, the goal is likely to slip by. Few people ever prepare a road map or plan that will lead them to their goals.

Many people who would like to write a book have asked me how to go about it. My answer is to begin small. See if you can get a letter to the editor published in a newspaper. Then you might try writing an article for the school newspaper. After you have accomplished that, branch out into articles for magazines. This advice is essentially an action plan for building your competence in writing step-by-step so that you will eventually be able to achieve your long-range goal of writing a book. In the same way, if your goal were to build your own log cabin, part of your action plan would be to learn how to operate a buzz saw, to read a handbook on log-cabin building, to learn how to operate a tractor, and so forth.

Some goals are so difficult to reach that your action plan might encompass hundreds of separate activities. You would then have to develop separate action plans for each step of the way. If your goal is to lead a rewarding and satisfying career, the techniques presented in this book can help you formulate many of your action plans. Among these skill-building techniques are assertiveness, resolving conflict, developing good work habits, and managing your money wisely.

Some immediate goals do not really require an action plan. A mere statement of the goal may point to an obvious action plan. If your goal were to start painting your room, it would not be necessary to draw up a formal action plan such as: "Go to hardware store, purchase paint, brush, and rollers; borrow ladder and drop cloth from Ken; put furniture in center of room"; and so on.

GUIDELINES FOR GOAL SETTING

Goal setting is an art in the sense that some people do a better job of goal setting than others. The following paragraphs provide suggestions on setting effective goals—those that lead to achieving what you hoped to achieve.

Formulate Specific Goals. A goal such as "to attain success" is too vague to serve as a guide to daily action. A more useful goal would be to state specifically what you mean by success and when you expect to achieve it. For example, "I want to be the manager of customer service at a telephone company by January 1, 2003."

Formulate Concise Goals. A useful goal can usually be expressed in a short, punchy statement. An example: "Decrease input errors in bank statements so that customer complaints are decreased by 25 percent by

I WISH I HAD MORE OUT OF LIFE.

September 30 of this year." People new to goal setting typically commit the error of formulating lengthy, rambling goal statements. These lengthy goals involve so many different activities that they fail to serve as specific guides to action.

Describe What You Would Actually Be Doing if You Reached Your Goal.   An effective goal specifies the behavior that results after the goal is achieved. A nonspecific goal for a sales representative would be "become a more effective salesperson." A more useful goal would be "increase the percent of leads I turn into actual sales." The meaning of a "more effective salesperson" is specified in the second goal (a higher conversion rate for leads).

Similarly, if your goal is to "get into good shape," you need to specify what signifies "good shape." It could mean such things as "weigh between 195 and 205 pounds," "run a mile in less than seven minutes," or "decrease the amount of time lost from work due to illness."

Use Past Performance as a Guide.   A good starting point in setting goals is to set them based on what you have achieved in the past. Past behavior gives as a guide to capabilities. This information becomes a foundation for defining ordinary and reasonable levels, barring any unforeseen changes or events. For example, your current grade point average is a good basis for setting goals for a future grade point average.

Set Realistic Goals.   A realistic goal is one that represents the right amount of challenge for the person pursuing the goal. On the one hand, easy goals are not very motivational—they may not spring you into action. On the other hand, goals that are too far beyond your capabilities may lead to frustration and despair because there is a good chance you will fail to reach them. The extent to which a goal is realistic depends upon a person's capabilities. An easy goal for an experienced person might be a realistic goal for a beginner.

Set Goals for Different Time Periods.   Goals are best set for different time periods, such as daily, short-range, medium-range, and long-range. Daily goals are essentially a "to do" list. Short-range goals cover the period from approximately one week to one year into the future. Finding a new job, for example, is typically a short-range goal. Medium-range goals relate to events that will take place within approximately two to five years. They concern such things as the type of education or training you plan to undertake and the next step in your career.

Long-range goals refer to events taking place five years into the future and beyond. As such they relate to the overall lifestyle you wish to achieve, including the type of work and family situation you hope to have. Although every person should have a general idea of a desirable lifestyle, long-range goals should be flexible. You might, for example, plan to stay single until age forty. But while on vacation next summer you might just happen to meet the right partner for you.

Include Some Fantasy in Your Personal Goal Setting.   Fantasy goals can bridge the gap between personal and career goal setting. A fantasy goal would be difficult to attain at any stage in your life. Fantasy goals also reflect your vision of the ideal type of life you would like to lead. They help you dream the impossible dream. However difficult to attain, *some* people do eventually live out their wildest dreams.

Here is a sampling of fantasy goals found in the career reports of students in a career development course:

> "I'd like to become a big tycoon by owning about ten office buildings in Manhattan, along with the San Francisco Forty-Niners and the Boston Red Sox."

> "I hope to become a freelance photographer for major news magazines. My specialty would be shooting civil unrest and border wars."

> "I hope to become a multimillionaire philanthropist, and have a high school named after me in a poor neighborhood."

Aside from being exciting to pursue, fantasy goals are important for another reason. Research suggests that your fantasy life can help with personal adjustment and overcoming stress. A well-developed fantasy can result in a pleasurable state of physical and mental relaxation. Furthermore, fantasy goals can help you cope with an unpleasant current situation by giving you hope for the future.[13]

Review Your Goals from Time to Time. A sophisticated goal setter realizes that all goals are temporary to some extent. In time one particular goal may lose its relevance for you, and therefore may no longer motivate you. At one time in your life you may be committed to earning an income in the top 10 percent of the population. Along the way toward achieving that goal, some other more relevant goal may develop. You might decide that the satisfactions of being self-employed are more important than earning a particular amount of money. You might therefore open an antique store with the simple financial goal of "meeting my expenses." Human Relations Skill-Building Exercise 2-2 gives class members an opportunity to improve their goal-setting skills.

PROBLEMS SOMETIMES CREATED BY GOALS

Despite the many advantages of goals, they can create problems. A major problem is that *goals can create inflexibility.* People can become so focused on reaching particular goals that they fail to react to emergencies, such as neglecting a much-needed machine repair to achieve quota. Goals can also make a person inflexible with respect to missing out on opportunities. Sales representatives sometimes neglect to invest time in cultivating a prospective customer because of the pressure to make quota. Instead, the sales rep goes for the quick sale with an established customer.

Goals can contribute to a *narrow focus, thus neglecting other worthwhile activities.* Students who have established goals for achieving a high grade sometimes face this problem. They might be tempted to concentrate their efforts on the details they think will appear on a forthcoming test and

HUMAN RELATIONS SKILL-BUILDING EXERCISE 2-2

Goal Sharing and Feedback

Each person selects one work and one personal goal from Skill-Building Exercise 2-1 that he or she would be willing to share with other members of the class. In turn, every class member presents those two goals to the rest of the class exactly as they are stated on the worksheet. Other class members have the opportunity of providing feedback to the person sharing his or her goals. Here are a few types of errors commonly made in goal setting that you should avoid:

1. Is the goal much too lengthy and complicated? Is it really a number of goals, rather than one specific goal?

2. Is the goal so vague that the person will be hard-pressed to know if he or she has reached the goal? (Such as, "I intend to become a good worker.")

3. Is the action plan specific enough to serve as a useful path for reaching that goal?

4. Does the goal sound sincere? (Admittedly, this is a highly subjective judgment on your part.)

neglect to review other beneficial aspects of the course. Another problem is that *performance goals can sometimes detract from an interest in the task.* People with a performance-goal orientation (focusing on being judged as competent) will sometimes lose interest in the task. The loss of interest is most likely to occur when the task is difficult.[14] This potential problem could be stated in another way. If you focus too much on success (as defined by reaching a goal), you will become frustrated when the means to reaching the goal is difficult.

Assume that your primary reason for working as a salesperson is to perform well enough so that you will be in line for promotion. If selling your product or service encounters some hurdles, you may readily become frustrated with selling. However, if your orientation is primarily to learn how to sell effectively, you will not be readily frustrated when you encounter problems. You might even look on it as a learning opportunity.

Consider also that *goals can interfere with relaxation.* A preoccupation with goals makes it difficult to relax. Instead of improving one's life, goals then become a source of stress. In the words of one purchasing agent, "Ever since I caught on to goal setting as a way of life, I feel as if I'm a basketball player racing from one end of the court to another. Even worse, nobody ever calls a time out." If the person is already under pressure, taking on another goal may be overwhelming.[15]

Despite the problems that can arise in goal setting, goals are valuable tools for managing your work and personal life. Used with common sense, and according to the ideas presented in this chapter, they could have a major, positive impact on your life.

SELF-MOTIVATION TECHNIQUES

Many people never achieve satisfying careers and never realize their potential because of low motivation. They believe they could perform better but admit, "I'm just not a go-getter" or "my motivation is low." Earlier we described how identifying your most important needs could enhance motivation. Here we describe six additional techniques for self-motivation.

1. *Set goals for yourself.* As shown throughout this chapter, goal setting is one of the most important techniques for self-motivation. If you set long-range goals and back them up with a series of smaller goals set for shorter time spans, your motivation will increase. Assume you knew that once you had passed a real estate broker's licensing exam, you would be guaranteed a lucrative job as a commercial real estate broker. You would have two clearly defined goals: attaining the new position and passing your exam. If the position were important to you, you would be strongly motivated to pass the exam. Your longer-range goal of having a satisfying career would lead you to set daily goals, such as 'Study for the broker exam for two hours today."

2. *Attempt to find self-determining work.* **Self-determining work** allows the person performing the task some choice in initiating and regulating his or her own actions.[6] Exerting such control over your work (being self-determining) enhances motivation. An extreme form of self-determining work would occur when an employee says to the employer, "These are the projects I have decided to work on this week." A more realistic form of self-determination would occur when an employee is given leeway in deciding how to get certain assignments accomplished, and in what sequence to get them done. To the extent that you can find self-determining work, your motivation is likely to increase. The self-discipline model presented later will give you another ideal for performing self-motivating work.

3. *Get feedback on your performance.* Few people can sustain a high level of motivation without receiving information about how well they are doing. Even if you find your work challenging and exciting, you will need feedback. One reason feedback is valuable is that it acts as a reward. If you learn that your efforts achieved a worthwhile purpose, you will feel encouraged. For example, if a graphics display you designed was well received by company officials, you would probably want to prepare another graphics display.

4. *Apply behavior modification to yourself.* **Behavior modification** is a system of motivating people that emphasizes rewarding them for doing the right things and punishing them for doing the wrong things. Behavior modification has been used by many people to change their own behavior. Specific purposes include overcoming eating disorders, tobacco addiction, nail biting, and procrastination.

To boost your own motivation through behavior modification, you would have to first decide what specific motivated actions you want to increase (such as working 30 minutes longer each day). Second, you would have to decide on a suitable set of rewards and punishments. You may choose to use rewards only, since rewards are generally better motivators than punishments.

5. *Improve your skills relevant to your goals.*   The **expectancy theory of motivation** states that people will be motivated if they believe that their efforts will lead to desired outcomes. According to this theory, people hold back effort when they are not confident that their efforts will lead to accomplishments. You should therefore seek adequate training to ensure that you have the right abilities and skills to perform your work. The training might be provided by the employer, or on your own through a course or self-study. Appropriate training gives you more confidence that you can perform the work. The training also increases your feelings of self-efficacy (as described in Chapter 1).[17] By recognizing your ability to mobilize your own resources to succeed, your self-confidence for the task will be elevated.

6. *Raise your level of self-expectation.*   A final strategy for increasing your level of motivation is to simply expect more of yourself. If you raise your level of self-expectation, you are likely to achieve more. Because you expect to succeed, you do succeed. The net effect is the same as if you had increased your level of motivation.

The technical term for improving your performance through raising your own expectations is the **Galatea effect.** In one experiment, for example, the self-expectations of subjects was raised in brief interviews with an organizational psychologist. The psychologist told the subjects they had high potential to succeed in the undertaking they were about to begin (a problem-solving task). The subjects who received the positive information about their potential did better than those subjects who did not receive such encouragement.[18]

High self-expectations and a positive mental attitude take a long time to develop. However, they are critically important for becoming a well-motivated person in a variety of situations.

7. *Develop a strong work ethic.*   A highly effective strategy for self-motivation is to develop a strong work ethic. If you are committed to the idea that most work is valuable and that it is joyful to work hard, you will automatically become strongly motivated. A person with a weak work ethic cannot readily develop a strong one, because the change requires a profound value shift. Yet if a person gives a lot of serious thought to the importance of work, and follows the right role models, a work ethic can be strengthened. The shift to a strong work ethic is much like a person who has a casual attitude toward doing fine work becoming quality conscious.

DEVELOPING THE SELF-DISCIPLINE TO ACHIEVE GOALS AND STAY MOTIVATED

Another perspective on achieving goals and staying motivated is that it requires **self-discipline,** the ability to work systematically and progressively toward a goal until it is achieved. The self-disciplined person works toward achieving his or her goals without being derailed by the many distractions faced each day. Self-discipline incorporates self-motivation, because it enables you to motivate yourself to achieve your goals without being nagged or prodded with deadlines. Our discussion of how to develop self-discipline follows the model shown in Figure 2-5. You will observe that the model incorporates several of the ideas about goals already discussed in this chapter. Without realizing it, you have already invested mental energy into learning the self-discipline model.

Component 1. *Formulate a mission statement.*   Who are you? What are you trying to accomplish in life? If you understand what you are trying to accomplish in life, you have the fuel to be self-disciplined. With a mission, activities that may appear mundane to others become vital stepping stones for you. An example would be learning Spanish grammar to help you become an international business person. To help formulate your mission statement, answer two questions: What are my five biggest wishes? What do I want to accomplish in my career during the next five years?

Component 2. *Develop role models.*   An excellent method of learning how to be self-disciplined is to model your behavior after successful achievers who are obviously well-disciplined. To model another person does not mean you will slavishly imitate every detail of that person's life. Instead, you will follow the general pattern of how the person operates in spheres related to your mission and goals. An ideal role model is the type of person whom you would like to become, not someone you feel you could never become.

Component 3. *Develop goals for each task.*   Your mission must be supported by a series of specific goals that collectively will enable you to achieve your mission. Successfully completing goals eventually leads to

Figure 2-5   The Self-Discipline Model

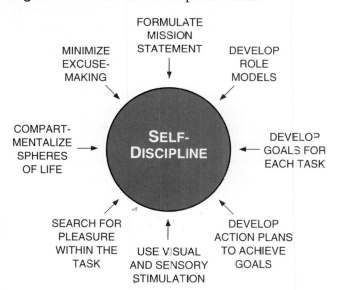

SOURCE: Andrew J. DuBrin, *Getting It Done: The Transforming Power of Self-Discipline* (Princeton, NJ: Peterson's, 1995), p. 18.

fulfilling a mission. Each small goal achieved is a building block toward larger achievements.

Component 4. *Develop action plans to achieve goals.*   Self-disciplined people carefully follow their action plans because they make goal attainment possible. It is helpful to chart your progress against the dates established for the subactivities.

Component 5. *Use visual and sensory stimulation.*   A self-disciplined person relentlessly focuses on a goal and persistently pursues that goal. To accomplish this consistent focus, self-disciplined people form images of reaching their goals—they actually develop a mental image of the act of accomplishing what they want. As mysterious as it sounds, visualization helps the brain convert images into reality. The more senses you can incorporate into your visual image, the stronger its power. Imagine yourself seeing, tasting, hearing, smelling, and touching your goal. Can you imagine yourself sitting in your condo overlooking the ocean, eating a great meal to celebrate the fact that the business you founded now has 10,000 employees?

Component 6. *Search for pleasure within the task.*   A self-disciplined person finds joy, excitement, and intense involvement in the task at hand, a situation referred to as **intrinsic motivation.** Instead of focusing on the extrinsic (or external) reward, the love of the task helps the person in pursuit of the goal. An axiom of becoming wealthy is not to focus on getting rich. Instead, focus on work. If the task at hand does not thrill you, at least focus on the pleasure from the most enjoyable element within the task. A thruway toll collector might not find the total task intrinsically motivating, but perhaps he or she enjoys meeting so many people on the job!

Component 7. *Compartmentalize spheres of life.*   Self-disciplined people have a remarkable capacity to divide up (or compartmentalize) the various spheres of their lives to stay focused on what they are doing at the moment. While working, develop the knack of concentrating on work and putting aside thoughts about personal life. In the midst of social and family activities, concentrate on them rather than half-thinking about work. This approach will contribute to both self-discipline and a better integration of work and family life.

Component 8. *Minimize excuse making.*   Self-disciplined people concentrate their energies on goal accomplishment, rather than making excuses for why work is not accomplished. Instead of trying to justify why they have been diverted from a goal, high-achieving, self-disciplined people circumvent potential barriers. Undisciplined people, in contrast, seem to look for excuses. If you are an excuse maker, conduct a self-audit writing down all the reasons blocking you from achieving any current goal. Be brutally honest in challenging each one of your excuses. Ask yourself, "Is this a valid excuse, or is it simply a rationalization for my getting sidetracked?"

SUMMARY

Self-motivation is important for achieving success in work and personal life. A well-accepted explanation of human behavior is that people have needs and motives propelling them toward achieving certain goals. The central idea behind need theory is that unsatisfied needs motivate us until they become satisfied. After satisfaction of one need, the person usually pursues satisfaction of another, higher need.

Work and personal life offer the opportunity to satisfy many different needs and motives. Among the more important needs and motives are achievement, power, affiliation, recognition, dominance, and order. The need for thrill seeking is also important for some people.

According to Maslow's need hierarchy, people have an internal need pushing them on toward self-actualization. However, needs are arranged into a five-step ladder. Before higher-level needs are activated, certain lower-level needs must be satisfied. In ascending order, the groups of needs are physiological, safety, social, esteem, and self-actualization (such as self-fulfillment).

Need theory helps in self-motivation. First identify which needs you want to satisfy, and then focus your efforts on an activity that will satisfy those needs.

A goal is an event, circumstance, object, or condition a person strives to attain. Goals are valuable because they (1) focus effort in a consistent direction, (2) improve your chances for success, and (3) improve motivation and satisfaction.

One explanation for the contribution of goals is that they create a discrepancy between what individuals have and what they aspire to achieve. Self-dissatisfaction with this discrepancy serves as an incentive to achieve. Goals also create a state of arousal, which readies people for accomplishment.

Goals can be aimed at either learning or performing. A learning-goal orientation means that an individual is focused on acquiring new skills and mastering new situations. A performance-goal orientation is aimed at wanting to demonstrate and validate the adequacy of your competence by seeking favorable judgments of competence. People with a learning-goal orientation are more likely to seek feedback on how well they are performing.

Goal setting is widely used on the job. Goals set by employees at lower levels in an organization are supposed to contribute to goals set at the top. Frequently, individual employees are asked to participate in goal setting by contributing ideas of their own. An important part of goal setting, both on and off the job, is priority setting. To increase the motivational impact of goals, some managers encourage workers to track their own performances.

Goal setting in personal life can contribute to life satisfaction. For maximum advantage, personal goals should be integrated with career goals. Areas of life in which personal goals may be set include (1) social and family, (2) hobbies and interests, (3) physical and mental health, and (4) financial. To increase their effectiveness, goals should be supported with action plans.

Effective goals are specific and concise. You should describe what you would actually be doing if you reached your goal. Past performance should be used as a guide, and goals should be realistically challenging. Set goals for different time periods, and include some fantasy in your personal goal setting.

Goals have some problems associated with them. They can create inflexibility and can lead you to a narrow focus, thus neglecting other worthwhile activities. Performance goals can detract from an interest in the task, and goals can interfere with relaxation.

Key techniques of self-motivation include: (1) Set goals for yourself; (2) engage in self-determining work; (3) get feedback on your performance; (4) apply behavior modification to yourself; (5) improve your skills relevant to your job, (6) raise your level of self-expectation, and (7) develop a strong work ethic.

Achieving goals and staying motivated requires self-discipline. A model presented here for developing self-discipline consists of eight components: (1) Formulate a mission statement; (2) develop role models; (3) develop goals for each task; (4) develop action plans; (5) use visual and sensory stimulation; (6) search for pleasure within the task; (7) compartmentalize spheres of life; and (8) minimize excuse making.

Questions and Activities

1. How would the need theory of motivation explain the fact that shortly after being promoted, many people begin thinking about their next possible promotion?

2. Give an example from your own life of how a lower-level need had to be satisfied first before you were able to concentrate on a higher-level need.

3. How might having a strong need for power create problems in an individual's personal life?

4. How might having a strong need for affiliation retard a person's career advancement?

5. Identify any self-actualized person you know and explain why you think that person is self-actualized.

6. Why does a learning-goal orientation often contribute to more peace of mind than a performance-goal orientation?

7. How can people who are not sure what field they want to enter, nevertheless set long-range goals?

8. Explain how you might be able to use the Galatea effect to improve the success you achieve in your career and personal life.

9. In what way does the self-discipline model presented in this chapter go beyond goal setting as a method of improving your chances for success?

10. Ask a person who has achieved career success how much self-discipline contributed to his or her success.

A HUMAN RELATIONS CASE PROBLEM

Motivating the Kitchen Staff at the Blue Gardenia

Jimmy Gomez aspires to someday be the manager of a large hotel. To help reach that goal he is working part-time on a degree in food and hotel administration. He attends classes at various times to fit his demanding full-time position as the kitchen staff supervisor at the Blue Gardenia, a well-established downtown hotel. Gomez supervises a staff of about 45 kitchen workers including food preparers, butchers, bakers, and cooks. The highly paid chefs report to the restaurant manager, Sonya Rosato, who is also Gomez's manager.

The average wage is $7.75 per hour for the kitchen staff reporting to Gomez. Half of these workers work part time and receive almost no benefits. The full-time staff receive a few modest benefits, such as vacation, a $20,000 life insurance policy, and medical insurance. Blue Gardenia management believes strongly that they pay competitive wages for kitchen staff, and that paying them much more would eat into profits too much.

During a goal-setting conference with Rosato, Gomez agreed that an important area for improvement in his operation would be to reduce turnover and increase productivity among the kitchen staff. Rosato pointed out that although the turnover rate for Jimmy's employees was about average for kitchen staff in the geographic area (25 percent per year), it was still too high. If the turnover rate could be trimmed down to about 15 percent, it would save the hotel thousands of dollars in hiring and training costs. Also, less food would be wasted because trainees make so many mistakes in food preparation. Skilled workers also drop fewer dishes and glasses.

Rosato and Gomez also agreed that lower turnover would mean more kitchen staff would have good job skills and would therefore be able to produce more. For example, a skilled salad-maker can make twice as many salads as a beginner. Another concern Rosato expressed was that many of the kitchen staff seemed lazy.

During the week following the meeting with his boss, Gomez kept thinking about the problem. He decided tentatively that he was really dealing with a motivational issue. Jimmy reasoned that if the staff were better motivated, they would stay with the job longer, and obviously not appear lazy. As a starting point in attempting to better motivate the kitchen staff, he conducted a few informal interviews with them during breaks and toward the end of the work day. Jimmy asked 12 of the kitchen workers what Blue Gardenia management could do to keep kitchen staff on the job longer and to motivate them to work harder. A few of the comments Jimmy collected were as follows:

"What do you expect for $7.50 an hour? Some kind of superman? I work as hard as a factory worker, but I don't get paid like a factory worker."

"This is like a dead-end job. If I could find a job with a better future, I'd be out of here in no time."

"I like this job fine. But just like a few of the other guys here, I've got a problem. My wife and I are expecting a child. If I stay in this job, I won't be able to support my child. My wife wants to drop out of work for a year to care for the baby."

(Continued)

"Not me, but I think some of the workers here think management doesn't care much about them. So if they can find another job that pays even 25 cents more per hour, they're gone."

Questions

1. How effective do you think it was for Jimmy Gomez to interview members of the kitchen staff to investigate possible motivational problems?

2. What does the information revealed by the kitchen staff tell you about their motivational needs?

3. What recommendations can you make to Blue Gardenia management about decreasing the turnover and increasing the productivity of the kitchen staff?

REFERENCES

[1] Phil Ebersole, "Our Work Ethic: Many Companies Thrive Despite What Polls Say," Rochester *Democrat and Chronicle,* March 10, 1997, p. 6 of *Monday Business.*

[2] David C. McClelland, *The Achieving Society* (New York: Van Nostrand Reinhold, 1961).

[3] David C. McClelland and Richard Boyatzis, "Leadership Motive Pattern and Long-term Success in Management," *Journal of Applied Psychology,* December 1982, p. 737.

[4] Research cited in "What Makes Them Do It?" *Time,* January 15, 1996, p. 60; Marvin Zuckerman, "The Search for High Sensation," *Psychology Today,* February 1978, pp. 38–40, 43, 46, 96–99.

[5] The original statement is Abraham H. Maslow, "A Theory of Human Motivation," *Psychological Review,* July 1943, pp. 370–396. See also Maslow, *Motivation and Personality* (New York: Harper & Row, 1954).

[6] James L. Gibson, John M. Ivancevich, and James H. Donnelly, Jr., *Organizations: Behavior, Structure, Processes,* 6th ed. (Plano, TX: Irwin, 1988), p. 111.

[7] "Getting There: 1983 *Success* Magazine Goal-Setting Guide," *Success,* January 1983, p. A10.

[8] Edwin A. Locke and Gary P. Latham, *A Theory of Goal Setting and Task Performance* (Upper Saddle River, NJ: Prentice Hall, 1990), pp. 27–62.

[9] P. Christopher Earley and Terri R. Lituchy, "Delineating Goals and Efficacy: A Test of Three Models," *Journal of Applied Psychology,* February 1991, pp. 81–82.

[10] Ian R. Gellatly and John P. Meyer, "The Effects of Goal Difficulty on Physiological Arousal, Cognition, and Task Performance," *Journal of Applied Psychology,* October 1992, p. 695.

[11]Don VandeWalle and Larry L. Cummings, "A Test of the Influence of Goal Orientation on the Feedback-Seeking Process," *Journal of Applied Psychology,* June 1997, pp. 390–400.

[12]"Employee Motivation: Set Them on Fire Without Burning Them Out," *Executive Edge,* August 1996, p. 10.

[13]Stephen Sprinkel, "Not Having Fantasies Can Be Hazardous to Your Health Counselor Says," Gannett News Service, April 10, 1992.

[14]VandeWalle and Cummings, "A Test of the Influence of Goal Orientation," p. 392.

[15]P. Christopher Earley, Terry Connolly, and Goran Ekegran, "Goals, Strategy Development, and Task Performance: Some Limits to the Efficacy of Goal Setting," *Journal of Applied Psychology,* February 1989, p. 24.

[16]Edward L. Deci, James P. Connell, and Richard M. Ryan, "Self-Determination in a Work Organization," *Journal of Applied Psychology,* August 1989, p. 580.

[17]Earley and Lituchy, "Delineating Goal Effects," p. 96.

[18]Taly Dvir, Dov Eden, and Michal Lang Banjo, "Self-Fulfilling Prophecy and Gender: Can Women Be Pygmalion and Galatea?" *Journal of Applied Psychology,* April 1995, p. 268.

ADDITIONAL READING

Barrick, Murray K., Mount, Michael K., and Strauss, Judy P. "Conscientiousness and Performance of Sales Representatives: Test of the Mediating Effects of Goal Setting." *Journal of Applied Psychology,* October 1993, pp. 715–722.

Chandler, Steve. *100 Ways to Motivate Yourself.* Chicago: Career Press, 1996.

DeShon, Richard P., Brown, Kenneth G., and Greenis, Jennifer L. "Does Self-Regulation Require Cognitive Resources? Evaluation of Resource Allocation Models of Goal Setting." *Journal of Applied Psychology,* October 1996, pp. 596–608.

Muchnick, Marc. *Naked Management: Bare Essentials for Motivating the X-Generation at Work.* Delray Beach, FL: St. Lucie Press, 1996.

Nelson, Bob. "Dump the Cash: Load on the Praise." *Personnel Journal,* July 1996, pp. 65–69.

Nelson, Bob. *1001 Ways to Reward Employees.* New York: Workman Publishing, 1995.

Schmidt, Laura C., and Frieze, Irene Hanson. "A Mediational Model of Power, Affiliation and Achievement Motives and Product Involvement." *Journal of Business and Psychology,* Summer 1997, pp. 425–447.

Straub, Joseph T. "Prioritizing Goals." *Getting Results,* June 1996, p. 8.

Wilson, Susan R. *Goal Setting.* New York: AMACOM, 1993.

CHAPTER
3

PROBLEM SOLVING AND CREATIVITY

Learning Objectives

After studying the information and doing the exercises in this chapter, you should be able to:

▼ Understand how personal characteristics influence the ability to solve problems and make decisions

▼ Explain the four decision-making styles as defined by the Myers-Briggs Type Indicator

▼ Apply the problem-solving and decision-making steps to complex problems

▼ Summarize the characteristics of creative people

▼ Describe various ways of improving your creativity

*L*arry Baras, a financial planner based in Boston, frequently found himself eating on the run. This usually meant grabbing a bagel and cream cheese at a convenience store. But he usually ended up with more cheese on his tie and steering wheel than on the bagel. Baras said, "They call it a convenience food, but I know there had to be a better way."

So Baras, cashing in on the boom in the bagel business, worked with a bakery to develop a bagel that could be pumped full of cream cheese after baking. The UnHoley Bagel looks unorthodox, more like a dinner roll than the traditional bagel. Baras knows that purists might not be interested. "People will think that not having the hole is sacrilegious. But they'll realize the hole is a pain. The filling always squirts out the middle."

The UnHoley Bagel comes frozen, in a variety of flavors, as well as with regular, light, or fat-free cream cheese. Baras was able to quickly get his bagel product into several national food chains. A food critic remarked that "I think this has a lot of possibilities. Bagels have become so common that people are open to new alternatives."[1]

Baras' Boston-based beige bagels (your tongue twister for the day) may not rival the light bulb or the computer as creative brilliance. Yet it does illustrate a few basic facts about problem solving, decision making, and creativity. Baras found a **problem,** a gap between what exists and what you want to exist. Baras wanted a drip-free bagel, but could only find bagels with center holes. **Decision making** refers to choosing one alternative from the various alternative solutions that can be pursued. Baras no doubt thought through other alternatives to a dripless bagel, such as shaping it like an ice-cream cone. And the act of generating the various alternatives is a major aspect of creativity.

The general purpose of this chapter is to help you become a more effective and creative problem solver when working individually or in groups. Whether you are solving problems by yourself or as part of a group, most of the principles apply equally well. The problems we refer to are unique and/or major decisions such as developing a new product, purchasing major equipment, or weighing a job offer. Very minor decisions, such as choosing a bagel with or without a hole, do not require formal study in decision making for most people.

PERSONAL CHARACTERISTICS THAT INFLUENCE YOUR PROBLEM-SOLVING ABILITY

Many personal characteristics and traits influence the type of problem solver and decision maker you are now or are capable of becoming. Fortunately, some personal characteristics that influence your decision-making ability can be improved through conscious effort. For instance, if you make bad decisions because you have limited information, you can take steps to become a more knowledgeable person. Most of the personal characteristics described next can be strengthened though the appropriate education, training, and self-discipline. Before reading more about problem solving, do Human Relations Self-Assessment Exercise 3-1. It is designed for you to take stock of your present problem-solving tendencies.

FLEXIBILITY VERSUS RIGIDITY

Some people are successful problem solvers and decision makers because they approach every problem with a fresh outlook. They are able to avoid developing rigid viewpoints. Flexible thinking enables the problem solver to think of original—and therefore creative—alternative solutions to solving a problem. Another perspective on the same issue is that being open-minded helps a person solve problems well. For example, a person might face the problem of wanting to purchase a high-quality PC but lacks sufficient funds. So the person keeps searching for a high-quality PC at a bargain price. If the person were more open-minded, he or she might investigate a "Net PC." Such a computer is low-priced because, instead of having a hard drive of its own, it temporarily downloads programs from the Internet. The link between flexibility and creativity will be described in more detail in the discussion of the characteristics of creative people.

INTELLIGENCE, EDUCATION, AND EXPERIENCE

In general, if you are intelligent, well educated, and well experienced you will make better decisions than people without these attributes. Intelligence helps because, by definition, intelligence denotes the ability to solve problems. Education improves the problem-solving and decision-making process because it gives you a background of principles and facts to rely on.

Experience facilitates decision making because good decisions tend to be made by people who have already faced similar situations in the past. This is one of the many reasons why experienced people command higher salaries. All things being equal, would you prefer to take your computer problem to an experienced or inexperienced specialist?

HUMAN RELATIONS SELF-ASSESSMENT EXERCISE 3-1

Problem-Solving Quiz

Indicate if the following statements are true or false about you. Then read on for the scoring and an explanation:

_____   1. Most problems solve themselves in one way or another.

_____   2. I'm known to be a perfectionist when it comes to solving problems.

_____   3. It's usually true that the first answer that comes to mind is the one to follow.

_____   4. I often shelve vexing problems and hope that they will go away.

_____   5. I often become rattled by tough problems.

_____   6. I often let others make decisions for me.

_____   7. I would prefer a job where I didn't have the burden of making decisions.

_____   8. I've never been able to judge how well I did on an exam.

_____   9. It's hard for me to admit that a solution of mine isn't working out well.

_____ 10. It's hard to accept a solution from someone who is younger than I am or below my professional level.

Scoring: All items in the quiz are examples of pitfalls common to poor problem solvers. Give yourself 1 point for each item you answered true. Then consider the following interpretations:

   0 to 3 points: You have a solid approach to solving problems. You are the person to ask when a good solution to a problem is needed.

   4 to 6 points: You are an average problem solver. Some conflicts you find easy to solve, but others are more difficult.

   7 to 10 points: You are weak as a problem solver. You rely too heavily upon your assumptions instead of examining the facts. Try to be more open-minded and flexible about solutions.

Explanation: Many people fall into problem-solving traps. Many of us have strong tendencies to deny that problems even exist in our daily lives. This is wishful thinking, and items 1 and 4 give such examples. Another trap in problem solving is to fall into a rigid mental set. This one-sided outlook hampers our flexibility to arrive at good solutions. More will be said about overcoming rigid mental sets at several places in this chapter. Problem-solving ability cannot be improved without improving mental flexibility.

SOURCE: Adapted with permission from the files of Salvatore Didato.

DECISIVENESS AND PERFECTIONISM

Some people are ill-suited to solving problems and making decisions because they are fearful of committing themselves to any given course of action. "Gee, I'm not sure, what do you think?" is their typical response to a decision forced upon them. If you are indecisive, this characteristic will have to be modified if you are to become a success in your field. A manager has to decide which person to hire. And a photographer has to decide which setting is best for the subject. As the old saying goes, at some point "you have to fish or cut bait."

People can be indecisive because they are perfectionists. In regard to decision making, **perfectionism** is a pattern of behavior in which the individual strives to accomplish almost unattainable standards of flawless work. Psychologist J. Clayton Lafferty explains that "Perfectionism is a way of thinking and behaving that seems like a search for excellence and perfection but actually brings great unhappiness, poor health, and massive imperfection."[2] Perfectionism leads people toward indecisiveness and delay in making decisions because they usually believe that they need more information before making a choice. Have you ever noticed how a perfectionist goes about purchasing an expensive piece of consumer electronics equipment? He or she might visit many stores, ask the opinions of many people, and search for extensive written material before making a choice. At the electronics store, the person barrages the store associate with a long series of picky questions.

SELF-CONFIDENCE AND RISK TAKING

Effective decision makers are confident of the courses of action they choose. They recognize that making a major decision involves some risk, yet are reasonably confident that they can make a good decision. An example is George Fisher, the top executive at Eastman Kodak, and formerly the president of Motorola Incorporated. He faced considerable criticism when he made the decision for Motorola to forge ahead into the cellular telephone and pager business. Fisher reflects back on his decision and compares it to his decision to push Kodak forward into the photo CD business.

> You saw what happened in the cellular paging business. "Who wants a pager?" There are 30 million pagers out there now. "Who wants a cellular telephone? You want to talk to somebody while you're driving? You've got to be crazy." Let me tell you what. It's a wonderful business. You have to do the same sort of thinking in imaging.
>
> Photo CD is going to be, and is already becoming, a work standard. And there are a lot of naysayers who would have shot at my head way prematurely, and they would have shot cellular telephone. I [Motorola] was losing $50 million to $70 million a year on cellular telephone for several years and a lot of the wise people of the financial world were saying "Why are you doing that? That's stupid. You're never going to get that thing up." Let me tell you, it's a $5 billion dollar business today, and that was in less than 10 years.[3]

High self-confidence and a risk-taking attitude are assets to a decision maker, as exemplified by Fisher. Yet being too self-confident can lead to needless risks and a decision-making error. Overconfidence usually results from approaching a problem from a limited perspective. People tend to see the world through their own perspectives and think that their viewpoints are the correct and only ones. In reality, each of their views of reality is but one perspective. A man invested his total inheritance into an auto detailing (total cleaning) service because he assumed most people shared the importance he attached to an immaculate car. He also assumed people would be willing to pay approximately $95 to have their cars "detailed." Unfortunately, not enough customers showed up to pay his operating expenses.

To avoid the error of overconfidence, seek other perspectives on a problem before making your decision.[4] Seek input from people with different interests and backgrounds. The man just referred to might have spoken to people who are not so concerned about auto cleanliness.

CONCENTRATION

Mental concentration is an important contributor to making good decisions. Many people who solve problems poorly do so because they are too distracted to immerse themselves in the problem at hand. In contrast, effective problem solvers often achieve the **flow experience**—total absorption in their work. When flow occurs, things seem to go just right. The person feels alive and fully attentive to what he or she is doing. As a by-product of the flow experience, a good solution to a problem may surface.

INTUITION

Effective decision makers do not rely on careful analysis alone. Instead, they also use their **intuition,** a method of arriving at a conclusion by a quick judgment or "gut feel." Intuition takes place when the brain gathers information stored in memory and packages it as a new insight or solution. Intuitions, therefore, can be regarded as stored information that is reorganized or repackaged.[5] Developing good intuition may take a long time because so much information has to be stored. Considerable attention has been drawn to the importance of intuition in managerial decision making. Managers must still analyze problems systematically. Yet they also need to be able to respond to situations rapidly. Robert Eaton, the chairman of Chrysler Corporation, puts it this way: "We've put so much faith in analysis and quantification and other areas of left-brain thinking, we've often missed the forest for all the well-examined trees. Over the past few years I've been on sort of a personal crusade at Chrysler to legitimatize what I refer to as right-brain (intuitive) thinking."[6]

To use intuition to your advantage, you have to know when to rely on facts and figures and when to rely on intuitive skills. Intuition is often required when the facts and figures in a situation still leave you with uncertainty. One way of sharpening your intuition is to keep an idea journal. Whenever an insight comes to you, record it on paper or electronically. If you notice that you shut off these insights without carefully processing them, you will know that you must learn to give them more careful thought.[7]

EMOTIONAL FACTORS

Problem solving and decision making are not entirely rational processes. Instead, emotion plays a key role in all stages of decision making. Have you ever decided to blow off a day instead of studying for an exam, although the facts in the situation suggest that you should stay home and study? Intellect, reason, and emotion enter into most decisions. Even when decisions appear to be based almost entirely on hard data, *which* data are included in making the decision is influenced by emotion and feeling.

It is not necessarily wrong to be influenced by your emotions, but you should try to recognize when you are not being rational. You might say to yourself, for example, "Is this home-entertainment center really worth going into debt for? Or am I buying it just to impress my friends?"

Fear of making the wrong decision is another significant emotional factor that influences decision making. Each time you make a decision, you run the risk that someone will disagree with you or not like your decision. (Remember George Fisher, the business executive?) A person who is too fearful will hesitate to make important decisions. Keep in mind that you will never please everyone, so use facts and intuition to make the best-possible decision.[8]

PROBLEM-SOLVING STYLES

People go about solving problems in various ways. You may have observed, for example, that some people are more analytical and systematic while others are more intuitive. The most widely used method of classifying problem-solving styles is the Myers-Briggs Type Indicator (MBTI).[9] A key aspect of the MBTI is to understand how people gather and evaluate information to solve problems.

To solve problems it is necessary to gather information. Styles of gathering information range from sensation to intuition. **Sensation-type individuals** prefer routine and order. They search for precise details when gathering information to solve a problem. These people would prefer to work with established facts rather than to search for new possibilities. **Intuitive-type individuals** prefer an overall perspective—the big picture. Such people enjoy solving new problems. In addition, they dislike routine and would prefer to look for possibilities rather than work with facts.

When shopping for an automobile, a sensation-type individual would want to gather a large number of facts about such matters as miles per gallon, provisions of the warranty, finance charges, and resale value. In contrast, the intuitive-type individual would be more concerned about the overall style of the car and how proud he or she would be as the owner.

The evaluation aspect of problem solving involves judging how to deal with information after it has been collected. Styles of information evaluation range from an emphasis on feeling to an emphasis on thinking. **Feeling-type individuals** have a need to conform, and they attempt to adapt to the wishes of others. Because of these tendencies, they try to avoid problems that might result in disagreements. **Thinking-type individuals** rely on reason and intellect to deal with problems. They downplay emotion in problem solving and decision making.

Assume that the manager asks group members their opinions on an idea for a new product. Feeling-type people in the group are likely to look for the good in the proposal and express approval for the new project. Thinking-type group members are likely to be more independent in their evaluation of the new product idea. As a result, they will express their opinion even if it is not what the manager wants to hear. (The people who told George Fisher that pagers and cellular phones had no future might have been thinking-type individuals.)

The two dimensions of information gathering and evaluation are combined to produce a four-way classification of problem-solving styles, as shown in Exhibit 3-1. The four styles are (1) sensation-thinking, (2) sensation-feeling, (3) intuitive-thinking, and (4) intuitive-feeling. Listed below each type are examples of occupations well suited for people of that particular type.

EXHIBIT 3-1

FOUR PROBLEM-SOLVING STYLES AND WORK MATCHUP

Sensation-Thinking: decisive, dependable, alert to details
   Accounting and bookkeeping
   Computer programming
   Manufacturing technology

Intuitive-Thinking: creative, progressive, perceptive
   Design of systems
   Law, paralegal work
   Middle manager

Sensation-Feeling: pragmatic, analytical, methodical, and conscientious
   Supervision
   Selling
   Negotiating

Intuitive-Feeling: colorful, people person, helpful
   Customer service
   Business communications
   Human resources

If you take the Myers-Briggs Type Indicator, often available in career centers, you will discover your type. You can also study these four types and make a tentative judgment as to your problem-solving style. Recognizing your problem-solving style can help you identify work that you are likely to perform well. For example, a person with an intuitive-feeling style is likely to be skillful in resolving customer complaints. The same person might not be well suited by temperament to bookkeeping.

PROBLEM-SOLVING AND DECISION-MAKING STEPS

Whatever complex problem you face, it is best to use the standard problem-solving and decision-making steps as a guide. These steps are similar to the systematic approach used in the scientific method. Although based on the scientific method, the decision-making steps presented here do not exclude the role of intuition. Rather, finding creative alternatives to your problem is actually at the heart of the method. Figure 3-1 summarizes the steps involved in problem solving and decision making. It is based on the assumption that decision making should take place in an orderly flow of steps.

Figure 3-1   Decision-Making Steps

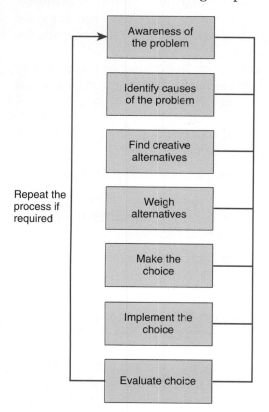

Awareness of the Problem

Problem solving and decision making begin when somebody is aware that a problem exists. In most decision-making situations, problems are given to another person. At other times, people create their own problems to solve, or they find problems. When one man decided that there were too many potholes in the streets of his town, he campaigned for the town supervisor to take decisive action on the town's pothole problem.

After you have identified the problem, recognize that it may represent an important opportunity. Paul Hawken, a company founder and author, says that a mess is a pile of opportunities.[10] For example, if you are bothered enough by a problem facing your company, you might volunteer to be the person in charge of overcoming the problem.

Identify Causes of the Problem

The causes of problems should be diagnosed and clarified before any action is taken because they are not always what they seem to be on the surface. Some may be more complicated than suspected, or may even be the wrong problem you need to solve in a particular situation. The person who found the potholes was thinking about treating the symptoms and not the real problem. Although it certainly would be advisable for the town to patch its potholes, the best solution is to attend to the cause of potholes. The town would never be able to change the weather conditions, of course, but it could strengthen all new pavement. One petroleum company, for example, has developed a webbing that dramatically reduces potholes when placed beneath the surface of a street.

Identifying the root cause of a problem can sometimes be facilitated by asking a series of questions. Five key elements to ask questions about (along with some sample questions) are as follows:

- *People.* What do the people involved contribute to the problem? Are they competent? Do they have an attitude problem?

- *Materials.* Do we have the right materials available? Is the quality of the materials adequate?

- *Machines and facilities.* Do we have the right machines and facilities to do the job? Have the machines and facilities changed?

- *Physical environment.* Is anything wrong with the environment (such as toxic fumes making people sick)? Has the environment changed?

- *Methods.* Are the processes and procedures adequate? Have new methods been introduced that workers do not understand?

An associate in a consumer electronics shop used the above questions to quickly identify why a customer's brand-new CD player played music with such a muffled sound. In asking about the physical environment, the associated identified the fact that the customer placed the CD on a thick carpet, leading to a "muffled sound."

FIND CREATIVE ALTERNATIVES

Here creativity and imagination enter into problem solving and decision making. Successful decision makers have the ability to think of different alternatives. The person who pushes to find one more alternative to a problem is often the person who finds a breakthrough solution. Creativity plays such an important role in decision making that it will be discussed again in the next two major sections of this chapter.

WEIGH ALTERNATIVES

This stage refers simply to examining the pros and cons of the various alternatives in the previous stages. In a major decision, each alternative would have to be given serious consideration. In practice, weighing alternatives often means jotting down the key good and bad points of each possible choice.

A source of error when weighing alternatives is to rely too much on the first information you receive. The information anchors some people to their first alternatives, thereby overshadowing data and impressions that come later.[11] Anchoring can be somewhat minimized by remembering that decision making is incomplete until many alternatives have been explored.

MAKE THE CHOICE

The essence of decision making is selecting the right course of action to follow. You have to choose an alternative, even if it is not to go ahead with a new plan of action. For instance, after conducting a job campaign, you could decide *not* to change jobs. Experienced business executives have often criticized well-educated young people for their lack of decisiveness. Instead of coming to a decision, the young people are accused of over-analyzing a problem. Do you suffer from "analysis paralysis," or do you make up your mind after a reasonable amount of thought?

In choosing an alternative, it is helpful to remember that most problems really have multiple solutions. You therefore do not have to be overly concerned with finding the only correct answer to your problem. For instance, there might be several effective ways of reducing the costs of running a department.

IMPLEMENT THE CHOICE

After you decide which course of action to take, you have to put the choice into effect. Some decisions are more difficult to implement than others. Decisions made by top management, for example, are sometimes so difficult to implement that they have to be reversed. An executive announced a new policy that all employees would be restricted to 45-minute lunch breaks. Few employees took the edict seriously, and they continued to spend about 60 minutes at lunch. The executive gave up and reconsidered the decision in terms of its effect on morale.

EVALUATE THE CHOICE

The decision-making sequence is not complete until the decision has been evaluated. Evaluation may take a considerable period of time because the results of your decision are not always immediately apparent. Suppose you receive two job offers. It might take several months to a year to judge whether you are satisfied with the job you accepted. It would be necessary to look at the factors you think are most important in a job. Among them might be: "Is there opportunity for advancement?" "Are the people here friendly?" "Is the work interesting?" Evaluating your choice would be further complicated by the difficulty of determining how you might have fared in the job you didn't accept. Now and then you might obtain some information to suggest what that alternative held in store for you, as did a woman who turned down a job offer with a new and promising company. She questioned that decision until she read one morning a year later that the company had gone into bankruptcy.

What happens when your evaluation of a decision is negative? You go back to the drawing board, as the line and arrow on the left-hand side of

Figure 3-1 indicates. Since your first decision was not a good one, you are faced with another problem situation.

A helpful decision-making aid is to visualize what you would do if the alternative you chose proved to be dreadful—the **worst-case scenario.** Suppose, for example, you choose a job that proves to be unsuited to your talents. Would you resign as soon as your mistake became apparent, or would you sweat it out for a year to show some employment stability? Or would you retain the job while starting to look around for a more suitable job? Developing a worst-case scenario helps prevent you from becoming overwhelmed by a bad decision.

To gain practice in developing your skills in making major decisions, do Human Relations Skill-Building Exercise 3-1. You will be given some additional practice in using the problem-solving method in the end-of-chapter case problem.

CREATIVITY IN DECISION MAKING

Creativity is helpful at any stage of decision making, but is essential for being aware of problems, analyzing their causes, and searching for alternative solutions. Simply put, **creativity** is the ability to develop good ideas that can be put into action. When many people see or hear the word *creativity,* they think of a rarefied talent. A more helpful perspective is to recognize that not all creativity requires wild imagination. According to creativity expert Michael Kirton, two types of creativity exist. *Adaptive creativity* involves improving an existing system, such as identifying what is wrong in a customer billing system and correcting the problem. *Innovative creativity* involves creating something new. Instead of trying to correct the invoicing system, the person using innovative creativity would discard it and start all over.[12]

MEASURING YOUR CREATIVE POTENTIAL

One way to understand creativity is to try out exercises used to measure creative potential, such as those presented in Human Relations Self-Assessment exercises 3-2 and 3-3. Both exercises measure creativity based on verbal ability. Human Relations Skill-Building Exercise 3-2 demonstrates how visualizing objects and shapes is important for creative problem solving. In order to solve this problem, you will need to rely on intuition to find a correct solution. Persistence alone will not lead to the correct solution.

CHARACTERISTICS OF CREATIVE WORKERS

Creative workers tend to have different intellectual and personality characteristics from their less-creative counterparts. In general, creative

HUMAN RELATIONS SKILL-BUILDING EXERCISE 3-1

Using the Problem-Solving Process

Imagine that you have received $1,000,000 in cash with the gift taxes already paid. The only stipulation is that you will have to use the money to establish some sort of enterprise, either a business or a charitable foundation. Solve this problem, using the worksheet provided below. Describe what thoughts you have or what actions you will take for each step of problem-solving and decision making.

I. *Identify causes of the problem:* Have you found your own problem or was it given to you?

II. *Diagnose the problem:* What is the true decision that you are facing? What is your underlying problem?

III. *Find creative alternatives:* Think of the many alternatives facing you. Let your imagination flow and be creative.

IV. *Weigh alternatives:* Weigh the pros and cons of each of your sensible alternatives.

Alternatives	Advantages	Disadvantages
1.		
2.		
3.		
4.		
5.		

V. *Make the choice:* Based on your analysis in step IV, choose the best alternative.

VI. *Implement the choice:* Outline your action plan for converting your chosen alternative into action.

VII. *Evaluate the choice:* Do the best you can here by speculating how you will know if the decision you reached was a good one.

HUMAN RELATIONS SELF-ASSESSMENT EXERCISE 3-2

Creative Personality Test

Answer each of the following statements as "mostly true" or "mostly false." We are looking for general trends, so do not be concerned that under certain circumstances your answer might be different in response to a particular statement.

	Mostly True	Mostly False
1. I think novels are a waste of time, so I am more likely to read a nonfiction book.	_____	_____
2. You have to admit, some crooks are ingenious.	_____	_____
3. I pretty much wear the same style and colors of clothing regularly.	_____	_____
4. To me most issues have a clear cut right side or wrong side.	_____	_____
5. I enjoy it when my boss hands me vague instructions.	_____	_____
6. When I'm surfing the Internet, I sometimes investigate topics I know very little about.	_____	_____
7. Business before leisure activities is a hard and fast rule in my life.	_____	_____
8. Taking a different route to work is fun, even if it takes longer.	_____	_____
9. From time to time I have made friends with people of a different sex, race, religion, or ethnic background from myself.	_____	_____
10. Rules and regulations should be respected, but deviating from them once in a while is acceptable.	_____	_____
11. People who know me say that I have an excellent sense of humor.	_____	_____
12. I have been known to play practical jokes or pranks on people.	_____	_____
13. Writers should avoid using unusual words and word combinations.	_____	_____
14. Detective work would have some appeal to me.	_____	_____
15. I am much more likely to tell a rehearsed joke than make a witty comment.	_____	_____
16. Almost all national advertising on television bores me.	_____	_____

(Continued)

17. Why write letters to friends when there are so many clever greeting cards already available in the stores?   _____   _____

18. For most important problems in life, there is one best solution available.   _____   _____

19. Pleasing myself means more to me than pleasing others.   _____   _____

20. I'm enjoying taking this test.   _____   _____

Score: _____

Scoring: Give yourself a plus 1 for each answer scored in the creative direction as follows:

1. Mostly False	6. Mostly True	11. Mostly True	16. Mostly False
2. Mostly True	7. Mostly False	12. Mostly True	17. Mostly False
3. Mostly False	8. Mostly True	13. Mostly False	18. Mostly False
4. Mostly False	9. Mostly True	14. Mostly True	19. Mostly True
5. Mostly True	10. Mostly True	15. Mostly False	20. Mostly True.

Interpretation: A score of 15 or more suggests that your personality and attitudes are similar to those of a creative person. A score of between 9 and 14 suggests an average similarity with the personality and attitudes of a creative person. A score of 8 or less suggests that your personality is dissimilar to that of a creative person. You are probably more of a conformist and not highly open-minded in your thinking at this point in your life. To become more creative, you may need to develop more flexibility in your thinking and a higher degree of open-mindedness.

people are more mentally flexible than others, which allows them to overcome the traditional ways of looking at problems. This flexibility often shows up in practical jokes and other forms of playfulness. Laurie, a computer whiz, knew that Sergio, one of her coworkers, had been working for a month on an inventory project. Laurie decided to play a high-tech joke on Sergio. One day when he booted his computer, a message flashed across the screen: "Sorry Sergio, your files have been dumped by the Great Computer Virus." After a five-second pause, another message flashed: "Sorry to frighten you Sergio. Everything is back to normal now. Press return to continue." Later that morning, Laurie confessed her prank. Sergio said he went through five seconds of agony, but had a good laugh when he realized that he was the victim of a practical joke.

The characteristics of creative workers can be grouped into four broad areas: knowledge, intellectual abilities, personality, and social habits and upbringing.[13]

Knowledge

Creative thinking requires a broad background of information, including facts and observations. Knowledge supplies the building blocks for generating and combining ideas. This is particularly true because, according to some experts, creativity always comes down to combining things in a new and different way. For example, a fax machine is a combination of a telephone and a photocopier.

HUMAN RELATIONS SELF-ASSESSMENT EXERCISE 3-3

Rhyme and Reason

A noted creativity expert says that exercises in rhyming release creative energy; they stir imagination into action. While doing the following exercises, remember that rhyme is frequently a matter of sound and does not have to involve similar or identical spelling. This exercise deals with light and frivolous emotions.

After each "definition," write two rhyming words to which it refers.

Examples

1. Large hog   Big _____   pig _____
2. Television   Boob _____ tube _____
3. A computer control for the home   house _____ mouse _____

Now try these

1. Happy father
2. False pain
3. Formed like a simian
4. Highest-ranking police worker
5. Voyage by a large boat
6. Corpulent feline
7. Melancholy fellow
8. Clever beginning
9. Heavy and unbroken slumber
10. Crazy custom
11. Lengthy melody
12. Weak man
13. Instruction at the seashore
14. Criticism lacking in effectiveness
15. A person who murders for pleasurable excitement
16. Musical stringed instrument with full, rich sounds
17. Courageous person who is owned as property by another
18. Mature complaint
19. Strange hair growing on the lower part of a man's face
20. Drooping marine crustacean
21. A computer whiz with a ridiculous sense of humor.

(Continued)

Answers and Interpretation: The more of these rhymes you were able to come up with, the higher your creative potential. You would also need an advanced vocabulary to score very high (for instance, what is a "simian" or a "crustacean"?). Ten or more correct rhymes would tend to show outstanding creative potential, at least in the verbal area. Here are the answers:

1. Glad dad	8. Smart start	15. Thriller killer
2. Fake ache	9. Deep sleep	16. Mellow cello
3. Ape shape	10. Mad fad	17. Brave slave
4. Top cop	11. Long song	18. Ripe gripe
5. Ship trip	12. Frail male	19. Weird beard
6. Fat cat	13. Beach teach	20. Limp shrimp
7. Sad lad	14. Weak critique	21. Absurd nerd

If you can think of a sensible substitute for any of these answers, give yourself a bonus point. For example, for number 21, how about a freak geek?

SOURCE: The current test is an updated version of Eugene Raudsepp with George P. Hough, Jr., *Creative Growth Games* (New York: Harcourt Brace Jovanovich, 1977). Reprinted with permission.

Intellectual Abilities

In general, creative workers tend to be bright rather than brilliant. Extraordinarily high intelligence is not required to be creative. Yet creative people are good at generating alternative solutions to problems in a short period of time. Creative people also maintain a youthful curiosity throughout their lives. And the curiosity is not centered on just their own field of expertise. Instead, their range of interests encompasses many areas of knowledge, and they generate enthusiasm toward almost any puzzling

HUMAN RELATIONS SKILL-BUILDING EXERCISE 3-2

The Nine-Dot Problem

Connect the dots by drawing only four straight lines. Do not retrace any lines, and do not lift your pencil from the paper.

Several answers to this problem are found at the end of the chapter.

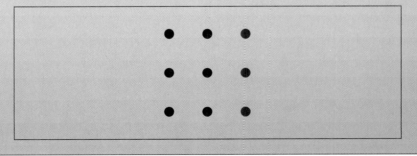

problem. It has also been observed that creative people are open and responsive to feelings and emotions in the world around them.

Personality

The emotional and other nonintellectual aspects of a person heavily influence creative problem solving. Creative people tend to have a positive self-image without being blindly self-confident. Because they are self-confident, creative people are able to cope with criticism of their ideas. Creative people have the ability to tolerate the isolation necessary for developing ideas. Talking to others is a good source of ideas. Yet at some point, the creative problem solver has to work alone and concentrate.

Creative people are frequently nonconformists, and do not need strong approval from the group. Many creative problem solvers are thrill seekers who find developing imaginative solutions to problems to be a source of thrills. Creative people are also persistent, which is especially important for seeing that a new idea is implemented. Selling a creative idea to the right people requires considerable follow-up. Creative people enjoy dealing with uncertainty and chaos. A creative person, for example, would enjoy the challenge of taking over a customer service department that was way behind schedule and ineffective. Less-creative people become frustrated quickly when their jobs are unclear and disorder exists.

Social Habits and Upbringing

Contrary to their stereotype, most creative people are not introverted loners or nerds. Many creative people enjoy interacting with people and exchanging ideas. The majority of creative adults lacked a smooth and predictable childhood environment. Family upheavals caused by financial problems, family feuds, and divorce are common occurrences. During their childhood, many people who became creative adults sought escape from family turmoil by pursuing ideas.

THE CONDITIONS NECESSARY FOR CREATIVITY

Creativity is not just a random occurrence. For creativity to occur, ability, intrinsic motivation, certain mental activities, and the right environmental conditions are needed.[14] These necessary conditions are not surprising considering our discussion of creativity up to this point. *Ability* is the knowledge in the area in which the individual works, combined with the skills to process information to produce a useful, novel solution. A mind disciplined through study is therefore a major contributor to creativity.

Intrinsic (or *internal*) *motivation,* as mentioned in Chapter 2, is a fascination with the task. Even if you have the potential, you are unlikely to be creative unless you intensely enjoy the work. Creative people are usually wrapped up in their work.

For creativity to occur, the person must engage in certain cognitive (or mental) activities. Most of these cognitive activities are included in the decision-making steps outlined in Figure 3-1. For example, to be creative, the individual must define the problem, gather information, and evaluate the solution. Added to these cognitive activities is unconscious thinking about the problem. If you are seriously interested in solving a problem, the unconscious thinking may take place automatically.

Environmental conditions are also important for facilitating creativity. One key condition is an environmental need to stimulate the setting of a goal. (As you have heard many times, "Necessity is the mother of invention.") Here's an example for animal lovers:

> A dairy farmer in Ontario, Canada, was concerned that his cows suffered so many diseases from the bacteria that accumulate in their surroundings. Bacteria is also hazardous because it can contaminate milk. Another adverse environmental condition the farmer noticed was that cows took too many falls, often suffering serious injuries. The farmer's solution to the problem was a cow mattress. (Just think of the size of the untapped market.) Farmers in Canada, the east coast of the United States, and Europe have been the biggest customers for the mattresses because they are especially effective in cold, rainy climates. The mattresses, made of thick tarp and stuffed with ground-up auto tires, are installed on slanted concrete foundations. The slant keeps rainwater and manure from collecting and becoming a breeding ground for bacteria. The rubber-filled columns on the mattresses serve as shock absorbers that prevent the cows from slipping and injuring themselves.
>
> A California dairy farmer observed that after installing the mattresses, milk production increased, diseases decreased, and the cows were more blissful. Pointing to a cow lying on a mattress and lazily chewing her feed, the farmer said, "See how peaceful and stress-free she looks? That's a happy cow."[15]

Another environmental condition that enhances creativity is a moderate degree of conflict. With too much harmony, there is a risk that people will not push themselves to make suggestions that differ from standard thinking. An irritant on the staff can provoke others into imaginative ideas. For example, at the Cadillac division of GM, several insiders kept arguing that the division had to do something radically different to attract people under age 60. The result was the entry-level luxury car, the Catera. It proved to be a big hit with the older Baby Boomers.

Finally, humor is a key environmental condition for enhancing creativity. Humor has always been linked to creativity. Humor gets the creative juices flowing, and effective humor requires creativity. Thomas Edison started every workday with a joke-telling session. Mike Vance, chairman of the Creative Thinking Association of America, says that "Humor is unmasking the hypocritical. What makes us laugh often is seeing how things are screwed up—then sometimes seeing how we can fix them. Whenever I go into a company and don't hear much laughter, I know it's not a creative place."[16]

IMPROVING YOUR CREATIVITY

Because of the importance of creative problem solving, many techniques have been developed to improve creativity. Let us look at both specific techniques and general strategies for becoming more creative. The goal of these experiences is to think like a creative problem solver. Such a person lets his or her imagination wander. He or she ventures beyond the constraints that limit most people.

CONCENTRATE INTENSELY ON THE TASK AT HAND

The ability to concentrate was mentioned earlier as a characteristic that contributes to effective problem solving in general. The ability to eliminate distractions also contributes mightily to generating new ideas. At times we think we are thinking intently about our problem (such as how to make cows more comfortable), yet in reality we may be thinking about something that interferes with creativity.[17] Among the office distractions that interfere with concentration are phone calls, a computer beep informing you of an incoming message, a fax machine in the receiving mode, and a friendly hello from a work associate walking past your cubicle. All of the methods that follow for creativity enhancement require concentration.

OVERCOME TRADITIONAL MENTAL SETS

An important consequence of becoming more intellectually flexible is that you can overcome a **traditional mental set,** a fixed way of thinking about objects and activities. Overcoming traditional mental sets is important because the major block to creativity is perceiving things in a traditional way. All creative examples presented so far in this chapter involved this process.

According to traditional thinking, business firms have the right to develop their own 800 numbers. The restrictions, of course, are that nobody else has the number and that the letter combination chosen is not offensive. You would think that if AT&T wanted to use the number (800) COLLECT it would be free to do so. You might also think that an automobile manufacturer might be able to claim rights to the number (800) MINIVAN.

A creative individual challenged traditional thinking about who has the rights to use which 800 numbers. His firm scouted for interesting and potentially useful 800 numbers that had meaningful spellings. He then secured the rights to them. As a result, AT&T has to pay him a royalty if the company wants to use (800) COLLECT. Does a salt company have the right to use (800) EAT SALT? What about (800) COW REST?

An effective way of overcoming a traditional mental set is to challenge the status quo. If you want to develop an idea that will impress your boss, or turn around an industry, you must use your imagination. Question the old standby that things have always been done in a particular way. To make the information superhighway possible, many old standby assumptions had to be questioned. Among them were that (1) the only way to obtain videos for home use is to bring a videocassette into the home, and (2) only telephone cables can be used to transmit digital information.

Discipline Yourself to Think Laterally

A major challenge in developing creative thinking skills is to learn how to think laterally in addition to vertically. **Vertical thinking** is an analytical, logical, process that results in few answers. The vertical thinker is looking for the one best solution to a problem, much like solving an equation in algebra. In contrast, **lateral thinking** spreads out to find many different alternative solutions to a problem. In short, critical thinking is vertical and creative thinking is lateral.

A vertical thinker might say, "I must find a part-time job to supplement my income. My income is not matching my expenses." The lateral thinker might say, "I need more money. Let me think of the various ways of earning more money. I can find a second job, get promoted where I am working, cut my expenses, run a small business out of my home. . . ."

To learn to think laterally, you have to develop the mental set that every problem has multiple alternative solutions. Do not leave the problem until you have sketched out multiple alternatives. Use a pencil or pen and paper or a computer screen, but do not walk away from your problem until you have thought of multiple alternatives.

Conduct Brainstorming Sessions

The best-known method of improving creativity is **brainstorming,** a technique by which group members think of multiple solutions to a problem. Using brainstorming, a group of six people might sit around a table generating new ideas for a product. During the idea-generating part of brainstorming, potential solutions are not criticized or evaluated in any way. In this way spontaneity is encouraged. The original device for programming VCRs by simply punching one number was a product of brainstorming. The product retails for about $75. It is designed for people who are unable or unwilling to learn how to program a VCR. Rules for brainstorming are presented in Exhibit 3-2. Brainstorming has many variations, including an electronic approach, creative twosomes, brainwriting, and forced associations.

Electronic Brainstorming

In electronic brainstorming, group members simultaneously enter their suggestions into a computer. The ideas are distributed to the screens of other group members. Although the group members do not talk to each other, they are still able to build on each other's ideas and combine ideas.

Electronic brainstorming helps overcome certain problems encountered in traditional brainstorming. Shyness, domination by one or two members, and participants who loaf tend to be less troublesome than in face-to-face situations. An experiment indicated that, with large groups, electronic brainstorming produces more useful ideas than the usual type.[18]

Creative Twosomes

Some of the advantages of brainstorming can be achieved by thinking through a challenging problem with a partner. Creative twosomes are a

---

EXHIBIT 3-2

RULES AND GUIDELINES FOR BRAINSTORMING

1. Use groups of about five to seven people.

2. Encourage the spontaneous expression of ideas. All suggestions are welcome, even if they are outlandish or outrageous. The least workable ideas can be edited out when the idea-generation phase is completed.

3. Quantity and variety are very important. The greater the number of ideas, the greater the likelihood of a breakthrough idea.

4. Encourage combination and improvement of ideas. This process is referred to as "piggybacking" or "hitchhiking."

5. One person serves as the secretary and records the ideas, perhaps posting them on a chalkboard.

6. In many instances, it pays to select a moderator who helps keep the session on track. The moderator can prevent one or two members from dominating the meeting. If the moderator takes notes, a secretary is not needed.

7. Do not overstructure by following any of the above rules too rigidly. Brainstorming is a spontaneous process.

8. To broaden idea generation, think about how a characteristic of something might be if it were modified: how something might be if it were larger or more frequent; if it were smaller or less frequent; or if something else could be used instead.

---

favorite of the music business (for example, Rodgers and Hammerstein). Many researchers work in twosomes. Part of the creative-twosome technique is to audiotape your problem-solving session. After exhausting your ideas, return and listen to your tape together. Listening to previous ideas helps spur new thoughts. The next time you face a creative assignment, try teaming up with a compatible partner and a tape recorder.[15]

Brainwriting

In many situations, brainstorming by yourself produces as many or more useful ideas than does brainstorming in groups. **Brainwriting,** or solo brainstorming, is arriving at creative ideas by jotting them down yourself. The creativity-improvement techniques discussed so far will help you to develop the mental flexibility necessary for brainstorming. After you have loosened up your mental processes, you will be ready to tackle your most vexing problems. Self-discipline is very important for brainwriting because some people have a tendency to postpone something as challenging as thinking alone.

An important requirement of brainwriting is that you set aside a regular time (and perhaps place) for generating ideas. The ideas discovered in the process of routine activities can be counted as bonus time. Even five minutes a day is much more time than most people are accustomed to spend thinking creatively about job problems. Give yourself a quota with a time deadline.

A variation of brainwriting is to seat participants around a table and give each of them a set of index cards. Each person writes one idea on the index card and passes it along to the person on the right. As the cards pass around the table, each person uses the idea on each card as a stimulus for new ideas to contribute.[20]

Forced Associations

A widely used method of releasing creativity is the **forced-association technique.** Using this technique, individuals or groups solve a problem by making associations between the properties of two objects. A link is found between the properties of the random object and the properties of the problem object. The forced association is supposed to help solve the problem. An individual (working alone or in a group) selects a word at random from a dictionary or text book. If you happen to choose a preposition, try again until you find a noun to give you something more to work with. Next, the person (or group) lists many of the properties and attributes of this word. Assume you randomly chose the word *ladder.* Among its attributes are "durable," "foldable," "aluminum or wood," "moderately priced," and "easy to use." If you were trying to improve a bow tie to increase sales, for example, you might make the tie more durable and easier to use.

In the various types of brainstorming just discussed, collecting wild ideas is just the start of the process. After ideas are collected, the group or each member carefully evaluates and analyzes the various alternatives. It is usually important to also specify the implementation details. For example, how do you make a bow tie easier to use other than by adding a clip?

Human Relations Skill-Building Exercise 3-3 will give you an opportunity to practice brainstorming in an area familiar to every reader of this book.

BORROW CREATIVE IDEAS

Copying the successful ideas of others is a legitimate form of creativity. Be careful, however, to give appropriate credit. Knowing when and which ideas to borrow from other people can help you behave as if you were an imaginative person. Creative ideas can be borrowed through such methods as:

Speaking to friends, relatives, classmates, and coworkers

Reading newspapers, newsmagazines, trade magazines, textbooks, nonfiction books, novels, and surfing the Internet

Watching television and listening to radio programs

Subscribing to computerized information services (expensive but worth it to many ambitious people)

HUMAN RELATIONS SKILL-BUILDING EXERCISE 3-3

1-800-INSIGHT

Using conventional brainstorming or one of its variations, huddle in small groups. Your task is to develop 800, 888, or 900 telephone numbers for firms in various fields. Keep in mind that the best 800 (or 888, or 900) numbers are easy to memorize and have a logical connection to the goods or services provided. After each group makes up its list of telephone numbers (perhaps about three for each firm on the list), compare results with the other groups. Here is the list of enterprises:

- A nationwide chain of funeral homes

- An air conditioning firm

- A software problem help line for Microsoft Corp.

- A used car chain

- A prayer service (a 900 number)

- An introduction (dating) service (a 900 number)

Business firms borrow ideas from each other regularly as part of quality improvement. The process is referred to as *benchmarking* because another firm's product, service, or process is used as a standard of excellence. Benchmarking involves representatives from one company visiting another to observe firsthand the practices of another company. The company visited is usually not a direct competitor. It is considered unethical to visit a competitor company for the purpose of appropriating ideas.

It is difficult to capitalize on your creative ideas unless you keep a careful record of them. A creative idea entrusted to memory may be forgotten under the pressures of everyday living. An important new idea kept on your list of daily errands or duties may become lost. Because creative ideas carry considerable weight in propelling your career forward, they deserve to be recorded in a separate notebook, such as a daily planner.

CHALLENGE YOUR RUTS

A major hurdle to thinking creatively is getting locked into so many habits and routines that our thinking becomes too mechanical. According to Kathleen R. Allen, "We do the same things, the same way, every day. This is a primary barrier to creativity. Often we need to feel a little uncomfortable—we need to experience new things—to get creative sparks."[21] Challenging your ruts, or habitual way of doing things, can assist you in developing mental flexibility. Anything you do that forces you out of your normal environment will help you see things in new and different ways. Here is a sampling of challenging everyday ruts:

- Eating lunch with the same friends at work or school
- Watching the same television shows or reading only the same sections of the newspaper
- Restricting your Internet browsing to the same few bookmarks
- Befriending only those people in your same demographic group, such as age range, race, and ethnic background
- Engaging in the same pastimes exclusively
- Using the same form of physical exercise each time you exercise
- _____ (Your turn to select a rut.)

PLAY THE ROLES OF EXPLORER, ARTIST, JUDGE, AND LAWYER

A method for improving creativity has been proposed that incorporates many of the suggestions already made. The method calls for you to adopt four roles in your thinking.[22]

1. *Be an explorer.*   Speak to people in different fields and get ideas that you can use. For example, if you are a telecommunications specialist, speak to salespeople and manufacturing specialists.

2. *Be an artist by stretching your imagination.*   Strive to spend about 5 percent of your day asking "what if" questions. For example, a sales manager at a fresh-fish distributor might ask, "What if some new research suggests that eating fish causes intestinal cancer in humans?" Also, remember to challenge the commonly perceived rules in your field. For example, a bank manager challenged why customers needed their canceled checks returned each month. This questioning led to some banks not returning canceled checks unless the customer paid an additional fee for the service. (As a compromise, some banks send customers photocopies of about ten checks on one page.)

3. *Know when to be a judge.*   After developing some wild ideas, at some point you have to evaluate them. Do not be so critical that you discourage your own imaginative thinking. However, be critical enough to prevent attempting to implement weak ideas.

4. *Achieve results by playing the role of a lawyer.*   Negotiate and find ways to implement your ideas within your field or place of work. The explorer, artist, and judge stages of creative thought might take only a short time to develop a creative idea. Yet you may spend months or even years getting your brainstorm implemented. For example, it took a long time for the developer of the electronic pager to finally get the product manufactured and distributed on a large scale.

SUMMARY

Problem solving occurs when you try to remove an obstacle that is blocking a path you want to take, or when you try to close the gap between what exists and what you want to exist. Decision making takes place after you encounter a problem. It refers to selecting one alternative from the various courses of action that can be pursued.

Many traits and characteristics influence the type of problem solver you are now or are capable of becoming. Among them are (1) flexibility versus rigidity, (2) intelligence, education, and experience, (3) decisiveness and perfectionism, (4) self-confidence and risk taking, (5) concentration, (6) intuition, and (7) emotional factors.

The Myers-Briggs Type Indicator is a widely used method of problem-solving styles. Information gathering is divided into two main types. Sensation-type individuals prefer routine and order. Intuitive-type individuals prefer an overall perspective. Information evaluation is also divided into two types. Feeling-type individuals have a need to conform. Thinking-type individuals rely on reason and intellect to deal with problems. The two dimensions of information gathering and evaluation are combined to produce a four-way classification of problem-solving styles. Recognizing your problem-solving style can help you identify work you are likely to perform well. (See Exhibit 3-2.)

The decision-making process outlined in this chapter uses both the scientific method and intuition for making decisions in response to problems. Decision making follows an orderly flow of events:

1. You are aware of a problem or create one of your own.

2. You identify causes of the problem.

3. You find creative alternatives.

4. You weigh the alternatives.

5. You make the choice.

6. You implement the choice.

7. You evaluate whether you have made a sound choice. If your choice was unsound, you are faced with a new problem and the cycle repeats itself.

Creativity is the ability to look for good ideas that can be put into action. Adaptive creativity involves improving an existing system, whereas innovative creativity involves creating something new. Creative workers tend to have different intellectual and personality characteristics than their less-creative counterparts. In general, creative people are more mentally flexible than others, which allows them to overcome the traditional way of looking at problems.

Creative thinking requires a broad background of information, including facts and observations. Creative workers tend to be bright rather than brilliant. The emotional and other nonintellectual aspects of a person heavily influence creative problem solving. For example, creative people are frequently nonconformists and thrill seekers. Creative people tend not to be loners, but many experienced troubled family situations during childhood.

For creativity to occur, ability, intrinsic motivation, certain cognitive activities, and the right environmental conditions are needed. Among the cognitive activities are going through the problem-solving process and subconscious thinking about the problem. Key environmental conditions include an environmental need to stimulate goal setting, a moderate degree of conflict, and the presence of humor.

Methods of improving your creativity include (1) concentrating intensely on the task at hand, (2) overcoming traditional mental sets, (3) disciplining yourself to think laterally, (4) conducting brainstorming sessions, (5) borrowing creative ideas, (6) challenging your ruts, and (7) playing the roles of explorer, artist, judge, and lawyer.

Brainstorming has several variations, including electronic brainstorming in which people enter ideas into a computer. Creative twosomes involve interaction with a partner; brainwriting is essentially solo brainstorming. The forced-association technique requires problem solving by making associations between the properties of two objects.

Questions and Activities

1. What would be some of the symptoms or signs of a "rigid thinker"?

2. How might being a perfectionist create performance problems for an industrial sales representative? For a paralegal? For a computer programmer?

3. Why does concentration improve problem solving?

4. Why is intuition often referred to as a "sixth sense"?

5. Which of the four problem-solving styles shown in Exhibit 3-1 do you think fits you best? Explain your reasoning.

6. Give two examples of decisions you have faced, or will face, that justify running through the problem-solving and decision-making steps.

7. Think of the most creative person you know. Describe his or her personal characteristics and compare them to the characteristics of creative people presented in this chapter.

8. Give an example of one work problem and one personal problem for which brainstorming might be useful.

9. Why might doing the exercises and self-assessment quizzes in this chapter help a person become more creative?

10. Ask an experienced manager or professional how important creative thinking has been in his or her career. Be prepared to report back to class with your findings.

A HUMAN RELATIONS CASE PROBLEM

A Bad Day at Citron Beverages

Julia Anderson worked as the production manager at Citron Beverages, a manufacturer of lemon-flavored soft drinks. She looked forward to another fast-paced workday this Monday morning. Although Citron was not a major player in the vast soft-drink market, it had a solid group of loyal customers in the Northwest United States and Canada. A warm spell had increased demand for its top seller, Citron Power. However, production was able to keep up with demand.

At 9:15 A.M., Ramesh Sharma, a production supervisor, rushed into Anderson's office. "We've got to talk, Julia," said Ramesh with a worried look on his face. Anderson motioned for Sharma to sit down.

"Something awful may have happened on the production line," said Ramesh. "One of the maintenance workers said he found an empty container of lemon-scented liquid cleaner next to a production vat. He's worried that somebody may have dumped the cleaner into the vat as a joke or as sabotage.

"I had one of the quality control technicians test the vat for impurities. Her tests were inconclusive. We use so much artificial lemon flavoring in Citron Power, anyway, that it makes the testing more difficult."

"Oh how terrible," said Julia, "You mean to say a vat of Citron Power syrup might have been contaminated with liquid cleanser?"

"We don't know for sure. But it seems too late to do much about it now. We've already bottled and canned several hundred cases of Citron Power from the batch of syrup in question. Besides that, one bottle of liquid cleaner in one vat of Citron Power syrup might not be detectable to the consumer."

"Ramesh, I question your judgment. All it takes is one foamy-mouthed Citron drinker to lodge a complaint. Then the place will fall apart."

"Julia, keep in mind that if we attempt to recall any possible contaminated shipment the company will really fall apart."

"Okay Ramesh. Let me just think this problem through for ten minutes or so."

Questions

1. Why is this case problem included in a chapter on problem solving and decision making?

2. Which problem-solving style would be best suited to dealing with the dilemma faced by Anderson and Sharma?

3. Offer Julia a creative suggestion.

REFERENCES

[1] Cathy Hainer, "Entrepreneurial Financial Planner Banks on a Bagel Without A Hole," Gannett News Service, March 12, 1997.

[2] Joanne Cole, "The Problem with Being Perfect," *Getting Results,* July 1997, p. 1.

[3]Adapted from "Focusing on the Customer," interview with George Fisher, Rochester, NY, *Democrat and Chronicle,* February 16, 1994, p. 7A; updated with Geoffrey Smith, "What Kodak is Developing in Digital Photography," *Business Week,* July 7, 1997, pp. 108–109.

[4]Orlando Behling and Normal L. Eckel, "Making Sense Out of Intuition," *Academy of Management Executive,* February 1991, p. 46.

[5]Roger Frantz, "Intuition at Work," *Innovative Leader,* April 1997, p. 4.

[6]Cited in Ibid., pp. 1, 4.

[7]"When to Go with Your Intuition," *Working Smart,* May 27, 1991, pp. 1–2.

[8]Eleanor Davidson, "Overcoming the Fear of Decision Making," *Supervisory Management,* October 1991, p. 12.

[9]The Myers-Briggs Type Indicator (MBTI) is published by Consulting Psychological Press, Inc., Palo Alto, CA 94306; David A. Whetton and Kim S. Cameron, *Developing Management Skills,* 2nd ed. (New York: HarperCollins, 1991), p. 66.

[10]"More on Problem Solving," *Personal Report for the Executive,* December 1, 1987, p. 4.

[11]"Decision-Making Flaws," *Personal Report for the Executive,* February 15, 1988, pp. 5–6.

[12]Cited in "Team Talent: Bringing Creativity on Board," *Supervisory Management,* April 1995, p. 7.

[13]Richard W. Woodman, John E. Sawyer, and Ricky W. Griffin, "Toward a Theory of Organizational Creativity," *The Academy of Management Review,* April 1993, pp. 293–321; Robert R. Godfrey,, "Tapping Employee's Creativity," *Supervisory Management,* February 1986, pp. 17–18; Greg R. Oldham and Anne Cummings, "Employee Creativity: Personal and Contextual Factors at Work," *Academy of Management Journal,* June 1996, pp. 607–634.

[14]Christina E. Shalley, "Effects of Productivity Goals, Creativity Goals, and Personal Discretion on Individual Creativity," *Journal of Applied Psychology,* April 1991, pp. 179–180.

[15]"Cows Now Count Sheep on Comfy Mattresses," Knight-Ridder, May 11, 1997.

[16]Cited in Robert McGarvey, "Turn It On," *Entrepreneur,* November 1996, pp. 156–157.

[17]Frederick D. Buggie, "Overcoming Barriers to Creativity," *Innovative Leader,* May 1997, p. 5.

[18]R. Brente Gallupe et al., "Electronic Brainstorming and Group Size," Academy of Management Journal, June 1992, pp. 350–359.

[19]"The Two-Person Technique," *The Pryor Report,* July 1992, p. 1; Michael LeBoeuf, *Imagineering: How to Profit from Your Creative Powers* (New York: Berkeley Books, 1985).

[20]"How to Produce More Creative Ideas," interview with Michael Michalko, *Getting Results,* November 1996, p. 6.

[21]Quoted in Mark Hendricks, "Good Thinking: Knock Down the Barriers to Creativity—and Discover a Whole World of New Ideas," *Entrepreneur,* May 1996, p. 158.

[22]"Be a Creative Problem Solver," *Executive Strategies,* June 6, 1989, pp. 1–2.

ADDITIONAL READING

Buggie, Frederick D. "Overcoming Barriers to Creativity." *Innovative Leader,* May 1997, pp. 1, 4–5.

Csikszentmihalyi, Mihaly. *Creativity: Flow and the Psychology of Discovery and Invention.* New York: HarperCollins, 1997.

DeBono, Edward. *Serious Creativity.* New York: Harper Business, 1992.

Foster, Jack. *How to Get Ideas.* San Francisco: Berrett-Koehler Publishers, 1996.

Kao, John. *Jamming: The Art and Discipline of Business Creativity.* New York: Harper Business, 1996.

Mattimore, Bryan W. *99% Inspiration: Tips, Tales & Techniques for Liberating Your Business Creativity.* New York: AMACOM, 1993.

Rhea, Kathlyn *Mind Sense: Fine Tuning Your Intellect and Intuition.* Berkeley, CA.: Celestial Arts, 1994.

Roth, William, Ryder, James, and Voehl, Frank. *Problem Solving for Results.* Delray Beach, FL: St. Lucie Press, 1996.

Solomon, Charlene Marmer. "Creativity Training," *Personnel Journal,* May 1990, pp. 64–71.

von Oech, Roger. *Whack on the Side of the Head.* New York: Warner Books, 1990.

SOLUTIONS TO THE NINE-DOT PROBLEM

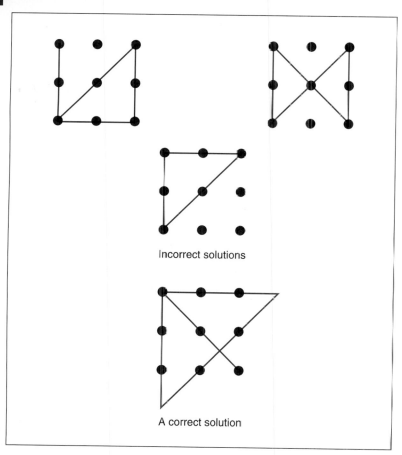

Incorrect solutions

A correct solution

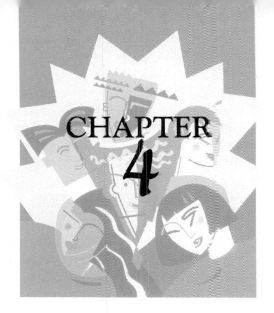

CHAPTER 4

ACHIEVING WELLNESS AND MANAGING STRESS

Learning Objectives

After studying the information and doing the exercise in this chapter, you should be able to:

▼ Explain the meaning of wellness and how it can be attained

▼ Describe the meaning of stress, its physiology, and consequences

▼ Identify several positive and negative consequences of stress

▼ Pinpoint potential stressors in personal and work life

▼ Describe key methods for managing the potential adverse effects of stress

*R*enee Dziekan, administrator of health services at Northwestern Mutual Life Insurance Co. (NML), said, "Being a life insurance company, we have long focused on the health and well-being of our employees—as well as our policy owners." The company's modern fitness center is

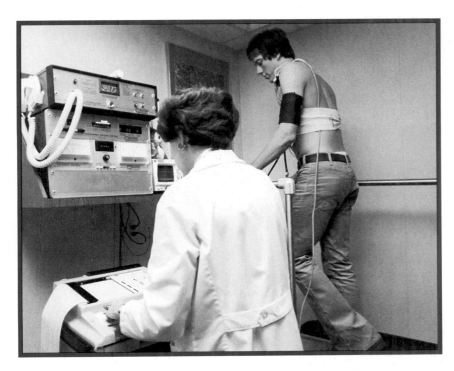

open to its employees 24 hours a day. The center offers aerobic exercise as well as weight training and the expertise of a part-time fitness consultant. Dziekan says the center is used by almost half the employees. Although for employees who want some variety, NML still offers reimbursements on YMCA and YWCA memberships.

To provide employees with positive health choices, the company offers a variety of facilities and services. Medical screening programs make up an important part of these services. Not only does NML provide testing for blood pressure and cholesterol, it also offers ergonomic assessments, weight reduction programs, smoking cessation and stress management programs. Employees are able to adjust their working hours to schedule these seminars.

Dziekan emphasizes how much support the company provides employees: "People who are trying to make healthy lifestyle choices need a lot of support, and we support with a very warm, caring environment at NML. The work environment provides the human connection and social support needed to make lifestyle changes."[1]

The time and money the large insurance company described above invests in employee health, including stress management, illustrates an important workplace reality. To be successful in a competitive business world, it is not enough simply to cope with job pressures and overcome health problems. You also have to feel and be at your best. Similarly, treating and curing physical and mental health problems is still important, but considerable emphasis is now being placed on preventing illness and staying well. Well people are not simply those who are not sick. Instead, they are vibrant, relatively happy, and able to cope with life's problems.

In this chapter we describe the achievement of wellness, the nature and cause of stress, and managing personal and work stress. In the next chapter we continue with a stress-related topic: coping with personal problems.

STRATEGIES FOR ACHIEVING WELLNESS

An increasing number of people believe that we can live longer, healthier lives if we choose to do so. An important principle of behavioral medicine is now widely accepted—that the body and mind must work together for a healthy lifestyle. Consider also that lifestyle decisions contribute to seven of the ten principal causes of mortality. And about half of the deaths resulting from these causes could be prevented by changes in behavior.[2] A person who smokes two packs of cigarettes per day, eats mostly fatty food and sweets, drinks a liter of wine per day, and leads a sedentary life, has a below-average life expectancy. Note that all of these life-threatening activities are under the person's control.

Wellness is a formalized approach to preventive health care. By promoting health, company wellness programs help prevent employees from developing physical and mental problems often associated with excessive job pressures. Wellness programs focus on preventive health, rather than treating problems after they have occurred. Companies with such programs usually have an atmosphere that encourages employee health (like NML).[3] In this section we describe achieving wellness through exercise, diet, competence, resilience, developing a health-prone personality, and minimizing health and safety risks. Another key component of achieving wellness—stress management—is described later.

EXERCISING PROPERLY

The right amount and type of physical exercise contributes substantially to wellness. To achieve wellness it is important to select an exercise program that is physically challenging but that does not lead to overexertion and muscle injury. Competitive sports, if taken too seriously, can actually increase a person's stress level. The most beneficial exercises are classified as aerobic, because they make you breathe faster and raise your heart rate.

Most of a person's exercise requirements can be met through everyday techniques such as walking or running upstairs, vigorous housework, yard work, or walking several miles per day. Avoid the remote control for your television; getting up to change the channel can burn off a few calories! Another exercise freebie is to park your car in a remote spot in the parking lot. The exercise you receive from walking to and from your car is an investment in your wellness.

The physical benefits of exercise include: increased respiratory capacity; increased muscle tone; improved circulation; increased energy; increased rate of metabolism; reduced body weight and improved fat metabolism; and slowed-down aging processes. Of enormous importance, physical activity strengthens the heart and reduces harmful cholesterol (LDL) while increasing the level of beneficial cholesterol (HDL).

The mental benefits of exercise are also plentiful. A major benefit is the euphoria that often occurs when morphinelike brain chemicals called *endorphins* are released into the body. The same experience is referred to as "runner's high." Other mental benefits of exercise include: increased self-confidence; improved body image and self-esteem; improved mental functioning, alertness, and efficiency; release of accumulated tensions; and relief from mild depression.[4]

MAINTAINING A HEALTHY DIET

Eating nutritious foods is valuable for mental as well as physical health. To illustrate, many nutritionists and physicians believe that eating fatty foods, such as red meat, contributes to colon cancer. Improper diet, such as consuming less than 1,300 calories per day, can weaken you physically. In turn, you become more susceptible to stress.

The subject of proper diet has been debated continually. Advice abounds on what to eat and what not to eat. Some of this information is confusing and contradictory, partly because not enough is known about nutrition to identify an ideal diet for each individual. For example, many people can point to an 85-year-old relative who has been eating the wrong food (and perhaps consuming considerable alcohol) most of his or her life. The implication is that if this person has violated sensible habits of nutrition and has lived so long, how important can good diet be?

The food requirements for wellness differ depending on age, sex, body size, physical activity, and other conditions such as pregnancy and illness. A workable dietary strategy is to follow the guidelines for choosing and preparing food developed by the U.S. Department of Agriculture[5] as shown in Figure 4-1. At each successive layer of the pyramid, a food group should be eaten less frequently.

At the base of the pyramid are grains (bread, cereal, rice, and pasta) which should comprise 6 to 11 servings per day. At the next level are fruits and vegetables of which we should consume from two to five servings per day. At the next-narrower level of the pyramid are found two groups of food of which we should eat only about two to three servings per day. One group is milk, yogurt, and cheese. The other is meat, poultry, fish, dry beans, eggs, and nuts. At the top of the pyramid are foods low in nutritional value, such as fats, oils, and sweets. It is recommended that these foods be eaten sparingly. Pizza, meat sausage, and milk shakes should therefore be an occasional treat, not a daily event.

The Department of Agriculture also recommends that if you drink alcoholic beverages, do so in moderation. Alcoholic beverages are high in calories and low in nutrients. Heavy drinkers, especially those who also smoke, frequently develop nutritional deficiencies. They also develop more serious diseases such as cirrhosis of the liver and certain types of cancer. This is partly true because of the loss of appetite, poor food intake, and impaired absorption of nutrients. One or two standard-size drinks per day appear to cause no harm in normal, healthy, nonpregnant adults. Some medical specialists believe that moderate doses of alcohol help prevent heart disease by preventing arteries from becoming clogged with fatty deposits.

For a thumbnail overview of good nutrition, consider the guidelines developed by the Center for Science in the Public Interest. According to

Figure 4-1   The Food Guide Pyramid: A Guide to Daily Food Choices

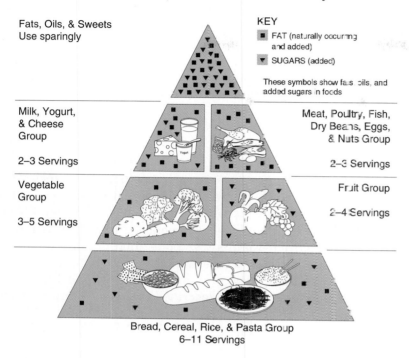

SOURCE: U.S. Department of Agriculture, 1992.

their research, the best diets are rich in whole grains, beans, and fresh vegetables and fruit. Such diets include small portions of low-fat animal foods like skim or 1% fat milk, yogurt, cottage cheese, fish, and skinless chicken or turkey. Vegetarians should replace meat with beans, peas, and lentils.[6]

The above dietary guidelines are intended only for populations with food habits similar to those of people in the United States. Also, the guidelines are for people who are already healthy and do not require special diets because of diseases or conditions that interfere with normal nutritional requirements. No guidelines can guarantee health and well-being. Health depends on many things, including heredity, lifestyle, personality traits, mental health, attitudes, and the environment, in addition to diet. However, good eating habits based on moderation and variety keep you healthy and even improve your health.

DEVELOPING COMPETENCE

Emory L. Cowen says that **competence** is an important part of wellness. Competence refers to both job skills and social skills, including the ability to solve problems and control anger. The presence of these skills has been shown to be related to wellness, and their absence to poor adaptation to your environment. Although acquiring such capabilities is a lifelong undertaking, Cowen recommends that childhood is the best time to lay the groundwork for competency.[7] If you are a well-rounded person who has performed satisfactorily in school and on the job, and you have a variety of friends, you have probably achieved competency.

The importance of competence in developing wellness illustrates how different wellness strategies produce similar results. Developing competence improves self-confidence and self-esteem. Physical exercise also contributes to enhancements in self-confidence and self-esteem.

DEVELOPING RESILIENCE

The ability to overcome setback is an important characteristic of successful people. It therefore follows that **resilience,** the ability to withstand pressure and emerge stronger for it, is a strategy for achieving wellness. Most people at times in their lives experience threats to their wellness. Among these threats are death of a loved one, having a fire in your home, a family breakup, or a job loss. Recovering from such major problems helps a person retain wellness and become even more well in the long term. Learning how to manage stress, as described later, is an important part of developing resilience.

A key contributor to becoming resilient is to develop **psychological hardiness.** A psychologically hardy individual tends to profit from a stressful situation instead of developing negative symptoms. Psychologically hardy people are committed to the various parts of their lives, such as being devoted to work and parenting. The same people also feel a greater sense of control over events in their lives.[8] Psychologically hardy people also see change as more of a challenge than a threat.

People with a hardy attitude take the major problems in life in stride. When they encounter a stressful event, they are likely to consider it interesting, and they believe they can influence the outcome. Furthermore, they see major challenges as an opportunity for personal development.

DEVELOPING A HEALTH-PRONE PERSONALITY

Tentative evidence has been gathered that people can be taught to develop a personality that helps ward off cancer and heart disease. In one study, people prone to cancer and heart disease were taught to express their emotions more readily, and to cope with stress. The training was a step-by-step form of mental healing called *behavior therapy*. Equally important, the physically ill people were taught to become less emotionally dependent on others and to be more self-reliant.

The results from the behavior training were astonishing. Fifty of the people with cancer-prone personalities received training and fifty did not. Many more people died of cancer (and of other causes) in the no-therapy group than in the therapy group. Thirteen years later, 45 people who received therapy were still alive. Only 19 in the no-therapy group were still alive. Similar encouraging results were achieved in studies conducted by other psychologists and researchers.[9]

The implication of these studies is that a person might be able to develop a well personality by becoming more emotionally expressive and self-reliant. Even if these behaviors did not prolong life, the person's enjoyment of life would increase. If you are already emotionally expressive and self-reliant, no changes need to be made.

A more general approach to developing a health-prone personality is to have a varied social life and a variety of interests. According to a study of 276 people in the United States, those individuals who lead an active, balanced life are less likely to become physically sick from infections. A possible explanation offered for these results is that being happy helps a person develop a strong immune system. Another consideration is that people with a variety of satisfactions in life take better care of themselves because they feel their lives have meaning.[10] What has been your experience? Do you think happy people are more immune to sickness such as the common cold?

MINIMIZE OBVIOUS RISKS TO HEALTH AND SAFETY

Part of staying well is staying alive. Perhaps the most effective strategy for achieving wellness is to minimize exposure to activities that can readily contribute to disease, injury, and death. The list of these environmental threats is endless, including riding in helicopters, skydiving, bungee jumping, inhaling cleaning fluid or rubber cement, playing "highway chicken," walking in a high-crime area at night, or having unprotected sex with prostitutes and intravenous drug users. Add to the list drunken driving, not wearing seat belts, and motorcycle riding or bicycle riding without a helmet. All of the activities just mentioned have a common element: They are conscious behavioral acts that can in almost all cases be avoided.

To relate the concept of wellness and stress to yourself, now take Human Relations Self-Assessment Exercise 4-1. Taking the inventory will give you many useful ideas for improving your well-being.

THE PHYSIOLOGY AND CONSEQUENCES OF STRESS

An important part of learning about stress is to understand its meaning, underlying physiology, and consequences to the person. **Stress** is an internal reaction to any force that threatens to disturb a person's equilibrium. The internal reaction usually takes the form of emotional discomfort. A **stressor** is the external or internal force that brings about the stress. Your perception of an event or thought influences whether a given event is stressful. Your confidence in your ability to handle difficult situations also influences the amount of stress you experience. If you believe you have the resources to conquer the potentially stressful event, you are much less likely to experience stress. A computer whiz would therefore not be stressed by the prospect of having to install a new computer system.

HUMAN RELATIONS SELF-ASSESSMENT EXERCISE 4-1

The Wellness Inventory

Answer Yes or No to each question.

1.	I rarely have trouble sleeping.	Yes	No
2.	My energy level is high when I get up in the morning and it stays high until bedtime.	Yes	No
3.	In the past year, I've been incapacitated by illness less than five days.	Yes	No
4.	I am generally optimistic about my chances of staying well.	Yes	No
5.	I do not smoke or drink alcoholic beverages habitually.	Yes	No
6.	I am pain-free except for minor ailments, which heal quickly.	Yes	No
7.	I am generally considered to be slim, not fat.	Yes	No
8.	I am careful about my diet. I restrict my intake of alcohol, sugar, salt, caffeine and fats.	Yes	No
9.	I am moderate in food and drink, and I choose fresh, whole foods over processed ones.	Yes	No
10.	I strenuously exercise at least three times a week for at least 20 minutes.	Yes	No
11.	I do not need any medicine (prescribed or self-prescribed) every day or most days to function.	Yes	No
12.	My blood pressure is 120/80 or lower.	Yes	No
13.	I am concerned about the future, but no one fear runs through my mind constantly.	Yes	No
14.	My relationships with those around me are usually easy and pleasant.	Yes	No
15.	I have a clear idea of my personal goals and choices.	Yes	No
16.	Disappointments and failures might slow me down a bit, but I try to turn them to my advantage.	Yes	No
17.	Taking care of myself is a high priority for me.	Yes	No
18.	I spend at least 20 minutes a day by myself, for myself.	Yes	No
19.	I know how much sleep I require, and I get it.	Yes	No
20.	I accept the fact that daily life can be stressful, and I am confident I can handle most problems as they arise.	Yes	No
21.	I have at least one hobby or form of creative expression (e.g., music, art, or gardening) that is a passion for me.	Yes	No

(Continued)

22. I can share my feelings with others and allow them to share their feelings with me.   Yes   No

23. I enjoy and respect my connection to nature and the environment.   Yes   No

24. I am aware of what my body feels like when I am relaxed and when I am experiencing stress.   Yes   No

25. I find meaning in life and generally anticipate death with minor fear.   Yes   No

Score: _____

Scoring: Give yourself four points for each Yes answer.

88–100: Excellent health/wellness awareness. You are probably well adapted to handle stress.
76–88: Good awareness, but there are areas where improvement is needed. Look at your No answers again.
Less than 76: You need to evaluate your health and lifestyle habits to improve the quality of your life and your ability to handle stressful situations.

SOURCE: Anita Schambach, wellness coordinator of the Holistic Health & Wellness Center at Mercy Hospital Anderson, Cincinnati, Ohio. Reprinted with permission.

The physiological changes taking place within the body are almost identical for both positive and negative stressors. Riding a roller coaster, falling in love, or being fired, for example, make you feel about the same inside. The experience of stress helps activate hormones that prepare the body to fight or run when faced with a challenge. This battle against the stressor is referred to as the **fight-or-flight response.** (The "response" is really a conflict because you are forced to choose between struggling with the stressor or fleeing from the scene.) It helps you deal with emergencies.

An updating of the fight-or-flight response explains that, when faced with stress, the brain acts much like a thermostat. When outside conditions deviate from an ideal point, the thermostat sends a signal to the furnace to increase heat or air conditioning. The brain senses stress as damage to well-being and therefore sends out a signal to the body to cope. The purpose of coping is to modify the discrepancy between the ideal (low-stress) and actual (high-stress) conditions.[11] The brain is thus a self-regulating system that helps us cope with stressors.

The activation of hormones when the body has to cope with a stressor produces a short-term physiological reaction. Among the most familiar reactions are an increase in heart rate, blood pressure, blood glucose, and blood clotting. To help you recognize these symptoms, try to recall the internal bodily sensations the last time you were almost in an automobile accident or heard some wonderful news. Less familiar changes are a redirection of the blood flow toward the brain and large muscle groups and a release of stored fluids from places throughout the body into the bloodstream.

If stress is continuous and accompanied by these short-term physiological changes, annoying and life-threatening conditions can occur. A stressful life event usually leads to a high cholesterol level (of the unhealthy type) and high blood pressure. Other conditions associated with stress are cardiac disease, migraine headaches, ulcers, allergies, skin disorders, and cancer. To make matters worse, stress can hamper the immune system, thus increasing the severity of many diseases and disorders. For example, people whose stress level is high recover more slowly from colds and injuries, and are more susceptible to sexually transmitted diseases.

Stress symptoms vary considerably from one person to another. A sampling of common stress symptoms is listed in Exhibit 4-1.

Despite all the problems just mentioned, stress also plays a positive role in our lives. The right amount of stress prepares us for meeting difficult challenges and spurs us on to peak intellectual and physical performance. An optimum of stress exists for most people and most tasks.

In general, performance tends to be best under moderate amounts of stress. If the stress is too great, people become temporarily ineffective; they may freeze or choke. Under too little stress, people may become lethargic and inattentive. Figure 4-2 depicts the relationship between stress and performance. An exception to this relationship is that certain negative forms of stress are likely to lower performance even if the stress is moderate.[12] For example, the stress created by an intimidating boss or worrying about radiation poisoning—even in moderate amounts—will not improve performance.

The optimum amount and type of stress is a positive force that is the equivalent of finding excitement and challenge. Your ability to solve problems and deal with challenge is enhanced when the right amount of adren-

---

EXHIBIT 4-1

A VARIETY OF STRESS SYMPTOMS

Mostly Physical

Shaking or trembling	Upper- and lower-back pain
Dizziness	Frequent headaches
Heart palpitations	Low energy and stamina
Difficulty breathing	Stomach problems
Chronic fatigue	Constant cravings for sweets
Unexplained chest pains	Increased alcohol or cigarette consumption
Frequent teeth grinding	Frequent need to eliminate
Frequent nausea and dizziness	

Mostly Emotional and Behavioral

Difficulty concentrating	Anxiety or depression
Nervousness	Forgetfulness
Crying	Restlessness
Anorexia	Frequent arguments with others
Declining interest in sex	Feeling high strung much of the time

Figure 4-2 The Relationship Between Stress and Job Performance

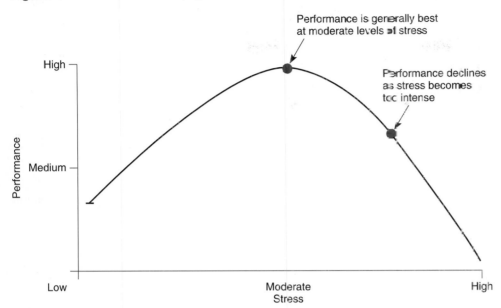

aline flows in your blood to guide you toward peak performance. In fact, highly productive people are sometimes said to be hooked on adrenaline.

Where does burnout fit into the stress picture? One of the major problems of prolonged stress is that it may lead to **burnout,** a condition of emotional, mental, and physical exhaustion in response to long-term job stressors. The burned-out person often becomes cynical. Burnout is most likely to occur among those whose jobs call for frequent and intense interactions with others, such as a social worker, teacher, or customer service representative. Yet people in other occupations also suffer from burnout, especially when not much support from others is present and the rewards are few.[13] Students can also experience burnout because studying is hard work. Conscientiousness and perfectionism also contribute to burnout because people with these characteristics feel stressed when they do not accomplish everything they would like.

SOURCES OF STRESS IN PERSONAL LIFE

Almost any form of frustration, disappointment, setback, inconvenience, or crisis in your personal life can cause stress. The list is dynamic because new sources of stress emerge continuously. For example, recent legislation in the province of Québec forbids recent drivers from having even one alcoholic beverage before driving. Drinkers who recently obtained an operator's license would have something new to worry about. Our life stage also helps determine which events are stressors. Being snubbed by a friend at age 17 may be more stressful than being snubbed at age 40. Presented next are major categories of stressful events in personal life.

TABLE 4-1

THE TOP 25 STRESSORS AS MEASURED BY LIFE-CHANGE UNITS

1. Death of a spouse	14. Change in financial status
2. Divorce	15. Number of arguments with spouse
3. Marital separation	16. Major mortgage
4. Jail term/imprisonment	17. Foreclosure of a loan
5. Death of a family member	18. Change in responsibilities at work
6. Personal injury or illness	19. Son or daughter leaves home
7. Marriage	20. Trouble with in-laws
8. Fired from the job	21. Outstanding personal achievement
9. Marital reconciliation	22. Spouse begins or stops work
10. Retirement	23. Begin or end school
11. Change in health of family member	24. Change in living conditions
12. Pregnancy	25. Revision of personal habits
13. Sexual difficulties	

SOURCE: These stressors have changed over time. This version is from Thomas H. Holmes and Richard H. Rahe, "The Social Adjustment Rating Scale," *Journal of Psychosomatic Research,* 15, 1971, pp. 210–223, with an interview updating from Sue MacDonald, "Battling Stress," *The Cincinnati Enquirer,* October 23, 1995, p. C4.

SIGNIFICANT LIFE CHANGE

A general stressor that encompasses both work and personal life is having to cope with significant change. According to many years of research conducted by Thomas Holmes and Richard Rahe, the necessity of a significant change in an individual's life pattern creates stress. The more significant the change you have to cope with in a short period of time, the greater the probability of experiencing a stress disorder.[14] As shown in Table 4-1, the maximum negative change is the death of a spouse. Twenty-four other stressors created by change are listed in the table, in decreasing order of impact. Individual differences are important in understanding the stressful impact of life changes. The rank order shown in Table 4-1 are averages and do not hold true for everybody. For example, a person who could fall back into working for a family business might not find being fired from the job (number 8) to be so stressful.

LOW SELF-ESTEEM

A subtle cause of stress is having low self-esteem. People who do not feel good about themselves often find it difficult to feel good about anything. Low self-esteem has several links to stress. One is that being in a bad mood continually functions like a stressor. People with low self-esteem drag themselves down into a funk which creates stress. Another link between low self-esteem and stress-proneness is that people with low self-esteem get hurt more by insults. Instead of questioning the source of the criticism, the person with self-doubt will accept the opinion as valid.[15] An insult accepted as valid acts as a stressor because it is a threat to our well-being.

Low self-esteem is linked to stress in yet another way. People with low self-esteem doubt their ability to work their way out of problems. As a result, minor challenges appear to be major problems. For example, a person with low self-esteem will often doubt he or she will be successful in conducting a job search. As a result, having to conduct a job search will represent a major stressor. A person with high self-esteem might feel better prepared mentally to accept the challenge. (As you will recall, your perception of an event influences whether it is stressful.)

EVERYDAY ANNOYANCES

Managing everyday annoyances can have a greater impact on your health than major life catastrophes. Among these everyday annoyances are losing keys or wallet, crashing a computer file, being stuck in traffic, having your car break down, having one of your checks bounce, being overdrawn on your credit card, and being lost on the way to an important appointment. People who have the coping skills to deal with everyday annoyances are less likely to be stressed out over them. A major reason everyday annoyances act as stressors is because they are frustrating—they block your path to an important goal such as getting your work accomplished.

SOCIAL AND FAMILY PROBLEMS

Friends and family are the main source of love and affection in your life. But they can also be the main source of stress. Most physical acts of violence are committed among friends and family members. One of the many reasons we encounter so much conflict with friends and family is that we are emotionally involved with them.

PHYSICAL AND MENTAL HEALTH PROBLEMS

Prolonged stress produces physical and mental health problems, and the reverse is also true. Physical and mental illness can act as stressors—the fact of being ill is stressful. Furthermore, thinking that you might soon contract a life-threatening illness is stressful. Many people who find they are HIV positive (yet do not have AIDS) experience overwhelming stress. Each day they worry about their condition turning into a potentially terminal disease. Some people who fear they may have contracted the AIDS virus avoid being tested. The resulting cloud of uncertainty acts as a recurring stressor. If you receive a serious injury, that too can create stress. The stress from being hospitalized can be almost as severe to some patients as the stress from the illness or injury that brought them to the hospital.

FINANCIAL PROBLEMS

A major life stressor is financial problems. Although you may not be obsessed with money, not having enough money to take care of what you consider the necessities of life can lead to anxiety and tension. If you do not have enough money to replace or repair a broken or faulty personal computer or automobile, the result can be stressful. Even worse, imagine the stress of being hounded by bill collectors. Lack of funds can also lead to embarrassment and humiliation (both stressors). A member of the work team said he chose not to accompany the group to a restaurant after work. The team leader said, "What's the matter, can't you afford to go out to dinner?" The team member said, "I hate to admit it, but I have no money to go out to dinner, and I can't afford to put anything else on my credit card."

SCHOOL-RELATED PROBLEMS

The life of a student can be stressful. Among the stressors to cope with are exams in subjects you do not understand well, having to write papers on subjects unfamiliar to you, working your way through the complexities of registration, or having to deal with instructors who do not see things your way. Another source of severe stress for some students is having too many competing demands on their time. On most campuses you will find someone who works full-time, goes to school full-time, and has a family. This type of three-way pull often leads to marital problems.

PERSONALITY FACTORS AND STRESS-PRONENESS

Some people are more stress-prone than others because of personality factors. Three key personality factors predisposing people to stress are Type A behavior, belief that their lives are controlled by external forces, and a negative disposition.

TYPE A BEHAVIOR

People with **Type A behavior** characteristics have basic personalities that lead them into stressful situations. Type A behavior has two main components. One is a tendency to try to accomplish too many things in too little time. This leads the Type A individual to be impatient and demanding. The other component is free-floating hostility. Because of this combined sense of urgency and hostility, these people are irritated by trivial things. On the job, people with Type A behavior are aggressive and hard-working. Off the job, they keep themselves preoccupied with all kinds of errands to run and things to do.

Certain features of the Type A behavior pattern are related to coronary heart disease. Hostility, anger, cynicism, and suspiciousness lead to heart problems, whereas impatience, ambition, and work-driven are not associated with coronary disease.[16] Many work-driven people who like what they are doing—including many business executives—are remarkably healthy and outlive less competitive people.

The vast majority of people reading this book probably are Type B personalities—those who are easygoing and can relax readily. People who display Type B behavior rarely suffer from impatience or a sense of time urgency, nor are they excessively hostile.

BELIEF IN EXTERNAL LOCUS OF CONTROL

If you believe that your fate is controlled more by external than internal forces, you are probably more susceptible to stress. People with an **external locus of control** believe that external forces control their fate. Conversely, people with an **internal locus of control** believe that fate is pretty much under their control.

The link between locus of control and stress works in this manner: If people believe they can control adverse forces, they are less prone to the stressor of worrying about them. For example, if you believed that you can always find a job, you will worry less about unemployment. At the same time, the person who believes in an internal locus of control experiences a higher level of job satisfaction. Work is less stressful and more satisfying when you perceive it to be under your control.

What about your locus of control? Do you believe it to be internal? Or is it external?

NEGATIVE AFFECTIVITY

A major contributor to being stress-prone is **negative affectivity,** a tendency to experience aversive (intensely disliked) emotional states. In more detail, negative affectivity is a predisposition to experience emotional stress that includes feelings of nervousness, tension, and worry. Furthermore, a person with negative affectivity is likely to experience emotional states such as anger, scorn, revulsion, guilt, self-dissatisfaction.[17] Such negative personalities seem to search for discrepancies between what they would like and what exists. Instead of attempting to solve problems, they look for them.

People with negative affectivity are often distressed even when working under conditions that coworkers perceive as interesting and challenging. In one company, a contest was announced that encouraged customer-contact workers to compete against each other in terms of improving customer service. An employee with a history of negative affectivity said: "Here we go again. We're already hustling like crazy to please customers. Now we're being asked to dream up even more schemes to make sure the customer is right. It's about time the company thought of ways to please employees as well as customers."

SOURCES OF WORK STRESS

No job is without potential stressors for some people. When work is lacking stressful elements, it may not have enough challenge to prompt employees to achieve high performance. Here we describe five major job stressors you might encounter or have already encountered, as listed in Figure 4-3.

HIGH JOB DEMANDS—LOW JOB CONTROL

Many workers experience stress when they are faced with a heavy work load combined with limited ability to control key features of the job.[18] Among these features would be how many phone calls to handle, when to perform certain tasks, and how fast to perform the work. Imagine being required to write more reports than you thought you could handle, yet being unable to concentrate on them for more than a few minutes at a time. The impediments to your concentration might include demands from customers, coworkers, and your boss.

Figure 4-3   Frequent Job Stressors

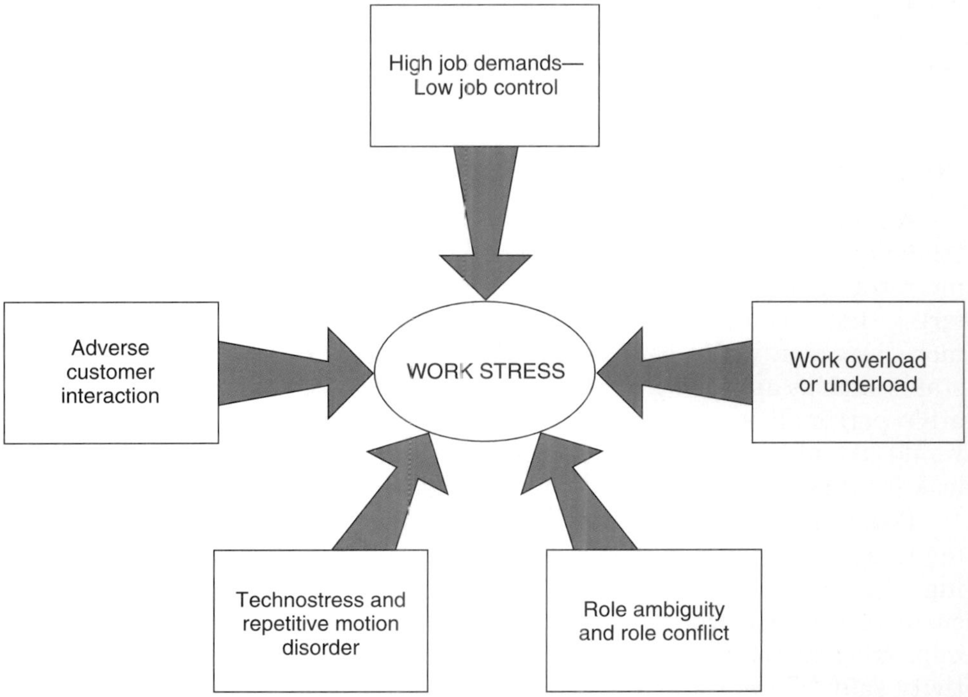

High job demands—
Low job control

Adverse
customer
interaction

WORK STRESS

Work overload
or underload

Technostress and
repetitive motion
disorder

Role ambiguity
and role conflict

Why a combination of high demand and low control creates stress can be explained as follows: High job demands produce a state of arousal that is typically reflected in such responses as increased heart rate and flow of adrenaline. When the worker has low control, the arousal cannot be properly channeled into a coping response. As a result, the physiological stress reaction is even larger and persists for a longer time.[19]

A service station mechanic suffered from migraine headaches. Asked by a health professional if he was experiencing job stress, the mechanic replied: "My job is killing me. Half the time we're shorthanded. That means while I'm doing repair work I also have to work the cash register. Sometimes I have to pump gas for the people who don't use self-serve. Every time the bell rings I have to stop what I'm doing. I can't do decent repair work when I'm being jerked around like this."

WORK OVERLOAD OR UNDERLOAD

As just described, having limited control over a heavy work load creates job stress. A heavy work load itself, however, can also be a stressor. **Role overload,** a burdensome work load, can create stress for a person in two ways. First, the person may become fatigued and thus be less able to tolerate annoyances and irritations. Think of how much easier it is to become provoked over a minor incident when you lack proper rest. Second, a person subject to unreasonable work demands may feel perpetually behind schedule, a situation that in itself creates an uncomfortable, stressful feeling.

When work overload goes to extremes it can lead to heart attack and death. In Japan where managerial workers are expected to sacrifice most of their personal life for the good of the organization, heart attacks through overwork is referred to as **karoshi.** In one such case, a Japanese middle manager worked 80 consecutive hours without sleep before dying. Karoshi affects more than 10,000 Japanese workers annually.[20]

Another form of work overload is demanding higher and higher speed from workers. Speed is important to companies because delivering goods and services very quickly brings a competitive edge. The most stressful situation occurs when a company first *downsizes* (reduces its workforce to operate more efficiently and save money). Next, the remaining workers are expected to carry a heavier workload, at a faster pace than previously. The combination of additional responsibility and high speed can be a major stressor. Among the problems are that the hurried employees have very little time to ask for help, or to carefully study what they are doing.

A disruptive amount of stress can also occur when people experience **role underload,** or too little to do. Some people find role underload frustrating because it is a normal human desire to want to work toward self-fulfillment. Also, making a contribution on the job is one way of gaining self-esteem. As with any facet of human behavior, there are exceptions. Some people find it relaxing not to have much to do on the job. One direct benefit is that it preserves their energy for family and leisure activities.

A DISRUPTIVE AMOUNT OF STRESS CAN ALSO OCCUR
WHEN PEOPLE EXPERIENCE ROLE UNDERLOAD

ROLE AMBIGUITY AND ROLE CONFLICT

Not being certain of what they should be doing is a stressor for many people. **Role ambiguity** is a condition in which the job holder receives confusing or poorly defined expectations. A typical complaint is "I'm not really sure I know what I'm supposed to be doing around here." You will recall, however, that creative people enjoy ambiguity because they can define problems for themselves when clear directions are lacking. Role ambiguity is related to job control. If you lack a clear picture of what you should be doing, it is difficult to get your job under control.

Role conflict refers to having to choose between two competing demands or expectations. Many workers receive conflicting demands from two or more managers. Imagine being told by your manager to give top priority to one project. You then receive a call from your manager's manager who tells you to drop everything and work on another project. It's often up to you to resolve such a conflict. If you don't, you will experience stress.

TECHNOSTRESS AND REPETITIVE-MOTION DISORDER

The computerization of the workplace and home, especially information technology, has created a significant stressor labeled as **technostress.** The condition refers to a stress reaction caused by an inability to cope with computer technologies in a constructive manner.[21] One contributor to technostress is the demand for continuous learning as software changes so rapidly. At the same time, software problems surface at unpredictable times often leaving the computer operator feeling incompetent and helpless. (What to do when the computer screen freezes and you have not saved your valuable data or words, and no one else available knows how to help?)

Another contributor to technostress is that computer work can become so consuming that the person loses interest in human interaction. As a result, interpersonal relationships suffer. (The next chapter includes a section about one of the worst computer-related problems, on-line addictions.) Working at a computer monitor for prolonged periods of time can lead to adverse physical and psychological reactions. The symptoms include headaches; fatigue; and hot, tired, watery eyes and blurred vision.

Technostress also comes in the form of a repetitive-motion disorder as a consequence of prolonged keyboarding. The repetitive-motion disorder (or repetitive-stress disorder) most frequently associated with keyboarding, and the use of optical scanners, is **carpal tunnel syndrome.** The syndrome occurs when repetitive flexing and extension of the wrist causes the tendons to swell, thus trapping and pinching the median nerve. Carpal tunnel syndrome creates stress because of the pain and misery. The thoughts of having to permanently leave a job requiring keyboarding is another potential stressor.

Much of repetitive-motion disorders can be prevented by computer workers taking frequent rest breaks and using a well-designed combination of the work table, chair, and monitor. Being comfortable while working prevents much physical strain. Figure 4-4 presents the basics of a work

Figure 4-4   How to Minimize Cumulative Trauma Disorder

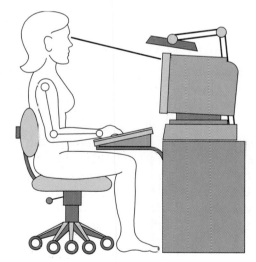

An Ergonomic Workstation

- Keep the screen below your eye level.
- Keep your elbows on the same level with home-key row, with your wrists and lower arms parallel to floor.
- Support your back and thighs with a well constructed chair.
- Position your feet flat on the floor.
- Use lamp to supplement inadequate room lighting.

station designed on *ergonomic* principles. (Ergonomics has to do with making machines and equipment fit human capabilities and demands.)

ADVERSE CUSTOMER INTERACTION

Interviews conducted with 93 employees revealed that interactions with customers can be a major stressor. Stressful events frequently cited were customers losing control, using profanity, badgering employees, harassing employees, and lying. The employees interviewed said that these adverse interactions with customers negatively affected the quality of their work environment.[22] Part of the problem is that the sales associate often feels helpless when placed in conflict with a customer. The sales associate is told that "the customer is always right." Furthermore, the store manager usually sides with the customer in a dispute with the sales associate.

MANAGING STRESS

Because potentially harmful stressors surround us in work and personal life, virtually everybody needs a program of stress management to stay well. Stress management techniques are placed here into three categories: attacking the source of the stress, getting social support, and relaxation techniques. Your challenge is to select those techniques that best fit your circumstances and preferences.

DEALING WITH STRESS BY ATTACKING ITS SOURCE

Stress can be dealt with in the short range by indirect techniques such as exercise and relaxation. However, to manage stress in the long range and stay well, you must also learn to deal directly with stressors. Several of these techniques are described in the next few paragraphs.

Eliminating or Modifying the Stressor.   The most potent method of managing stress is to eliminate the stressor giving you trouble. For example, if your job is your primary stressor, your stress level would be reduced if you found a more comfortable job. At other times, modifying the stressful situation can be equally helpful. Using the problem-solving method, you search for an alternative that will change the stressor. Here is a useful model to follow:

> A retailing executive repeatedly told her boss that she wanted to open a new branch of the business. He agreed with her but took no action. Feeling rejected, frustrated, and stressed, she took another approach to the problem. She drew up the plans for opening a new branch, presented them to her boss, and informed him she was ready to move ahead. To the executive's surprise, he said, "Great! I was only hesitating to ask you to do this because I thought you were overworked."
> Everything worked out just as she wanted after she pursued the alternative of restating her plans in writing.[23]

Placing the Stressful Situation in Perspective. Stress comes about because of our perception of the situation. If you can alter your perception of a threatening situation, you are attacking the source. A potentially stressful situation can be put into perspective by asking, "What is the worst thing that could happen to me if I fail in this activity?"

The answer to the above question is found by asking a series of questions, starting with the grimmest possibility. For instance, you are late with a report that is due this afternoon. Consider the following questions and answers:

- Will my reputation be damaged permanently? (*No.*)

- Will I get fired? (*No.*)

- Will I get reprimanded? (*Perhaps, but not for sure.*)

- Will my boss think less of me? (*Perhaps, but not for sure.*)

Only if the answer is yes to either of the first two questions is negative stress truly justified. The thought process just described allows stressful situations to be properly evaluated and kept in perspective. You therefore avoid the stress that comes from overreacting to a situation.

Gaining Control of the Situation. As implied in the discussion of low job control, feeling that a bothersome situation is out of control is almost a universal stressor. A key method of stress management is therefore to attack the stressor by gaining control of the situation. A multipurpose way of gaining control is to improve your work habits and time management, as described in Chapter 12. By being "on top of things," you can make heavy work and school demands less stressful.

A study conducted with middle managers supports the idea that gaining control of the situation helps reduce stress. Middle managers were selected for the study because of the worries about job security and time pressures they faced. The two stress-management strategies studied both involved gaining control of the situation: resolving conflict and clarifying work expectations. (The rationale is that conflict is stressful and so is role ambiguity, as described previously.) The study demonstrated that managers who were able to resolve conflict and clarify their work expectations perceived potential stressors as less threatening. Also of importance, the managers experienced less overall stress.[24]

Finding the Humor in the Situation. An indirect way of gaining control of the situation to reduce stress is to find the humor in the situation. By finding humor in the potentially stressful situation, the situation becomes less threatening and therefore less likely to produce stress. Quite often situations that were frustrating at the time become funny after time has passed. An example would be thinking back to how funny it was to have called in sick on your first day of work at your present job.[25] Humor is a stress reliever also because it deepens breathing, lowers blood pressure, loosens tight muscles, and releases endorphins.

Reducing Stress through Social Support. An ideal way of managing stress is one that provides side benefits. Getting close to people falls into this category. You will reduce some stress symptoms and form healthy relationships with others in the process. Becka Barbatis, a bioenergy healer, puts it this way: "We need to view ourselves as social beings and we very much need to know that we're related to one another."[26] By getting close to others, you build a **support system,** a group of people on whom you can rely for encouragement and comfort. The trusting relationship you have with these people is critically important. People within your support network include family members, friends, coworkers, and other students. In addition, some people in turmoil reach out to strangers to discuss personal problems.

The usual method of reducing stress is to talk over your problems while the other person listens. Switching roles can also help reduce stress. Listening to others will make you feel better because you have helped them. Another advantage to listening to the feelings and problems of others is that it helps you to get close to them.

Relaxation Techniques for Handling Stress

"Relax" is the advice many people have always offered the stressed individual. Stress experts give us similar advice but also offer specific techniques. Here we describe four techniques that can help you relax and, consequently, help you reduce stress and its symptoms In addition, Exhibit 4-2 lists a variety of "stress busters," many of which are relaxation-oriented. Recognize that many of these techniques contribute directly to wellness, and that stress-management is a major component of wellness. Pick and choose among stress-management techniques until you find several that effectively reduce your stress.

Relaxation Response. A standard technique for reducing stress is to achieve the relaxation response. The **relaxation response** is a bodily reaction in which you experience a slower respiration and heart rate, lowered blood pressure, and lowered metabolism. By practicing the relaxation response, you can counteract the fight-or-flight response associated with stress.

According to cardiologist Herbert Benson, four things are necessary to practice the relaxation response: a quiet environment, an object to focus on, a passive attitude, and a comfortable position. You are supposed to practice the relaxation response 10 to 20 minutes, twice a day. To evoke the relaxation response, Benson advises you to close your eyes. Relax. Concentrate on one word or prayer. If other thoughts come to mind, be passive, and return to the repetition.[27] Human Relations Skill-Building Exercise 4-1 gives you an opportunity to practice the relaxation response.

Similar to any other relaxation technique, the relaxation response is harmless and works for most people. However, some very impatient people find it annoying to disrupt their busy day to meditate. Unfortunately, these may be the people who most urgently need to learn to relax.

Deep Breathing. The natural process of inhaling and exhaling slowly, filling your lungs with air and slowly letting it escape is a powerful stress reducer for many people. Deep breathing has immediate and long-term benefits. It lowers the heart rate and blood pressure and increases your skin temperature. Deep breathing also relaxes you emotionally and

EXHIBIT 4-2

STRESS BUSTERS

- Take a nap when facing heavy pressures. "Power napping" is regarded as one of the most effective techniques for reducing and preventing stress.

- Give in to your emotions. If you are angry, disgusted, or confused admit your feelings. Suppressing your emotions adds to stress.

- Take a brief break from the stressful situation and do something small and constructive like washing your car, emptying a waste basket, or getting a haircut.

- Get a massage because it can loosen tight muscles, improve your blood circulation, and calm you down.

- Get help with your stressful task from a coworker, boss, or friend.

- Concentrate intensely on reading, surfing the Internet, a sport, or hobby. Contrary to common sense, concentration is at the heart of stress reduction.

- Have a quiet place at home and have a brief idle period there every day.

- Take a leisurely day off from your routine.

- Finish something you have started, however small. Accomplishing almost anything reduces some stress.

- Stop to smell the flowers, make friends with a young child or elderly person, or play with a kitten or puppy.

- Strive to do a good job, but not a perfect job.

- Work with your hands, doing a pleasant task.

- Hug somebody you like, and whom you think will hug you back.

- Minimize drinking caffeinated or alcoholic beverages, and drink fruit juice or water instead. Grab a piece of fruit rather than a can of beer.

helps you gain perspective. Barbatsis explains how to use deep breathing for stress reduction:

1. Sit or lie down in a quiet spot. Place one hand on your waist, the other in the center of your chest. Breathe several times. The hand on your belly should move more because it indicates you are breathing from your diaphragm.

2. Now inhale slowly, filling up the lungs. As you exhale slowly, push air out from the bottom of your lungs.

3. Take long, slow breaths. If you become dizzy or lightheaded, you are breathing too fast.

HUMAN RELATIONS SKILL-BUILDING EXERCISE 4-1

The Relaxation Response

Think of one of the most stressful moments you have experienced in recent weeks. Visualize yourself as experiencing stress. If you are currently experiencing significant stress, visualization will not be necessary. Now carry out the relaxation response. Close your eyes. Relax. Concentrate on one simple word. Repeat the word several times.

Describe to yourself in writing, how effective this technique has been in reducing your stress. Share experiences with the rest of the class. Discuss what you see as the strengths and limitations of this technique.

4. As you inhale, elevate your shoulders and collarbone slightly to fill the lungs fully with air.

5. After you have mastered the breathing technique, with each outward breath blow out your worrisome thoughts and pains. Breathe in relaxation and calmness.[28]

Visualizing a Pleasant Experience.   Perhaps the most effortless and enjoyable relaxation technique when under stress is to visualize a calm and pleasant experience. Visualization means to picture yourself doing something that you would like to do. Whatever fantasy suits your fancy will work, according to the advocates of this relaxation technique. Visualizations that work for some people include: fishing on a sunny day, floating on a cloud, caressing a baby, petting a kitten, and walking in the woods. Notice that all of these scenes are relaxing rather than exciting. What visualization would work for you?

Muscle Monitoring.   An important part of many stress-reduction programs is to learn to relax your muscles. Learn to literally loosen up and

HUMAN RELATIONS SKILL-BUILDING EXERCISE 4-2

The Stress-Buster Survey

Each class member thinks through carefully which techniques he or she uses to reduce work or personal stress. Class members then come to the front of the room individually to make a brief presentation of their most effective stress-reduction technique. After the presentations are completed, class members analyze and interpret what they heard. Among the issues to explore are:

1. Which are the most popular stress-reduction techniques?

2. How do the stress-reduction techniques used by the class compare to those recommended by experts?

be less uptight. Muscle monitoring involves becoming aware that your muscles have tightened and then consciously relaxing them. If your jaw muscles are tightening up in a tense situation, you learn to relax your jaw enough to overcome the stress effects.

Try to determine whether muscle tautness occurs in association with some recurring event. Pay attention to the tautness of your muscles on those occasions. For example, you might experience a tightening of your neck muscles whenever it is time to pay the rent. Take a few moments to be aware of that muscle tension. After a while you will learn to relax as the day approaches for paying your rent.

Human Relations Skill-Building Exercise 4-2 will give you and your class mates an opportunity to learn more about what stress-management techniques others use.

SUMMARY

Wellness is a formalized approach to preventive health care. By promoting health, company wellness programs help prevent employees from developing physical and mental problems often associated with excessive job pressures.

Four strategies for achieving wellness were described in this chapter. (1) The right amount and type of physical exercise contributes substantially to wellness. (2) Maintaining a healthy diet is valuable for mental and physical health. The Food Guide Pyramid (Figure 4-1) contains many useful suggestions. (3) Developing competence, including both job and social skills, helps us stay well. (4) Being resilient is another wellness strategy. Psychological hardiness contributes to resiliency (5) Developing a health-prone personality (emotional expressiveness and self-reliance) helps use to be well. (6) Minimizing obvious risks to health and safety improves the chances of achieving wellness.

The body's battle against a stressor is the fight-or-flight response. Stress always involves physiological changes such as an increase in heart rate, blood cholesterol, and blood pressure. The right amount of stress can be beneficial. Performance tends to be best under moderate amounts of stress, yet certain negative forms of stress almost always decrease performance.

Prolonged stress may lead to burnout, a condition of emotional, mental, and physical exhaustion in response to long-term job stressors. Occupations that require frequent and intense interaction with others often lead to burnout. Yet the condition can happen whenever not much support from others is present, and the rewards are few.

Almost any form of frustration, disappointment setback, inconvenience, or crisis in your personal life can cause stress. The categories of situations that can produce stress include: significant life changes; low self-esteem; everyday annoyances; social and family problems; physical and mental health problems; financial problems; and school-related problems.

Personality factors contribute to stress-proneness. People with Type A behavior are impatient and demanding, and have free-floating hostility all of which leads to stress. People with an external locus of control (believing that external forces control their fate) are more susceptible to stress. Negative affectivity (a predisposition to negative mental states) also contributes to stress.

Sources of job stress are quite varied. Among them are high job demands and low job control; work overload, including time pressures, and work underload; role ambiguity and role conflict; technostress and repetitive-motion disorder; and averse customer interaction.

To successfully manage stress in the long range, you have to deal with the stressors directly. Four direct approaches are: eliminate or modify the stressor; place the situation in perspective; gain control of the situation; and find humor in the situation. Reducing stress through emotional support by others is an effective stress-management technique. Four relaxation techniques for handling stress are: the relaxation response; deep breathing; visualizing a pleasant experience; and muscle monitoring.

Questions and Activities

1. How can a company wellness program improve profits and productivity?

2. If exercise contributes so much to wellness, how come so many athletes are stressed out?

3. Does a "well person" ever eat such foods as pizza, hamburgers, and hot dogs, and drink milk shakes and beer? Explain.

4. Give an example of a "psychologically hardy" individual you either know personally or through the media. What is the basis for your conclusion?

5. What responsibility should an employer have in helping employees minimize obvious risks to health and safety?

6. Some researchers have suggested that the term *challenge* be substituted for the term *stress*. What do you think of the merit of their suggestion?

7. How does a person judge the strength or impact of a stressor he or she is facing?

8. Repeated case histories have revealed that people who win large cash prizes in government lotteries wind up suffering severe stress disorders. Explain why this situation could be true.

9. How can a person who suffers from technostress compete in the modern world?

10. Speak to a person you consider to be much more relaxed than most people. Ask your contact which (if any) of the relaxation or stress-busting techniques listed in this chapter he or she uses. Report your findings back to class.

A HUMAN RELATIONS CASE PROBLEM

The New Marketing Assistant

One year ago Wanda Diaz returned enthusiastically to the workforce after 12 years of being a full-time homemaker and a part-time direct sales representative for beauty products. Diaz's major motive for finding a full-time professional job was to work toward her career goal as a marketing manager in a medium-size or large company. To help prepare for this career, Diaz completed a business administration degree over a five-year period.

Another compelling reason for returning to full-time employment was financial need. Diaz's husband owned and operated an appliance and electronics store that was becoming less profitable each year. Several large appliance stores had moved into the area resulting in fewer customers for Northside Appliances (the name of the family business). Diaz and her husband Miguel concluded that the family could not cover its bills unless Wanda earned the equivalent of a full-time income.

After three months of searching for full-time employment, Wanda responded to a newspaper ad for a marketing assistant position. The ad described the position as part of a management training program with an excellent future. Ten days after submitting her cover letter and résumé, Wanda was invited for an interview. The company proved to be a national provider of long-distance telephone service. The human resources interviewer and hiring manager both explained that Wanda's initial assignment would be as a telemarketer. Both people advised Wanda that large numbers of people were applying for these telemarketing positions.

Wanda would be required to telephone individual consumers and small-business owners, and make a sales pitch for them to transfer their long-distance telephone service to her company. The company supplied an almost inexhaustible computerized list of names and telephone numbers across the country. In this way Wanda could take advantage of time-zone differences to telephone people during their dinner time, as well as other times. Wanda would receive a small commission for customers who made the switch to her company. Her major responsibility in addition to telephone soliciting would be to enter the results of her conversations into a computer, as well as prepare summaries.

One week after the interviews, Wanda was extended a job offer. She accepted the offer despite some concern that the position was a little too far removed from the professional marketing position she sought. Wanda was assigned to a small cubicle in a large room with about 25 other telemarketers. She found the training program exciting, particularly with respect to techniques for overcoming customer resistance. Wanda reasoned that this experience combined with her direct selling of beauty products would give her excellent insights into how consumers think and behave. For the first two weeks Wanda found the calls to be uplifting. She experienced a surge of excitement when a customer agreed to switch to her company. As was the custom in the office, she shouted "Yes" after concluding each customer conversion to her company.

As the weeks moved slowly on, Wanda became increasingly restless and concerned about the job. Her success ratio was falling below the company standard of a 3 percent success rate on the cold calls. A thought kept running through Wanda's mind.

(Continued)

"Even if I'm doing well at this job, 97 percent of people I call will practically hang up on me. And I can't stand keyboarding all these worthless reports explaining what happened as a result of my calls. It's a horrible waste of time."

Wanda soon found it difficult to sleep peacefully, often pacing the apartment after Miguel had fallen asleep. She also noticed that she was arguing much more with Miguel and the two children. Wanda's stomach churned so much that she found eating uncomfortable. She often poked at her food, but drank coffee and diet soft drinks much more than previously. After six months of working at the long-distance carrier, her weight plunged from 135 pounds to 123 pounds. Wanda's left thumb and wrists were constantly sore. One night when Miguel asked her why she was rubbing the region below her thumb, Wanda said, "I keep pushing around the mouse so much during the day that my thumb feels like it's falling off."

During the next several months, Wanda spoke with her supervisor twice about her future in the company. Both times the supervisor explained that the best telemarketers become eligible for supervisory positions, providing they have proved themselves for at least three years. The supervisor also cautioned Wanda that her performance was adequate, but not exceptional. Wanda thought to herself, "I'm banging my head against the wall, and I'm considered just average."

As Wanda approached a full year in her position, she and Miguel reviewed the family finances. He said, "Sales at the store are getting worse and worse. I predict that this year your salary will be higher than profits from the store. It's great that we can count on at least one stable salary in the family. The kids and I really appreciate it."

Wanda thought to herself, "Now is the worst time to tell Miguel how I really feel about my job. I'm falling apart inside, and the family needs my salary. What a mess."

Questions

1. What aspects of work stress are revealed in this case?

2. What suggestions can you make to the company for decreasing the stressors in the position of telemarketer?

3. What advice can you offer Wanda to help her achieve wellness?

 REFERENCES

[1]Gillian Flynn, "Companies Make Wellness Work," *Personnel Journal,* February 1995, pp. 65–66.

[2]Dot Yandle, "Staying Well May Be Up to You," *Success Workshop Folio* (a supplement to *The Pryor Report Management Newsletter*), February 1994, pp. 2–3.

[3]Flynn, "Companies Make Wellness Work," pp. 63–64.

[4]Philip L. Rice, *Stress and Health: Principles and Practices for Coping and Wellness* (Monterey, CA.: Brooks/College Publishing Company, 1987), pp. 353–354.

[5]*Dietary Guidelines for Americans,* 3rd ed., U.S. Department of Agriculture, U. S. Department of Health and Human Services, 1990; updated with food pyramid, May 1992.

[6]Quoted in *Top Health: The Health Promotion and Wellness Letter,* February 1995, p. 4.

[7]Emory L. Cowen, "In Pursuit of Wellness," *American Psychologist,* April 1991, p. 406.

[8]James M. Kouzes and Barry Z. Posner, *The Leadership Challenge: How to Get Extraordinary Things Done in Organizations* (San Francisco: Jossey-Bass, 1987), pp. 65–67.

[9]Hans J. Eysenck, "Health's Character," *Psychology Today,* December 1988, pp. 28–35.

[10]Research cited in "Happy People Get Sick Less," Associated Press, June 28, 1997.

[11]Jeffrey R. Edwards, "A Cybernetic Theory of Stress, Coping, and Well-Being in Organizations," *Academy of Management Review,* April 1992, p. 248.

[12]R. Douglas Allen, Michael A. Hitt, and Charles R. Greer, "Occupational Stress and Perceived Organizational Effectiveness: An Examination of Stress Level and Stress Type," *Personnel Psychology,* Summer 1982, pp. 359–370.

[13]Raymond T. Lee, and Blake E. Ashforth, "A Meta-Analytic Examination of the Correlates of Three Dimensions of Job Burnout," *Journal of Applied Psychology,* April 1996, p. 123.

[14]Rabi S. Bhagat, "Effects of Stressful Life Events on Individual Performance and Work Adjustment Processes Within Organizational Settings: A Research Model," *Academy of Management Review,* October 1983, pp. 660–670.

[15]"Building Self-Esteem," http://www.ashland.com/education/self-esteem/best_shot.html.

[16]T.M. Dembrowski and P.T. Costa, Jr., "Coronary-Prone Behavior: Components of the Type A Pattern and Hostility," *Journal of Personality,* Vol. 55, 1987, pp. 211–235; Ray H. Rosenman, *Type A Behavior and Your Heart* (New York: Fawcett, 1975).

[17]Peter Y. Chen and Paul E. Spector, "Negative Affectivity as the Underlying Cause of Correlations Between Stressors and Strains," *Journal of Applied Psychology,* June 1991, p. 398.

[18]Marilyn L. Fox, Deborah J. Dwyer, and Daniel C. Ganster, "Effects of Stressful Job Demands and Control on Physiological and Attitudinal Outcomes in a Hospital Setting," *Academy of Management Journal,* April 1993, pp. 290–291.

[19]Ibid.

[20]Robert McGarvey, "On the Edge," *Entrepreneur,* August 1995, p. 76.

[21]Craig Bond, *Technostress: The Human Cost of the Computer Revolution* (Reading, MA.: Addison-Wesley, 1984), p. 16.

[22]James D. Brodzinski, Robert P. Scherer, and Karen A. Goyer, "Workplace Stress: A Study of Internal and External Pressures Placed on Employees," *Personnel Administrator,* July 1989, pp. 77–78.

[23]"Making Stress Work for You," *Executive Strategies,* October 3, 1989, p. 5.

[24]David Antonioni, "Two Strategies for Responding to Stressors: Managing Conflict and Clarifying Work Expectations," *Journal of Business and Psychology,* Winter 1996, pp. 287–295.

[25]John Roger and Peter McWilliams, *Wealth 101: Getting What You Want—Enjoying What You've Got* (Los Angeles: Prelude Press, 1993).

[26]Quoted in Sue McDonald, "Relax: Stress Can Be Managed," *The Cincinnati Enquirer,* October 25, 1995, p. D6.

[27]Herbert Benson (with William Proctor), *Beyond the Relaxation Response* (New York: Berkley Books, 1995), pp. 96–97.

[28]Sue McDonald, "Take a Deep Breath," *The Cincinnati Enquirer,* October 24, 1995, p. D3.

 ## ADDITIONAL READING

Bachler, Christopher J. "Workers Take Leave of Job Stress." *Personnel Journal,* January 1995, pp. 38–48.

Carlton, Susie. "Getaways from Stress," *Working Woman,* January 1996, pp. 70–74, 81, 86.

"De-Stressing News: Don't Worry, You're Happy Despite All That Stress." *Working Woman,* January 1997, pp. 46–47.

Edwards, Jeffrey R. "An Examination of Competing Versions of the Person-Environment Fit Approach to Stress." *Academy of Management Journal,* April 1996, pp. 292–339.

Geber, Sara Zeff. *How to Manage Stress for Success.* New York: AMACOM, 1996.

Keita, Gwendolyn Puryear, and Hurrell, Joseph J., Jr. *Job Stress in a Changing Workforce: Investigating Gender, Diversity, and Family Issues.* Washington, DC: American Psychological Association, 1994.

Leatz, Christine A. *Career Success/Personal Stress: How to Stay Healthy in a High Stress Environment.* New York: McGraw-Hill, 1992.

Phillips, Debra. "Healthy, Wealthy Wise: A Fit Body and Mind Keep Your Business in Peak Condition." *Entrepreneur,* March 1996, pp. 125–127.

Potter, Beverly. *Finding a Path with a Heart: How to Go from Burnout to Bliss.* Berkeley, CA: Ronin Publishing, 1995.

CHAPTER 5

DEALING WITH PERSONAL PROBLEMS

Learning Objectives

After studying the information and doing the exercises in this chapter, you should be able to:

▼ Recognize how self-defeating behavior contributes to personal problems

▼ Explain the nature of addictive behavior and its link to craving for dopamine

▼ Explain how alcohol and drug abuse interfere with career and personal success, and how to deal with these problems

▼ Develop insights into dealing with the loss of a relationship

▼ Describe how depression and neurobiological disorders can lower job productivity

▼ Develop a strategy for dealing with anger

*L*arry, an automotive technology student, had a well-paying, part-time job as an automobile mechanic. A year-and-a-half later he dropped out of school and lost his job. Larry hoped to someday become a service manager in a large automobile dealership. He first showed his talents for automotive repair at age ten, when he helped his father do simple car repairs. Larry also developed an interest in computers at around the same

time. His software library contained about 40 different computer games plus the latest joy sticks.

At school, Larry was allowed almost unlimited access to the computer laboratory. After completing his computer course work, Larry would stay at the lab for additional exploration. Soon he began visiting different web sites related to automotive technology. Then came a search for web sites about sports, automotive clubs, stock market information, chat rooms, and airline reservation systems. To give himself more time to surf the Web, Larry convinced his parents to buy a computer for the home. After coming home from the lab at 9 P.M., Larry would surf for a few more hours at home. Soon he drifted into a pattern of staying up all night, except for a few brief naps, several times a week. Larry rarely left his computer on weekends.

Next Larry started skipping classes and lab assignments so that he could stay in his room and stay on-line. He also began missing work, or showing up in such a state of fatigue that his manager sent him home. Now Larry had one more excuse to stay on-line: He could conduct his job search by computer. Larry's friends stopped calling him or dropping by, because he only wanted to communicate by Internet. Larry skipped so many meals that he lost 20 pounds.

As Larry became more and more isolated from the outside world, his parents persistently urged him to get help for his problems. Larry finally enrolled in the Center for Online Addiction. The psychologist running the program thinks Larry's chances for recovery are reasonably good. Soon he might be able to spend time on-line without it consuming his life.

Larry's addictive behavior is but one of the personal problems that can create havoc with work and personal life described in this chapter. Until he conquers his problems, he cannot achieve wellness or manage his stress. How many people have you known or heard about who damaged their career or an important relationship because of personal problems?

Our approach to understanding and overcoming personal problems will be to first describe self-defeating behavior in general, and how to reverse the trend. We then describe various forms of self-defeating behavior including addictions, and absenteeism and tardiness. We also describe two types of personal problems that are much less under a person's control: depression and neurobiological disorders (such as attention-deficit disorder). Finally, we describe dealing with anger.

SELF-DEFEATING BEHAVIOR

Many problems on the job and in personal life arise because of factors beyond our control. A boss may be intimidating and insensitive, an employer might lay you off, or a significant other might abruptly terminate your relationship. Many personal problems, nevertheless, arise because of **self-defeating behavior.** A person with self-defeating tendencies intentionally or unintentionally engages in activities or harbors attitudes that work against his or her best interest. A person who habitually is late for important meetings is engaging in self-defeating behavior. Dropping out of school for no reason other than being bored with studying is another of many possible examples. Let's examine several leading causes of self-defeating behavior, and how to reverse the pattern.

WHY PEOPLE ENGAGE IN SELF-DEFEATING BEHAVIOR

Many different forces lead people to work against their own best interests, often sabotaging their careers. The major cause of self-defeating behavior is a *loser life script.*[1] Early in life, our parents and other influential forces program our brains to act out certain life plans. These plans are known as *scripts.* People fortunate enough to have winner scripts consistently emerge victorious. When a tough assignment needs doing, they get the job done. For example, they figure out how to get a jammed computer program running again that baffles everybody else in the office.

In contrast, others have scripts that program them toward damaging their careers and falling short of their potential. Much of this damage paradoxically occurs just when things seem to be going well. A person might steal equipment from a company shortly after receiving an outstanding performance appraisal.

The simplest explanation for self-defeating behavior is that some people suffer from a personality that fosters defeat. People with a *self-defeating personality pattern* have three notable characteristics. First, they repeatedly fail at tasks they have the ability to perform. Second, they place themselves in very difficult situations and respond helplessly. Third, they typically refuse to take advantage of escape routes, such as accepting advice and counsel from a manager.[2]

Self-defeating beliefs put many people on the road to career self-sabotage. In this context, a self-defeating belief is an erroneous belief that creates the conditions for failure. For example, some people sabotage their job campaigns before even starting. They think to themselves: "I lack the right experience," "I'm not sharp enough," "I'm too old," "I'm too young," and so forth.

Fear of success is yet another contributor to career self-sabotage. People who fear success often procrastinate to the point of self-defeat. The same people worry that being successful will lead to such negative outcomes as an overwhelming work load or loss of friends. They also worry that success will bring about unrealistic expectations from others, such as winning a big suggestion award every year.

To examine your present tendencies toward self-defeating behavior, take the self-sabotage quiz presented in Human Relation Self-Assessment Exercise 5-1. Taking the quiz will help alert you to many self-imposed behaviors and attitudes that could potentially harm your career and personal life.

Strategies and Techniques for Overcoming and Preventing Self-Defeating Behavior

Overcoming self-defeating behavior requires hard work and patience. Here we present six widely applicable strategies for overcoming and preventing self-defeating behavior. Pick and choose among them to fit your particular circumstance and personal style.

Examine Your Script and Make the Necessary Changes.   Much importance has been attached to the influence of early-life programming in determining whether a person is predisposed to self-defeat. Note carefully the word *predisposed*. A person may be predisposed to snatch defeat from the jaws of victory, but that does not mean the predisposition makes defeat inevitable. It does mean that the person will have to work harder to overcome a tendency toward self-sabotage. A good starting point is to look for patterns in your setbacks:

- Did you blow up at people who have the authority to make the administrative decisions about your future?

- Did you get so tense during your last few command performances that you were unable to function effectively?

- Did you give up in the late stages of several projects, saying "I just can't get this done"?

Stop Blaming Others for Your Problems.   Blaming others for our problems contributes to self-defeating behavior and career self-sabotage.[3] Projecting blame onto others is self-defeating because doing so relieves you of most of the responsibility for your setback and failure. Consider this example: If someone blames favoritism for not receiving a promotion, he or she will not have to worry about becoming a stronger candidate for future promotions. Not to improve your suitability for promotion is self-sabotaging. If you accept most of the blame for not being promoted, you are more likely to make the changes necessary to qualify in the future.

HUMAN RELATIONS SELF-ASSESSMENT EXERCISE 5-1

The Self-Sabotage Questionnaire

Indicate how accurately each of the statements below describes or characterizes you, using a five-point scale: (0) very inaccurately, (1) inaccurately, (2) midway between inaccurately and accurately, (3) accurately, (4) very accurately. Consider discussing some of the questions with a family member, close friend, or work associate. Another person's feedback may prove helpful in providing accurate answers to some of the questions.

Answer

1. Other people have said that I am my worst enemy. _____

2. If I don't do a perfect job, I feel worthless. _____

3. I am my own harshest critic. _____

4. When engaged in a sport or other competitive activity, I find a way to blow a substantial lead right near the end. _____

5. When I make a mistake, I can usually identify another person to blame. _____

6. I have a sincere tendency to procrastinate. _____

7. I have trouble focusing on what is really important to me. _____

8. I have trouble taking criticism, even from friends. _____

9. My fear of seeming stupid often prevents me from asking questions or offering my opinion. _____

10. I tend to expect the worst in most situations. _____

11. Many times I have rejected people who treat me well. _____

12. When I have an important project to complete, I usually get sidetracked, and then miss the deadline. _____

13. I choose work assignments that lead to disappointments, even when better options are clearly available. _____

14. I frequently misplace things, such as my keys, then get very angry at myself. _____

15. I am concerned that, if I take on much more responsibility, people will expect too much from me. _____

16. I avoid situations, such as competitive sports, where people can find out how good or bad I really am. _____

17. People describe me as the "office clown." _____

18. I have an insatiable demand for money and power. _____

(Continued)

19. When negotiating with others, I hate to grant any concessions. _____

20. I seek revenge for even the smallest hurts. _____

21. I have an overwhelming ego. _____

22. When I receive a compliment or other form of recognition, I usually feel I don't deserve it. _____

23. To be honest, I choose to suffer. _____

24. I regularly enter into conflict with people who try to help me. _____

25. I'm a loser. _____

Total score _____

Scoring and Interpretation: Add your answers to all the questions to obtain your total score. Your total score provides an approximate index of your tendencies toward being self-sabotaging or self-defeating. The higher your score, the more probable it is that you create conditions to bring about your own setbacks, disappointments, and failures. The lower your score, the less likely it is that you are a self-saboteur.

0–25: You appear to have very few tendencies toward self-sabotage. If this interpretation is supported by your own positive feelings toward your life and yourself, you are in good shape with respect to self-defeating behavior tendencies. However, stay alert to potential self-sabotaging tendencies that could develop at later stages in your life.

26–50: You may have some mild tendencies toward self-sabotage. It could be that you do things occasionally that defeat your own purposes. Review actions you have taken during the past six months to decide if any of them have been self-sabotaging.

51–75: You show signs of engaging in self-sabotage. You probably have thoughts, and carry out actions, that could be blocking you from achieving important work and personal goals. People with scores in this category characteristically engage in negative self-talk that lowers their self-confidence and makes them appear weak and indecisive to others. People in this range frequently experience another problem. They sometimes sabotage their chances of succeeding on a project just to prove that their negative self-assessment is correct. If you scored in this range, carefully study the suggestions offered in this chapter.

76–100: You most likely have a strong tendency toward self-sabotage. (Sometimes it is possible to obtain a high score on a test like this because you are going through an unusually stressful period in your life.) Study this chapter carefully and look for useful hints for removing self-imposed barriers to your success. Equally important, you might discuss your tendencies toward undermining your own achievements with a mental health professional.

An underlying theme to the suggestions for preventing and overcoming self-defeating behavior is that we all need to engage in thoughts and actions that increase our personal control. This is precisely the reason that blaming others for our problems is self-sabotaging. By turning over control of your fate to forces outside yourself, you are holding them responsible for your problems.

Solicit Feedback on Your Actions. Feedback is essential for monitoring whether you are sabotaging your career or personal life. A starting point is to listen carefully to any direct or indirect comments from your superiors, subordinates, coworkers, customers, and friends about how you are coming across to them. Consider the case of Bill, a technical writer.

Bill heard three people in one week make comments about his appearance. It started innocently with, "Here, let me fix your collar." Next, an office assistant said, "Bill, are you coming down with something?" The third comment was, "You look pretty tired today. Have you been working extra hard?" Bill processed this feedback carefully. He used it as a signal that his steady late-night drinking episodes were adversely affecting his image. He then cut back his drinking enough to revert to his normal healthy appearance.

An assertive and thick-skinned person might try the technique described for soliciting feedback described in Chapter 1. Approach a sampling of people both on and off the job with this line of questioning: "I'm trying to develop myself personally. Can you think of anything I do or say that creates a bad impression in any way? Do not be afraid of offending me. Only people who know me can provide me with this kind of information."

Take notes to show how serious you are about the feedback. When someone provides any feedback at all, say, "Please continue, this is very useful." Try not to react defensively when you hear something negative. You asked for it, and the person is truly doing you a favor.

Learn to Profit from Criticism. As the above example implies, learning to profit from criticism is necessary to benefit from feedback. Furthermore, to ignore valid criticism can be self-defeating. People who benefit from criticism are able to stand outside themselves while being criticized. It is as if they are watching the criticism from a distance and looking for its possible merits. People who take criticism personally experience anguish when receiving negative feedback. Here are several specific suggestions for benefiting from valid criticism.[4]

1. *See yourself at a distance.* Place an imaginary plexiglass shield between you and the person being criticized. Attempt to be a detached observer looking for useful information.

2. *Ask for clarification and specifics.* Ask politely for more details about the negative behavior in question, so that you can change if change is warranted. If your boss is criticizing you for being rude with customers, you might respond: "I certainly don't want to be rude. Can you give me a couple of examples of how I was rude? I need your help in working on this problem." After asking questions, you can better determine if the criticism is valid.

3. *Decide on a response.* An important part of learning from criticism is to respond appropriately to the critic. Let the criticizer know what you agree with. Apologize for the undesirable behavior, such as saying, "I apologize for being rude to customers. I know what I can do differently now. I'll be more patient, so as not to appear rude." If the feedback was particularly useful in helping you overcome self-defeating behavior, thank the person for the constructive feedback.

Stop Denying the Existence of Problems. Many people sabotage their careers because they deny the existence of a problem and therefore do not take appropriate action. Denial takes place as a defensive maneuver against a painful reality. An example of a self-sabotaging form of denial is to ignore the importance of upgrading one's credentials despite overwhelming evidence that it is necessary. Some people never quite complete a degree program that has become an informal qualification for promotion. Consequently, they sabotage their chances of receiving a promotion for which they are otherwise qualified. Many people in recent years have damaged their chances for career progress by not upgrading their computer skills.

Visualize Self-Enhancing Behavior.   Visualization is a primary method for achieving many different types of self-improvement. It is therefore an essential component of overcoming self-defeating behavior. To apply visualization, program yourself to overcome self-defeating actions and thoughts. Imagine yourself engaging in self-enhancing, winning actions and thoughts. Picture yourself achieving peak performance when good results count the most.

A starting point in learning how to use visualization for overcoming career self-sabotage is to identify the next job situation you will be facing that is similar to ones you have flubbed in the past. You then imagine yourself mentally and physically projected into that situation. Imagine what the room looks like, who will be there, and the confident expression you will have on your face. Visualization is akin to watching a video of yourself doing something right. An example:

> Matt, an actuary in a life insurance company, has an upcoming meeting with top management to discuss his analysis of how insurance rates should be changed to factor in the impact of AIDS on mortality rates. Based on past experience, Matt knows that he becomes flustered and too agreeable in high-level meetings about controversial topics (such as rate increases). Matt also knows that to behave in this way is self-defeating.
>
> As he prepares for the meeting, he visualizes himself calmly listening to challenges to his analysis. In response, he does not back off from his position, but smiles and presents his findings in more detail. Matt visualizes the people who challenged him changing their attitudes as he knowledgeably explains his case. By the end of the meeting Matt is warmly thanked for his recommendations on making rate changes to meet the incidence of AIDS in the population. The president congratulates him on how well he stood up to the challenges to his forecasts.

 # UNDERSTANDING AND CONTROLLING ADDICTIONS

Wellness is blocked by a variety of addictions, and addictive behavior is also a personal problem. Furthermore, people with personal problems often seek relief by lapsing into addictive behavior. An **addiction** (or **substance dependence**) is a compulsion to use substances or engage in activities that lead to psychological dependence and withdrawal symptoms when use is discontinued. A caffeine addict would suffer adverse symptoms such as headaches and tension if deprived of caffeine for an entire day. A person with a work addiction would feel ill at ease and tense if forced to say away from work for several days.

Recent research about brain chemistry and behavior helps explain why addictions to substances are so widespread. The moment a person ingests a substance such as tobacco, alcohol, marijuana, or chocolate, trillions of strong molecules surge through the bloodstream and into the brain. The molecules trigger a flood of chemical and electrical events that result in a temporary state of pleasure and euphoria.

The common thread to all these mood-altering drugs is their ability to elevate levels of a chemical substance in the brain called **dopamine,** a neurotransmitter that is associated with pleasure and elation. (A neurotransmitter is a molecule in the brain that transports messages from one neuron in the brain to another. It moves across the connectors among brain cells called synapses.) Dopamine is so effective that it is regarded by some scientists as the master molecule of addiction.[5] The chemical is elevated by the common addictive drugs such as heroin, amphetamines, cocaine and crack, marijuana, alcohol, nicotine, and caffeine. However dopamine can also be elevated by a hug, sexual attraction, praise from a key person, and presumably by finding an exciting new web site or book. In short, people develop addictions to get their shot of dopamine.

The balance of our study of substance abuse and addictions concentrates on alcohol abuse and a variety of other drugs. Other forms of substance abuse include inhaling intoxicants such as rubber cement or cleaning fluid. Nicotine, caffeine, chocolate, and sugar could be added to the list. With the exception of nicotine, however, their symptoms are not life threatening.

ALCOHOL ABUSE

A major concern about consuming large amounts of alcohol is that health may be adversely affected. What constitutes a large amount of alcohol depends on a person's size and tolerance level. For the average-size adult, more than four alcoholic beverages per day would be considered a large amount. Alcohol consumption leads to marked changes in behavior. Even low doses significantly impair the judgment and coordination required to drive an automobile safely.

Moderate to high doses of alcohol cause marked impairment in higher mental functions. The brain damage that results can severely alter a person's ability to learn and remember information. Very high doses of alcohol cause respiratory depression and death. Heavy alcohol consumption over a prolonged period of time contributes to heart disease. (Consuming up to three alcoholic beverages a day, however, may help prevent heart disease by stimulating the heart and unclogging arteries.)

Long-term consumption of large quantities of alcohol, particularly when combined with poor nutrition, can lead to permanent damage to vital organs such as the brain and liver. Drinking large quantities of alcohol during pregnancy may result in newborns with fetal alcohol syndrome. These infants have irreversible physical abnormalities and mental retardation.

As with other drugs, repeated use of alcohol can lead to dependence. Abrupt cessation of alcohol consumption can produce withdrawal symptoms including severe anxiety, tremors, hallucinations, and convulsions. Severe withdrawal symptoms can be life threatening.

Work and Personal Life Consequences of Alcohol Abuse

Heavy consumption of alcohol has many adverse consequences for a person's career and personal life. Heavy drinking will eventually interfere with work performance, resulting in some of the following behaviors:[6]

- Low productivity and quality of work

- Erratic performance

- Erratic and unusual behavior such as swearing at coworkers during a meeting

- Excessive tardiness and absenteeism

- Increased difficulty in working cooperatively with supervisors

- Increased difficulty in working cooperatively with coworkers

- Carelessness, negligence, or disinterest

Alcohol consumption is potentially disruptive to personal and family life. Even moderate doses of alcohol increase the incidents of a variety of aggressive acts, including partner and child abuse. Purchasing alcoholic beverages can lead to family problems because household bills may go unpaid. Many alcoholics lose friends because they are uncomfortable to be around when drinking. Sexual desire and performance often decline with heavy alcohol abuse. Many male drinkers suffer from impotency. Alcohol abuse often leads to divorce and other broken relationships.

Overcoming Alcohol Abuse

A person's approach to overcoming alcohol abuse depends to some extent on whether he or she regards alcoholism as a disease or as maladaptive behavior. Regarding alcoholism as a disease is the majority viewpoint among mental health specialists and the general public. People who regard alcoholism as a disease are likely to seek medical or psychological help. To conquer alcoholism they would therefore seek help from physicians and counselors. Such help might consist of outpatient visits to mental health practitioners, often at clinics for substance abusers. People with severe alcoholism might volunteer to become inpatients at a hospital specializing in the treatment of alcoholism.

Another viewpoint is to regard alcoholism as self-defeating behavior that is somewhat under a person's control. People who accept the *bad habit* view of alcohol abuse might seek professional assistance with their problem. Yet the thrust of their efforts to overcome alcoholism will be to discipline themselves to change their counterproductive ways. Looking upon alcoholism as maladaptive behavior runs contrary to groups such as Alcoholics Anonymous. Such groups label alcoholism as a sickness over which the victim has no control, and therefore insist on abstinence. A person who believes that alcohol abuse is under his or her control could take the following precautions to prevent a major drinking problem[7]:

- Limit the consumption of alcoholic beverages to three on any given day, but average no more than two per day. Remember that in order of increasing strength, popular alcoholic beverages are ranked as follows: wine cooler, beer, wine, and whiskey. Whiskey should therefore be consumed in smaller quantities than the other three types of beverages.

- Abstain from alcoholic beverages for at least two consecutive days each week.

- Drink only standard-size beverages: one ounce of whiskey in a mixed drink; 12 ounces of beer; or 5 ounces of wine.

- Don't drink on an empty stomach.

- Drink slowly and intersperse alcoholic beverages with nonalcoholic beverages while at parties.

- When you have the urge for an alcoholic beverage, on occasion substitute a glass of fruit juice or water.

- Make friends with people whose social life does not revolve around drinking alcoholic beverages. Associate with responsible drinkers.

- Regard drinking before 6 P.M. as a personal taboo.

The above suggestions are useful because they assume that mature adults can enjoy moderate alcohol consumption without falling prey to alcohol abuse. The same suggestions can be used to convert problem drinking into relatively safe drinking. Implementing these suggestions requires considerable self-discipline, as do approaches to overcoming other forms of self-defeating behavior.

DRUG ABUSE

Another major personal problem many people face is drug abuse. The use of illegal drugs is often perceived more harshly than alcohol abuse because drinking alcoholic beverages is legal. Similarly, the abuse of prescription drugs is not considered as wrong as the abuse of illegal drugs. The health effects and personal life consequences of abusing both illegal and prescription drugs are similar to those of alcohol abuse. Human Relations Self-Assessment Exercise 5-2 will help sensitize you to the many similarities of behavioral consequences of drug and alcohol abuse. Here we will summarize the effects of five major categories of drugs, and then describe how drug abusers can be helped.

Use and Effects of Controlled Substances

The term *drug* refers to a variety of chemicals with different chemical compositions and effects. One individual might purchase heroin for recreational use, while another person might sniff paint thinner to achieve the

HUMAN RELATIONS SELF-ASSESSMENT EXERCISE 5-2

Symptoms of Alcohol and Drug Abuse

People with alcohol or drug abuse problems are often poor judges of the extent of their problem. Nevertheless, it is helpful to use the symptoms mentioned below as a checklist to help identify an alcohol or drug problem you might be experiencing. Review the symptoms listed below and indicate whether each one applies to you.

Alcohol Abuse	Yes	No
Sudden decreases in my job performance	_____	_____
Decreases in my mental alertness	_____	_____
Many long lunch hours	_____	_____
Tardiness for work and social appointments	_____	_____
Wobbling instead of walking straight	_____	_____
Many absences from work or school	_____	_____
Comments by others that my speech is slurred	_____	_____
Frequent use of breath freshener	_____	_____
Frequent depressed moods	_____	_____
Trembling of my hands and body	_____	_____
Errors in judgment and concentration	_____	_____
Many financial problems because of my drinking	_____	_____
Comments by others that my eyes look sleepy	_____	_____
Much lost time due to physical illness	_____	_____
Elaborate alibis for not getting work done on the job or at home	_____	_____
Denying a drinking problem when I know I have one	_____	_____

Interpretation: If five or more of the above symptoms fit you, you may have a problem with alcohol abuse. Act on the remedial measures described previously.

Drug Abuse	Yes	No
Sudden decreases in my job performance	_____	_____
Decreases in my mental alertness	_____	_____
Hiding out on company premises	_____	_____
Many absences from work or school	_____	_____
My pupils appear dilated when I look in the mirror	_____	_____
Unusual bursts of energy and excitement	_____	_____
Prolonged and serious lethargy	_____	_____
States of apathy and elation I cannot explain	_____	_____
Errors in concentration and judgment	_____	_____
Many financial problems because of drug purchases	_____	_____
Comments by others that my eyes look sleepy	_____	_____

(Continued)

Frequent sniffing

People telling me that I look "out of it"

Elaborate alibis for not getting work done on the job or
   at home

Frequent dry, irritated coughing

Denying a drug problem when I know I have one

Interpretation: If five or more of the above symptoms fit you, you may have a problem with drug abuse. Act on the remedial measures described previously.

same effect. The United States government has compiled a five-way classification of frequently used drugs.[8] Each of the five categories of drugs has different possible effects and different consequences for overdoses. Each category of drug has both illegal and legitimate uses. For example, stimulants include both crack and a drug with the trade name Dexedrine.

Narcotics: A **narcotic** is a drug that dulls the senses, facilitates sleep, and is addictive with long-term use. Well-known narcotics include opium, morphine, codeine, and heroin. The possible effects of narcotics include euphoria, drowsiness, and decreased breathing. A narcotic user may also experience constricted pupils and nausea. Overdosing on narcotics may lead to slow and shallow breathing, clammy skin, convulsions, and coma. Death is also possible. People who use narcotics frequently do severe damage to their careers and personal lives in the long run.

Depressants: A **depressant** is a drug that slows down vital body processes. Barbiturates are the best-known depressant (or sedative). Alcohol is also classified as a depressant. Heavy doses of depressants can lead to slurred speech and disorientation. A depressant user will show drunken behavior without the odor of alcohol. An overdose of depressants leads to shallow breathing, clammy skin, and dilated pupils. With extreme overdoses, the person may lapse into coma and then death.

Many anxious people are convinced they must take legally prescribed sedatives to calm down. The trade-off is the risk of lacking the mental alertness to perform at their peak. Frequent users of depressants make poor companions because they lack vitality.

Stimulants: The class of drugs known as **stimulants** produces feelings of optimism and high energy. Cocaine and amphetamines are the two best-known stimulants. Taking stimulants leads to increased alertness, excitation, and euphoria. The user will also experience increased pulse rate and blood pressure, insomnia, and loss of appetite. (Many diet pills are really stimulants.) Overdoses of stimulants lead to agitation, increased body temperature, hallucinations, convulsions, and possible death. Stimulant abusers are regarded by others as being "hyper," and may be too agitated to do high-quality work.

The stimulant methamphetamine requires separate mention because of the violent behavior associated with its use. Similar to cocaine, it can be smoked, snorted, or injected. The hazardous side effects of methampetamine include hallucinations, depression, paranoia, and violent rages. Police report that many of the most brutal crimes today are committed by "meth" users.[9]

Hallucinogens: In small doses the class of drugs known as **hallucinogens** produce visual effects similar to hallucinations. Three well-known hallucinogens are LSD, mescaline, and peyote. Hallucinogens lead to illusions (misperceptions) and poor perception of time and distance. Overdoses of hallucinogens can produce "trip" episodes, psychosis (severe mental disorder), and possible death. While under the influence of a hallucinogen, a person is unfit for work. The bizarre behavior of hallucinogen abusers leads to a deterioration of their relationships with people.

Cannabis: The class of drugs known as **cannabis** are derived from the hemp plant and generally produce a state of mild euphoria. Marijuana and hashish are placed in the cannabis category. A study conducted by the U. S. Department of Human Services indicates that marijuana use among youths (ages 12 to 17) has doubled in recent years. Nevertheless, alcohol remains the leading form of drug abuse among high school students.[10] Cannabis use leads to euphoria, relaxed inhibitions, and increased appetite. The same drug may cause disorientation. Cannabis abuse may lead to fatigue, paranoia, and possible psychosis. Because marijuana is used as a cigarette, it may cause lung cancer and cardiovascular damage. Used in moderate doses, cannabis does much less damage to career and personal life than the other drugs described here.

Getting Help for Drug Abuse Problems

Many forms of assistance are available for drug abusers. The comments made earlier in relation to alcohol abuse also apply to drug abuse. Drug abusers can seek help from physicians and from mental health specialists (some of whom are physicians). At the same time, the drug abuser may view his or her problem as a form of maladaptive behavior that can be controlled through concentrated effort. Assume, for example, a person says, "I simply cannot get through the day without an amphetamine pill. Life is too boring for me if I don't have an upper."

The antidote is for the person to say something to the following effect: "This week, I won't take an amphetamine on Monday. Next week, no amphetamine on Monday or Tuesday. I'll keep adding a day until I have gone an entire week drug-free." Self-management of this type can work for many people.

An avenue of help for an employed person with a drug abuse problem is the company employee assistance program. A major purpose of these programs is to help employees overcome personal problems that drain productivity. Typically, the assistance program coordinator refers the troubled employee to an outside treatment facility. Some larger organizations have their own treatment facilities located on or off company premises. The program is confidential, sometimes to the extent that the company does not know which employees have referred themselves for help.

Many of the problems dealt with by the employee assistance program involve forms of self-defeating behavior in addition to drug abuse. Among them are other forms of substance abuse, cigarette addiction, compulsive gambling, financial problems, and physical abuse of family members. Employees can also spend one or two sessions with the assistance counselor to talk about self-defeating behavior in general. If the counselor thinks multiple sessions are required, an appropriate referral is made.

Seeking help from an assistance counselor rather than going to a mental health practitioner on your own has an important advantage. Employee assistance counselors work regularly with people whose personal problems are hurting job performance. Also, the company usually pays the entire fee.

COPING WITH THE LOSS OF A RELATIONSHIP

A major personal problem many people encounter is the loss of a valued personal relationship. The loss may take the form of separation, divorce, or a nonmarried couple splitting up. A more subtle loss is when a couple stays together, yet the intimacy in a relationship vanishes. Loneliness and conflict result from the lost intimacy. Chapter 16 presents ideas on maintaining and revitalizing relationships. Our attention here is directed toward specific suggestions for dealing with the loss of an important personal relationship.

When you are emotionally and romantically involved with another person, the loss of that relationship usually has a big impact. Even if you believe strongly that splitting up is in your best interests, the fact that you cared at one time about that person leads to some hurt. The major reason we need tactics for dealing with lost relationships is that many upsetting feelings surface in conjunction with the loss.

A newly unattached person might feel lonely, guilty, angry, or frightened. Your role in the disengagement will usually dictate which emotion surfaces. For instance, if you dumped your partner, you will probably experience guilt. If you were the person dumped, you would probably experience anger. If you survive a spouse, you might feel guilty about not having been nice enough to your partner during your years together.

A number of suggestions are presented below to help a person recover from a lost relationship.[11] Choose the tactics that seem to fit your personality and circumstances. As with the other personal problems described in this chapter, professional counseling may be helpful in making a recovery.

1. *Be thankful for the good in the relationship.* An excellent starting point in recovering a broken relationship is to take stock of what went right when the two of you were together. Looking for the good in the relationship helps place the situation in proper perspective. It also helps prevent you from developing the counterproductive attitude that your time together was a total waste.

2. *Find new outlets for spare time.* Some of the energy you were investing in your partnership can now be invested in spare-time activities. This activity provides a healthy form of the defense mechanism called *compensation* or *substitution.*

3. *Get ample rest and relaxation.* A broken relationship is a stressor. As a result, most people need rest and relaxation to help them overcome the emotional pain associated with the departure of a partner.

4. *Pamper yourself.* Pampering involves finding little ways of doing nice things for yourself. These could take the form of buying yourself a new outfit, taking a weekend vacation, eating pizza at midnight, or getting a body massage.

5. *Get emotional support.* A highly recommended antidote to a broken relationship is to obtain emotional support from others. Friends and relatives are often the most important source of emotional support to help you cope with postseparation blues. Be careful, however, not to let your loss of a relationship dominate conversations with friends to the point of boring them. Another source of emotional support are groups specifically designed to help people cope with recent separation or divorce. Parents without Partners is an example of such a group. A caution here is that some people stay too long with such groups rather than taking the initiative to find a new partner.

6. *Get out and go places.* The oldest suggestion about recovering from a lost relationship is perhaps the most valid—keep active. While you are doing new things you tend to forget about your problems. Also, as you go places and do things, you increase your chances of making new friends. And new friends are the only true antidote to the loneliness of being unattached.

7. *Give yourself time to heal.* The greater the hurt, the more time it will take to recover from the broken relationship. Recognizing this fact will help to curb your impatience over disentangling yourself emotionally from the former spouse or partner.

8. *Anticipate a positive outcome.* While you are on the path toward rebuilding your social life, believe that things will get better. Also believe that all the emotional energy you have invested into splitting and healing will pay dividends. Self-fulfilling prophecies work to some extent in social relationships. If you believe you will make a satisfactory recovery from a broken relationship, your chances of doing so will increase. The underlying mechanism seems to be that if you believe in yourself, you exude a level of self-confidence that others find appealing.

 ## ABSENTEEISM AND TARDINESS

Absenteeism and tardiness are the leading causes of employee discipline. Employer tolerance for absenteeism and lateness varies from industry to industry and from job level to job level. Yet as a rule of thumb, latenesses and absences in excess of five constitute a problem.[12] Developing a poor record of attendance and punctuality is also a form of career self-sabotage. Employees who are habitually late or absent develop a poor reputation and receive negative employment references. It becomes difficult to find a good job with another employer after establishing a poor record of attendance and punctuality.

Maintaining good attendance and punctuality is important because worldwide competition has forced many private organisations to trim costs. Government organizations are also under constant pressure to control costs. The employee who is habitually absent or late therefore risks termination.

During a person's career, many unexpected situations arise in which it is necessary to be absent or late. Accidents, illnesses, severe family problems, and family deaths all may require time away from the job. A serious-minded worker should therefore strive to attain near perfect attendance and punctuality when not faced with an emergency. Some suggestions follow to help a person develop the right mental set for achieving an excellent record of attendance and punctuality.

1. *Recognize that not to have excellent attendance and punctuality is self-defeating.* For reasons already described, poor attendance and punctuality can lead to a poor reputation and job loss. Why self-handicap your chances for career success?

2. *Look upon your job as self-employment.* Few people operating their own business will take a day off, or begin late, for no valid reason. The smaller the business, the better the attendance and punctuality, because so little help is available. You can therefore improve your attendance and punctuality by imagining that your area of responsibility is your own business.

3. *Regard your job responsibilities as being as important as those of the person in charge of opening the bank's doors in the morning.* People in charge of opening banks, department stores, movie theaters, and other retail businesses have excellent records of attendance and punctuality. To do otherwise would create panic, especially in the case of the bank. To improve your attendance and punctuality, think of your responsibilities as being as important as opening the doors in the morning.

4. *Reward yourself for good attendance and punctuality and punish yourself for the opposite.* Following the suggestions for self-motivation described in Chapter 2, modify your behavior in relation to attendance and punctuality. Treat yourself after six months of excellent attendance and punctuality. Punish yourself for a poor record. For example, if you miss one day of work for a flimsy reason, punish yourself by working all day on a national holiday.

5. *Think through carefully the consequences if all company employees were absent and late frequently.*   Some people argue that they are entitled to take the maximum number of sick days allowable under company policy. If everybody took the maximum number of sick days and were late as often as possible without incurring discipline, the company would suffer. Customer service would deteriorate, productivity would decrease, and more people would have to be hired just to cover for employee "no-shows." Less money might be available for salary increases and employee benefits. Even worse, the company might have to lay off employees because of low profits.

6. *Imagine being fired by two employers for poor attendance and punctuality.*   Being fired once for poor attendance and punctuality might adversely affect your career. Being fired twice for the same reason could place you at the bottom of the labor pool in terms of employability.

7. *Think of the consequences to coworkers if you are absent and late frequently.*   Being absent or late may hurt the company. The same behavior can adversely affect your relationships with coworkers. Coworkers become annoyed and irritated quickly when they have to cover for a negligent peer. The worker who is frequently absent and late runs the risk of losing the cooperation of coworkers when he or she needs assistance.

8. *Remember that unwarranted absenteeism and tardiness violates company policy.*   Some people with poor attendance and punctuality seem to ignore the reality that they are violating company policy—and that such behavior can lead to termination.

DEPRESSION AND NEUROBIOLOGICAL DISORDERS

Many employees perform poorly on the job because of reasons beyond their control. They would like to perform well, but disturbed emotions or brain malfunctioning interfere with handling some aspects of their job responsibilities well. To illustrate this problem, we describe two problems faced by many workers, depression and neurobiological disorders (defined later).

Depression

A widespread emotional disorder is **depression.** A depressed person has such difficulties as sadness; changes in appetite; sleeping difficulties; and a decrease in activities, interests, and energy. Approximately 19 million Americans and Canadians will suffer depression serious enough during their lives to interfere with happiness and productivity.

Being depressed on the job creates many problems. Depression drains energy and reduces productivity and quality. The reduced effectiveness triggers a cycle of failure. As effectiveness decreases, the person's thinking, acting, and feeling become more damaged. As relationships with coworkers and job performance deteriorates, the person becomes more depressed.[13] Here is an example of how depression affects job behavior:

> A sales manager known for his exuberance and enthusiasm slowly began to withdraw from face-to-face contact with team members. During one team meeting, the manager abruptly terminated the meeting, telling the group, "I'm just too emotionally drained to continue today." Soon he rarely communicated with others in the firm except through e-mail. At times he was observed just staring out the window. Reports of his unusual behavior soon reached his manager, who in turn urged the sales manager to visit a mental health professional. A combination of antidepressant drugs and psychotherapy helped the sales manager to overcome his problems enough to function satisfactorily on the job.

Human Relations Self-Assessment Exercise 5-3 will help you better appreciate the symptoms of depression as they apply to the job. These symptoms are easier to recognize in another person than in yourself. Having more than a few of these symptoms is an indicator that treatment by a mental health professional is important. Most people who attempt or commit suicide are extremely depressed, and about 15 percent of people with severe depression eventually take their own lives.[14]

NEUROBIOLOGICAL DISORDERS

Personal problems on the job are sometimes the result of **neurobiological disorders,** a quirk in the chemistry or anatomy of the brain that creates a disability. The quirk is usually inherited, but could also be caused by a brain injury or poisoning, such as exposure to harmful vapors. The disabilities take the form of reduced ability to control one's behavior, movements, emotions, or thoughts.[15] If you experience sudden changes in your job behavior, a thorough neurological examination is strongly recommended. The most common neurobiological disorders on the job are described next. Depression, already described is sometimes classified as a neurobiological disorder when it stems from chemical or anatomical factors.

Attention-Deficit Disorder. People with this disorder have difficulty concentrating that may be accompanied by hyperactivity. The person might therefore engage in a flurry of activity on the job, yet much of the activity might be wasted effort. Many difficulties in paying attention in school are attributed to attention deficit disorder.

Obsessive-Compulsive Disorder. People with this disorder have uncontrollable and recurring thoughts or behavior relating to an unreasonable fear. A job example of obsessive-compulsive disorder would be a person who becomes obsessed with cleaning his or her work area. The person could be motivated by fear of being contaminated by impurities in the ventilation system.

HUMAN RELATIONS SELF-ASSESSMENT EXERCISE 5-3

Symptoms of Depression on the Job

Workers suffering from depression often experience a combination of one or more of the following symptoms. Not every depressed person will experience them all. (Most of these symptoms are also present off the job.)

- Slow movement, drooped posture

- Decreased energy, fatigue, and frequent complaints of being tired

- Decreased ability to concentrate, remember, or make decisions

- Taking an unusually long time to complete tasks

- Speaking only when spoken to

- Crying on the job

- Attributing any personal successes to luck

- Loss of interest in activities that were once enjoyable, such as having lunch with coworkers

- Mentions of suicide, even in a joking manner

- Deterioration in grooming such as rumpled clothing, unkempt hair, neglected facial shaving

- Increased absenteeism

- Alcohol and drug abuse

- Increasing intensity and frequency of any of the above symptoms

SOURCE: Canadian Mental Health Association, 1995; *Health Guide,* America's Pharmaceutical Research Companies, 1996 (www.phrma.org); John Lawrie, "Coping with Depression on the Job," *Supervisory Management,* June 1992, pp. 6–7.

Narcolepsy. People with this disorder have uncontrollable sleepiness, even after receiving adequate sleep. A person with narcolepsy may fall asleep at the desk or while driving a company vehicle or operating dangerous machinery.

Tourette Syndrome. People suffering from this disorder experience uncontrollable movement or utterances, and often shout profanities at inappropriate times. A person with Tourette syndrome is often misinterpreted as consciously attempting to create a disturbance.

Although damaging to work performance, neurobiological disorders can be treated successfully. In addition to the proper medication, the person usually needs a supportive environment both at home and on the job.

Most people with neurobiological disorders can function close to normally after appropriate medication is determined and they are taught how to cope with their symptoms.

Training individuals to understand their condition is an important part of the treatment. The person with Tourette syndrome, for example, should explain to coworkers that at times he or she may appear insulting and abusive. Furthermore, coworkers can be advised not to take such behavior seriously, and that the behavior is under medical control and may soon disappear entirely. Discussing a personal problem with coworkers may help to reduce their fears about your problem and lead to better understanding.

DEALING WITH ANGER

Limited ability to manage anger damages the career and personal life of many people. **Anger** is a feeling of extreme hostility, displeasure, or exasperation. The emotion of anger creates stress, including the physiological changes described in Chapter 4. One noticeable indicator of anger is enlargement of the pupils, causing the wide-eyed look of people in a rage. Blood may rush to the face, as indicated by reddening in light-skinned people. Anger often leads to aggression, which is the verbal or physical attacking of another person, animal, or object. Workplace violence, such as an ex-employee shooting a former boss who fired him, is an extreme point in expressing anger. What angry behavior have you observed on the job?

The ability to manage anger is an important interpersonal skill, now considered to be part of **emotional intelligence.** This concept refers to qualities such as understanding your feelings, empathy for others, and the regulation of emotion to enhance living.[15] A person who cannot manage anger well cannot take good advantage of his or her regular intelligence. As an extreme example, a genius who swears at the boss regularly will probably lose his or her job despite being so talented. Our concern here is with several suggestions that will help you manage (not necessarily eliminate) anger so it does not jeopardize your career or personal success.

A starting point is to recognize that at its best, *anger can be an energizing force.* Instead of being destructive, channel your anger into exceptional performance. If you are angry because you did not get the raise you thought you deserved, get even by performing so well that there will be no question you deserve a raise next time. Develop the habit of *expressing your anger before it reaches a high intensity.* Tell your companion that you do not appreciate his or her using a cell phone while you are having dinner together the first time the act of rudeness occurs. If you wait too long, you may wind up grabbing the cell phone and slamming it to the floor.

As you are about to express anger, *slow down.* (The old technique of counting to 10 is still effective.) Slowing down gives you the opportunity to express your anger in a way that does not damage your relationship with the other person. Following your first impulse, you might say to another person, "You're a stupid fool." If you slow down, this might translate into,

---

HUMAN RELATIONS SKILL-BUILDING EXERCISE 5-1

Learning to Manage Anger

The next few times you are really angry with somebody or something, use one or more of the good mental health statements described below. Each statement is designed to remind you that you are in charge, not your anger. For starters, visualize something that has made you angry recently. Practice making the statements below in relation to that angry episode.

- I'm in charge here, not my emotional outbursts.
- I'll breathe deeply a few times and then deal with this.
- I feel _____ when you _____.
- I can handle this.
- I'm going to take time out to cool down before I deal with this.
- Yes, I'm angry and I'll just watch what I say or do.

Now describe the effect making the above statements had on your anger.

SOURCE: Based on Lynne Namka, "A Primer on Anger: Getting a Handle on Your Mads," http://members.aol.com/AngriesOut/grown2.htm, (July 7, 1997) p. 4.

"You need training on this task." Closely related to slowing down is to say to yourself as soon as you feel angry, "Oops, I'm in the anger mode now. I had better calm down before I say something or do something I will regret later." To gauge how effectively you are expressing your anger, ask for *feedback*. Ask a friend, coworker, or manager, "Am I coming on too strong when I express my negative opinion?"[17]

Human Relations Skill-Building Exercise 5-1 will give you an opportunity to develop your anger-management skills. However, the exercise will require some work outside of class.

 ## SUMMARY

Unless personal problems are kept under control, a person's chances of achieving career and personal success diminish. Many personal problems arise out of self-defeating behavior. The major cause of this behavior is a loser life script, a life plan of coming out a loser in important situations. Other causes of self-defeating behavior include a self-defeating personality pattern, self-defeating beliefs, and fear of success. Approaches to overcoming and preventing self-defeating behavior include:

1. Examine your script and make the necessary changes.

2. Stop blaming others for your problems.

3. Solicit feedback on your actions.

4. Learn to profit from criticism.

5. Stop denying the existence of problems.

6. Visualize self-enhancing behavior.

Wellness is blocked by a variety of addictions, and addictive behavior is also a personal problem. Addictive behavior toward certain substances such as alcohol and marijuana comes about because these substances elevate dopamine, a chemical substance in the brain that is associated with pleasure and elation. Dopamine can also be elevated by psychological events such as a hug.

Alcohol abuse often adversely affects health. Moderate to high doses of alcohol cause marked impairment in mental functions. Alcohol consumption is associated with heart and liver disease and fetal alcohol syndrome. Very high doses of alcohol cause respiratory depression and death. Alcohol abuse adversely affects job performance and career success. Alcoholism can be treated as a disease or as maladaptive (counterproductive) behavior. Precautions can be taken to prevent alcohol abuse, such as not drinking during the day.

The health effects and personal life consequences of abusing both illegal and prescription drugs are similar to those of alcohol abuse. The various categories of drugs have different possible effects and different consequences for overdoses. The five drug categories are (1) narcotics, (2) depressants, (3) stimulants, (4) hallucinogens, and (5) cannabis. Many forms of professional help are available for drug abusers, yet self-management of the problem is also an important form of help. Employee assistance programs sponsored by employers can help with drug abuse problems.

A major personal problem many people encounter is the loss of a valued personal relationship. Suggestions for dealing with the problem include: (1) Be thankful for the good in the relationship, (2) find new outlets for spare time, (3) get ample rest and relaxation, (4) pamper yourself, (5) get emotional support, (6) go places, (7) give yourself time to heal, and (8) anticipate a positive outcome.

Absenteeism and tardiness are the leading causes of employee discipline, and thus can be a major problem. Workers must develop the right mental set to achieve excellent attendance and punctuality. For example, a person might look upon the job as self-employment.

Many employees perform poorly on the job because they are depressed. Depression drains energy and reduces productivity and quality. As job performance deteriorates, the person becomes more depressed. Many job problems are also caused by neurobiological disorders, a quirk in the chemistry or anatomy of the brain that creates a disability. The disabilities take the form of reduced ability to control your behavior, movements, emotions, or thoughts. Major neurobiological disorders are attention deficit disorder, obsessive-compulsive disorder, narcolepsy, and Tourette syndrome. These disorders can be treated with medication, but a supportive environment is also needed.

Limited ability to deal with anger damages the career and personal life of many people. The ability to manage anger is an important interpersonal skill, now considered to be part of emotional intelligence. To manage anger well, recognize that it can be an energizing force. Express anger before it reaches a high intensity. As you are about to express anger, slow down, and then express it constructively. Ask others for feedback on how well you are expressing anger.

Questions and Activities

1. What is the difference between making a bad mistake once and self-defeating behavior?

2. Describe a person you know who appears to have a winner life script, and justify your reasoning.

3. Identify three celebrities who have recently engaged in self-defeating behavior, and also mention what they did wrong.

4. If it is really true that chocolate releases dopamine the same as nicotine and alcohol do, is munching on chocolate a way to curb cigarette and alcohol abuse? Explain your reasoning.

5. A medical study released in 1997 indicated that passive smoking kills more children than all accidents combined. Why are these results unlikely to virtually eliminate smoking among parents of children at home?

6. How can looking upon substance abuse as a bad habit help substance abusers overcome their problem?

7. Find a recent magazine, journal, or Internet article about new developments in treating drug or alcohol abuse. Share this information with classmates.

8. Some companies offer awards for good attendance. Why is this necessary from a motivational standpoint?

9. What is the difference between "having the blues" and being depressed?

10. Why is it that hockey players become so angry that they regularly physically attack their opponents, whereas tennis and golf players almost never act this way?

REFERENCES

[1]John Wareham, *Wareham's Way: Escaping the Judas Trap* (New York: Atheneum, 1983), p. 107.

A HUMAN RELATIONS CASE PROBLEM

High Flying Eduardo

Eduardo was an excellent college student at Penn State University. He majored in business administration and was the president of a student organization. With a wealthy family backing him, Eduardo drove a Corvette and took lavish vacations during school breaks. After graduation from college, Eduardo went on to receive a master's degree in international business at the Thunderbird School at the University of Arizona. He was heavily recruited by several major business corporations.

Eduardo accepted an attractive offer from a multinational company based in the United States that produced manufacturing control systems. His goal was someday to become the vice president of international marketing. As part of his management training program, Eduardo was given assignments in general accounting, auditing, credit, and sales. He was immediately placed on the company's fast track, reserved for new management recruits of exceptional promise.

After a three-year stint in company headquarters, Eduardo was promoted to marketing manager of the company's branch in Mexico City. During this assignment, Eduardo remained single and pursued the lifestyle of an affluent bachelor. After six months in Mexico City, reports began to trickle back to headquarters that Eduardo was having problems.

Eduardo's job performance was erratic, particularly with respect to getting field reports completed on time. He was also getting into disputes with local management about sales strategies. Eduardo's position was that the Mexico City branch relied too much on existing customers to increase business. He believed that new customers must be pursued more aggressively.

Eduardo entertained prospective customers lavishly, including taking them to bullfights. He especially enjoyed the bullfights because he was in training to become an amateur matador. Local management was also concerned that Eduardo was using his expense account to entertain too many women who could not influence sales.

Around 1:00 A.M. on a Tuesday, Eduardo drove a company car into a tree on the way back from a nightclub. He escaped with facial cuts and a severely sprained wrist, but his companion was killed. Police reports suggested that Eduardo was driving beyond a safe speed and, though not drunk, he had been drinking heavily. Headquarters responded by recalling Eduardo to the United States and reassigning him to a market research analyst position. Eduardo feels remorse about the accident, his family is angry at him, and he wonders how he will regain his career thrust.

Questions

1. What evidence of self-defeating behavior does Eduardo display?

2. Does Eduardo qualify as having an alcohol abuse problem?

3. How could Eduardo's problems have been prevented?

4. What should Eduardo do now to rebuild his career?

HUMAN RELATIONS SKILL-BUILDING EXERCISE 5-2

Helping a Work Associate Role Play

One person assumes the role of one of Eduardo's work associates. Another person assumes the role of Eduardo. Troubled by recent events in his career, Eduardo comes to his work associate to discuss his problems. He is also seeking friendly advice on dealing with his problems. The work associate contacted by Eduardo is motivated to be helpful and constructive, and will offer whatever sensible advice he or she can give. The two role players spend about ten minutes in front of the class with their role play. Observers provide feedback as to how well the session accomplished its purpose.

[2]Thomas A. Widiger and Allen J. Frances, "Controversies Concerning the Self-Defeating Personality Disorder," in Rebecca C. Curtis (ed.), *Self-Defeating Behaviors* (New York: Plenum Press, 1989), p. 304.

[3]Seth Allcorn, "The Self-Protective Actions of Managers," *Supervisory Management,* January 1989, pp. 3–7.

[4]Connirae Andreas and Steve Andreas, *Heart of the Mind* (Moab, UT: Real People Press, 1991).

[5]J. Madeleine Nash, "Addicted," *Time,* May 5, 1997, pp. 69–76.

[6]Jonathan A. Segal, "Alcoholic Employees and the Law," *HRMagazine,* December 1993, pp. 87–88.

[7]Based mostly on Harriet B. Braiker, "What All Career Women Need to Know about Drinking," *Working Women,* August 1989, p. 72.

[8]Based on information in the Drug-Free Workplace Act of 1988, and Drug-Free Schools and Communities Act of 1989.

[9]Anastasia Toufexis, "There Is No Safe Speed," *Time,* January 8, 1996, p. 37.

[10]Cited in Lance Morrow, "Kids & Pot," *Time,* December 9, 1996, p. 28.

[11]Andrew J. DuBrin, *Bouncing Back: How to Handle Setbacks in Your Work & Personal Life* (Upper Saddle River, NJ: Prentice Hall, 1982), pp. 85–102; Melba Colgrove, Harold H. Bloomfeld, and Peter McWilliams, *How to Survive the Loss of a Love* (New York: Bantam Books, 1976).

[12]Jeff Stinson, "Company Policy Attends to Chronic Absentees," *Personnel Journal,* August 1991, p. 82; "Managing Poor Attendance," *Working Smart,* July 1997, p. 6.

[13]John Lawrie, "Coping with Depression on the Job," *Supervisory Management,* June 1992, pp. 6–7.

[14]"New Hope for Depression and Other Mental Illnesses," *Health Guide,* published by America's Pharmaceutical Research Companies, Washington, D.C., 1996.

[15]Peggy Stuart, "Tracing Workplace Problems to Hidden Disorder," *Personnel Journal,* June 1992, p. 84. Our discussion of neurobiological disorders is based on the Stuart article.

[16]Daniel Goleman, *Emotional Intelligence: Why It Can Matter More Than IQ* (New York: Bantam Books, 1995).

[17]Fred Pryor, "Is Anger Really Healthy?" *The Pryor Report Management Newsletter,* February 1996, p. 3.

ADDITIONAL READING

Breuer, Nancy L. "Honor Their Last Will When Terminally Ill Employees Choose to Work." *Workforce,* May 1997, pp. 58–67.

DuBrin, Andrew J. *Your Own Worst Enemy: How to Overcome Career Self-Sabotage.* New York: AMACOM, 1992.

Jeffreys, J. Shep. *Coping with Workplace Change: Dealing with Loss and Grief.* Menlo Park, CA: Crisp Publications, 1995.

Oliver, Bill. "How to Prevent Drug Abuse in Your Workplace." *HRMagazine,* December 1993, pp. 78–81.

Potera, Carol. "Trapped in the Web." *Psychology Today,* March/April 1998, pp. 66–72.

Rosse, Joseph G., Ringer, Richard C., and Miller, Janice. "Personality and Drug Testing: An Exploration of the Perceived Fairness of Alternatives to Urinalysis." *Journal of Business and Psychology,* Summer 1996, pp. 459–475.

Stuart, Peggy. "The Hidden Addiction." *Personnel Journal,* November 1991, pp. 103–108.

Wisman, Eric W. "Peer Pressure Curbs Drug Use." *Personnel Journal,* November 1990, pp. 29–30.

CHAPTER 6

COMMUNICATING WITH PEOPLE

Learning Objectives

After studying the information and doing the exercises in this chapter, you should be able to:

▼ Explain the basic communication process

▼ Describe the nature and importance of nonverbal communication in the workplace

▼ Identify the challenges to interpersonal communication created by information technology

▼ Identify and overcome many roadblocks to communication

▼ Enhance your listening skills

▼ Overcome many gender and cross-cultural communication barriers

*T*he chief executive officer (CEO) of a company that makes interiors for corporate jets was touring its largest manufacturing site. The CEO stopped by the department that installs seating. He asked the supervisor, Herb, how well his department was meeting its goals. Herb replied: "Like I don't know. You know we have lots of goals, you know. Like it's tough figuring out what you guys really want. You know, it's crazy down here. You know where I'm coming from?"

The CEO wasn't exactly sure where Herb was coming from. But he was sure where Herb wasn't going. The CEO told the plant manager that Herb was not to be promoted. In addition, the CEO requested the plant manager to carefully review Herb's performance to make sure he was an effective supervisor.

Maybe you feel sorry for Herb and believe that the CEO judged him too harshly based on a brief interaction. Yet an inescapable point is that you can create communication barriers between yourself and key people in the organization if you use choose the wrong communication style. Communication is so vital that it has been described as the glue that holds organizations and families together. Most job foul-ups and marital disputes are considered to be communication problems. Furthermore, to be successful in work or personal life, you usually have to be an effective communicator. You can't make friends or stand up against enemies unless you can communicate with them. And you can't accomplish work through others unless you can send and receive messages effectively.

In this chapter we explain several important aspects of interpersonal communication such as the communication process and overcoming various communication barriers. As with other chapters in this text, explanation should also lead to skill improvement. For example, if you understand the steps involved in getting a message across to another person, you may be able to prevent many communication problems.

HOW COMMUNICATION TAKES PLACE

A convenient starting point in understanding how people communicate is to look at the steps involved in communicating a message. **Communication** is the sending and receiving of messages. A diagram of how the process takes place is shown in Figure 6-1. The theme of the model is that two-way communication involves three major steps and that each step is

Figure 6-1 The Communication Process

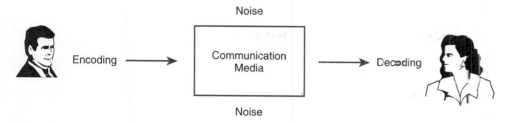

Noise

Encoding → Communication Media → Decoding

Noise

subject to interference or noise. Assume that Crystal, a customer, wishes to inform Tony, a used-car sales representative, that she is willing to make an offer of $5,000 on a used car. The price tag on the car is $5,500.

Step 1. *Encoding the message.* **Encoding** is the process of organizing ideas into a series of symbols, such as words and gestures, designed to communicate with the receiver. Word choice has a strong influence on communication effectiveness. The better a person's grasp of language, the easier it is for him or her to encode. Crystal says, "Tony, this car obviously is not in excellent condition, but I am willing to give you $5,000 for it."

Step 2. *Transmission over communication media.* The message is sent via a communication medium, such as voice, telephone, paper, or e-mail. It is important to select a medium that fits the message. It would be appropriate to use the spoken word to inform a coworker that he swore under his breath at a customer. It would be less appropriate to send the same message through e-mail. Many messages on and off the job are sent nonverbally, through the use of gestures and facial expressions. For example, a smile from a superior during a meeting is an effective way of communicating the message, "I agree with you." Crystal has chosen the oral medium to send her message.

Step 3. *Decoding.* In **decoding,** the receiver interprets the message and translates it into meaningful information. Decoding is the process of understanding a message. Barriers to communication are most likely to surface at the decoding step. People often interpret messages according to their psychological needs and motives. Tony wants to interpret Crystal's message that she is very eager to purchase this car. He may therefore listen attentively for more information demonstrating that she is interested in purchasing the car.

Decoding the message leads naturally to action—the receiver does something about the message. If the receiver acts in the manner the sender wants, the communication has been successful. If Tony says, "It's a deal," Crystal had a successful communication event.

Noise. Many missteps can occur between encoding and decoding a message. **Noise,** or unwanted interference, can distort or block a message. If Crystal has an indecisive tone and raises her voice at the end of her statement, it could indicate she is not really serious about offering a maximum of $5,000 for the car.

NONVERBAL COMMUNICATION (SENDING AND RECEIVING SILENT MESSAGES)

So far we have been talking mostly about spoken communication. However, much of the communication among people includes nonspoken and nonwritten messages. These nonverbal signals are a critical part of everyday communication. As a case in point, *how* you say "Thank you" makes a big difference in the extent to which your sense of appreciation registers. In **nonverbal communication** we use our body, voice, or environment in numerous ways to help put a message across. Sometimes we are not aware how much our true feelings color our spoken message.

One problem of paying attention to nonverbal signals is that they can be taken too seriously. Just because some nonverbal signals (such as yawning or looking away from a person) might reflect a person's real feelings, not every signal can be reliably connected with a particular attitude. Jason may put his hand over his mouth because he is shocked. Lucille may put her hand over her mouth because she is trying to control her laughter about the message, and Ken may put his hand over his mouth as a signal that he is pondering the consequences of the message. Here we look at seven categories of nonverbal communication that are generally reliable indicators of a person's attitude and feelings.[1]

Environment or Setting

Where you choose to deliver your message indicates what you think of its importance. Assume that a neighbor invites you over for dinner to discuss something with you. You will think it is a more important topic under these circumstances than if it were brought up when the two of you met in the supermarket. Other important environmental cues include room color, temperature, lighting, and furniture arrangement. A person who sits behind an uncluttered large desk, for example, appears more powerful than a person who sits behind a small, cluttered desk.

Distance from the Other Person

How close you place your body relative to another person's also conveys meaning when you send a message. If, for instance, you want to convey a positive attitude toward another person, get physically close to him or her. Putting your arm around someone to express interest and warmth is another obvious nonverbal signal. However, many people in a work setting abstain from all forms of touching (except for handshakes) because of concern that touching might be interpreted as sexual harassment.

Cultural differences must be kept in mind in interpreting nonverbal cues. To illustrate, a French male is likely to stand closer to you than a British male, even if they had equally positive attitudes toward you. A set of useful guidelines has been developed for estimating how close to stand to another person (at least in many cultures).[2] They are described in the following and diagramed in Figure 6-2.

Figure 6-2   Four Circles of Intimacy

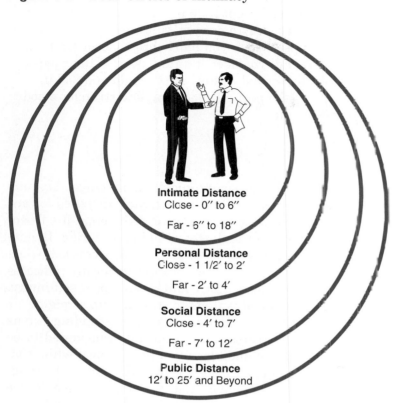

Intimate Distance
Close - 0″ to 6″

Far - 6″ to 18″

Personal Distance
Close - 1 1/2′ to 2′

Far - 2′ to 4′

Social Distance
Close - 4′ to 7′

Far - 7′ to 12′

Public Distance
12′ to 25′ and Beyond

Intimate distance covers actual physical contact to about 18 inches. Usually it is reserved for close friends and loved ones or other people you feel affectionate toward. Physical intimacy is usually not called for on the job, but there are exceptions. For one, confidential information might be whispered within the intimate distance zone.

Personal distance covers from about 1.5 to 4 feet. In this zone it is natural to carry on friendly conversation and discussions. Also, you can touch the other person if you wish to maintain a feeling of privacy. When people engage in a heated argument, they sometimes enter the personal distance zone. One example is a baseball coach getting up close to an umpire and shouting in his face.

Social distance covers from 4 to 12 feet and in general is reserved for interaction that is businesslike and impersonal. We usually maintain this amount of distance between ourselves and strangers such as retail sales associates and cab drivers.

Public distance covers from 12 feet to the outer limit of being heard. This zone is typically used in speaking to an audience at a large meeting or in a classroom, but a few insensitive individuals might send ordinary messages by shouting across a room. The unstated message suggested by such an action is that the receiver of the message does not merit the effort of walking across the room.

People sometimes manipulate personal space in order to dominate a situation. A sales representative might move into the personal or intimate circle of a customer just to intimidate him or her. Many people become upset when you move into a closer circle than the situation calls for. They consider it an invasion of their personal space, or their "territorial rights." How would you feel if, while waiting in line at the post office, a complete stranger stood within 4 inches of your face?

Posture

Certain aspects of your posture communicate a message. Leaning toward another individual suggests that you are favorably disposed toward his or her message. Leaning backward communicates the opposite. Openness of the arms or legs serves as an indicator of liking or caring. In general, people establish closed postures (arms folded and legs crossed) when speaking to people they dislike. Standing up straight generally indicates high self-confidence. Stooping and slouching could mean a poor self-image. In any event, there is almost no disadvantage to standing up straight.

Related to posture are the nonverbal signals sent by standing versus sitting. Sitting down during a conversation is generally considered to be more intimate and informal than standing. If you do sit down while conversing, be sure to stand up when you wish the conversation to end. Standing up sends a message to the other person that it is time to leave. It also gives you the chance to be more attentive and polite in saying goodbye.[3]

Hand Gestures

An obvious form of body language is hand gestures. Hand gestures are universally recognized as conveying specific information to others. If you make frequent hand movements, you will generally communicate a positive attitude. If you use few gestures, you will convey dislike or disinterest. An important exception here is that some people wave their hands vigorously while arguing. Some of their hand movements reflect anger. Another example is that open-palm gestures toward the other person typically convey positive attitudes.

Head, Face, and Eye Signals

"Here comes a live one," said one fellow to another at a sports bar. "I can tell she's interested in getting to know me. Just look into her eyes and at the expression on her face." The young man who spoke these words may have a valid point. When used in combination, the head, face, and eyes provide the clearest indications of attitudes toward other people. Lowering your head and peering over your glasses, for instance, is the nonverbal equivalent of the expression, "You're putting me on." As is well known, maintaining eye contact with another person improves communication with that person. To maintain eye contact, it is usually necessary to correspondingly move your head and face. Moving your head face, and eyes away from another person is often interpreted as a defensive gesture or one suggesting a lack of self-confidence. Would you lend money to someone who didn't look at you directly?

The face is often used as a primary source of information about how we feel. We look for facial clues when we want to determine another person's attitude. You can often judge someone's current state of happiness by looking at his or her face. The expression "sourpuss" attests to this observation. Happiness, apprehension, anger, resentment, sadness, contempt, enthusiasm, and embarrassment are but a few of the emotions that can be expressed through the face.

Blinking is a specific eye movement that communicates meaningful messages. According to experiments conducted by John Stern, blinks are punctuation marks. People blink at psychologically important times. After they have listened to and understood a question, people typically take time out for a blink. People in control of a situation, such as a pilot in control of an aircraft, are less likely to blink. Many people use rapid blinking to send the message, "I have no idea what you are talking about."

VOICE QUALITY

More significance is often attached to the *way* something is said than to *what* is said. A forceful voice, which includes a consistent tone without vocalized pauses, connotes power and control. Closely related to voice tone are volume, pitch, and rate of speaking. Anger, boredom, and joy can often be interpreted from voice quality. Anger is noted when the person speaks loudly, with a high pitch and fast rate. Boredom is indicated by a monotone. A tip-off to joy is when the person speaks loudly, with a high pitch and fast rate. Joy is also indicated by loud volume.

Avoiding an annoying voice quality can make a positive impact on others. The research of voice coach Jeffrey Jacobbi provides some useful suggestions. He surveyed a nationwide sample of 1,000 men and women, and asked, "Which irritating or unpleasant voice annoys you the most?" The most irritating quality was a whining, complaining, or nagging tone.

Jacobbi notes that we are judged by the way we sound. He also notes that careers can be damaged by voice problems such as those indicated in the survey. Jacobbi continues: "We think about how we look and dress. And that gets most of the attention. But people judge our intelligence much more by how we sound than how we dress."[5] Human Relations Self-Assessment Exercise 6-1 provides more details about his findings.

PERSONAL APPEARANCE

Your external image plays an important role in communicating messages to others. Job seekers show recognition of this aspect of nonverbal communication when they carefully groom for a job interview. People pay more respect and grant more privileges to people they perceive as being

HUMAN RELATIONS SELF-ASSESSMENT EXERCISE 6-1

Voice Quality Checkup

Jacobbi's study of voice quality (cited in the text) ranked voice quality, in decreasing order of annoyance, as follows:

- Whining, complaining, or nagging tone—44.0 percent
- High-pitched, squeaky voice—15.9 percent
- Mumblers—11.1 percent
- Very fast talkers—4.9 percent
- Weak and wimpy voice—3.6 percent
- Flat, monotonous tone—3.5 percent
- Thick accent—2.4 percent

Ask yourself, and two other people familiar with your voice, if you have one or more of the above voice-quality problems. If your self-analysis and feedback from others does indicate a serious problem, get started on self-improvement. Tape your voice and attempt to modify the biggest problems. Another avenue of improvement is to consult with a speech coach or therapist.

EXHIBIT 6-1

ADVICE FROM AN IMAGE CONSULTANT

Fingernails tell more about a person than the clothes he or she wears, says Paul Glick, an image consultant. "Fingernails are an indication of your ability to manage details. You must have noticed someone with very dirty glasses on, or one with bad breath, or one with dirty fingernails. They aren't fully there. You don't make the assessment consciously. But if someone is put together physically we can pretty well assume he or she is well adjusted."

Like it or not, says Glick, how you look is a statement about who you are socially and intellectually, so he advocates being concerned about presentation and making the best of what you have.

"Put a wardrobe together—the right shirts, blouses, ties, jackets, shapes of clothing, the right glasses, the right hairstyling, the right management of all your grooming aspects—so that it all can be done within an hour," said Glick.

"The right appearance is the one most appropriate for the context in which you will be presenting yourself. The right appearance might be jeans and a T-shirt. The right appearance could be a business suit. It's where you are going and whom you are going to be with."

SOURCE: Adapted with permission from Karol Stonger, "Stylist: Looks Are Not Necessarily Deceiving," Associated Press story, June 11, 1989.

EXHIBIT 6-2

BODY BASICS

Patricia Ball, former president of the National Speakers Association and founder of a corporate communications consulting firm, believes strongly in body language. She says that any basic body vocabulary should include the most positive body language you can muster. When you're on a sales call or in negotiations and want to say or hear an affirmative, here are the signals to look for or send:

- *Leaning forward.*   Leaning back sends the message of aloofness or rejection.

- *No leg crossing.*   Keep your feet flat on the floor (both men and women).

- *A vertical handshake.*   Some people shake with the palm down, forcing the other person to hold his or her palm up in a submissive, uncomfortable position.

- *An appropriate smile.*   Smiling continuously may be interpreted as powerlessness.

- *Direct eye contact.*   A direct look is permissable in the United States and Canada, but in many Asian and Middle-Eastern cultures, a direct look is disrespectful.

- *Mirroring the other person's body language.*   Ball warns against being an obvious mimic. However, if the other person has his or her leg crossed toward you and is leaning toward you, then crossing your leg in his or her direction and assuming that person's body language posture basically says, "I think like you. I'm with you."

SOURCE: Adapted from Mark Hennricks, "More Than Words," *Entrepreneur,* August 1995, p. 55.

well dressed and attractive. Furthermore, some research indicates that a favorable personal appearance leads to higher starting salaries and, later, salary increases.[6] The observations of an image consultant about the messages sent by personal appearances are presented in Exhibit 6-1.

Exhibit 6-2 helps integrate the information about nonverbal communication by giving you advice about using a positive basic body vocabulary.

INTERPERSONAL COMMUNICATION AND INFORMATION TECHNOLOGY

Rapid advances in information technology may enable workers to communicate more easily, rapidly, and quickly than they could even a few years ago.[7] Quite often the influence has been positive, but at other times the effectiveness of interpersonal communication has decreased. Two developments that illustrate the impact of information technology on interpersonal communication are e-mail and home-office systems.

E-MAIL AND COMMUNICATION AMONG PEOPLE

Aside from the telephone, e-mail is the information technology system with the most dramatic impact on interpersonal communication. E-mail is frequently used as an efficient substitute for telephone calls, letters, hard-copy memos, and in-person visits. For both work and personal life, e-mail is typically less formal than a letter but more formal than a telephone conversation. The major impact of e-mail on interpersonal communication is that written messages replace many telephone and in-person exchanges. Team members often keep in regular contact with each other without having lengthy meetings or telephone conversations. Several potential communication problems e-mail creates should be kept in mind to minimize these problems.

A major problem with e-mail is that it encourages indiscriminate sending of messages. Some managers receive an average of 300 e-mail messages per day. An executive in a telecommunications firm sends weekly e-mail messages of his "thoughts for the week" to each company employee. Some companywide e-mail announcements describe a battered file cabinet that is available to a "good home." Some workers conduct virtual joke-telling contests over e-mail, with some of the jokes being perceived as offensive by many other workers. Others constantly Spam (constantly send multiple messages to) others. The proliferation of electronic junk mail has prompted some company officials to take corrective action, such as warning employees about the problems with mass mailings and restricting the use of e-mail during certain hours.

E-mail has become a new tool for office politicians who search for ways to look good themselves and make others look bad. Many office politicians use e-mail to give credit to themselves for their contributions to a project, perhaps using a companywide distribution list. When something goes wrong, such as a failed project, the office politician will inform hundreds of people that is it was not his or her fault.

Some managers, and others whose job should involve considerable contact, prefer to remain in their offices or cubicle, firing off e-mail messages to people. Such behavior resembles a mild form of on-line addiction. As one systems analyst said, "I only see my boss about once every two months. She only relates to me by e-mail."

Many supervisors and other workers use e-mail to reprimand others because, by sending a message over the computer, they can avoid face-to-face confrontation. A telecommunications consultant says "e-mail is perfect for managers who would rather do anything other than walk down the hall."[8] Harsh messages sent over e-mail create several problems. First, it is shocking to be reprimanded or insulted in writing. Second, the person cannot offer a defense except by writing back an e-mail message explaining his or her position. Third, the recipient, not knowing what to do about the harsh message, may brood and become anxious.

A final caution about e-mail is that it can breed indecisiveness. Rather than making an independent decision, the worker sends an e-mail to the boss, asking him or her to choose the best alternative. Even though the worker has the authority to make the decision, he or she sends a message to the boss wanting a recommendation. An example: "The purchasing agent at Hunt Systems wants to cancel an order for $1,500 worth of merchandise that we already shipped. What should I tell her? I have to respond by 5 this afternoon." The message sender would be less likely to telephone the boss, send a hard-copy memo, or request an in-person visit over the same issue.

HOME-OFFICE SYSTEMS

Home-office systems are configurations of electronic equipment that make it easier for employees to work at home. Because of home-office systems, telecommuting is possible. A **telecommuter** is an employee who works at home full-time or part-time, and sends output electronically to a central office. Recent estimates indicate that about 38 percent of U.S. households contain at least one person doing income-generating work at home.[9] Electronic equipment for telecommuters includes computers, printers, fax machines, telephones and modems, and video hookups for teleconferencing.

Telecommuters can communicate abundantly via electronic devices, but they miss out on the face-to-face interactions so vital for dealing with complex problems. Another communication problem telecommuters face is feeling isolated from activities at the main office, and missing out on the encouragement and recognition that take place in face-to-face encounters. (Of course, many telecommuters prefer to avoid such contact.) Many telecommuters have another communications problem: Because they have very little face-to-face communication with key people in the organization, they believe they are passed over for promotion.

ROADBLOCKS TO COMMUNICATION

Communication rarely proceeds as effectively as we would like. Many different factors filter out a message on its way to the intended receiver, shown as noise in Figure 6-1. In this section we look at some of the human roadblocks to communication. If you are aware of their presence, you will be better able to overcome them.

Routine or neutral messages are the easiest to communicate. Communication roadblocks are most likely to occur when a message is complex, emotionally arousing, or clashes with the receiver's mental set. An emotionally arousing message would deal with such topics as a relationship between two people or money. A message that clashes with a receiver's mental set requires that person to change his or her familiar pattern of receiving messages. The next time you order a meal in a restaurant, order dessert first and an entrée second. The server will probably not "hear" your dessert order because it deviates from the normal ordering sequence.

LIMITED UNDERSTANDING OF PEOPLE

If you do not understand people very well, your communication effectiveness will be limited. To take a basic example, if you frame your message in terms of what can be done for you, you may be in trouble. It's much more effective to frame your message in terms of what you can do for the other person. Suppose a person in need of money wants to sell magazine subscriptions to a friend. Mentioning financial need is a very self-centered message. It could be made less self-centered:

Very self-centered: "You've got to buy a few subscriptions for me. I can't meet my credit card payments."

Less self-centered: "Would you be interested in subscribing to a few magazines that would bring you enjoyment and help you get ahead in your career? If your answer is yes, I can help you."

Limited understanding of people can also take the form of making false assumptions about the receiver. The false assumption serves as a communication roadblock. A supervisor might say to a telemarketer (a person who sells over the phone), "If you increase sales by 15 percent, we will give you an outside sales position." When the telmarketer does not work any harder, the supervisor thinks the message did not get across. The false assumption the supervisor made was that the telemarketer wanted an outside sales position. What false assumptions have you made lately when trying to communicate with another person?

Guidelines for helping a person overcome a limited understanding of people are presented in Exhibit 6-3.

One-Way Communication

Effective communication proceeds back and forth. An exchange of information or a transaction takes place between two or more people. Per-

---

EXHIBIT 6-3

A SHORT COURSE IN HUMAN RELATIONS

The *six* most important words are "I admit I made a mistake."
The *five* most important words are "You did a good job."
The *four* most important words are "What is your opinion?"
The *three* most important words are "If you please."
The *two* most important words are "Thank you."
The *one* most important word is "We."
The one *least* important word is "I."

Some people who first read this "short course" react to it negatively. Among their reservations are that "It is corny," "It's so obvious. Anybody with common sense knows that," or "Good for people in kindergarten." Yet if you put these seven rules into practice, you will find they do help overcome the communication roadblock called *limited understanding of people.* As one example, if you use "I" too frequently in your conversation, you will create communication roadblocks.

son A may send messages to person B to initiate communication, but B must react to A to complete the communication loop. One reason written messages (including electronic mail) fail to achieve their purpose is that the person who writes the message cannot be sure how it will be interpreted. One written message that is subject to many interpretations is "Your idea is of some interest to me." (How much is *some*?) Face-to-face communication helps to clarify meanings.

Different Interpretation of Words (Semantics)

Semantics is the study of the meaning and changes in the meaning of words. These different meanings can create roadblocks to communication. Often the problem is trivial and humorous; at other times, semantic problems can create substantial communication barriers. Consider first an example of trivial consequence:

> Two first-time visitors to Montréal, Québec (a French-Canadian province), entered a restaurant for dinner. After looking over the menu, the husband suggested they order the shrimp cocktail *entrées*. He said to his wife, "A whole shrimp dinner for $9.95 Canadian is quite a deal. I guess it's because Montréal is a seaport." When the entrées arrived, the visitors were sadly disappointed because they were the size of an *appetizer*.
>
> The husband asked the server why the entrées were so small in Montréal. With a smile, the server replied: "You folks must be Americans. In French-speaking countries the entrée is the beginning of the meal, like the word enter. In the United States it's just the reverse, the entrée is the main meal. Are you now ready to order your main meal?"

Of greater consequence is the experience of a trainer of airplane pilots who inadvertently contributed to a crash. As a rookie pilot navigated down the runway, the trainer shouted, "Takeoff power." The pilot shut off the engine and skidded off the runway. What the trainer really meant was to *use* takeoff power—a surge of energy to lift the airplane off the ground. He was using takeoff as an *adjective,* not a *verb.*

Distortion of Information

A great problem in sending messages is that people receiving them often hear what they want to hear. Without malicious intent, people modify your message to bolster their self-esteem or improve their situation. An incident that occurred between Jennifer and her mother is fairly typical of this type of communication roadblock. Jennifer asked her mother if she might have a digital camera system for Christmas. Regarding the request as farfetched and beyond her means, Jennifer's mother replied, "Why should I buy you a camera system like that when you never even take pictures of your little brother with your present camera?"

Jennifer *heard* her mother say, "If you take pictures of your little brother, I would then buy you that camera system." Three weeks later Jennifer presented her mother with a surprise gift—a small album containing 20 photographs of her little brother. "Mom," said Jennifer, "Here's the album you ordered. Now let me tell you in more detail about that digital outfit you said you would get me for Christmas." Her mother replied, "I never said that. Where did you get that idea?"

The reason some people are so difficult to criticize or insult is that they ward off your message just as a duck wards water off its feathers. What messages of yours has someone not heard recently? Can you think of any messages that bounced off you lately?

Different Perspectives and Experiences (Where Are You Coming From?)

People perceive words and concepts differently because their experiences and vantage points differ. On the basis of their perception of what they have heard, many Hispanic children believe that the opening line of the "Star-Spangled Banner" is "José, can you see . . ." (note that few children have *seen* the national anthem in writing).

Young people with specialized training or education often encounter communication barriers in dealing with older workers. A minority of older workers think that young people are trying to introduce impractical and theoretical ideas. It takes time to break down this type of resistance to innovation and the application of current knowledge.

Emotions and Attitudes

Have you ever tried to communicate a message to another person while that person is emotionally aroused? Your message was probably distorted considerably. Another problem is that people tend to say things when emotionally aroused that they would not say when calm. Similarly, a person who has strong attitudes about a particular topic may become emotional when that topic is introduced. The underlying message here is try to avoid letting strong emotions and attitudes interfere with the sending or receiving of messages. If you are angry at someone, for example, you might miss the merit in what that person has to say. Calm down before proceeding with your discussion or attempting to resolve the conflict.

Communication Overload

A major communication barrier facing literate people is being bombarded with information. **Communication** (or **information**) **overload** occurs when people are so overloaded with information that they cannot respond effectively to messages. As a result, they experience work stress. Workers at many levels are exposed to so much printed, electronic, and spoken information that their capacity to absorb it is taxed. The problem is worsened when low-quality information is competing for your attention. One example is receiving a lengthy letter informing you that you are one of 100 select people to receive a sweepstakes prize. (All you need to do is send $24.95 to cover the shipping and handling costs for your valuable prize.) The human mind is capable of processing only a limited quantity of information at a time.

IMPROPER TIMING

Many messages do not get through to people because they are poorly timed. You have to know how to deliver a message, but you must also know *when* to deliver it. Sending a message when the receiver is distracted with other concerns or is rushing to get somewhere is a waste of time. Furthermore, the receiver may become discouraged and therefore will not repeat the message later.

The art of timing messages suggests not to ask for a raise when your boss is in a bad mood, or to ask a new acquaintance for a date when he or she is preoccupied. On the other hand, do ask your boss for a raise when business has been good. And do ask someone for a date when you have just done something nice for that person and have been thanked.

POOR COMMUNICATION SKILLS

A message may fail to register because the sender lacks effective communication skills. The sender might garble a written or spoken message so severely that the receiver finds it impossible to understand. Also, the sender may deliver the message so poorly that the receiver does not take it seriously. Communication barriers can result from deficiencies within the receiver. A common barrier is a receiver who is a poor listener. Improving listening skills is such a major strategy for improving communication skills that it receives separate mention later in this chapter.

 # BUILDING BRIDGES TO COMMUNICATION

With determination and awareness that communication roadblocks and barriers do exist, you can become a more effective communicator. It would be impossible to remove all barriers, but they can be minimized. The following techniques are helpful in building better bridges to communication.

1. Appeal to human needs and time your messages.
2. Repeat your message, using more than one channel.
3. Discuss differences in paradigms.
4. Check for comprehension and feelings.
5. Minimize defensive communication.
6. Counter information overload.
7. Use mirroring to establish rapport.
8. Improve your telephone and voice-mail communications skills.

APPEAL TO HUMAN NEEDS AND TIME YOUR MESSAGES

People are more receptive to messages that promise to do something for them. In other words, if a message promises to satisfy a need that is less than fully satisfied, you are likely to listen. The person in search of additional money who ordinarily does not hear low tones readily hears the whispered message, "How would you like to earn $300 in one weekend?"

Timing a message properly is related to appealing to human needs. If you deliver a message at the right time, you are taking into account the person's mental condition at the moment. A general principle is to deliver your message when the person might be in the right frame of mind to listen. The right frame of mine includes such factors as not being preoccupied with other thoughts, not being frustrated, being in a good mood, and not being stressed out. (Of course, all this severely limits your opportunity to send a message!)

REPEAT YOUR MESSAGE, USING MORE THAN ONE CHANNEL

You can overcome many roadblocks to communication by repeating your message several times. It is usually advisable not to say the same thing so as to avoid annoying the listener with straight repetition. Repeating the message in a different form is effective in another way: The receiver may not have understood the message the first way in which it was delivered.

Repetition, like any other means of overcoming communication roadblocks, does not work for all people. Many people who repeatedly hear the message "Drinking and driving do not mix" are not moved by it. It is helpful to use several methods of overcoming roadblocks or barriers to communication.

A generally effective way of repeating a message is to use more than one communication channel. For example, follow up a face-to-face discussion with an e-mail message or telephone call or both. Your body can be another channel or medium to help impart your message. If you agree with someone about a spoken message, state your agreement and also shake hands over the agreement. Can you think of another channel by which to transmit a message?

DISCUSS DIFFERENCES IN PARADIGMS

Another way of understanding differences in perspectives and experiences is to recognize that people often have different paradigms that influence how they interpret events. A **paradigm** is a model, framework, viewpoint, or perspective. When two people look at a situation with different paradigms, a communication problem may occur. For instance, one person may say, "Let's go to Las Vegas for the computer show." The other person may respond, "A ridiculous idea. It costs too much money and takes too much time. Besides, the company would never approve." These objections are based on certain unstated beliefs:

- Air travel is the most suitable mode of transportation.

- Traveling over 500 miles a day by auto is fatiguing and dangerous.

- Traveling over a weekend for business and using vacation days cannot be considered seriously.

- Paying for such a trip with personal money is out of the question.

The other person has a different set of unstated beliefs:

- It is possible, traveling on interstate highways and using two drivers, to cover 500 miles in one day.

- Traveling over a weekend and taking vacation days is sensible.

- Paying for the trip with personal money is a sound educational investment.

The solution to this communication clash is to discuss the paradigms. Both people live by different rules or guidelines (a major contributor to a paradigm). If the two people can recognize that they are operating with different paradigms, the chances for agreement are improved. Keep in mind that people can change their paradigms when the reasons are convincing.[10] For example, the first person in the preceding situation may never have thought about using personal funds for a trip as being an educational investment.

CHECK FOR COMPREHENSION AND FEELINGS

Don't be a hit-and-run communicator. Such a person drops a message and leaves the scene before he or she is sure the message has been received as intended. It is preferable to ask receivers their understanding or interpretation of what you said. For example, you might say after delivering a message, "What is your understanding of our agreement?" Also use nonverbal indicators to gauge how well you delivered your message. A blank expression on the receiver's face might indicate no comprehension. A disturbed, agitated expression might mean that the receiver's emotions are blocking the message.

In addition to looking for verbal comprehension and emotions when you have delivered a message, check for feelings after you have received a message. When a person speaks, we too often listen to the facts and ignore the feelings. If feelings are ignored, the true meaning and intent of the message is likely to be missed, thus creating a communication barrier. Your boss might say to you, "You never seem to take work home." To clarify what your boss means by this statement, you might ask, "Is that good or bad?" Your boss's response will give you feedback on his or her feelings about getting all your work done during regular working hours.

When you send a message, it is also helpful to express your feelings in addition to conveying the facts. For example, "Our defects are up by 12 percent [fact], and I'm quite disappointed about those results [feelings]." Because feelings contribute strongly to comprehension, you will help overcome a potential communication barrier.

Minimize Defensive Communication

Distortion of information was described previously as a communication barrier. Such distortion can also be regarded as **defensive communication,** the tendency to receive messages in such a way that our self-esteem is protected. Defensive communication is also responsible for people sending messages to make themselves look good. For example, when criticized for achieving below-average sales, a store manager might shift the blame to the sales associates in her store.

Overcoming the barrier of defensive communication requires two steps. First, people have to acknowledge the existence of defensive communication. Second, they have to try not to be defensive when questioned or criticized. Such behavior is not easy because of **denial,** the suppression of information we find uncomfortable. For example, the store manager just cited would find it uncomfortable to think of herself as being responsible for below-average performance.

Defensive communication sometimes takes the form of answering the wrong question. Being touchy about a particular issue, you might regard a request for information as a criticism. David's manager might say to him, "Have you collected the data yet that we need for the trade show?" Angrily defensive because he feels criticized, David might say, "You know that I'm covering for two employees who are out ill." If he had simply said, No, the boss might have said, "Oh, I just wanted to offer my help."[11]

Combat Information Overload

You will recall that a flood of information reaching a person acts as a communication barrier because people have a tendency to block out new information when their capacity to absorb information becomes taxed. You can decrease the chances of suffering from communication overload by such measures as carefully organizing and sorting information before plunging ahead with reading. Speed reading may help, provided you stop to read carefully the most relevant information. Or you can scan through reports and magazines, looking for key titles and words that are important to you. Recognize, however, that many subjects have to be studied carefully to derive benefit. It is often better to read thoroughly a few topics than to skim through lots of information.

Being selective about your e-mail and Internet reading goes a long way toward preventing information overload. Suppose you see an e-mail message titled "Car Lights Left On in Parking Lot." Do not retrieve the message if you distinctly remember having turned off your lights or you did not drive to work. E-mail programs are being developed to help users sort messages according to their needs. Also, Internet software such as Pointcast can bring information of your choosing to your attention.

You can help prevent others from suffering from communication overload by being merciful in the frequency and length of your messages. Also, do not join the ranks of pranksters who send loads of jokes on e-mail, and who prepare bogus Web sites that look authentic but are unofficial (and unreliable) sources of information.

USE MIRRORING TO ESTABLISH RAPPORT

Another approach to overcoming communication barriers is to improve rapport with another person. A form of nonverbal communication called **mirroring** can be used to establish such rapport. To mirror someone is to subtly imitate that individual. The most successful mirroring technique for establishing rapport is to imitate another's breathing pattern. If you adjust your own breathing rate to someone else's, you will soon establish rapport with that person. Mirroring sometimes takes the form of imitating the boss in order to communicate better and win favor. Many job seekers now use mirroring to get in sync with the interviewer. Is this a technique you would be willing to try?

Mirroring takes practice to contribute to overcoming communication barriers. It is a subtle technique that requires a moderate skill level. If you mirror (or match) another person in a rigid, mechanical way you will appear to be mocking that person. And mocking, of course, erects rather than tears down a communication barrier.

IMPROVE YOUR TELEPHONE AND VOICE-MAIL COMMUNICATION SKILLS

A direct way of overcoming communication barriers is to use effective telephone and voice-mail communication skills because these two communication media often create communication problems. Also, many businesses attract and hold onto customers because their representatives interact positively with people through the telephone and voice mail. Many other firms lose money, and nonprofit organizations irritate the public because their employees have poor communication and voice-mail skills. Furthermore, despite the widespread use of computer networks, a substantial amount of work among employees is still conducted via telephone and voice mail. Most of the previous comments about overcoming communication barriers apply to telephone communications. A number of suggestions related specifically to improving telephone and voice-mail communications are also worth considering. The general goal of the suggestions presented in Exhibit 6-4 is to help people who communicate by telephone sound courteous, cheerful, cooperative, and competent.[12]

ENHANCING YOUR LISTENING SKILLS

Although many workers spend more time at computers than they do communicating orally, face-to-face communication is still a major part of life. Improving your receiving of messages is another part of developing better communication skills. Unless you receive messages as they are intended, you cannot perform your job properly or be a good companion. Listening has even been described as our primary communication activity. About 45 percent of the time we spend communicating with people is spent listening. Listening is a particularly important skill for anybody whose job

EXHIBIT 6-4

EFFECTIVE TELEPHONE AND VOICE-MAIL COMMUNICATION SKILLS

1. When answering the telephone, give your name and department. Also, give the company name if the call is not a transfer from a main switching center.

2. When talking to customers or clients, address them by name, but not to the point of irritation.

3. Vary your voice tone and inflection to avoid sounding bored or uninterested in your job and the company.

4. Speak at a moderate pace of approximately 150 to 160 words per minute. A rapid pace conveys the impression of impatience, while a slow rate might suggest disinterest.

5. Smile while speaking on the phone—somehow a smile gets transmitted over the telephone wires or optic fibers!

6. If the caller does not identify him- or herself, ask "Who is calling, please?" Knowing the caller's name gives a human touch to the conversation.

7. Be particularly tactful in your choice of words because you cannot look at the caller's face to determine if he or she is irked by your phrases. For example, the statement, "I'll tell you once more" can sound even harsher over the phone than in person.

8. Use voice mail to minimize "telephone tag" rather than to increase it. If your greeting specifies when you will return, callers can choose to call again or to leave a message. When you leave a message, suggest a good time to return your call. Another way to minimize telephone tag is to assure the person you are calling that you will keep trying.

9. Place an informative and friendly greeting (outgoing message) on your voice mail (or answering machine). Used effectively, a voice-mail greeting will minimize the number of people irritated by not talking to a person.

10. When you respond to a voice-mail outgoing message, leave specific, relevant information. As in the suggestions for minimizing telephone tag, be specific about why you are calling and what you want from the person called. The probability of receiving a return call increases when you leave honest and useful information. If you are selling something or asking for a favor, be honest about your intent.

11. When leaving your message, avoid the most common voice-mail error, by stating your name and telephone number clearly enough to be understood. Most recipients of a message dislike intensely listening to it several times to pick up identifying information.

12. Use upbeat, modern language. Given that it's more difficult to make a positive impression over the phone than in person, sprinkle your phone conversation with modern, "in" words. For example, you might say that some of your customers like "modern primitive." It refers to the revival of body modification processes like tattooing and piercing. Or try, "dead tree edition," referring to the paper version of a newspaper or magazine that also appears in electronic form.

involves troubleshooting, since you need to gather information in order to solve problems.

Another reason that improving employee listening skills is important is that insufficient listening is extraordinarily costly. Listening mistakes lead to reprocessing letters, rescheduling appointments, reshipping orders, and recalling defective products. Effective listening also improves interpersonal relationships because the people listened to feel understood and respected.

A major component of effective listening is to be an **active listener.** The active listener listens intensely, with the goal of empathizing with the speaker. **Empathy** is simply understanding another person's point of view. If you know "where the other person is coming from," you will be a better receiver and sender of messages. Empathy does not necessarily mean that you sympathize with the other person. For example, you may understand why some people are forced to beg in the streets, but you may have very little sympathy for their plight.

A useful way of showing empathy is to accept the sender's figure of speech. By so doing, the sender feels understood and accepted. Also, if you reject the person's figure of speech by rewording it, the sender may become defensive. Many people use the figure of speech, "I'm stuck," when they cannot accomplish a task. You can facilitate smooth communication by a response such as, "What can I do to help you get unstuck?" If you respond with something like, "What can I do to help you think more clearly?," the person is forced to change mental channels, and may become defensive.[13]

As a result of listening actively, the listener can feed back to the speaker what he or she thinks the speaker meant. Feedback of this type relies on both verbal and nonverbal communication. Active listening also involves **summarization.** When you summarize, you pull together, condense, and thereby clarify the main points the other person communicates. Here are two examples of summarization statements:

> "What I heard you say during our meeting is that . . ."
> "As I understand it, your position is that . . ."

To be an active listener, it is also important to **paraphrase,** or repeat in your own words what the sender says, feels, and means. You might feel awkward the first several times you paraphrase. Therefore, try it with a person with whom you feel comfortable. With some practice it will become a natural part of your communication skill kit. Here is an example of how you might use paraphrasing:

Other Person: I'm getting ticked off at working so hard around here. I wish somebody else would pitch in and do a fair day's work.

You: You're saying that you do more than your fair share of the tough work in our department.

Other Person: You bet. Here's what I think we should be doing about it. . . .

Human Relations Skill-Building Exercise 6-1 gives you an opportunity to practice your listening skills.

HUMAN RELATIONS SKILL-BUILDING EXERCISE 6-1

Active Listening

Before conducting the following role plays, review the suggestions for active listening in this chapter. The suggestion about paraphrasing the message is particularly relevant because the role plays involve emotional topics.

The Elated Coworker.   One student plays the role of a coworker who has just been offered a promotion to supervisor of another department. She will be receiving 10 percent higher pay and be able to travel overseas twice a year for the company. She is eager to describe full details of her good fortune to a coworker. Another student plays the role of the coworker to whom the first coworker wants to describe her good fortune. The second worker decides to listen intently to the first worker. Other class members will rate the second student on his or her listening ability.

The Discouraged Coworker.   One student plays the role of a coworker who has just been placed on probation for poor performance. His boss thinks that his performance is below standard and that his attendance and punctuality are poor. He is afraid that if he tells his girlfriend, she will leave him. He is eager to tell his tale of woe to a coworker. Another student plays the role of a coworker he corners to discuss his problems. The second worker decided to listen intently to his problems but is pressed for time. Other class members will rather the second student on his or her listening ability.

OVERCOMING GENDER AND CROSS-CULTURAL BARRIERS TO COMMUNICATION

Another strategy for overcoming communication barriers is to deal effectively with cultural differences. Two major types of cultural differences are those related to gender (male versus female) and those related to geographic differences. Of course, not everybody agrees that men and women are from different cultures.

GENDER DIFFERENCES IN COMMUNICATION STYLE

Despite the movement toward equality of sexes in the workplace, substantial interest has arisen in identifying differences in communication style between men and women. Interest in this topic was fueled by the extraordinarily successful book, *Men are from Mars, Women are from Venus.*[14] People who are aware of these differences face fewer communication problems between themselves and members of the opposite sex. As we describe these differences, recognize that they are group stereotypes. Individual differences in communication style are usually more important than group (men versus women). Furthermore, many research studies fail to show significant gender differences in communication style.[15] Here we will describe the major findings of gender differences in communication patterns.[16]

1. *Women prefer to use conversation for rapport building.* For most women, the intent of conversation is to build rapport and connections with people. It has been said that men are driven by transactions while women are driven by relations. Women are therefore more likely to emphasize similarities, to listen intently, and to be supportive.

2. *Men prefer to use talk primarily as a means to preserve independence and status by displaying knowledge and skill.* When most men talk, they want to receive positive evaluation from others and maintain their hierarchical status within the group. Men are therefore more oriented to giving a *report* while women are more interested in establishing *rapport*.

3. *Women want empathy, not solutions.* When women share feelings of being stressed out, they seek empathy and understanding. If they feel they have been listened to carefully, they begin to relax. When listening to the woman, the man may feel blamed for her problems or that he has failed the woman in some way. To feel useful, the man might offer solutions to the woman's problem.

4. *Men prefer to work out their problems by themselves, whereas women prefer to talk out solutions with another person.* Women lock on having and sharing problems as an opportunity to build and deepen relationships. Men are more likely to look on problems as challenges they must meet on their own. The communication consequences of these differences is that men may become uncommunicative when they have a problem.

5. *Men tend to be more directive and less apologetic in their conversation, while women are more polite and apologetic.* Women are therefore more likely to frequently use the phrases "I'm sorry" and "Thank you," even when there is no need to express apology or gratitude. Men less frequently say they are sorry for the same reason they rarely ask directions when they are lost while driving: They perceive communications as competition, and they do not want to appear vulnerable.

6. *Women tend to be more conciliatory when facing differences, while men become more intimidating.* Again, women are more interested in building relationships, while men are more concerned about coming out ahead.

7. *Men are more interested than women in calling attention to their accomplishments or hogging recognition.* One consequence of this difference is that men are more likely to dominate discussion during meetings. Another consequence is that women are more likely to help a coworker perform well. In one instance a sales representative who had already made her sales quota for the month turned over an excellent prospect to a coworker. She reasoned, "It's somebody else's turn. I've received more than my fair share of bonuses for the month."

8. *Men and women interrupt others for different reasons.* Men are more likely to interrupt to introduce a new topic or complete a sentence for someone else. Women are more likely to interrupt to clarify the other person's thought or offer support.

9.   *Women are more likely to us a gentle expletive, while men tend to be harsher.*   For example, if a woman locks herself out of the car she is likely to say, "Oh dear." In the same situation a man is likely to say, "Oh _____." (Do you think this difference really exists?)

How can this information just presented help overcome communication problems on the job? As a starting point, remember that gender differences often exist. Understanding these differences will help you interpret the communications behavior of people. For example, if a male coworker is not as polite as you would like, remember that he is simply engaging in gender-typical behavior. Do not take it personally.

A woman can remind herself to speak up more in meetings because her natural tendency might be toward holding back. She might say to herself, "I must watch out to avoid gender-typical behavior in this situation." A man might remind himself to be more polite and supportive toward coworkers. The problem is that, although such behavior is important, his natural tendency might be to skip saying thank you.

A woman should not take it personally when a male coworker or subordinate is tight-lipped when faced with a problem. She should recognize that he needs more encouragement to talk about his problems than would a woman. If a man persists in not wanting to talk about the problem, the woman might say: "It looks like you want to work out this problem on your own. Go ahead. I'm available if you want to talk about the problem."

Men and women should recognize that when women talk over problems, they might not be seeking hard-hitting advice. Instead, the may simply be searching for a sympathetic ear so they can deal with the emotional aspects of the problem.

Cross-Cultural Communication Barriers

Another potential communication barrier in the workplace is that communication takes place between and among people from different cultures. Personal life, too, is often more culturally diverse today than previously. Understanding how to react to cultural differences is important because the workforce has become more culturally diverse in two major ways. More subgroups from within our own culture have been assimilated into the work force. In addition, there is increasing interaction with people from other countries.

Because of this diversity, many workers face the challenge of preventing and overcoming communication barriers created by differences in language and customs. Here we describe several strategies and specific tactics to help overcome cross-cultural communication barriers.

Be Alert to Cultural Differences in Customs and Behavior.   To minimize cross-cultural communication barriers, recognize that many subtle job-related differences in customs and behavior may exist. For example, Asians typically feel uncomfortable when asked to brag about themselves in the presence of others. From their perspective, calling attention to yourself at the expense of another person is rude and unprofessional.

Use Straightforward Language and Speak Slowly and Clearly. When working with people who do not speak your language fluently, speak in an easy-to-understand manner. Minimize the use of idioms and analogies specific to your language. For example, in North America the term "over the hill" means outdated or past one's prime. A person from another culture may not understand this phrase, yet be hesitant to ask for clarification.

Speaking slowly is also important because even people who read and write a second language at an expert level may have difficulty catching the nuances of conversation. Facing the person from another culture directly also improves communication because your facial expressions and lips contribute to comprehension.

Observe Cultural Differences in Etiquette. Violating rules of etiquette without explanation can erect immediate communication barriers. A major rule of etiquette is that in many countries people address each other by last name unless they have worked together for a long time. Letitia Baldrige recommends that you explain the difference in custom to prevent misunderstanding. Imagine this scenario in which you are working with a man from Germany, and you are speaking:

> Herr Schultz, in my country by now I would be calling you Heinrich and you would be calling me Charlie. Would you be comfortable with that? Because if you wouldn't, I would be glad to call you Herr Schultz until you tell me it's time to call you Heinrich.[17]

Be Sensitive to Differences in Nonverbal Communication. Stay alert to the possibility that your nonverbal signal may be misinterpreted by a person from another culture. A problem happened to an engineer for a New Jersey company who was asked a question by a German coworker. He responded OK by making a circle with his thumb and forefinger. The German worker stormed away because in his native country the same gesture is a personal insult.[18]

Do Not Be Diverted by Style, Accent, Grammar, or Personal Appearance. Although these superficial factors are all related to business success, they are difficult to interpret when judging a person from another culture. It is therefore better to judge the merits of the statement or behavior.[19] A brilliant individual from another culture may still be learning your language and thus make basic mistakes in speaking your language. He or she might also not have developed a sensitivity to dress style in your culture.

SUMMARY

Communication is the sending and receiving of messages. Therefore, almost anything that takes place in work and personal life involves communication. The steps involved in communication are encoding, transmission over a communication medium, and decoding.

Nonverbal communication, or silent messages, are important parts of everyday communication. Nonverbal communication includes: the environment or setting in which the message is sent; distance from the other person; posture; gestures; head, face, and eye signals; voice quality; and personal appearance.

Despite its many advantages, information technology can create communication problems. The widespread use of e-mail creates some problems. One problem is that it encourages indiscriminate sending of messages. E-mail is also used for such negative purposes as making yourself look good and others look bad. Some managers and other workers use e-mail to avoid direct contact with people, including discipline. Some people find it difficult to handle harsh messages sent over e-mail. Another problem with e-mail is that it can breed indecisiveness because a worker can readily ask the boss to choose an alternative decision.

Telecommuters can communicate abundantly via electronic devices, but they miss out on the face-to-face interactions so vital for dealing with complex problems. Telecommuters can also face the problem of having so little face-to-face communication with people in the office that they are passed over for promotion.

Many potential roadblocks or barriers to communication exist. These roadblocks are most likely to occur when messages are complex, emotional, or clash with the receiver's mental set. Communication roadblocks include: limited understanding of people; one-way communication; semantics; distortion of information; different perspectives and experiences; emotions and attitudes; communication overload; improper timing; and poor communication skills.

Strategies to overcome communication roadblocks include: Appeal to human need and time your messages; repeat your message using more than one channel; discuss differences in paradigms; check for comprehension and feelings; minimize defensive communication; combat information overload; and use mirroring to establish rapport. Also, a direct way of overcoming communication barriers is to use effective telephone and voice-mail communication skills because these media often create communication problems. For example, vary your voice tone and inflection to avoid sounding bored or uninterested in your job and the company.

Improving your receiving of messages is another part of developing better communication skills. Unless you receive messages as intended, you cannot perform your job properly or be a good companion. A major component of effective listening is to be an active listener. The active listener uses empathy and can feed back to the speaker what he or she thinks the speaker meant. Active listening also involves summarizing the speaker's key ideas and paraphrasing what the speaker says, feels, and means.

Some opinion and evidence exists about gender differences in communication style. For example, women prefer to use conversation for rapport building, and men prefer to use talk primarily as a means to preserve independence and status by displaying knowledge and skill. Understanding gender differences will help you interpret the communications behavior of people.

To help overcome cross-cultural communication barriers, consider the following: Be alert to cultural differences in customs and behavior; use straightforward language and speak slowly and clearly; observe differences in etiquette; be aware of nonverbal differences; and do not be diverted by superficial factors.

Questions and Activities

1. How can knowing the three major steps in communication help a person communicate more effectively?

2. Why is nonverbal communication so important for the effectiveness of a manager or sales representative?

3. In what type of situation are you the most likely to give mirroring a try? Explain your reasoning.

4. In what way is a handshake a form of nonverbal communication?

5. During your next several work- or school-related phone calls, analyze what the people you speak to are doing right and wrong from the standpoint of telephone communication. Be prepared to report your findings back to the class.

6. Based on your own observations, identify a term or phrase that creates semantic problems.

7. Identify a barrier to communication that typically exists in a classroom. What can be done to reduce this barrier?

8. How does being "politically correct" help overcome communication barriers?

9. So what if differences in communication patterns between men and women have been identified? What impact will this information have on your communications with men and women?

10. Find an example of a cross-cultural barrier to communication by speaking to an informed person or by reading. Be prepared to report your findings back to the class.

REFERENCES

[1]Walter D. St. John, "You Are What You Communicate," *Personnel Journal,* October 1985, pp. 40–43.

[2]Edward T. Hall, "Proxemics—A Study of Man's Spatial Relationships," in *Man's Image in Medicine and Anthropology* (New York: International Universities Press, 1963); Pauline E. Henderson, "Communication Without Words," *Personnel Journal,* January 1989, pp. 28–29.

A HUMAN RELATIONS CASE PROBLEM

Just Call Me "Kat."

Katherine Matthews had worked for many years in a variety of retail positions, including a three-year assignment as an assistant manager at a woman's clothing store. Matthews was then involved in an automobile accident as the passenger in a friend's car. Although she was wearing a seat belt, Matthews was severely injured. Her right leg and ankle were broken as the door on her side caved in upon impact with a tree.

After four months of rehabilitation, Matthews walked well with the assistance of a cane. Yet she could not walk for long without enduring pain. Katherine and the team of medical specialists assisting her, agreed that an on-the-feet job was not appropriate for her in the foreseeable future. Katherine assessed her financial situation and decided she needed to return to work soon. Her disability payments were ending soon, and her savings were depleted down to $350.

To make the transition back to full-time employment, yet in another field, Katherine signed on with OfficeTemps, a well-established temporary placement agency. Katherine explained that she sought work which was mentally challenging but not physically demanding on her right leg and ankle. After carefully assessing Katherine's capabilities and experiences, the employment interviewer, Jack Radison, created a computer file for her. Radison said, "I'll call you as soon as I find a suitable assignment."

One week later Radison called Katherine with good news. He had located a nine-month assignment for her as a telephone interviewer for a market research firm. The market research firm was hiring several people to conduct telephone interviews with dealers and retailers about the acceptability of a relatively new product, a personal air cooler. The cooler is about the size of the central processing unit on a personal computer, and would fit easily on a desk or adjacent to a television set. The air cooler evaporates water, thereby lowering the temperature by 12 degrees F (6.7° C) in a 7-foot area. Using an air cooler, a person would have less need for air conditioning. With the cooler operating, a person could either eliminate air conditioning, or set it at a higher temperature. The manufacturer of the cooler was interested in estimating the potential market for the product, now being sold primarily by mail order.

Katherine's task was to telephone specific people (usually store managers or owners) from a long list of names. Completing an interview would require about 30 minutes, and involved obtaining answers to 20 separate questions. Each market research interview was given a quota of six completed interviews per day.

As the interviewers perceived the task, a major challenge was to keep the interviewee on the line long enough to answer all the detailed questions. Quite often the interviewer had to dig for additional information (such as sales of room air conditioners and fans), or request that the interviewee search his or her files for appropriate information. The several interviewers also agreed that an even bigger challenge was to get the people on the list to cooperate. Among the problems were reaching a voice mail system instead of the actual person, excuses about being too busy to be interviewed, and outright rejection and rudeness.

Following closely the script provided by the market research firm, Katherine began her pitch in this manner: "Hello this is Katherine from Garson Research Asso-

(Continued)

ciates in Chicago. I'm asking for your cooperation to participate in an important study about an exciting new product, personal coolers. My interview should only take approximately 30 minutes. May we conduct the interview right now, or would you prefer another time in the next few days?"

Four weeks into the job, Katherine was behind quota by an average of two interviews per day. Feeling fatigued one day, she slipped into introducing herself as "Kat," the name used by family members and close friends. The interviewee prospect responded, "Oh sure, Kat, I can talk now." Two days later, Katherine made a personal call to a friend, thus prompted to think of herself as "Kat." She inadvertently introduced herself as "Kat" to the next person on her list. Again, the prospective interviewee responded with enthusiasm: "Hey Kat, I'm ready to talk."

Prompted by the second cooperative response, Katherine then shifted to introducing herself as "Kat." The percentage of prospects willing to be interviewed jumped from 10 percent to 20 percent. Katherine explained this unusual result to her supervisor, who said that using a nick name and achieving good results was probably just a coincidence, that maybe she had simply become more confident. The increased confidence was therefore responsible for the higher success ratio in obtaining interviews.

Katherine responded, "I'm not so sure. There must be some other reasons that "Kat" gets more interviews than "Katherine."

Questions

1. How can information about overcoming communication barriers help explain why "Kat" gets more interviews than "Katherine"?

2. How might the sex of the receiver be related to the different success ratios of "Kat" and "Katherine" in obtaining interviews?

3. Based on Kat's good results, what recommendations can you offer the research firm to help them increase the percentage of people who agree to be interviewed?

[3]Merrill E. Douglas, "Standing Saves Time," *Executive Forum,* July 1989, p. 4.

[4]Research cited in Marco R. della Cava, "In the Blink of an Eye. Researcher Learns about Humans," Gannett News Service, May 7, 1988.

[5]Jeffrey Jacobi, *The Vocal Advantage* (Upper Saddle River, NJ: Prentice-Hall, 1996).

[6]Irene Hanson Frieze, Josephine E. Olson, and Jane Russell, "Attractiveness and Business Success: Is It Important for Women or Men?" paper presented at the Academy of Management, Washington, D.C., August, 1989.

[7]Betty S. Johnson, "Communication in a Changing Environment," in *The Changing Dimensions of Business Education* (Reston, VA: National Business Education Association, 1997), pp. 112.

[8]S. C. Gwynne and John F. Dickerson, "Lost in the E-mail," *Time,* April 21, 1997, p. 89.

[9]Amy Dunkin, "Taking Care of Business without Leaving the House," *Business Week,* April 17, 1995, p. 106; Elizabeth Sheley, "Flexible Work Options: Beyond 9 to 5," *HRMagazine,* February 1996, pp. 52–58.

[10]Suzette Haden Elgin, *Genderspeak* (New York: Wiley, 1993).

[11]Ibid.

[12]Janice Alessandra and Tony Alessandra, "14 Telephone Tips for Ernestine," *Management Solutions,* July 1988, pp. 35–36; Donna Deeprose, "Making Voice Mail Customer Friendly," *Supervisory Management,* December 1992, pp. 7–8; Steven Daly and Nathaniel Wice, *alt. culture* (New York: HarperCollins, 1996).

[13]Daniel Araoz, "Right-Brain Management (RBM): Part 2," *Human Resources Forum,* September 1989, p. 4.

[14]John Gray, *Men Are from Mars, Women Are from Venus* (New York: HarperCollins, 1992).

[15]Mary Crawford, *Talking Difference: On Gender and Language* (Newbury Park, CA: Sage Publications, 1995).

[16]Deborah Tannen, *Talking from 9 to 5* (New York: William Morrow, 1994); Tannen, *You Just Don't Understand* (New York: Ballentine, 1990); Gray, *Men Are from Mars;* Tannen, "The Power of Talk: Who Gets Heard and Why," *Harvard Business Review,* September-October 1995, pp. 138–148.

[17]"Letitia Baldrige: Arbiter of Business Manners and Mores," *Management Review,* April 1992, p. 50.

[18]Roger E. Axtell, *Gestures: The Do's and Taboos of Body Language Around the World* (New York: Wiley, 1991).

[19]David P. Tulin, "Enhance Your Multi-Cultural Communication Skills," *Managing Diversity,* Vol. 1, 1992, p. 5.

ADDITIONAL READING

Dilenschneider, Robert. *A Briefing for Leaders: Communication as the Ultimate Exercise of Power.* Burr Ridge, Ill.: Business One Irwin.

Gladis, Stephen D. *Write Type: Personality Types and Writing Styles.* Amherst, MA.: HRD Press, 1996.

Heyman, Richard. *Why Didn't You Say That in the First Place?* San Francisco: Jossey-Bass/Pfeiffer, 1997.

Joinson, Carla. "Re-creating the Indifferent Employee." *HRMagazine,* August 1996, pp. 76–80.

Parshall, Gerald. "Buzzwords." *U.S. New & World Report,* December 30, 1996/January 6, 1997, pp. 80–81.

Ryan, Kathleen, Oestrich, Dan. and Orr, George. *The Courageous Messenger: How to Successfully Speak Up at Work.* San Francisco: Jossey-Bass/Pfeiffer, 1997.

Shenk, David. *Data Smog: Surviving the Information Glut.* New York: HarperCollins, 1997.

Truitt, John. *Phone Tactics for Instant Influence.* New York: Dembern Books/W.W. Norton & Co., 1990.

HANDLING CONFLICT AND BEING ASSERTIVE

Learning Objectives

After studying the information and doing the exercises in this chapter, you should be able to:

▼ Identify reasons why conflict between people takes place so often

▼ Pinpoint several helpful and harmful consequences of conflict

▼ Choose an effective method of resolving conflict

▼ Improve your negotiating skills

▼ Improve your assertion skills

A manager was so concerned about a problem facing her in the office that she wrote to a business columnist: "I am a manager in a small office. My problem is that one of the staff people (a man who is 12 years older than I) is verbally harassing me, telling me that I don't know what I'm doing and that I'm incompetent. A lot of times, I just avoid dealing with him. Instead of saying something I'll regret, I figure I'm better off

walking away. This man doesn't report directly to me. He reports to someone else but I have authority over his work. What are my rights here? How should I handle this?"

The columnist who consulted several human relations specialists, responded: "What a tense situation! And what obnoxious remarks! You're probably dreading the thought of any direct confrontation with this man. Unfortunately, however, that's exactly what the experts want you to do—talk directly with the offender about his behavior."[1]

The situation just described illustrates a reality about the workplace and personal life. Conflict takes place frequently, and being able to manage it well contributes to your feeling of well being. **Conflict** is a condition that exists when two sets of demands, goals, or motives are incompatible. For example, if a person wants a career in retailing, yet also wants to work a predictable eight-hour day with weekends off, that person faces a conflict. He or she cannot achieve both goals. When two people have differences in demands, it often leads to a hostile or antagonistic relationship between them. A conflict can also be considered a dispute, feud, or controversy. The two people described above are in conflict because the man wants to insult the woman and the woman wants a peaceful relationship.

Conflict is important to study because it is far more complex than it appears on the surface. Many delicate human feelings are involved when two people are in conflict. The noted counseling psychologist, Carl Rogers, observed that most conflict between people includes four elements. First, each side thinks he or she is right and the other side is wrong. Second, communication breaks down as people do not hear each other. Third, there are distortions in perceptions as both sides ignore evidence that does not fit their viewpoints. Fourth, people distrust each other.[2]

A major purpose of this chapter is to describe ways of resolving conflict so that a win-win solution is reached. Both sides should leave the conflict feeling that their needs have been satisfied without having had to resort to extreme behavior. Both parties get what they deserve, yet preserve the dignity and self-respect of the other side. Another purpose of this chapter is to explain assertiveness, because being assertive helps to prevent and resolve conflict.

WHY SO MUCH CONFLICT EXISTS

Many reasons exist for the widespread presence of conflict in all aspects of life. All of these reasons are related to the basic nature of conflict—the fact that not every person can have what he or she wants at the same time. As with other topics in this book, understanding conflict helps you develop a better understanding of why people act as they do. Here we describe five key sources of conflict.

COMPETITION FOR LIMITED RESOURCES

A fundamental reason you might experience conflict with another person is that not everybody can get all the money, material, supplies, or human help they want. Conflict also ensues when employees are asked to compete for prizes such as bonuses based on individual effort or company-paid vacation trips. Because the number of awards is so limited, the competition becomes intense enough to be regarded as conflict. In some families, two or more children are pitted in conflict over the limited resources of money available for higher education.

Conflict stemming from limited resources has become prevalent as so many companies acquire others or decide to downsize. After one company takes over another, a decision is often made to eliminate a number of positions and to cut costs in other ways. People then squabble over which employees should be entitled to hold onto their jobs, and whose budget should be cut. In this instance, the positions in question and the money available become limited resources.

THE GENERATION GAP AND PERSONALITY CLASHES

Various personality and cultural differences among people contribute to workplace conflict. Differences in age, or the generation gap, can lead to conflict because members of one generation may not accept the values of another. Some observers see a clash between Baby Boomers and Generation X. The Baby Boomers are typically considered people born between 1946 and 1964, whereas Generation X are the group born approximately between 1965 and 1981. According to the stereotype, Boomers see Xers as disrespectful of rules, not willing to pay their dues, and being disloyal to employers. Generation X people see Boomers as worshipping hierarchy (layers of authority), being over cautious, and wanting to preserve the status quo.[3] Both groups, of course, see themselves in a more favorable light. Members of Generation X believe that employers have been disloyal to them, and baby boomers believe that the search for job security is highly sensible.

The generation gap as well as other forms of cultural diversity in the workforce have increased the potential for conflict. William L. Ury, a negotiation expert, says "Conflict resolution is perhaps the key skill needed in a diverse work force."[4] When these conflicts are properly resolved, diversity lends strength to the organization because the various viewpoints make an important contribution to solving a problem.

Many disagreements on the job stem from the fact that some people simply dislike each other. A **personality clash** is thus an antagonistic relationship between two people based on differences in personal attributes, preferences, interests, values, and styles. People involved in a personality clash often have difficulty specifying why they dislike each other. The end result, however, is that they cannot maintain an amiable work relationship. A strange fact about personality clashes is that people who get along well may begin to clash after working together for a number of years. Many business partnerships fold because the two partners eventually clash.

THE BUILDING OF STONE WALLS

The slow and steady growth of a conflict situation has been likened by Richard J. Mayer to the building of a stone wall. The seed of the conflict is usually a minor incident that is not dealt with openly. The minor incident is called a *pinch.* Next, the person pinched unconsciously gathers data to support his or her view of the situation because of a need to be right. Much of the data are subject to perceptual distortion (seeing things in a way that fits our needs). As a result, a wall of minor incidents is built. The incidents eventually become an insurmountable obstacle (or stone wall) for honest and candid interaction with the *pincher.*[5]

A typical pinch is when an employee fails to share credit for a good idea he or she received from a coworker. The coworker feels slighted and then looks for other incidents of the first person being dishonest. Communication breaks down between the two, and they are involved in frequent arguments. The employee who failed to share credit may be unaware of how or why the conflict began. If the pinched worker had confronted the issue early on, the conflict might not have festered.

SEXUAL HARASSMENT

Many employees face conflict because they are sexually harassed by a supervisor, coworker, or customer. **Sexual harassment** is generally defined as unwanted sexually oriented behavior in the workplace that results in discomfort and/or interference with the job. It can include an action as violent as rape or as subdued as telling a sexually toned joke. Sexual harassment creates conflict because the harassed person has to make a choice between two incompatible motives. One motive is to get ahead, keep the job, or have an unthreatening work environment. But to satisfy this motive, the person is forced to sacrifice the motive of holding on to his or her moral values or preferences. For example, a person might say, "I want to be liked by my coworkers and not be considered a prude. Yet to do this, must I listen to their raunchy jokes about the human anatomy?" Of even greater conflict, "I want a raise; but to do this, must I submit to being fondled by my boss?" Here we focus on the types and frequency of sexual harassment, guidelines for dealing with the problem and the potential problems of overreacting to mild forms of sexual harassment.

Types and Frequency of Harassment

Two types of sexual harassment are legally recognized. Both are violations of the Civil Rights Acts of 1964 and 1991, and are therefore a violation of your rights when working in the United States. Canada also has human rights legislation prohibiting sexual harassment. In quid pro quo sexual harassment, the individual suffers loss (or threatened loss) of a job benefit as a result of his or her response to a request for sexual favors. The demands of a harasser can be blatant or implied. An implied form of quid pro quo harassment might take this form: A manager casually comments to one of his or her employees, "I've noticed that workers who become very close to me outside of the office get recommended for bigger raises."

The other form of sexual harassment is hostile-environment harassment. Another person in the workplace creates an intimidating, hostile, or offensive working environment. No tangible loss has to be suffered under this form of sexual harassment. According to a 1993 U.S. Supreme Court ruling, the person does not have to suffer severe psychological injury for an act to be classified as harassing. So long as a "reasonable person" would be offended by the behavior in question, the act could be considered harassment. Mary C. Mattis has conducted extensive research about sexual harassment in business. She has found that 95 percent of sexual harassment charges concern hostile or offensive work environments, not quid pro quo.[6]

An employee who is continually subjected to sexually suggestive comments, lewd jokes, or requests for dates is a victim of hostile-environment harassment. When the offensive behavior stems from customers or vendors, it is still harassment. Although the company cannot readily control the actions of customers or vendors, the company may still be liable for such harassment. According to several legal decisions, it is a company's job to take action to remedy harassment problems involving employees.[7]

Sexual harassment of both types is widespread in the workplace, even if the vast majority of these complaints are related to a hostile environment. Sexual harassment through creating an intimidating environment received worldwide attention in 1991. The occasion was the Congressional hearing to determine if Judge Clarence Thomas, a Supreme Court justice nominee, had sexually harassed a former employee, Professor Anita F. Hill. Although Congress subsequently approved Thomas as a Supreme Court justice, employers became more sensitive to the problem of sexual harassment. Employees apparently perceived the climate to be more favorable for filing sexual harassment charges. During the next five years following the hearing, sexual harassment claims filed with the U.S. EEOC increased by 150 percent.[8]

Several other high-profile sexual harassment cases during the late 1990s also contributed to awareness of the problem. President Bill Clinton was accused of sexually harassing a state employee while he was governor of Arkansas. Multiple charges of sexual harassment and misconduct were levied against U.S. military officers and enlisted personnel. Around the same time, in one of the biggest federal sexual-harassment lawsuits in history, 29 women filed a class action suit against Mitsubishi Motor Manufacturing of America Inc. Female employees at the Normal, Illinois, plant complained of sexual misbehavior on the factory floor including obnoxious comments, the display of sexually oriented drawings, and forced sex play. Part of the lawsuit contended that the Japanese managers were complacent about charges.[9]

Guidelines for Preventing and Dealing with Sexual Harassment

A starting point in dealing with sexual harassment is to develop an awareness of the type of behaviors that are considered sexual harassment. Often the difference is subtle. Suppose, for example, you placed copies of two nudes painted by Renoir, the French painter, on a coworker's desk. Your coworker might call that harassment. Yet if you took that same coworker to a museum to see the originals of the same nude paintings, your behavior would usually not be classified as harassment. Education about the meaning of sexual harassment is therefore a basic part of any company program to prevent sexual harassment. Following is a sampling of the behaviors that will often be interpreted as environmental harassment:[10]

- *Inappropriate remarks and sexual implications.* Coworkers, subordinates, customers, and suppliers should not be referred to as sexual beings, and their appearance should not be referred to in a sexual manner. Telling a coworker she has gorgeous legs, or he as fabulous biceps, is out of place at work.

- *Terms of endearment.* Refrain from calling others in the workplace terms such as "cutie," "sweetheart," "honey," "dear," or "hunk." Even if these terms are not directly sexually suggestive, they might be interpreted as demeaning.

- *Suggestive compliments.* It is acceptable to tell another person he or she looks nice, but avoid sexually tinged comments such as mentioning that the person's clothing shows off his or her body to advantage.

- *Physical touching.* To avoid any appearance of sexual harassment, it is best to restrict physical touching to handshakes and an occasional sideways hug. Some people consider the "corporate A-frame" hug to be acceptable, whereby the two people's bodies only touch at the top. When a work associate is a long-term friend, the rules for hugging are more liberal.

- *Work-related kissing.* It is best to avoid all kissing in a work context—except perhaps a light kiss at an office party. It is much more professional to greet a work associate with a warm, sincere handshake.

The easiest way to deal with sexual harassment is to speak up before it becomes serious. The first time it happens, respond with statements such as: "I won't tolerate that kind of talk." "I dislike sexually oriented jokes." "Keep your hands off me." Write the harasser a stern letter shortly after the first incident. Confronting the harasser in writing dramatizes your seriousness of purpose in not wanting to be sexually harassed. If the problem persists, say something to the effect: "You're practicing sexual harassment. If you don't stop, I'm going to exercise my right to report you to management." Additional suggestions for dealing with sexual harassment are presented in Exhibit 7-1.

The Potential Problem of Overaggressive Enforcement of Harassment Laws and Guidelines

A major contributor to sexual harassment in the workplace is that people have not been sensitive enough to the issue. For example, many people who thought they were just displaying a sense of humor with their repeated sexual comments did not realize they were committing sexual harassment. A danger also exists at the other extreme: Some people may be accused of sexual harassment for minor mistakes in judgment. One example is the office worker who was accused of hostile-environment sexual harassment because there was a photo of a bikini-clad woman on display in his cubicle. When interviewed about his transgression, the man revealed that the photo was of his wife, taken on their recent honeymoon!

Recent legal rulings also support the idea that a danger exists in enforcing antisexual harassment laws too aggressively. In 1997 a Milwaukee, Wisconsin, jury awarded close to $27 million to a Miller Brewing Co. manager who was fired because of "unacceptable managerial performance." His per-

---

EXHIBIT 7-1

TIPS ON HARASSMENT

Here are some tips on dealing with sexual harassment from the New York State Division of Human Rights.

- Don't leave any room for doubt that the behavior or words you heard were unwelcome.
- If the behavior continues, report your complaint to a higher authority or the person your company or organization has designated to handle such complaints.
- Put the complaint in writing to reduce the chances of confusion.
- Keep concise yet accurate notes of incidents.
- If the matter isn't resolved internally, see a lawyer promptly for advice. The person can steer you through various legal options, possibly through federal or state court.

formance was deemed unacceptable based on alleged sexual harassment. His act of harassment consisted of repeating to a female coworker a sexually oriented joke he heard on the television show *Seinfeld*. The manager also showed the woman a photocopied dictionary page that contained the key word to the joke. The company claimed, however, the manager had also been accused of harassment in the past.[11]

Competing Work and Family Demands

Balancing the demands of work and family life is a major challenge facing workers at all levels. Yet achieving this balance, and resolving these conflicts, is essential for being successful in career and personal life. The challenge of achieving balance is particularly intense for employees who are part of a two-wage-earner family—a group that represents approximately 80 percent of the workforce. Attempting to meet work and family demands is a frequent source of conflict because the demands are often incompatible. A recent survey of 7,800 U.S. workers found that 42 percent of them said that work has a negative impact on their home life.[12] (Of course, unemployment would have an even bigger negative impact!)

The conflict over work versus family demands intensifies when the person is serious about both work and family responsibilities. The average professional working for an organization works approximately 55 hours per week, including 5 hours on weekends. Adhering to such a schedule almost inevitably results in some incompatible demands from work versus those from family members and friends. Conflict arises because the person wants to work sufficient hours to succeed on the job, yet still have enough time for personal life.

Employers have taken major steps in recent years to help employees balance the competing demands of work and family. One reason for giving assistance in this area, is that balancing work and family demands helps both the worker and the company. A survey of work and family strategies found that family-friendly business firms find big returns on their efforts. Absenteeism and turnover decrease, and productivity and profits increase.[13] Work/family programs are aimed directly at reducing the conflict that arises from competing work and family demands. A sampling of these programs and practices is as follows:

1. *Flexible work schedules.* Many employers allow employees to work flexible hours providing they work the full 40-hour schedule and are present at certain core times. A related program is the compressed workweek, whereby the person works 40 hours in four days or less. Some employees prefer the compressed workweek because it gives them longer weekends with their families. Yet compressed workweeks can also be family unfriendly and create major conflicts. An example is that for some workers, having to work three 12-hour days in one week creates family problems.

2. *Family-leave programs.* A major modification of work schedules is the opportunity to take extended time off from work to take care of family responsibilities. The employee's benefits continue while on leave, and the employee is guaranteed a job on return. The leave applies to any combination of family and/or medical leaves. Twelve weeks of such leave is required by the U.S. Family Leave Bill of 1933, applying to firms with 50 or more employees.

3. *Dependent-care programs.*   Assistance in dealing with two categories of dependents, children and elderly parents, lies at the core of programs and policies to help employees balance the demands of work and family. At one end of child-care assistance is a fully equipped nursery school on company premises. At the other end is simply a referral service that helps working parents find adequate child care. Many companies offer financial assistance for child care, including pretax expense accounts that allow employees to deduct dependent-care expenses.

4. *Abolishing early-morning and late-night meetings.*   An annoying conflict facing exempt (no overtime) workers can take place when they have an early or late business meeting. Often this means neglecting a family responsibility such as getting a child off to school or attending a social function with a partner. A product development group at Xerox Corporation banned early-morning and late-night meetings. The improvement in job satisfaction contributed to the first on-time launch of a product in the division's history.[14]

5. *Compassionate attitudes toward individual needs.*   An informal policy that facilitates balancing work and family demands is for the manager to decide what can be done to resolve individual conflicts. Yet the manager cannot make arrangements with employees that would violate company policy. Being sensitive to individual situations could involve such arrangements as allowing a person time off to deal with a personal crisis. After the crisis is resolved, the employee makes up the lost time in small chunks of extra work time.

Another reason that helping workers resolve work-family conflicts is important: Work and family have a profound impact on each other, as also suggested by the theme of this book. Good experiences at work can help absorb stress at home. At the same time, a healthy, low-stress family life can reduce work stress, decrease absenteeism, and improve the mental and physical health of employees.

THE GOOD AND BAD SIDE OF CONFLICT

Conflict over significant issues is a source of stress. We usually do not suffer stress over minor conflicts such as having to choose between wearing one sweater or another. Since conflict is a source of stress, it can have both positive and negative consequences to the individual. Like stress in general, we need an optimum amount of conflict to keep us mentally and physically energetic.

You can probably recall an incident in your life when conflict proved to be beneficial in the long run. Perhaps you and your friend or spouse hammered out an agreement over how much freedom each one has in the relationship. Handled properly, moderate doses of conflict can be beneficial.

Some of the benefits that might arise from conflict can be summarized around these key points:

1. *Talents and abilities may emerge in response to conflict.* When faced with a conflict, people often become more creative than they are in a tranquil situation. Assume that your employer told you that it would no longer pay for your advanced education unless you used the courses to improve your job performance. You would probably find ways to accomplish such an end.

2. *Conflict can help you feel better because it satisfies a number of psychological needs.* By nature, many people like a good fight. As a socially acceptable substitute for attacking others, you might be content to argue over a dispute on the job or at home.

3. *As an aftermath of conflict, the parties in conflict may become united.* Two adolescents engaged in a fistfight may emerge bloodied but good friends after the battle. And two warring supervisors may become more cooperative toward each other in the aftermath of confrontation.

4. *Conflict helps prevent people in the organization from agreeing too readily with each other, thus making some very poor decisions.* Groupthink is the situation that occurs when group members strive so hard to get along that they fail to critically evaluate each other's ideas.

Despite the positive picture of conflict just painted, it can also have some detrimental consequences to the individual, the organization, and society. These harmful consequences of conflict make it important for people to learn how to resolve conflict:

1. *Prolonged conflict can be detrimental to some people's emotional and physical well-being.* As a type of stress, prolonged conflict can lead to such problems as heart disease and chronic intestinal disorders. U.S. President Lyndon B. Johnson suffered his first heart attack after an intense argument with a young newspaper reporter.

2. *People in conflict with each other often waste time and energy that could be put to useful purposes.* Instead of fighting all evening with your roommate, the two of you might fix up your place. Instead of writing angry e-mail messages back and forth, two department heads might better invest that time in thinking up ideas to save the company money.

3. *The aftermath of extreme conflict may have high financial and emotional costs.* Sabotage—such as ruining machinery—might be the financial consequence. At the same time, management may develop a permanent distrust of many people in the workforce, although only a few of them are saboteurs.

4. *Too much conflict is fatiguing, even if it does not cause symptoms of emotional illness.* People who work in high-conflict jobs often feel spent when they return home from work. When the battle-worn individual has limited energy left over for family responsibilities, the result is more conflict. (For instance, "What do you mean you are too tired to go to the movies?" or "If your job is killing your appetite, find another job.")

5. *People in conflict will often be much more concerned with their own interests than with the good of the family, organization, or society.* A married couple in conflict might disregard the welfare of their children. An employee in the shipping department who is in conflict with his supervisor might neglect to ship an order. And a gang in conflict with another might leave a park or beach strewn with broken glass.

6. *Workplace violence erupts, including the killing of managers, previous managers, coworkers, customers, as well as spouses and partners.* The number of violent incidents at work causing death or serious injury has risen dramatically in recent years.[15] Disgruntled employees, such as those recently fired, may attempt revenge by assassinating work associates. People involved in an unresolved domestic dispute sometimes storm into the partner's workplace to physically attack him or her. According to one report, unresolved conflict and frustration from financial, marital, or other domestic problems increase the odds of a person "going ballistic" at work.[16]

CONFLICT-MANAGEMENT STYLES

The information presented so far is designed to help you understand the nature of conflict. Such background information is useful for resolving conflict because it helps you understand what is happening in a conflict situation. The next two sections offer more specific information about managing and resolving conflict. Before describing specific methods of resolving conflict, it is useful to understand five general styles, or orientations, of handling conflict. As shown in Figure 7-1, Kenneth Thomas identified

Figure 7-1 Conflict-Handling Styles According to Degree of Cooperation and Assertiveness

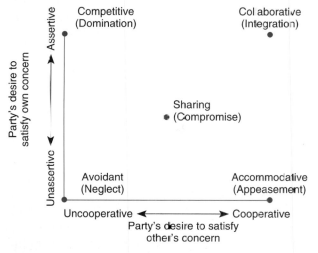

SOURCE: Kenneth W. Thomas, "Organizational Conflict," in Steven Kerr, ed., *Organizational Behavior* (Columbus, OH: Grid Publishing, 1979), p. 156.

five major styles of conflict management: competitive, accommodative, sharing, collaborative, and avoidance. Each style is based on a combination of satisfying your own concerns (assertiveness) and satisfying the concerns of others (cooperativeness).[17]

Competitive.   The competitive style is a desire to win your own concerns at the expense of the other party, or to dominate. A person with a competitive orientation is likely to engage in power struggles where one side wins and the other loses.

Accommodative.   The accommodative style favors appeasement, or satisfying the other's concerns without taking care of your own. People with this orientation may be generous or self-sacrificing just to maintain a relationship. An irate customer might be accommodated with a full refund, "just to shut him (or her) up." The intent of such accommodation might also be to retain the customer's loyalty.

Sharing.   The sharing style is halfway between domination and appeasement. Sharers prefer moderate but incomplete satisfaction for both parties, which results in a compromise. The term "splitting the difference" reflects this orientation and is commonly used in such activities as purchasing a house or car.

Collaborative.   In contrast to the other styles, the collaborative style reflects a desire to fully satisfy the desires of both parties. It is based on an underlying philosophy of **win-win,** the belief that after conflict has been resolved, both sides should gain something of value. The user of win-win approaches is genuinely concerned about arriving at a settlement that meets the needs of both parties, or at least does not badly damage the welfare of the other side. When collaborative approaches to resolving conflict are used, the relationships among the parties are built on and improved.

Here is an example of a win-win approach to resolving conflict. A manager granted an employee a few hours off on an occasional Friday afternoon if she were willing to be on call for emergency work on an occasional weekend. Both parties were satisfied with the outcome and both accomplished their goals.

Avoidant.   The avoider is a combination of uncooperative and unassertive. He or she is indifferent to the concerns of either party. The person may actually be withdrawing from the conflict or be relying upon fate. The avoidant style is sometimes used by a manager who stays out of a conflict between two team members who are left to resolve their own differences.

Human Relations Skill-Building Exercise 7-1 gives you an opportunity to practice a highly useful and desirable conflict management style.

In the following description of specific techniques for resolving conflict, you should be able to relate most of them to these five key styles. For example, you will see that the confrontation and problem-solving technique reflects the collaborative style.

HUMAN RELATIONS SKILL-BUILDING EXERCISE 7-1

Win-Win Conflict Management

The class is organized into groups of six, with each group being divided into conflict resolution teams of three each. The members of the team would like to find a win-win solution to the issue separating each side. The team members are free to invent their own pressing issue, or choose among the following:

- Management wants to control costs by not giving cost-of-living adjustments in the upcoming year. The employee group believes that a cost-of-living adjustment is absolutely necessary.

- The marketing team claims it could sell 250,000 units of a toaster large enough to toast bagels if the toasters could be produced at $10 per unit. The manufacturing group says it would not be feasible to get the manufacturing costs below $15 per unit.

- Starbucks Coffee would like to build in a new location, adjacent to an historic district in one of the oldest cities in North America. The members of the town planning board would like the tax revenue and the jobs that the Starbucks store would bring, but they still say they do not want a Starbucks store adjacent to the historic district.

After the teams have developed win-win solutions to the conflicts, the creative solutions can be shared with teammates.

TECHNIQUES FOR RESOLVING CONFLICTS WITH OTHERS

Because of the inevitability of conflict, a successful and happy person must learn effective ways of resolving conflict. Here we concentrate on methods of conflict resolution that you can use on your own. Most of them emphasize a collaborative or win-win philosophy. Several of the negotiating and bargaining tactics to be described may be close to the competitive orientation.

Confrontation and Problem Solving

The most highly recommended way of resolving conflict is **confrontation and problem solving.** It is a method of identifying the true source of conflict and resolving it systematically. The confrontation in this approach is gentle and tactful rather than combative and abusive. Reasonableness is important because the person who takes the initiative in resolving the conflict wants to maintain a harmonious working relationship with the other party.

Assume that Jason, the person working at the desk next to you, whistles loudly while he works. You find the whistling to be distracting and annoying; you think Jason is a noise polluter. If you don't bring the problem to Jason's attention, it will probably grow in proportion with time. Yet you are hesitant to enter into an argument about something a person might regard as a civil liberty (the right to whistle in a public place).

An effective alternative is for you to approach Jason directly in this manner:

You: Jason, there is something bothering me that I would like to discuss with you.

Jason: Go ahead, I don't mind listening to other people's problems.

You: My problem concerns something you are doing that makes it difficult for me to concentrate on my work. When you whistle it distracts me and grates on my nerves. It may be my problem but the whistling does bother me.

Jason: I guess I could stop whistling when you're working next to me. It's probably just a nervous habit.

An important advantage of confrontation and problem solving is that you deal directly with a sensitive problem without jeopardizing the chances of forming a constructive working relationship in the future. One reason that the method works so effectively is that the focus is on the problem at hand, and not upon the individual's personality.

Another approach to confrontation and problem solving is for each side to list what the other side should do. The two parties then exchange lists and select a compromise both sides are willing to accept. Laying out each side's demands in writing is an effective confrontation technique, especially if the items on the list are laid out factually without angry comments included. Several items on the list of a woman's conflict with her boyfriend might be:

- Please don't introduce me as "my current girlfriend." It makes our relationship sound temporary.

- Turn off the television set when we talk on the phone.

- At least once in awhile give me priority over your family when we are scheduling a social event together.

- Please open and close the car door for me when we are driving in your car.

All of these items relate to consideration and respect, so they are part of the same conflict. The partner can then point out where he can grant concessions. Of course, he will have his chance to produce a list.

Disarm the Opposition

The armament your criticizer has is valid negative criticism of you. The criticizer is figuratively clobbering you with knowledge of what you did wrong. If you deny that you have made a mistake, the criticism intensifies. A simple technique has been developed to help you deal with this type of manipulative criticism. **Disarm the opposition** is a method of conflict resolution in which you disarm the criticizer by agreeing with his or her criticism of you. The technique assumes that you have done something wrong. Disarm the opposition generally works more effectively than counterattacking a person with whom you are in conflict.

Agreeing with criticism made of you by a manager is effective because, by so doing, you are in a position to ask that manager's help in improving your performance. Most managers recognize that it is their responsibility to help employees to overcome problems, not merely to criticize them. Imagine that you have been chronically late in submitting reports during the last six months. It is time for a performance review and you know you will be reprimanded for your tardiness. You also hope that your boss will not downgrade all other aspects of your performance because of your tardy reports. Here is how disarming the situation would work in this situation:

Your Boss:	Have a seat. It's time for your performance review and we have a lot to talk about. I'm concerned about some things.
You:	So am I. It appears that I'm having a difficult time getting my reports in on time. I wonder if I m being a perfectionist. Do you have any suggestions?
Your Boss:	I like your attitude. I think you can improve on getting your reports in on time. Maybe you are trying to make your reports perfect before you turn them in. Try not to figure out everything to four decimal places. We need thoroughness around here, but we don't want to overdo it.

COGNITIVE RESTRUCTURING

An indirect way of resolving conflict between people is to lessen the conflicting elements in a situation by viewing them more positively. According to the technique of **cognitive restructuring,** you mentally convert negative aspects into positive ones by looking for the positive elements in a situation.[18] How you frame or choose your thoughts can determine the outcome of a conflict situation. Your thoughts can influence your actions. If you search for the beneficial elements in a situation, there will be less area for dispute. Although this technique might sound like a *mind game* to you, it can work effectively.

Imagine that a coworker of yours, Jennifer, has been asking you repeated questions about how to carry out a work procedure. You are about ready to tell Jennifer, "Go bother somebody else. I'm not paid to be a trainer." Instead, you look for the positive elements in the situation. You say to yourself, "Jennifer has been asking me a lot of questions. This does take time, but answering these questions is valuable experience. If I want to become a manager, I will have to help group members with problems."

After having completed this cognitive restructuring, you can then deal with the conflict more positively. You might say to Jennifer, "I welcome the opportunity to help you, but we need to find a mutually convenient time. In that way, I can better concentrate on my own work."

Appeal to a Third Party

Now and then you may be placed in a conflict situation in which the other party either holds most of the power or simply won't budge. Perhaps you have tried techniques such as confrontation and problem solving or disarming the opposition, yet you cannot resolve your conflict. In these situations you may have to enlist the help of a third party with power—more power than you or your adversary has. Among such third parties are your common boss, union stewards, or human resource managers. Taking your opponent to court is another application of the third-party technique.

In some situations, just implying that you will bring in a third party to help resolve the conflict situation is sufficient for you to gain advantage. One woman felt she was repeatedly passed over for promotion because of her sex. She hinted that if she were not given fairer consideration, she would speak to the Equal Employment Opportunity Commission (EEOC). She was given a small promotion shortly thereafter.

Negotiation and Bargaining Tactics

Conflicts can be considered situations calling for **negotiating and bargaining,** conferring with another person to resolve a problem. When you are trying to negotiate a fair price for an automobile, you are also trying to resolve a conflict. At first the demands of both parties seem incompatible. After haggling for a while, you will probably reach a price that is satisfactory to both sides.

Negotiation has many applications in the workplace, including buying, selling, arriving at a starting salary or raise, and deciding on a relocation allowance. Negotiation may also take place with coworkers when you need their assistance. For example, you might need to strike a bargain with a coworker to handle some of your responsibilities if you are faced with a temporary overload.

A sampling of negotiating tactics to help you resolve conflict successfully is presented next. As with the other techniques of resolving conflict already presented, choose the ones which best fit your style and the situation.

Create a Positive Negotiating Climate

Negotiation proceeds much more swiftly if a positive tone surrounds the session. So it is helpful to initiate a positive outlook about the negotiation meeting. A good opening line in a negotiating session is, "Thanks for fitting this meeting into your hectic schedule." Nonverbal communication such as smiling and making friendly gestures helps create a positive climate.

In negotiating with coworkers for assistance, a positive climate can often be achieved by phrasing demands as a request for help. Most people will be more accommodating if you say to them, "I have a problem that I wonder if you could help me with." The problem might be that you need the person's time and mental energy. By giving that person a choice of offering you help, you have established a much more positive climate than by demanding assistance.[19]

Allow Room for Compromise but Be Reasonable

The basic strategy of negotiation is to begin with a demand that allows room for compromise and concession. Anyone who has ever negotiated the price of an automobile, house, or used furniture recognizes this vital strategy. If you are a buyer, begin with a low bid. (You say, "I'll give you $35 for that painting" when you are prepared to pay $70.) If you are the seller, begin with a high demand. (You say, "You can have this painting for $100" when you are ready to sell it for as low as $70.) As negotiations proceed, the two of you will probably arrive at a mutually satisfactory price. This negotiating strategy can also be used for such purposes as obtaining a higher starting salary or dividing property after a divorce or legal separation.

Common sense propels many negotiators to allow *too much* room for compromise. They begin negotiations by asking way beyond what they expect to receive, or offering far less than they expect to give. As a result of these implausible demands, the other side may become hostile, antagonistic, or walk away from the negotiations. Assume you spotted a VCR that you really wanted in a retail store. The asking price was $298.95. In an attempt to negotiate the price, you offered the store manager $98.95 for the VCR. Most likely the store owner would move on to the next customer. However, if you began with a plausible offer such as $240, the store man-

COMMON SENSE PROPELS MANY NEGOTIATORS
TO ALLOW **TOO MUCH** ROOM FOR COMPROMISE

ager would take you seriously. Beginning with a plausible demand or offer is also important because it contributes to a positive negotiating climate.

Focus on Interests, Not Positions

Rather than clinging to specific negotiating points, keep your overall interests in mind and try to satisfy them. A negotiating point might be a certain amount of money or a concession that you must have. Remember that the true object of negotiation is to satisfy the underlying interests of both sides. Among the interests you and the other side might be trying to protect include money, lifestyle, power, or the status quo. For example, instead of negotiating for a particular starting salary, your true interests might be to afford a certain lifestyle. If the company pays all your medical and dental coverage, you can get by with a lower salary. Or your cost of living might be much lower in one city than in another. You can therefore accept a lower starting salary in the city with a lower cost of living.

Make a Last and Final Offer

In many circumstances, presenting a final offer will break a deadlock. You might frame your message something like this, "All I can possibly pay for your guitar is $250. You have my number. Call me when it is available at that price." Sometimes the strategy will be countered by a last and final offer from the other side: "Thanks for your interest. My absolute minimum price for this guitar is $300. Call us if that should seem OK to you." One of you will probably give in and accept the other person's last and final offer.

Allow for Face-Saving

We have saved one of the most important negotiating and conflict resolution strategies for last. Negotiating does not mean that you should try to squash the other side. You should try to create circumstances that will enable you to continue working with that person if it is necessary. People prefer to avoid looking weak, foolish, or incompetent during negotiation or when the process is completed. If you do not give your opponent an opportunity to save face, you will probably create a long-term enemy.

Face-saving could work in this way. A small-business owner winds up purchasing a computer, monitor, and printer for about twice what he originally budgeted. After the sale is completed, the sales rep says, "I know you bought a more professional rig than you originally intended. Yet I know you made the right decision. You will be able to do desktop publishing and save enough in printing costs to pay back the cost of the computer system in two years."

 ## DEVELOPING ASSERTIVENESS

Several of the techniques for resolving conflict require assertiveness. Without being forthright, confrontation and problem solving could not be achieved. Effective negotiation would also be difficult because assertiveness is required to carefully explain your demands. Learning to express your feelings and make your demands known is also an important aspect of becoming an effective individual in general. Expressing your feelings helps you establish good relationships with people. If you aren't sharing your feelings and attitudes with other people, you will never get close to them.

Another benefit from being emotionally expressive and, therefore, assertive, is that you get more of what you want in life. If you are too passive, people will neglect giving you what you want. Often it is necessary to ask someone when you want a raise, promotion, date, or better deal on a bank loan. Successful people usually make their demands known, yet only throw tantrums for an occasional effect, and rarely bully others. (Exceptions include flamboyant trial lawyers and athletic coaches.)

Let's examine the nature of assertiveness, and then describe several techniques for building assertiveness. However, first take Human Relations Self-Assessment Exercise 7-1 to relate assertiveness to yourself.

ASSERTIVE, NONASSERTIVE, AND AGGRESSIVE BEHAVIOR

As implied above, **assertive** people state clearly what they want or how they feel in a given situation without being abusive, abrasive, or obnoxious. People who are assertive are open, honest, and "up-front" because they believe that all people have an equal right to express themselves honestly. Assertive behavior can be understood more fully by comparing it to that shown by two other types of people. **Nonassertive** people let things happen to them without letting their feelings be known. **Aggressive** people are obnoxious and overbearing. They push for what they want with almost no regard for the feelings of others.

Suppose a stranger invites you to a party and you do not wish to go with that person. Here are the three ways of responding according to the three-way classification under discussion:

Assertive: Thank you for the invitation but I prefer not to go.
Nonassertive: I'm not sure, I might be busy. Could you call me again? Maybe I'll know for sure by then.
Aggressive: I'd like to go to a party, but not with you. Don't bother me again.

Gestures as well as words can communicate whether the person is being assertive, nonassertive, or aggressive. Exhibit 7-2 illustrates these differences.

BECOMING MORE ASSERTIVE AND LESS SHY

There are a number of everyday actions a person can take to overcome nonassertiveness or shyness. Even if the actions described here do not elevate your assertiveness, they will not backfire and cause you discomfort. After reading the following four techniques, you might be able to think of others that will work for you.[20]

HUMAN RELATIONS SELF-ASSESSMENT EXERCISE 7-1

The Assertiveness Scale

Answer each question Mostly True or Mostly False as it applies to you.

	Mostly True	Mostly False
1. It is extremely difficult for me to turn down a sales representative when that individual is a nice person.	_____	_____
2. I express criticism freely.	_____	_____
3. If another person were being very unfair, I would bring it to that person's attention.	_____	_____
4. Work is no place to let your feelings show.	_____	_____
5. No use asking for favors; people get what they deserve on the job.	_____	_____
6. Business is not the place for tact; I say what I think.	_____	_____
7. If a person looked as if he or she were in a hurry, I would let that person go in front of me in a supermarket line.	_____	_____
8. A weakness of mine is that I'm too nice a person.	_____	_____
9. If my restaurant bill is even 25¢ more than it should be, I demand that the mistake be corrected.	_____	_____
10. I have laughed out loud in public more than once.	_____	_____
11. I've been described as too outspoken by several people.	_____	_____
12. I have no misgivings about returning merchandise that has even the slightest defect.	_____	_____
13. I dread having to express anger toward a coworker.	_____	_____
14. People often say that I'm too reserved and emotionally controlled.	_____	_____
15. Nice guys and gals finish last in business.	_____	_____
16. I fight for my rights down to the last detail.	_____	_____
17. If I disagree with a grade on a test or paper, I typically bring my disagreement to my instructor's attention.	_____	_____
18. If I have had an argument with a person, I try to avoid him or her.	_____	_____
19. I insist on my spouse (or roommate or partner) doing his or her fair share of undesirable chores.	_____	_____

(Continued)

20. It is difficult for me to look directly at another person when the two of us are in disagreement.   _____   _____

21. I have cried among friends more than once.   _____   _____

22. If someone near me at a movie kept up a conversation with another person, I would ask him or her to stop.   _____   _____

23. I am able to turn down social engagements with people I do not particularly care for.   _____   _____

24. It is in poor taste to express what you really feel about another individual.   _____   _____

25. I sometimes show my anger by swearing at or belittling another person.   _____   _____

26. I am reluctant to speak up in a meeting.   _____   _____

27. I find it relatively easy to ask friends for small favors such as giving me a lift to work when my car is being repaired.   _____   _____

28. If another person were talking very loudly in a restaurant and it bothered me, I would inform that person.   _____   _____

29. I often finish other people's sentences for them.   _____   _____

30. It is relatively easy for me to express love and affection toward another person.   _____   _____

Scoring and Interpretation: Give yourself plus 1 for each of your answers that agrees with the scoring key. If your score is 15 or less, it is probable that you are currently a nonassertive individual. A score of 16 through 24 suggests that you are an assertive individual. A score of 25 or higher suggests that you are an aggressive individual. Retake this score about 30 days from now to give yourself some indication of the stability of your answers. You might also discuss your answers with a close friend to determine if that person has a similar perception of your assertiveness. Here is the scoring key.

1. Mostly False	11. Mostly True	21. Mostly True
2. Mostly True	12. Mostly True	22. Mostly True
3. Mostly True	13. Mostly False	23. Mostly True
4. Mostly False	14. Mostly False	24. Mostly False
5. Mostly False	15. Mostly True	25. Mostly True
6. Mostly True	16. Mostly True	26. Mostly False
7. Mostly False	17. Mostly True	27. Mostly True
8. Mostly False	18. Mostly False	28. Mostly True
9. Mostly True	19. Mostly True	29. Mostly True
10. Mostly True	20. Mostly False	30. Mostly True

EXHIBIT 7-2

ASSERTIVE, NONASSERTIVE, AND AGGRESSIVE GESTURES

Assertive	Nonassertive	Aggressive
Well-balanced	Covering mouth with hand	Pounding fists
Straight posture	Excessive head nodding	Stiff and rigid posture
Hand gestures, emphasizing key words	Tinkering with clothing or jewelry	Finger waving or pointing
	Constant shifting of weight	Shaking head as if other person isn't to be believed
	Scratching or rubbing head or other parts of body	Hands on hips
	Wooden body posture	

Set a Goal. Clearly establish in your mind how you want to behave differently. Do you want to date more often? Speak out more in meetings? Be able to express dissatisfaction to coworkers? You can only overcome shyness by behaving differently; feeling differently is not enough.

Appear Warm and Friendly. Shy people often communicate to others through their body language that they are not interested in reaching out to others. To overcome this impression, smile, lean forward, uncross your arms and legs, and unfold your hands.

Make Legitimate Telephone Calls to Strangers. Telephone conversations with strangers that have a legitimate purpose can help you start expressing yourself to people you do not know well. You might call numbers listed in classified ads to inquire about articles listed for sale. Try a positive approach: "Hello, my name is _____. I'd like to know about the condition of that piano you have for sale." Call the gas and electric company to inquire about a problem with your bill. Make telephone inquiries about employment opportunities in a firm of your choice. Call the library with reference questions. Call the federal government bureau in your town with questions about laws and regulations.

With practice, you will probably become more adept at speaking to strangers. You will then be ready for a more challenging self-improvement task.

Conduct Anonymous Conversations. Try starting a conversation with strangers in a safe setting such as a political rally, the waiting room of a medical office, a waiting line at the post office, or in a laundromat. Begin the conversation with the common experience you are sharing at the time. Among them might be:

"I wonder if there will be any tickets left by the time we get to the box office?"

"How long does it usually take before you get to see the doctor?"

"Where did you get that laundry basket? I've never seen one so sturdy before."

Greet Strangers. For the next week or so, greet every person you pass. Smile and make a neutral comment such as "How ya doing?" "Great day, isn't it." Since most people are unaccustomed to being greeted by a stranger, you may get a few quizzical looks. Many other people may smile and return your greeting. A few of these greetings may turn into conversations. A few conversations may even turn into friendships. Even if the return on your investment in greetings is only a few pleasant responses, it will boost your confidence.

SUMMARY

Conflict occurs when two sets of demands, goals, or motives are incompatible. Such differences often lead to a hostile or antagonistic relationship between people. A conflict can also be considered a dispute, feud, or controversy.

Among the reasons for widespread conflict are (1) competition for limited resources, (2) the generation gap and personality clashes, (3) the building of stone walls, (4) sexual harassment, (5) competing work and family demands. Sexual harassment is of two types: quid pro quo (a demand for sexual favors in exchange for job benefits), and creating a hostile environment. It is important for workers to understand what actions and words constitute sexual harassment, and how to deal with the problem. Many companies have programs to help their employees reduce work/family conflict including flexible work schedules and dependent care. Such programs increase productivity.

The benefits of conflict include the emergence of talents and abilities, constructive innovation and change, and increased unity after the conflict is settled. Among the detrimental consequences of conflict are physical and mental health problems, wasted resources, the promotion of self-interest, and workplace violence.

Five major styles of conflict management have been identified: competitive, accommodative, sharing, collaborative, and avoidant. Each style is based on a combination of satisfying your own concerns (assertiveness) and satisfying the concerns of others (cooperativeness). The collaborative style is effective because it leads to win-win solutions to conflict.

Techniques for resolving conflicts with others include:

1. Confrontation and problem solving—get to the root of the problem and resolve it systematically.

2. Disarm the opposition—agree with the criticizer and enlist his or her help.

3. Cognitive restructuring—mentally converting negative aspects into positive ones by looking for the positive elements in a situation.

4. Appeal to a third party (such as a government agency).

5. Use negotiation and bargaining tactics.

Negotiation and bargaining tactics include: (1) Create a positive negotiating climate; (2) allow room for compromise but be reasonable; (3) focus on interests, not positions; (4) make a last and final offer; and (5) allow for face saving.

Several of the techniques for resolving conflict require assertiveness, or stating clearly what you want and how you feel in a given situation. Being assertive also helps you develop good relationships with people and get more of what you want in life. People can become more assertive and less shy by using techniques such as: (1) Set a goal; (2) appear warm and friendly; (3) conduct anonymous conversations; and (4) greet strangers.

Questions and Activities

1. Why are conflict resolution skills considered so important in a culturally diverse workplace?

2. Give an example from your own life of how competition for limited resources can breed conflict.

3. Why might labeling a worker a "Generation Xer" create conflict?

4. One week after a woman joins a company, her team leader invites her to have dinner with him on a Saturday night. Explain whether the team leader is committing sexual harassment.

5. Many male managers who confer with a female worker in their offices leave the door open to avoid any charges of sexual harassment. Are these managers using good judgment, or are they being overly cautious?

6. Many older women in the workforce refer to young men and women as "dear," "honey," and "sweetie." Should these women be advised that they are committing sexual harassment?

7. Identify several occupations in which conflict-resolution skills are particularly important.

8. Suppose you are caught making a right turn on a red light without first stopping. Explain which method of conflict resolution would be best suited to resolving the conflict with the officer.

9. How might a person use cognitive restructuring to help deal with the conflict of having received a below-average raise, yet expecting an above-average raise?

10. Ask a successful person how much conflict he or she experiences in balancing the demands of work and personal life. Be prepared to report your findings in class.

A HUMAN RELATIONS CASE PROBLEM

Generation X Meets Baby Boomer

While studying hotel/restaurant management at college, Cindy worked two part-time jobs: a desk clerk at the Windmere Hotel and a hostess at a restaurant. As graduation approached, Cindy sent résumés to many hotels around the country. She received a few encouraging responses, mostly advising Cindy to contact the hotel after she had relocated to the area. In assessing her employment opportunities, Cindy decided that it would make sense to discuss a full-time position with the head manager at the Windmere.

Much to Cindy's delight and amazement, the manager offered her a full-time position as assistant general manager. Cindy expressed a little hesitation about her ability to handle so much responsibility at this stage in her career. The manager assured Cindy that he had observed her handle difficult situations as a desk clerk, and that she could easily become a competent assistant general manager. He also told Cindy that he and other staff members would be available to give her whatever assistance she needed.

Several weeks into her new position, Cindy felt confident that she was successfully handling her responsibilities with one exception. The exception took the form of Stephanie, a night auditor with 20 years of experience at the Windmere. While attending high school, Stephanie worked part-time in housekeeping. Shortly after graduation, she married and became a parent. Cramped for money after her second child was born, Stephanie returned to the Windmere as the bell desk coordinator. She soon recognized that working during the day was not profitable because of the large child-care expenses she incurred. Finally Stephanie transferred to the night auditor position, which she held for 14 years.

Stephanie was disturbed to learn that her new boss was Cindy, whom she described as "A Generation Xer half my age." Each night while auditing her boss's mistakes, Stephanie became increasingly frustrated. Finally, she decided to send Cindy an e-mail message about her unacceptable performance. Stephanie's e-mail message initiated a series of messages sent back and forth between the two women:

To: Cindy
From: Stephanie
I am starting to wonder if you are really qualified for your new position. I found loads of mistakes made by you and your staff in last night's audit. I knew this was going to happen! I have circled numerous errors from yesterday's transactions. Please fix them immediately.

To: Stephanie
From: Cindy
Thank you for your ever so kind note! It is unfortunate you're having difficulty dealing with me in my new position. I *am* your boss, you know. I can imagine that this is a difficult thing for you to accept, but it's the truth. Be patient with me and my staff. We are not perfect!!!!

(Continued)

To: Cindy
From: Stephanie

Your life as a student and part-time worker is over now. It's time you get cracking and take your new job a little bit more seriously. We've got a business to run here. Again, I remind you to inform your staff of their errors.

To: Stephanie
From: Cindy

We've got to stop meeting like this! Ha! Ha! Please forgive me. The desk clerks and I have been so wild and crazy that we haven't had a free minute to work. By the way, whatever transactions you have been referring to are no longer errors. If you would read the updated procedures manual you would know this. **Please** keep current on the many changes being made by management.

To: Cindy
From: Stephanie

Please find my letter of resignation in the envelop I placed on your desk this afternoon. Perhaps if the Windmere had hired an adult to replace Mr. Benton this would not have happened. Good luck finding a new night auditor who will stay with the hotel for 19.8 years. And one who was an entirely devoted employee.

Cindy thought to herself, "Did I do something terribly wrong, or am I dealing with a nut case? I wonder what I might have done differently. The general manager will not be too happy about Stephanie resigning."

SOURCE: Case researched by Nicole Harwood, Rochester Institute of Technology, May 1997.

Questions

1. What is the most likely source (or sources) of the conflict between Cindy and Stephanie?

2. What could Cindy have done to better resolve conflict with Stephanie?

3. What could Stephanie have done to better resolve conflict with Cindy?

HUMAN RELATIONS SKILL-BUILDING EXERCISE 7-2

Conflict Resolution

Imagine that before Stephanie resigned in a huff, Cindy took the initiative to resolve the conflict between them. One person plays the role of Cindy who is exasperated with Stephanie's behavior and wants to bring about a constructive working relationship. Another student plays the role of embittered Stephanie who resents the fact that Cindy is her manager. The role play might be carried out with three pairs of students playing the two roles. Others in the class can provide constructive criticism about how well the conflict was managed.

REFERENCES

[1]Kathleen Driscoll, "Manager Must Confront Disrespectful Employee, or Behavior Will Not Improve," Rochester, N.Y., *Democrat and Chronicle,* May 10, 1995, p. 1D.

[2]Carl Rogers, "Dealing with Psychological Tensions," *Journal of Applied Behavioral Science* 1, 1956, pp. 12–13.

[3]Gillian Flynn, "Xers vs. Boomers: Teamwork or Trouble?" *Personnel Journal,* November 1996, p. 88.

[4]Quoted in Sybil Evans, "Conflict Can Be Positive," *HRMagazine,* May 1992, p. 50.

[5]Richard J. Mayer, *Conflict Management: The Courage to Confront* (Columbus, OH: Batelle Press, 1990).

[6]Jennifer J. Laabs, "Sexual Harassment," *Personnel Journal,* February 1995, p. 39.

[7]Robert F. Prorok, "Employer Liability Extends to Customers, Clients, and Vendors," *HRfocus,* November 1993, p. 4; Jennifer J. Laabs, "What to Do When Sexual Harassment Comes Calling," *Personnel Journal,* July 1995, pp. 42–53.

[8]Kathleen Driscoll, "Sexual Harassment: Big Cases Causing Local Corporations to Stress Prevention," Rochester, New York, *Democrat and Chronicle,* May 19, 1996, p. 1E.

[9]Leon Jaroff, "Assembly-Line Sexism?" *Time,* May 6, 1996, pp. 56–57.

[10]Kathleen Neville, *Corporate Attractions: An Inside Account of Sexual Harassment with the New Sexual Roles for Men and Women on the Job* (Reston, VA: Acropolis Books, 1992).

[11]James L. Graff, "It Was a Joke!" *Time,* July 28, 1997, p. 62.

[12]Keith H. Hammonds, "Balancing Work and Family," *Business Week,* September 16, 1996, p. 75.

[13]Summary of Hammonds, "Balancing Work and Family," p. 4.

[14]Hammonds, "Balancing Work and Family," p. 80.

[15]Laurel R. Goulelt, "Modeling Aggression in the Workplace: The Role of Role Models," *Academy of Management Executive,* May 1997, p. 84.

[16]"Violent Employees: Cues, Clues, and Constructive Responses," *Getting Results,* June 1996, p. 6.

[17]Kenneth Thomas, "Conflict and Conflict Management," in Marvin D. Dunnette (ed.), *Handbook of Industrial and Organizational Psychology* (Chicago: Rand McNally College Publishing, 1976), pp. 900–902.

[18]Kenneth Kaye, *Workplace Wars and How to End Them: Turning Personal Conflicts into Productive Teamwork* (New York: AMACOM, 1994).

[19]Joseph D'O'Brian, "Negotiating with Peers: Consensus, Not Power," *Supervisory Management,* January 1992, p. 4.

[20]Philip Zimbardo, *Shyness: What It Is, What to Do About It* (Reading, MA: Addison-Wesley, 1977), pp. 220–226; Kevin Shyne, "Shyness: Breaking Through the Invisible Barrier to Achievement," *Success,* July 1982, pp. 14–16, 36–37.

ADDITIONAL READING

Amason, Allen C., Thompson, Kenneth R., Hochwarter, Wayne A., and Harrison, Allison W. "Conflict: An Important Dimension in Successful Management Teams." *Organizational Dynamics,* Autumn 1995, pp. 20–33.

Azar, Beth. "Quelling Today's Conflict Between Home and Work," *APA Monitor,* July 1997, pp. 1, 16.

Caudron, Shari. "Don't Make Texaco's $175 Million Mistake." *Workforce,* March 1997, pp. 58–66.

Hardman, Wendy. "When Sexual Harassment Is a Foreign Affair." *Personnel Journal,* April 1996, pp. 91–97.

Karras, Gary. *Negotiate to Close.* New York: Fireside/Simon & Schuster, 1993.

Laabs, Jennifer J. "What to Do When Sexual Harassment Comes Calling." *Personnel Journal,* July 1995, pp. 42–53.

Landauer, Jill. "Bottom-Line Benefits of Work/Life Programs." *HRFocus,* July 1997, pp. 3–4.

Leider, Richard J., and Shapiro, David A. *Repacking Your Bags: Lighten Your Load for the Rest of Your Life.* (San Francisco, CA: Berrett-Koehler, 1955).

CHAPTER 8

GETTING ALONG WITH YOUR MANAGER

Learning Objectives

After reading the information and doing the exercises in this chapter, you should be able to:

▼ Recognize the impact your manager has on your future

▼ Select several tactics for creating a favorable impression on your present or future manager

▼ Select several tactics for dealing with your manager in a constructive manner

▼ Deal effectively with a manager whom you perceive as being intolerable

*K*evin, an accounts receivable specialist, felt privileged to be asked to select the site for the company's annual meeting. However, he would need final approval from his manager before a site was approved. Kevin located a site in a nearby suburb that he thought would be ideal for the meeting. Twice he brought back information about the proposed sight to Arlene, his manager. Kevin talked in terms of the amount of square feet available, the number of seats, and dining facilities. Yet Arlene was non-committal about his proposal and asked Kevin to return again to discuss the matter further.

As Kevin looked around Arlene's office, a thought flashed through his mind: "Arlene isn't buying what I'm proposing because I'm relying too much on words, facts, and figures. She's the visual type who likes graphics, photos, and actually touching something."

Kevin returned two days later with several photos about the meeting site, including the room where the meeting would be held. He picked up a brochure from the hotel owner and also took a few instant photos of his own. Within five minutes after seeing the photos, Arlene said, "Great idea for the site. Please give me the necessary forms to sign."

Kevin was finally successful in accomplishing what he needed with his manager because he adapted to her style—a person who responds best to visual information. Understanding and adapting to your manager's style is but one of many approaches to establishing a good working relationship with him or her. And getting along well with your manager is the most basic strategy of getting ahead in your career. If you cannot gain favor with the boss, it will be difficult to advance to higher positions or earn much more money. The boss might be more of a traditional boss such as a person with the title of manager or supervisor. Or the boss might be a team leader who typically has less formal authority than a manager or supervisor. Our comments about relationships with managers generally apply equally well to team leaders.

Your manager or team leader is always the person who is contacted first when someone wants to determine what kind of employee you are. Usually this information is sought when you are being considered for transfer, promotion, or a position with another firm.

In this chapter we present a variety of approaches that lead to constructive relationships with an immediate superior. The approaches are grouped for convenience into three categories: creating a favorable impression on your manager or team leader, dealing with your manager directly, and coping with an intolerable manager.

Before reading further, do Human Relations Self-Assessment Exercise 8-1. It will sensitize you to the importance of getting along with your manager or team leader, even if you do not currently have one.

CREATING A FAVORABLE IMPRESSION ON YOUR MANAGER OR TEAM LEADER

The strategies and tactics in this section all help you create a favorable impression on the manager or team leader. The term *impression* refers to

---

HUMAN RELATIONS SELF-ASSESSMENT EXERCISE 8-1

How Well Do You and Your Manager Communicate?

Here's a quick way to measure the quality of your communications with your immediate superior. If you are not currently working, think back to the last time you had a manager. Read the following statements, and circle either A (*Agree*) or D (*Disagree*).

1. I can ask for help without feeling embarrassed.	A D
2. My manager recognizes the good things that I do.	A D
3. I understand what my manager expects of me.	A D
4. My manager coaches me toward improvement when I need it.	A D
5. I am aware of the reasons for the major decisions my manager made recently.	A D
6. My manager understands my personal goals.	A D
7. I am aware of at least two specific things I can do to get a better rating at my next performance review.	A D
8. My manager lets me know when I've made a mistake without putting me down.	A D
9. I feel free to disagree with my manager when we talk.	A D
10. My manager is aware of the basic problems I have to cope with in doing my job.	A D

Scoring and Interpretation: Count the number of As you have circled. If you circled 10, your communication with your manager is excellent; 9 or 8 is good; 7 or 6, about average; 5 or less, needs improvement.

SOURCE: Adapted from *Practical Supervision,* sample issue, 1996.

a true impression, not a false one. Following these straightforward suggestions helps you deserve a positive reputation.

DISPLAY GOOD JOB PERFORMANCE

Good job performance remains the most effective strategy for impressing your manager. When any rational manager evaluates a group member's performance, the first question asked is: "Is this employee getting the job done?" And you cannot get the job done if you are not competent. Many factors contribute to whether you can become a competent performer. Among them are your education, training, personality characteristics, job experience, and special skills such as being able to organize your work.

An advanced way of displaying good job performance is to assist your manager with a difficult problem he or she faces. Your manager, for example, might need to operate equipment outside his or her area of expertise. If you show the manager how to operate the equipment, he or she will think highly of your job performance. Another example would be helping your manager get ready for an important meeting with higher management by you preparing the slides.

DISPLAY A STRONG WORK ETHIC

In Chapter 2 a strong work ethic was described as a contributor to self-motivation. (A strong **work ethic** is a firm belief in the dignity and value of work.) Having a strong work ethic is also important for favorably impressing a manager. An employee with a strong work ethic will sometimes be excused if his or her performance is not yet exceptional. This is true because the manager assumes that a strong work ethic will elevate performance eventually. Six suggestions follow for demonstrating a strong work ethic.

1. *Work hard and enjoy the task.* By definition, a person with a strong work ethic works diligently and has strong internal motivation. The person may appreciate external rewards yet appreciates the importance of any work that adds value to society.

2. *Demonstrate competence even on minor tasks.* Attack each assignment with the recognition that each task performed well, however minor, is one more career credit. A minor task performed well paves the way for your being given more consequential tasks.

3. *Assume personal responsibility for problems.* An employee with a problem will often approach the manager and say, "We have a tough problem to deal with." The connotation is that the manager should be helping the employee with the problem. A better impression is created when the employee says, "I have a tough problem to deal with, and I would like your advice." This statement implies that you are willing to assume responsibility for the problem and for any mistake you may have made that led to the problem.

4. *Assume responsibility for free-floating problems.* A natural way to display a strong work ethic is to assume responsibility for free-floating (nonassigned) problems. Taking on even a minor task, such as ordering lunch for a meeting that is running late, can enhance the impression one makes on a manager.

5. *Get your projects completed promptly.* A by-product of a strong work ethic is an eagerness to get projects completed promptly. People with a strong work ethic respect deadlines imposed by others. Furthermore, they typically set deadlines of their own more tightly than those imposed by their bosses.

6. Accept undesirable assignments willingly. Another way of expressing a strong work ethic is to accept undesirable assignments willingly. Look for ways to express the attitude, "Whether this assignment is glamorous and fun is a secondary issue. What counts is that it is something that needs doing for the good of the company."

BE DEPENDABLE AND HONEST

Dependability is a critical employee virtue. If an employee can be counted on to deliver as promised and to be at work regularly, that employee has gone a long way toward impressing the boss. A boss is uncomfortable not knowing whether an important assignment will be accomplished on time. If you are not dependable, you will probably not get your share of important assignments. Honesty is tied to dependability because a dependable employee is honest about when he or she will have an assignment completed.

Dependability and honesty are important at all job levels. One of the highest compliments a manager can pay an employee is to describe the employee as dependable. Conversely, it is considered derogatory to call any employee undependable. As one company president put it when describing a subordinate: "When he's great, he's terrific; but I can't depend on him. I'd rather he be more consistent even if he delivered fewer peak successes—at least I could rely on him."[1]

BE LOYAL

A basic way to impress your manager is to be loyal. Loyalty can be expressed to the supervisor, the department, the division, or the entire firm. In whatever form it is expressed, loyalty tends to foster a good relationship with your immediate superior. A subordinate can express loyalty in many ways other than heaping flattery on the manager and the department. Loyalty can be expressed through staying with the company, attending company picnics and other functions, using the company's products, or even wearing the company insignia.

An important characteristic of a loyal subordinate is defending the manager when the latter is under attack by people from other departments. Defending your boss under such circumstances does not necessarily mean that you think your boss is entirely correct. You can defend what deserves credit without agreeing with the boss's entire position. Assume your manager was under attack from another department for being late with the processing of materials needed by them. Your manager contends that delays in shipments by suppliers have created the problem. You realize that inefficiencies in the department are also a contributing factor. You might publicly agree with your boss that supplier delays have created problems. In private, you might make suggestions to your boss for improving department efficiency.

APPRECIATE YOUR MANAGER'S STRENGTHS

You may not admire every manager or team leader to whom you report. If you focus only on the weaknesses of your boss, you will probably communicate many negative nonverbal messages to that individual. For example, when your boss is offering you suggestions, you might display a bored expression. Instead of thinking primarily about your manager's weaknesses, look for strengths. Look for answers to such questions as, "What knowledge does he or she have that can help me advance my career?" "What good points about my team leader led to his or her appointment as team leader?" or "What do my coworkers see as my manager's strengths?" The following anecdote illustrates the value of searching for a manager's good points:

> Bruce, a sales representative, recently graduated from business school. He was fired up with modern techniques of selling such as identifying the customer's most pressing problems. Bruce was perplexed about why his boss, Arnie, was considered such an outstanding sales manager. He displayed few of the techniques that Bruce had studied in school. Bruce then spoke to an aunt who worked in another department of the same company. "How come Arnie is so highly regarded? He doesn't seem to know much about sales techniques or management." The aunt replied, "You could be right. But Arnie knows how to read people and how to form good relationships. He's what is known as a good personal salesman."
>
> From that point forward Bruce looked for techniques of forming good relationships with people that Arnie used. As he showed a sincere interest in learning more from Arnie, their relationship improved.

SHOW AN INTEREST IN YOUR FIRM'S PRODUCTS OR SERVICES

Showing a genuine interest in your company and its products or services impresses superiors in both profit and nonprofit firms. This tactic works because so many workers do not identify with their employers. Many employees are not even familiar with what their organization is trying to accomplish. A natural opportunity for showing interest in your firm's products and services is to promote them. Find a way to promote your company's products or services, and you will endear yourself to top management. The next step is to casually mention that you are actively using the product. As an administrative assistant working for a printer manufacturer told a vice president:

My husband and I bought one of our desktop color printers two years ago. We've become the neighborhood print shop whenever somebody wants to prepare a fancy graphic. So far, the printer has never been back for service. Our neighbors are so impressed with the printer that two of them plan to buy one of their own.

STEP OUTSIDE YOUR JOB DESCRIPTION

Job descriptions are characteristic of a well-organized firm. If everybody knows what he or she is supposed to be doing, there will be much less confusion and goals will be achieved. This logic sounds impressive, but job descriptions have a major downside. If people engage only in work included in their job description, an "It's not my job" mentality pervades. An effective way to impress your manager is therefore to demonstrate that you are not constrained by a job description. If something needs doing, you will get it done whether or not it is your formal responsibility.

An impressive way of stepping outside your job description is to anticipate problems, even when the manager had not planned to work on them. Anticipating problems is characteristic of a resourceful person who exercises initiative. Instead of working exclusively on problems that have been assigned, the worker is perceptive enough to look for future problems. Anticipating problems impresses most managers because it reflects an entrepreneurial, take-charge attitude.

CREATE A STRONG PRESENCE

A comprehensive approach to impressing your manager or team leader and other key people in the workplace is to create a strong presence, or keep yourself in the forefront. Such actions impress key people and simultaneously help advance your career. Stephanie Sherman, a career consultant, offers this advice for creating a strong presence:

- Get involved in high-visibility projects such as launching a new product or redesigning work methods. Even an entry-level position on such a project can be impressive.

- Get involved in teams because they give you an opportunity to broaden your skills and knowledge.

- Get involved in social and community activities of interest to top management, such as those sponsored by the company. Behave professionally and use your best manners.

- Create opportunities for yourself by making constructive suggestions about earning or saving money. Even if an idea is rejected, you will still be remembered for your initiative.

- Show a willingness to take on some of the tasks that your manager doesn't like to do but would be forced to do if you did not step in.[2]

AVOID MIMICKING YOUR MANAGER OR TEAM LEADER

To favorably impress the manager, some workers virtually mimic him or her. Attempts at mimicking include wearing almost identical clothing, decorating your cubicle with the boss's favorite cartoon, and stacking your bookshelf with the boss's favorite management or human relations books. Instead of mimicking your manager's personal habits, it is better to find more substantial ways to develop rapport. At the top of the list would be to discuss mutual interests briefly as conversation warm-ups. Another rapport builder is to go along with your boss's sense of humor. For example, if your boss enjoys humorous anecdotes, emphasize these rather than rehearsed jokes.[3]

 # DEALING DIRECTLY WITH YOUR MANAGER

To develop a good relationship with your manager, you need to create a favorable impression, as already described. You also need to focus directly on your relationship with your manager in terms of your work transactions with him or her. In this section we emphasize techniques geared more toward transactions with the boss than focusing on the impression you create. (Do not be concerned about overlap in the categories.)

UNDERSTAND YOUR MANAGER

A crucial aspect of developing a good working relationship with the boss is to understand the boss, including the environment in which the boss works. An important starting point in understanding your manager is to recognize his or her style. A **style** is a person's way of doing things. Walter St. John identifies some questions that need to be answered to understand one's manager.[4]

1. What is your manager's position in the company hierarchy? What are his or her relationships with his or her manager?

2. What are your manager's blind spots, prejudices, pet peeves, and sore spots? What constitutes positive and negative words to your manager?

3. Does you manager understand better as a reader (should you send a memo) or as a listener (should you tell him or her in person)?

4. Is you manager a morning or evening person? When is the best time of the day to approach your manager?

5. What is your manager's preference for getting things done?

6. What is most important to your manager?

7. What nonverbal signals does your manager communicate to you?

Finding answers to these questions, including understanding your manager's style, may involve discussions with coworkers as well as with the boss directly. Concentrate on "how" questions, such as "This is my first report for Julie. How does she like it done? Does she want a one-page summary at the beginning of the report or at the end?" Speaking to coworkers can also reveal what kinds of attitudes your boss expects you to have. For example, does the boss really believe that the customer is always right? Your question may also reveal that your manager is jumping to please a demanding superior. If this is true, you may be expected to do the same.[5]

In addition to understanding your manager's or team leader's work style, you can also establish rapport with your boss by viewing him or her from a personal perspective. A career advisor suggests that you understand your boss as a person:

> This may not seem like a big deal, since it seems so obvious. But I'm astounded at the number of people who don't know anything personal about their boss. You work with this person at least 40 hours a week and don't know the names of her kids or what her hobbies are or what else she does when she's not at work? It isn't just knowing this stuff that matters. It's knowing it in *context*. That means seeing the boss as a whole person, with work demands, family demands and social demands. How can you really understand a boss without this fuller picture?[6]

FIND OUT WHAT YOUR MANAGER EXPECTS OF YOU

You have little chance of doing a good job and impressing your manager unless you know what you are trying to accomplish. Work goals and performance standards represent the most direct ways of learning your manager's expectations. Review your work goals and ask clarifying questions. An example would be, "You told me to visit our major customers who are 60 days or more delinquent on their accounts. Should I also visit the three of these customers who have declared bankruptcy?" In addition to having a clear statement of your goals, it is helpful to know the priorities attached to them. In this way you will know which task to execute first.

A **performance standard** is a statement of what constitutes acceptable performance. These standards can sometimes be inferred from a job description. For example, part of the job description of a payroll specialist is to "calculate and maintain local, state, and federal tax returns." The payroll specialist would therefore be meeting a standard by accurately computing these taxes. Performance standards are sometimes stated in quantitative terms, such as, "process an average of 50 medical insurance claims per day."

> The answer to what is expected of you can be surprising. Jeremy took a position as a management trainee in a bank. Wanting to do a good job, Jeremy actively campaigned among people in his network to transfer their checking accounts to the bank. Jeremy asked his manager, "I take it an important part of my job is to bring new accounts to the bank. That's what I've been doing with good results so far." The manager replied, "No, Jeremy, we actually lose money on most small checking accounts. If you are going to attract new business to the bank, make sure it's individuals who maintain large balances. Business accounts are even better."

Minimize Competitiveness with Your Manager

A delicate problem facing many ambitious workers is that they attempt to out perform their managers as if they were in competition with the manager. This situation is the most evident when the person receives frequent praise from the boss's boss. The manager of the person receiving the praise might develop feelings of envy. One way to lower the competitive threat is to search for opportunities to acknowledge the fact that your manager or team leader is expert in certain areas in which you lack expertise. Do not attempt to prove that you are smarter than your manager.[7] Such behavior will most likely breed conflict.

Another constructive method of decreasing competitiveness with your manager is to share your accomplishments with him or her. Sharing accomplishments is honest because most higher-level jobs are team efforts. A person who successfully completes a big project has received help from many people. Input and encouragement from the manager are usually part of the help received. Upon successful completion of the project, share credit for the accomplishment with your manager. The credit sharing reflects good courtesy on your part and will help you cement the relationship.

Bring Forth Solutions as well as Problems

An advanced tactic for developing a good working relationship with your immediate superior is to bring to your boss's attention solutions, not just problems. Too often, group members ask to see their bosses only when they have problems requiring help. A boss under pressure may thus anticipate additional pressure when a group member asks for an appointment. The subordinate who comes forth with a solved problem is thus regarded as a welcome relief. In short, you can ease your manager's suffering by walking into his or her office and saying, "Here's what I did about that mess that was plaguing us yesterday. Everything is under control now."

Minimize Complaints

In the previous chapter we extolled the virtues of being open and honest in expressing your feelings and opinions. Nevertheless, this type of behavior when carried to excess could earn you a reputation as a whiner. Few managers want to have a group member around who constantly complains about working conditions, coworkers, working hours, pay, and so forth. An employee who complains too loudly and frequently quickly becomes labeled a pill or a pest.

Another important reason a boss usually dislikes having a subordinate who complains too much is that listening to these complaints takes up considerable time. Most managers spend a disproportionate amount of time listening to the problems of a small number of ineffective or complaining employees. Consciously or unconsciously, a manager who has to listen to many of your complaints may find a way to seek revenge.

How then does an employee make valid complaints to the manager? The answer is to complain only when justified. And when you do offer a complaint, back it up with a recommended solution. Anyone can take pot-shots at something. The valuable employee is the person who backs up these complaints with a constructive action plan. Following are two examples of complaints, backed up by action plans for remedying the complaint:

1. "I've noticed that several of us get very tired feet by the end of the working day. Maybe we could perform this work just as well if we sat on high stools."

2. "We have a difficult time handling emergency requests when you are away from the department. I would suggest that when you will be away for more than one or two hours, one of us can serve as the acting supervisor. It could be done on a rotating basis to give each of us some supervisory experience."

AVOID BYPASSING YOUR MANAGER

A good way to embarrass and sometimes infuriate your manager is to repeatedly go to his or her superior with your problems, conflicts, and complaints. Such bypasses have at least two strongly negative connotations. One is that you don't believe your boss has the power to take care of your problem. Another is that you distrust his or her judgment in the matter at hand. A third is that you are secretly launching a complaint against your manager.

The boss bypass is looked on so negatively that most experienced managers will not listen to your problem unless you have already discussed it with your immediate superior. There *are* times, however, when running around your manager is necessary; for example, when you have been unable to resolve a conflict directly with him or her (see the following section). But even under these circumstances, you should politely inform your manager that you are going to take up your problem with the next level of management.

In short, if you want to keep on the good side of your manager, bring all problems directly to him or her. If your boss is unable or unwilling to take care of the problem, you might consider contacting your boss's superior. Nonetheless, considerable tact and diplomacy are needed. Do not imply that your manager is incompetent, but merely that you would like another opinion about the issues at stake.

SUGGEST IMPROVEMENTS DURING THE PERFORMANCE EVALUATION

An effective method of enhancing your relationship with your manager is to use the performance evaluation session as an opportunity to suggest a variety of work improvements. Making suggestions for improvement during the performance evaluation is logical because one purpose of an evaluation is to bring about improvements. After your manager has completed his or her agenda, volunteer ideas for such topics as:

- Helping the department run more smoothly
- Making better use of your skills
- Saving time or money for the company
- Increasing productivity and quality[8]

Suggesting ideas of this nature communicates the fact that you perceive performance evaluation as an opportunity for both individual and company improvements. An attitude of this type will usually strengthen the relationship with your manager. If your company uses a peer evaluation system (as described in Chapter 1), look for an opportunity to make improvement suggestions to peers as well.

RESOLVE COMPETING DEMANDS OF TWO MANAGERS

A substantial change in the modern workplace is that many workers report to more than one manager. A typical arrangement is for a person to report to a manager in his or her regular or *home* department. At the same time the person also reports to the head of a project, or task force, or team. Many people like this arrangement because it adds variety and excitement to the workday. An unfortunate consequence of having two bosses, however, is that you might be caught in conflict. One boss might make a demand that is incompatible with a demand made by the other boss. You might be asked to attend two meetings at the same time, or told by both bosses that some task has to be done immediately.

A recommendation for resolving the competing demands of two managers is to assemble a list of possible solutions that you can sell to both parties. After you have prepared your solutions, explain to both managers the pros and cons of each solution. Recommend which one you think would work best, and describe how it would be implemented. Get a reaction from each manager. After you have taken the steps just indicated, you and the two bosses might have a three-way discussion to resolve the issue.[9] The three of you might decide, for example, that the only way you can get both their projects done immediately is to hire an office temporary for the duration of the project.

USE DISCRETION IN SOCIALIZING WITH YOUR MANAGER

A constant dilemma facing employees is how much and what type of socializing with the manager is appropriate. Advocates of socializing contend that off-the-job friendships lead to more natural work relationships.

Opponents of socializing with the boss say that it leads to **role confusion** (being uncertain about what role you are carrying out). For example, how can your manager make an objective decision about your salary increase on Monday morning when he or she had dinner with you on Sunday? To avoid cries of favoritism, you might be recommended for a below-average increase.

One guideline to consider is to have cordial social relationships with the manager of the same kind shared by most employees. "Cordial" socializing includes activities such as company-sponsored parties, group invitations to the boss's home, and business lunches. Individual social activities, such as camping with the boss, double-dating, and so forth are more likely to lead to role confusion.

Socializing should not include a casual romantic involvement. Romantic involvements between a superior and a subordinate are disruptive to work and morale. Coworkers usually suspect that the manager's special friend is getting special treatment and resent the favoritism.

What should you do if you and your boss seem suited for a long-term commitment? Why walk away from Mr. or Ms. Right? My suggestion is that if you do become romantically involved, one of you should request a transfer to another department. Many office romances do lead to happy marriages and other long-term relationships. At the start of the relationship, however, use considerable discretion. Engaging in personal conversation during work time, or holding hands in the company cafeteria, is unprofessional and taboo.

ENGAGE IN FAVORABLE INTERACTIONS WITH YOUR MANAGER

The many techniques described previously support the goal of engaging in favorable interactions with your manager. A study of interactions between bank employees and their supervisors showed that purposely trying to create a positive impression on the supervisor led to better performance ratings.[10] Although the finding is not surprising, it is reassuring to know that it is backed by quantitative evidence. Human Relations Self-Assessment Exercise 8-2 contains a listing of behaviors used by employees in the study to create positive interactions with their supervisors. Use these behaviors as a guide for skill building.

Although favorable interactions with a manager are valuable for relationship building, there are times when a group member has to deliver bad news. For example, you might have to inform the manager about a burst water pipe in the mainframe computer room or a bunch of customer complaints about a new product. You want to avoid being the messenger who is punished because he or she delivered bad news. Attempt to be calm and businesslike. Do not needlessly blame yourself for the problem. Mention that *we* or *the company* is facing a serious challenge. If possible, suggest a possible solution such as, "I have already investigated a backup computer service we can use until the damage is repaired."

HUMAN RELATIONS SELF-ASSESSMENT EXERCISE 8-2

Supervisor Interaction Checklist

Use the following behaviors as a checklist for achieving favorable interactions with your present manager or a future one. The more of these actions you are engaged in, the higher the probability that you are building a favorable relationship with your manager.

1. Agree with your supervisor's major opinions outwardly even when you disagree inwardly. _____

2. Take an immediate interest in your supervisor's personal life. _____

3. Praise your supervisor on his or her accomplishments. _____

4. Do personal favors for your supervisor. _____

5. Do something as a personal favor for your supervisor even though you are not required to do it. _____

6. Volunteer to help your supervisor on a task. _____

7. Compliment your supervisor on his or her dress or appearance. _____

8. Present yourself to your supervisor as being a friendly person. _____

9. Agree with your supervisor's major ideas. _____

10. Present yourself to your supervisor as being a polite person. _____

SOURCE: Adapted from Sandy J. Wayne and Gerald R. Ferris, "Influence Tactics, Affect, and Exchange Quality in Supervisor-Subordinate Interactions: A Laboratory Experiment and Field Study," *Journal of Applied Psychology*, October 1990, p. 494.

COPING WITH A PROBLEM MANAGER

Up to this point we have prescribed tactics for dealing with a reasonably rational boss. At some point in their careers many people face the situation of dealing with a problem manager—one who makes it difficult for the subordinate to get the job done. The problem is sometimes attributed to the boss's personality or incompetence. At other times, differences in values or goals could be creating the problem. Our concern here is with constructive approaches to dealing with the delicate situation of working for a problem manager.

Reevaluate Your Manager

As noted by J. Kenneth Matejka and Richard J. Dunsing, some problem managers are not really a problem. Instead, they have been misperceived by one or more group members. Some employees think they have problem managers when those bosses simply have major role, goal, or value differences. (A role in this context is the expectations of the job.) The problem might also lie in conflicting personalities, such as being outgoing or shy. Another problem is conflicting perspectives, such as being detail-oriented as opposed to taking an overall perspective.

The differences just noted can be good or bad, depending on how they are viewed and used. For example, a combination of a detail-oriented group member with an "overall perspective" boss can be a winning combination.[11]

Confront Your Manager About the Problem

A general-purpose way of dealing with a problem manager is to use confrontation and problem solving as described in Chapter 7. Because your manager has more formal authority than you, the confrontation must be executed with the highest level of tact and sensitivity. A beginning point in confronting a manager is to gently ask for an explanation of the problem. Suppose, for example, you believed strongly that your team leader snubs you because he or she dislikes you. You might inquire gently, "What might I be doing wrong that is creating a problem between us?"

Another situation calling for confrontation would be outrageous behavior by the manager, such as swearing at and belittling group members. Since several members, or all group members, are involved, a group discussion of the problem might be warranted. You and your coworkers might meet as a group to discuss the impact of the manager's style on group morale and productivity. This tactic runs the risk of backfiring if the manager becomes defensive and angry. Yet career adviser Jim Miller believes it is worth the risk, because the problem of abuse will not go away without discussion.[12]

Confrontation can also be helpful in dealing with the problem of **micromanagement,** the close monitoring of most aspects of group member activities by the manager. "Looking over your shoulder" constantly is an everyday term for micromanagement. If you feel that you are being supervised so closely that it is difficult to perform well, confront the situation. Say something of this nature, "I notice that you check almost everything I do lately. Am I making so many errors that you are losing confidence in my work?"[13] As a consequence, the manager might explain why he or she is micromanaging or begin to check on your work less frequently.

Learn from Your Manager's Mistakes

Just as you can learn from watching your manager do things right, you can also learn from watching him or her do things wrong. In the first instance, we are talking about using your manager as a positive model. "Modeling" of this type is an important source of learning on the job. Using a superior as a negative model can also be of some benefit. As an elementary example, if your manager criticized you in public and you felt humiliated, you would have learned a good lesson in effective supervision: Never criticize a subordinate publicly. By serving as a negative example, your manager has taught you a valuable lesson.

An unfortunate mistake some workers make is to yell at their manager when he or she has made a mistake (such as yelling at *you* in public).

Learning from a problem manager's mistakes can also occur when a manager is fired. Should your manager be fired, analyze the situation to avoid the mistakes he or she made. Enlist the help of others in understanding what went wrong. Did the manager get along poorly with higher-level managers? Was the manager lacking in technical expertise? Did the manager work hard enough? Did the manager commit ethical or legal violations such as sexual harassment or stealing company property? Whatever the reason, you will learn quickly what behavior the company will not tolerate. If your manager was fired simply as a way to cut costs, there is still a lesson to be learned. Attempt to prove to the company that your compensation is a good investment for the company because your work is outstanding.

WHAT TO DO WHEN YOUR MANAGER TAKES CREDIT FOR YOUR ACCOMPLISHMENTS

Imagine that you have been assigned the job of making the arrangements for a company meeting. Everything runs so smoothly that at the banquet your manager is praised for his or her fine job of arranging the meeting. You smolder while he or she accepts all the praise without mentioning that you did all the work. How should you handle a problem manager of this type—one who takes credit for your accomplishments?

Remember, first, that in one sense your manager does deserve much of the credit. Managers are responsible for the accomplishments and failures of their subordinates. Your boss had the good sense to delegate the task to the right person. Nevertheless, a self-confident manager would share the credit with you. To get the credit you deserve for your ideas and accomplishments, try these suggestions:

1. *Supply the pieces, but let others fit them together.* Suppose, for example, you were talking to your boss's boss at the company meeting mentioned previously. You might state, "I'm happy that people enjoyed this meeting. I enjoyed being given so much responsibility for helping our department arrange this meeting." Your boss's boss may get the point without your disputing what your manager said.

2. *Try a discreet confrontation.* The manager who is taking credit for your accomplishments may not realize that you are being slighted. A quiet conversation about the issue could prevent recurrences. You might gently ask, for example, "At what point do I get recognition for doing an assigned task well? I noticed that my name was not mentioned when our department received credit for setting up a new billing system." (It was you who did 95 percent of the work on the system.)

3. *Take preventive measures.* A sensible way to receive credit for your accomplishments is to let others know of your efforts *while* you are doing the work. This is more effective than looking for recognition after your manager has already taken credit for your accomplishments. Casually let others know what you are doing, including your boss's boss and other key people. In this way you will not sound immodest or aggressive—you are only talking about your work.

4. *Present a valid reason for seeking recognition.* By explaining why you want recognition, you will not seem unduly ambitious or pushy to your manager. You might say "I am trying to succeed in this company. It would help me to document my performance. Would it therefore be possible for my name to also appear on the report of the new billing system?"[14]

HOW TO WORK WITH A DISORGANIZED BOSS

Many well-organized people report to disorganized managers, creating the opportunity for tension and personality clashes. Under these circumstances, the well-organized group member faces the challenge of creating a good working relationship. In contrast, a well-organized boss is unlikely to put up with a disorganized subordinate for long. Given that the well-organized group member cannot readily fire the boss, he or she faces the task of forever compensating for the boss's disorganization For example, many assistants have to spend time searching for the misplaced files of their bosses—both hard-copy and disk files.

According to management consultant Deborah Zeigler, you can take several steps to facilitate a good working relationship with a disorganized manager.[15] Begin by identifying goals and priorities. Find out what the organization and department are attempting to accomplish and what your boss expects of you. This basic information can be used as a wedge to encourage your boss to be better organized.

The second step is to communicate your concerns to your manager about how his or her work habits could be interfering with goal attainment. Tact and diplomacy are essential. You might say, for example, "I want to prepare a chart explaining our need for more salespeople, but I can't do it without the figures you promised me last week."

Third, rely on coworkers and others throughout the company to supplement your boss as an information source. When your manager is unavailable (disorganized people are often difficult to find) or does not have the information you need, network members might be able to help. In the previous example, maybe somebody else can provide the figures you need.

A fourth step is to become familiar with your boss's primary problems in organization. If you know your manager has difficulty getting projects completed on time, step in well before the deadline to offer encouragement and assistance. You might present a chart to your boss estimating how close the project should be to completion. If you offer help rather than criticism, your contribution will be valued.

HOW TO GENTLY GET AWAY FROM YOUR MANAGER

Perhaps you have tried long and hard to develop a better working relationship with your manager but the situation is still intolerable. Three alternatives remain: You can wait for your manager to leave; you can leave the company; or you can look for a job in the same firm. It generally makes the most sense to pursue the last course of action, particularly if you are satisfied with the firm.

The major strategy for getting away from your supervisor is to market yourself to other key managers in the company.[16] Make others aware of your accomplishments through such means as volunteering for committee work or getting your name in the company newsletter. Another method is to make personal contacts through such means as joining company teams or clubs.

While you are developing your contacts, speak to your manager about a transfer. Point out that, although you are satisfied with your job, you value broad experience at this point in your career. Unfortunately, weak managers generally are reluctant to recommend subordinates for transfer.

Another recommended approach is to speak directly to the human resources department about your dilemma. Point out quietly that you want to be considered a candidate for transfer to another department. Suggest that you could make a bigger contribution if you worked for a manager who gave you more responsibility. However, never say anything derogatory about your present manager. Such a practice is strictly taboo.

A unifying theme exists to the aforementioned seven approaches for dealing with a problem manager. Continue to perform well despite your short-term problems. If your manager is indeed a poor performer or has a personality problem, top management is probably aware of the situation. You will be admired for your ability to cope with the situation. Performing poorly because you perceive your manager as a problem is self-defeating.

SUMMARY

Developing a favorable relationship with your manager is the most basic strategy of getting ahead in your career. Your manager influences your future because he or she is often asked by other prospective superiors to present an opinion about your capabilities.

A general strategy for developing a good relationship with your manager is to create a favorable impression. Specific tactics of this type include:

1. Display good job performance.

2. Display a strong work ethic. (Use such means as demonstrating competence on even minor tasks, assuming personal responsibility for problems, and complete projects promptly.)

3. Be dependable and honest.

4. Be loyal.

5. Appreciate your manager's strengths.

6. Show an interest in your firm's products or services.

7. Step outside your job description (do job tasks not required).

8. Create a strong presence (keep yourself in the forefront).

9. Avoid mimicking your manager or team leader.

Many tactics for developing a good relationship with your manager require that you deal directly with him or her, including:

1. Understand your manager.

2. Find out what your manager expects of you.

3. Minimize competitiveness with your manager.

4. Bring forth solutions as well as problems.

5. Minimize complaints.

6. Avoid bypassing your manager.

7. Suggest improvements during the performance evaluation.

8. Resolve competing demands of two managers.

9. Use discretion in socializing with your manager.

10. Engage in favorable interactions with your manager.

Coping with a manager you perceive to be a problem is part of getting along with him or her. Reevaluate you manager to make sure you have not misperceived him or her. It is important to confront your manager about your problem. Often this problem is a case of being micromanaged. Learning from your problem manager's mistakes is recommended, including if he or she is fired.

When your manager takes credit for your accomplishments, consider these tactics: Give enough information to others so that they can figure out what you have done; discreetly confront your manager; take preventive measures by keeping others informed of work in progress; and present a valid reason for seeking recognition.

Working with a disorganized manager can lead to tension and a personality clash. Under these circumstances, tactfully explain how your manager's work habits create problems in attaining work goals. Rely on others to help you attain the information you need to accomplish work for your boss. Also, recognize your boss's biggest problems in organization and offer direct assistance.

When your relationship with your manager does not improve, it may be necessary to seek a transfer. The best method is to market yourself to other key managers in the company. This may involve establishing a network of contacts. Also, speak to your manager about a transfer without speaking of dissatisfaction, and present your case to the human resources department.

Questions and Activities

1. Suppose your manager reads this chapter. How might this influence the effectiveness of your using the strategies and tactics described here?

2. Identify three tactics described in this chapter that you think are the most relevant for entry-level workers. Explain.

3. Identify three tactics described in this chapter that you think are the most relevant for experienced workers. Explain.

4. Is the information presented in this chapter simply a question of "kissing up to the boss"? Explain.

5. Aside from the suggestions in the text, how else can a worker show an interest in the firm's products or services?

6. What are the disadvantages of appearing to be competitive with your manager?

7. Why is "creating a strong presence" considered to be a key strategy for getting ahead in the workplace?

8. Suppose you and a coworker are close friends. Your friend gets promoted and becomes your team leader. What should be your position about socializing with this person?

9. What would your boss have to do before you would be willing to organize a group confrontation about his or her behavior?

10. Interview an experienced manager. Ask his or her opinion about what an employee can do to create a favorable impression. Be prepared to discuss your findings in class.

REFERENCES

[1]William A. Cohen and Nuritt Cohen, "Get Promoted Fast," *Success,* July/August 1985, p. 6.

[2]Anita Bruzzese, "Get the Boss to Take Notice of You," Gannett News Service, April 21, 1997.

[3]"Should You Mimic Your Boss?" *Executive Strategies,* March 1997, p. 1.

[4]Walter D. St. John, "Successful Communications Between Supervisors and Employees," *Personnel Journal,* January 1983, p. 76.

[5]John H. Gabarro and John P. Kotter, "Managing Your Boss," *Harvard Business Review,* May-June 1993, p. 152. (*HBR Classic* reprint of article originally published in January-February 1980.)

A HUMAN RELATIONS CASE PROBLEM

The Boss Bypass

Fred was a hard-working supervisor whose demonstrated ability gave him a strong shot at a middle-management position. One morning Fred was reviewing next year's budget. He was distressed when he discovered that his budget was being cut and that he was losing one person in his department. "Sorry, things are tight and there's nothing we can do," said his manager, Ruth. Later, Fred found out that Phil, another supervisor (whose division was doing poorly), was getting a budget increase. Fred became furious and said to himself, "Of course Phil gets what he wants. He's always so buddy-buddy with Ruth."

Phil did take time to chat with Ruth. He would ask about her grandchild and offer to have lunch together. Fred had a cordial relationship with Ruth, but he mostly kept to himself and tended to his job.

Fred thought over who in the company might be able to help him work out his dispute with Ruth. He remembered that he and the president had struck up an acquaintance when they met at a music concert several months ago. "Maybe if I talk to him," Fred thought, "I can get my budget restored."

Fred sent an e-mail message to the president's office justifying why he wanted his budget and group member restored. The president thought Fred's points were sound, and he requested that Ruth reverse her decision. Although miffed, Ruth complied with the president's request.

Fred was relieved at first, but Ruth started making life miserable for him. Working over the problem in his head, Fred thought there might be one way Ruth would change her attitude toward him. "Maybe a well-placed memo asking why Ruth was never available until eleven in the morning, or saying that I can't ever talk with her because she's always showing Phil photos of her grandchild, might work."

Fred sent another electronic message to his "friend" the president, sending a copy to Ruth. He didn't hear from the president, but he did hear from Ruth. "I'm putting you on notice," she said, "for gross insubordination."

Fred said calmly, "We'll see about that." He then returned to his office and put a call through to the president, who was in a day-long meeting. Finally, at 3:00 P.M. the president called and asked him to come to his office. "Ah, sweet revenge," thought Fred.

"I understand you're not happy here, Fred," said the president.

"But . . ." Fred tried to protest.

"You know we would hate to lose someone as competent as you, but I do have some connections in other companies. I strongly suggest you let me help you find a suitable position elsewhere."

Questions

1. What errors in boss relationships did Fred commit?

2. How might Fred have attempted to improve his relationship with Ruth?

3. How should Fred respond to the president's suggestion about looking for another job elsewhere?

SOURCE: Adapted from George Milite, "Office Politics: It's Still Out There," *Supervisory Management,* July 1992, pp. 6–7.

HUMAN RELATIONS SKILL-BUILDING EXERCISE 8-1

Discussing a Sensitive Issue with Your Manager

Assume Fred decided to work directly with Ruth rather than go to the president with the budget controversy. Assume also Fred did learn about Phil receiving a budget increase. One student plays the role of Fred, who is trying to get back in Ruth's good graces. Another student plays the role of Ruth, who has granted Fred an appointment to further discuss the budget issue. The person who plays the role of Fred should work diligently at creating a favorable impression on Ruth.

[6]"How I Gained the Trust of a Difficult Boss," *Working Smart,* July 1997, p. 4.

[7]"When You Outshine Your Boss," *Working Smart,* April 1997, p. 7.

[8]"Using Evaluation Time to Improve Your Own Job," *Success Workshop* (Supplement to *Pryor Report*), May 1996, p. 2.

[9]Jay T. Knippen, Thad B. Green, and Kurt M. Sutton, "How to Handle Problems with Two Bosses," *Supervisory Management,* August 1991, p. 7.

[10]Sandy J. Wayne and Gerald R. Ferris, "Influence Tactics, Affect, and Exchange Quality in Supervisor-Subordinate Interactions: A Laboratory Experiment and Field Study," *Journal of Applied Psychology,* October 1990, pp. 487–499.

[11]J. Kenneth Matejka and Richard Dunsing, "Managing the Baffling Boss," *Personnel,* February 1989, p. 50.

[12]Quoted in Kathleen Driscoll, "Is a Tyrannical Boss Getting You Down? Don't Be Afraid to Confront Her." Rochester, N.Y., *Democrat and Chronicle,* June 14, 1995, p. 10B.

[13]"How's the View Back There?" *Working Smart,* December 1996, p. 1.

[14]*How to Win at Organizational Politics—Without Being Unethical or Sacrificing Your Self-Respect* (New York: The Research Institute of America, January 1985), pp. 7–8.

[15]"How to Work with a Disorganized Boss," *The Office Professional,* January 1994, pp. 1, 3–4.

[16]D. Keith Denton, "Survival Tactics: Coping with Incompetent Bosses," *Personnel Journal,* April 1985, p. 63.

 ## ADDITIONAL READING

Boccialetti, Gene. *It Takes Two: Managing Yourself When Working with Bosses and Other Authority Figures.* San Francisco: Jossey-Bass, 1995.

DuBrin, Andrew J. *Stand Out: 330 Ways to Gain the Edge with Bosses, Subordinates, Coworkers, and Customers.* Englewood Cliffs, NJ: Prentice Hall, 1993.

Fritz, Roger, and Kennard, Kristie. *How to Manage Your Boss,* 2nd ed. Hawthorne, NJ: Career Press, 1994.

Germer, Jim G. *How to Make Your Boss Work for You: More than 200 Hard-Hitting Strategies, Tips, and Tactics to Keep Your Career on the Fast Track.* Burr Ridge, Ill.: Business One Irwin, 1992.

Grothe, Mardy, and Wylie, Peter. *Problem Bosses.* New York: Facts on File Publications, 1987.

Hornstein, Harvey A. *Brutal Bosses and Their Prey.* New York: Riverhead Books (G.P. Putnam's Sons), 1996.

Parker, Glenn M. *Team Players and Teamwork: The New Competitive Business Strategy.* San Francisco: Jossey-Bass Publishers, 1990.

CHAPTER 9

GETTING ALONG WITH COWORKERS AND CUSTOMERS

Learning Objectives

After studying the information and doing the exercises in this chapter, you should be able to:

▼ Describe methods of taking the initiative to get along with coworkers

▼ Become an effective team player

▼ Specify methods of reacting constructively to the behavior of coworkers and teammates

▼ Specify approaches to building good relationships with customers

▼ Develop increased awareness of how to appreciate diversity among coworkers and customers

*T*ammy was a copywriter at an advertising agency that was hard hit by a decline in client advertising. Her message to the group was that advertising always runs in cycles. Tammy also noted that the bottom point had already been reached. Tammy encouraged the team by reminding them that management was attempting to increase advertising activity outside the usual channels. Tammy proved to be right. The com-

pany soon landed a few big contracts to conduct direct mail advertising. The payout to Tammy was that team spirit did not deteriorate, and two coworkers told Tammy they appreciated her support.

The brief anecdote about the copywriter illustrates the importance of making a deliberate effort to contribute to the welfare of group members. Tammy contributed to the team effort by encouraging her coworkers in times of trouble. Anyone with work experience is aware of the importance of getting along with coworkers and customers (including clients and patients). If you are unable to work cooperatively with others in the workplace, it will be difficult for you to do your job. You need their cooperation and support and they need yours. Furthermore, the leading reason employees are terminated is not poor technical skill but inability or unwillingness to form satisfactory relationships with others on the job.

In this chapter we describe a variety of approaches to help you build strong relationships with coworkers and customers. For convenience these strategies and tactics are classified into taking the initiative with coworkers, responding to coworkers, customer relationships, and appreciating diversity among coworkers and customers.

TAKING THE INITIATIVE IN COWORKER RELATIONSHIPS

The approaches in this section have one common thread—they all require you to take the initiative in establishing good relationships with coworkers. Instead of reacting to a coworker's behavior, you launch an offensive of goodwill. Expressed another way, you are *proactive* instead of *reactive*. Later we deal with reactive methods of getting along with coworkers. Remember, however, that several of the tactics and methods could fit either category.

DEVELOP ALLIES THROUGH BEING CIVIL

People who are courteous, kind, cooperative, and cheerful develop allies and friends in the workplace. Practicing basic good manners such as being pleasant and friendly is also part of being civil. Being civil helps make you stand out because many people believe that crude, rude, and obnoxious behavior has become a national problem.[1] Being civil also involves not snooping, spreading malicious gossip, or weaseling out of group presents such as shower or retirement gifts. In addition, it is important to be available to coworkers who want your advice as well as your help in times of crisis.

Closely related to being civil is maintaining a positive outlook. Everyone knows that you gain more allies by being optimistic and positive than by being pessimistic and negative. Nevertheless, many people ignore this simple strategy for getting along well with others. Coworkers are more likely to solicit your opinion or offer you help when you are perceived as a cheerful person.

From the supervisor's standpoint, an optimistic and positive employee is a greater asset than an employee with the opposite disposition. People who chronically complain are a drag on the morale of other employees in the office. People with a positive attitude tend to be asked first to try out new techniques and procedures. The reason is that they are more willing to accept change than are people with a negative outlook.

MAKE OTHER PEOPLE FEEL IMPORTANT

A fundamental principle of fostering good relationships with coworkers and others is to make them feel important. Sheila Murray Bethela advises

us to make use of the please-make-me-feel-important concept. Visualize that everyone in the workplace is wearing a small sign around the neck that says, "Please make me feel important."[2] Although the leader has primary responsibility for satisfying this recognition need, coworkers also play a key role. One approach to making a coworker feel important would be to bring a notable accomplishment of his or hers to the attention of the group. Human Relations Self-Assessment Exercise 9-1 gives you an opportunity to think through your tendencies to make others feel important.

MAINTAIN HONEST AND OPEN RELATIONSHIPS

In human relations we attach considerable importance to maintaining honest and open relationships with other people. Giving coworkers frank, but tactful, answers to their requests for your opinion is one useful way of developing open relationships. Assume that a coworker asks your opinion about a memo that he intends to send to his boss. As you read it, you find it somewhat incoherent and filled with spelling and grammatical errors. An honest response to this letter might be: "I think your idea is a good one. But I think your memo needs more work before that idea comes across clearly."

As described in Chapter 7, accurately expressing your feelings also leads to constructive relationships. If you arrive at work upset over a personal problem and appearing obviously fatigued, you can expect some reaction. A peer might say, "What seems to be the problem? Is everything all right?" A dishonest reply would be, "Everything is fine. What makes you think something is wrong?" In addition to making an obviously untrue statement, you would also be perceived as rejecting the person who asked the question.

If you prefer not to discuss your problem, an honest response on your part would be, "Thanks for your interest. I am facing some problems today. But I think things will work out." Such an answer would not involve you in a discussion of your personal problems. Also, you would not be perceived as rejecting your coworker. The same principle applies equally well to personal relationships.

BE A TEAM PLAYER

An essential strategy for developing good relationships with coworkers is to be a team player. A **team player** is one who emphasizes group accomplishment and cooperation rather than individual achievement and not helping others. Team play has surged in importance because of the current emphasis on having teams of workers decide how to improve productivity and quality. You will also have to be a team player if you reach the pinnacle of power in your organization. Executives are expected to be good team players as well as individual decision makers.

An opinion survey of high-level workers about effective tactics for getting things accomplished underscores the importance of team play. Forty-nine percent of men and 42 percent of women surveyed agreed that being a team player is an effective method of getting things accomplished on the job.[3]

HUMAN RELATIONS SELF-ASSESSMENT EXERCISE 9-1

How Important Do I Make People Feel?

Indicate on a one-to-five scale how frequently you act (or would act if the situation presented itself) in the ways indicated below: very infrequently (*VI*); infrequently (*I*); sometimes (*S*); frequently (*F*); very frequently (*VF*). Circle the number underneath the column that best fits your answer.

	VI	I	S	F	VF
1. I do my best to correctly pronounce a coworker's name.	1	2	3	4	5
2. I avoid letting other people's egos get too big.	5	4	3	2	1
3. I brag to others about the accomplishments of my coworkers.	1	2	3	4	5
4. I recognize the birthdays of friends in a tangible way.	1	2	3	4	5
5. It makes me anxious to listen to others brag about their accomplishments.	5	4	3	2	1
6. After hearing that a friend has done something outstanding, I shake his or her hand.	1	2	3	4	5
7. If a friend or coworker recently received a degree or certificate, I would offer my congratulations.	1	2	3	4	5
8. If a friend or coworker finished second in a contest, I would inquire why he or she did not finish first.	5	4	3	2	1
9. If a coworker showed me how to do something, I would compliment that person's skill.	1	2	3	4	5
10. When a coworker starts bragging about a family member's accomplishments, I do not respond.	5	4	3	2	1

Scoring and Interpretation: Total the numbers corresponding to your answers. Scoring 40 to 50 points suggests that you typically make people feel important; 16 to 39 points suggests that you have a moderate tendency toward making others feel important; 10 to 15 points suggests that you need to develop skill in making others feel important. Study this chapter carefully.

Here we describe a representative group of behaviors that contribute to team play. In addition, engaging in such behavior helps you be perceived as a team player.

1. *Share credit with coworkers.* A direct method of promoting team play is to share credit for good deeds with other team members. Instead of focusing on yourself as the person responsible for a work achievement, point out that the achievement was a team effort.

2. *Display a helpful, cooperative attitude.* Working cooperatively with others is virtually synonymous with team play. Cooperation translates into such activities as helping another worker with a computer problem, covering for a teammate when he or she is absent, and making sure a coworker has the input required from you on time.

3. *Share information and opinions with coworkers.* Teamwork is facilitated when group members share information and opinions. This is true because one of the benefits of group effort is that members can share ideas. The result is often a better solution to problems than would have been possible if people worked alone. The group thus achieves **synergy,** a product of group effort whereby the output of the group exceeds the output possible if the members worked alone.

4. *Provide emotional support to coworkers.* Good team players offer each other emotional support. Such support can take the form of verbal encouragement for ideas expressed, listening to a group member's concerns, or complimenting achievement. An emotionally supportive comment to a coworker who appears to be experiencing stress might be: "This doesn't look like one of your better days. What can I do to help?"

5. *Follow the golden rule.* The ancient adage, "Treat others the way you would like them to treat you" provides a firm foundation for effective teamwork. Although some may dismiss the golden rule as a syrupy platitude, it still works. For example, you would probably want someone to help you with a perplexing problem, so you take the initiative to help others when you have the expertise needed.

6. *To establish trust, keep confidential information private.* Confidential information shared with you by a teammate should not be shared with others. Trust is exceedingly difficult to regain after a person has been betrayed.

7. *Avoid becoming part of a clique within the group.* As a member of a clique, you stand a good chance of alienating members of the larger group. You will therefore be perceived as a poor team player.

8. *Avoid actions that could sabotage or undermine the group in any way.* Frequently criticizing group members directly or complaining about them to outsiders works against the best interest of the group. Members within the group, as well as the team leader, will most likely hear that you criticized them to an outsider, thus doing severe damage to your ability to work cooperatively with them.

9. *Engage in shared laughter.* Laughter is a natural team builder that enhances understanding and empathy, essential ingredients for team play. The individual can trigger laughter by making humorous comments related to a situation at hand, or making in-group jokes. A harmless prank, such as placing a stuffed animal collection on a teammate's desk, can also inject the right amount and type of humor.

10. *Attend company-sponsored social events.* A worker's reputation as a team player is often judged both on the job and in company-sponsored social events such as parties, picnics, and athletic teams. If you attend these events and participate fully, your reputation as a team player will be enhanced. Company-sponsored social events are also important because they provide an opportunity to build rapport with coworkers. Rapport, in turn, facilitates teamwork.

11. *Carefully manage the challenge of being the manager's favorite.* A natural tendency is for a manager to rely most heavily on one or two team members who are the hardest working or most talented. Other team members may become envious of the "boss's pet." As a consequence, the favored team member or members may find themselves alienated from the group. The favored team player can soften the problem in two ways. First, he or she should not mention being favored or brag about his or her relationship with the manager. Second, when receiving another plum assignment from the boss (such as a trade-show visit), the person might suggest that another team member deserves a turn at such an activity.

The eleven points just made contribute specifically to effective team play. Recognize also that all other actions directed toward good coworker relationships will enhance team play.

AVOID BACKSTABBING

A special category of disliked behavior is **backstabbing,** an attempt to discredit by underhanded means such as innuendo, accusation, or the like. A backstabber might drop hints to the boss, for example, that a coworker performs poorly under pressure or is looking for a new job. Sometimes the backstabber assertively gathers information to backstab a coworker. He or she might engage another worker in a derogatory discussion about the boss and then report the coworker's negative comments back to the boss.

Backstabbing tends to rise as the pressure for jobs increases. A career counselor noted that during a period of intense job competition, "People seem inclined to stab before they get stabbed themselves."[5] An implication to be drawn here is that, when jobs and promotions are in short supply, a person might be more inclined to backstab. The practice is still unethical and can backfire. A person who develops a reputation as a backstabber will receive poor cooperation from coworkers. The person might also be considered untrustworthy by management, thus retarding his or her own career.

REACTING CONSTRUCTIVELY TO THE BEHAVIOR OF COWORKERS

You are often forced to react to the actions and words of coworkers. How you react influences the quality of your relationship with them. In this section of the chapter, we describe a number of time-tested ways of reacting constructively to the behavior of coworkers. (**Behavior** refers to the tangible acts or decisions of people, including both their actions and words.)

FOLLOW GROUP STANDARDS OF CONDUCT

The basic principle to follow in getting along with coworkers is to follow **group norms.** These refer to the unwritten set of expectations for group members—what people ought to do. Norms become a standard of what each person should do or not do within the group. Norms also provide general guidelines for reacting constructively to the behavior of coworkers. Norms are a major component of the **organizational culture,** or values and beliefs of the firm that guide people's actions. In one firm, the norms and culture may favor hard work and high quality. In another firm, the norms and culture may favor a weaker work ethic.

Group norms also influence the social aspects of behavior on the job. These aspects of behavior relate to such things as the people to have lunch with, getting together after work, joining a company team, and the type of clothing to wear to work.

Workers learn about norms both through observation and direct instruction from other group members. If you do not deviate too far from these norms, much of your behavior will be accepted by the group. If you deviate too far, you will be subject to much rejection and the feeling of being isolated. In some instances, you might even be subjected to verbal abuse if you make the other employees look bad.

Getting along too well with coworkers has its price as well. The risk of conforming too closely to group norms is that you lose your individuality. You become viewed by your superiors as "one of the office gang" rather than a person who aspires to move up in the organization.

Express an Interest in the Work of Others

Almost everyone is self-centered to some extent. Thus, topics that are favored are ones closely related to themselves, such as their children, friends, hobbies, work, or possessions. Sales representatives rely heavily on this fact in cultivating relationships with established customers. They routinely ask the customer about his or her hobbies, family members, and work activities. You can capitalize on this simple strategy by asking coworkers and friends questions such as these:

How is your work going? (*Highly recommended.*)

How are things going for you?

How did you gain the knowledge necessary for your job?

How does the company use the output from your department?

How does your present job fit in with your career plans?

How did Mitzie do in the county cat show?

A danger in asking questions about other people's work is that some questions may not be perceived as well intentioned. There is a fine line between honest curiosity and snooping. You must stay alert to this subtle distinction.

Be a Good Listener

After you ask questions, you must be prepared to listen to the answers. The simplest technique of getting along with coworkers, friends, and acquaintances is to be a good listener. The topics you should be willing to listen to during working hours include job problems and miscellaneous complaints. Lunch breaks, beverage breaks, and after hours are better suited to listening to people talk about their personal lives current events, sports, and the like.

Becoming an effective listener takes practice. As you practice your listening skills try the suggestions offered in Chapter 5. The payoff is that listening builds constructive relationships both on and off the job. Too often, people take turns talking rather than listening to each other. The result is that neither party feels better as a result of the conversation.

USE APPROPRIATE COMPLIMENTS

An effective way of developing good relationships with coworkers and friends is to compliment something with which they closely identify, such as their children, spouses, hobbies, or pets. Paying a compliment is a form of **positive reinforcement,** rewarding somebody for doing something right. The right response is therefore strengthened, or reinforced. A compliment is a useful multipurpose reward.

Another way of complimenting people is through recognition. The suggestions made earlier about making people feel important are a way of recognizing people, and therefore compliments. Investing a small amount of time in recognizing a coworker can pay large dividends in terms of cultivating an ally. Recognition and compliments are more likely to create a favorable relationship when they are appropriate. *Appropriate* in this context means that the compliment fits the accomplishment. Praise that is too lavish may be interpreted as belittling and patronizing.

Let's look at the difference between an appropriate and an exaggerated compliment over the same issue. An executive secretary gets a fax machine operating that was temporarily not sending messages.

Appropriate compliment: Nice job, Stephanie. Fixing the fax machine took considerable skill. We can now resume sending important fax messages.

Exaggerated compliment: Stephanie, I'm overwhelmed. You're a world-class fax machine specialist. Are there no limits to your talents?

Observe that the appropriate compliment is thoughtful and is proportionate to what Stephanie accomplished. The exaggerated compliment is probably wasted because it is way out of proportion to the magnitude of the accomplishment.

DEAL EFFECTIVELY WITH DIFFICULT PEOPLE

A major challenge in getting along well with coworkers is dealing constructively with difficult people. A coworker is classified as difficult if he or she is uncooperative, touchy, defensive, hostile, or even very unfriendly. Exhibit 9-1 presents a humorous typology of negative or difficult people. Rather than attempt to list different tactics for dealing with specific types of difficult people, here we present five widely applicable approaches for dealing with such individuals.

Take Problems Professionally, Not Personally

A key principle in dealing with a variety of personalities is to take what they do professionally, not personally. Difficult people are not necessarily out to get you. You may just represent a stepping-stone for them to get what they want.[6] For example, if a coworker insults you because you need his help Friday afternoon, he probably has nothing against you personally. He just prefers to become mentally disengaged from work that Friday afternoon. Your request distracts him from mentally phasing out of work as early as he would like.

Use Tact and Diplomacy in Dealing with Annoying Behavior

Coworkers who irritate you rarely do annoying things on purpose. Tactful actions on your part can sometimes take care of these annoyances without your having to confront the problem. Close your door, for example, if noisy coworkers are gathered outside. Or try one woman's method of getting rid of office pests: She keeps a file open on her computer screen and gestures to it apologetically when someone overstays a visit.

Sometimes subtlety doesn't work, and it may be necessary to diplomatically confront the coworker who is annoying you. Jane Michaels suggests that you precede a criticism with a compliment. Here is an example of this approach: "You're one of the best people I've ever worked with, but one habit of yours drives me bananas. Do you think you could let me know when you're going to be late getting back to the office after lunch?"[7]

Use Humor in Dealing with Difficult People

Nonhostile humor can often be used to help a difficult person understand how his or her behavior is blocking others.[8] Also, the humor will help defuse conflict between you and that person. The humor should point to the person's unacceptable behavior, yet not belittle him or her. Assume that Kevin (who in your opinion is a difficult person) says that he will not sign off on your report because you used the decimal instead of the metric system. You need Kevin's approval, because the boss wants a consensus report from the group. You ask Kevin again the next day, and he still refuses to sign.

To gain Kevin's cooperation, you say: "I'm sorry we upset your scientific mind. But I swear on a stack of Bibles, one meter high, all future reports will use the metric system. Will you please affix your signature one centimeter below mine? By the way, did you see that 45.45-meter field goal the Ram kicker made in yesterday's game?" With a grin on his face, Kevin replies, "Okay, give me the report to sign." (The touch of humor here indicates that you respect Kevin's desire to convert to the metric system, but you also acknowledge that it can sometimes be impractical.)

EXHIBIT 9-1

THE MANY FACES OF NEGATIVITY

- *The jeer-leader.* Loves bad news, pokes fun at those who try and fail, puts down newcomers, especially those with new ideas and fresh enthusiasm.

- *The subtle saboteur.* Feigns enthusiasm for organization, career, teammates, but secretly works to upset the applecart whenever possible.

- *The carper.* Never a good word to say about anything or anybody. Skilled at finding fault, ridiculing, downplaying successes, exaggerating weaknesses.

- *The "grass is greener" type.* Wishes he or she were elsewhere, but has no intention of leaving.

- *The bottleneck.* Forever late on everything: projects, meetings, deadlines. Doesn't get serious about his or her work until everybody else is waiting.

- *The lone wolf.* Can't stand being part of anything: a team, a project, group functions. Independent to a fault—and makes no attempt to hide solitary preferences.

- *Chicken Little.* No matter how sunny things seem to be, he or she will always find a cloud to cast a shadow. ("What a great year we're having!" "Yeah, but wait until fourth-quarter sales come in.")

- *The bare minimum.* Will only do what's spelled out in writing. No more, no less. Chides others who give more than expected.

- *The topper.* Delights in one-upping everyone else's stories, experiences, and successes. First thing out of his or her mouth is usually something like, "Oh that's nothing. Wait until you hear what I did."

- *The sad sack.* "Nothing goes right, nobody likes me, I'll never be good enough." Plenty of self-pity, and loves to share it with anyone who'll listen."

- *The ostrich.* Head is in the sand about everything. Plays dumb to get attention, special treatment. Never on the same page as everyone else.

SOURCE: Reprinted with permission from a brochure for ETC w/Career Track, 3085 Center Green Drive, Boulder, CO, 80301-5408.

Listen and Respond

As usual, active listening improves many problems in human relations. Give the difficult person ample opportunity to express his or her concerns, doubts, anger, or other feelings. Then acknowledge your awareness of the person's position.[9] An example: "Okay, you tell me that management is really against us and, therefore, we shouldn't work so hard." After listening, present your perspective in a way such as this: "Your viewpoint may be valid based on your experiences. Yet so far, I've found management here to be on my side." This exchange of viewpoints is less likely to lead to failed communication than if you are judgmental with a statement such as, "You really shouldn't think that way."

Reduce Nonverbal Differences between You and the Other Person

To gain cooperation from the person you perceive to be difficult, blend a little with him or her. People naturally resist cooperating with somebody who is against them. A potentially useful tactic is, therefore, to reduce obvious differences such as body posture and voice volume (as in mirroring). Voice volume is a good example. If the obstinate person speaks softly, you speak softly. If he or she speaks loudly, elevate your voice volume. Two researchers who have studied difficult people note, "You synchronize your behavior, then take charge of the energy and take it where you want it to go."[10]

You may have to use a combination of the five tactics described in this section to deal effectively with a difficult person. The point of these tactics is not to out-manipulate or subdue a difficult person, but to establish a cordial and productive working relationship.

FACE MATURELY THE CHALLENGE OF THE OFFICE ROMANCE

As described in the discussion about socializing with the boss (Chapter 8), office romances can be disruptive to morale and productivity. Coworker romances are a more widespread potential problem, because more romances take place between coworkers on the same level than between superiors and subordinates. As more women have entered the workforce in professional positions, and as professionals work longer hours, the office has become a frequent meeting place. Many companies have policies against managers dating people below them in the hierarchy, but few companies attempt to restrict same-level romantic involvements. Nevertheless, sensitivity is required to conduct an office romance that does not detract from your professionalism.

Many companies are concerned about information leakage within their organization. If you date a person who has access to confidential information (such as trade secrets), management might be concerned that you are a security risk. You therefore might miss out on some opportunities for better assignments.

It is important not to abuse company tolerance of the co-worker romance. Do not invite the person you are dating to meals at company expense, take him or her on nonessential business trips, or create projects to work on jointly.

Strive to keep the relationship confidential and restricted to after hours. Minimize talking to coworkers about the relationship. Such behavior as holding hands or kissing in public view is regarded as poor office etiquette.

Should your coworker romance terminate, you face a special challenge. You must now work together cooperatively with a person toward whom you may have angry feelings. Few people have the emotional detachment necessary to work smoothly with a former romantic involvement. Extra effort will therefore be required on both your parts.

BUILDING GOOD RELATIONSHIPS WITH CUSTOMERS

Success on the job also requires building good relationships with both external and internal customers. *External customers* fit the traditional definition of customer that includes clients and guests. External customers can be classified as either retail or industrial. The latter represents one company buying from another, such as purchasing steel. *Internal customers* are the people you serve within the organization, or those who use the output from your job. For example, if you design computer graphics, the other people in the company who receive your graphics are your internal customers.

The information already presented about getting along with your manager (in Chapter 8) and coworkers dealt with internal customers. Here we emphasize providing good service (or delight) to external customers. As usual, categories overlap and some techniques for serving external customers would also work well with internal customers, and vice versa.

Research supports the widely accepted belief that good customer service is good for business. Figures gathered by a marketing consulting firm show that 68 percent of customers will remain loyal to a brand if they only needed one contact with a company to resolve a problem with a product. However, only 33 percent remain loyal if it requires three or more contacts to resolve a problem.[11] Another study documenting the importance of good customer service was conducted in the automobile service field. As shown in Figure 9-1, profits jump considerably as the customer is retained over time.[12] And good service is the primary factor that keeps customers coming back.

Before reading the suggestions for high-level customer service presented next,[13] do Human Relations Self-Assessment Exercise 9-1. The exercise is designed to help you think through your present tendencies toward serving others.

1. *Establish customer satisfaction goals.*   Decide jointly with your manager how much you intend to help customers. Find answers to questions such as the following: Is your company attempting to satisfy every customer within ten minutes of his or her request? Are you striving to provide the finest customer service in your field? Is your goal zero defections to competitors? Your goals will dictate how much and the type of effort you put into pleasing customers.

2. *Understand your customer's needs and place them first.*   The most basic principle of selling is to identify and satisfy customer needs. Many customers may not be able to express their needs clearly. Also, they many not be certain of their needs. To help identify customer needs, you may have to probe for more information. For example, an associate in a cor-

Figure 9-1   Profits Over Time Per Auto Servicing Customer

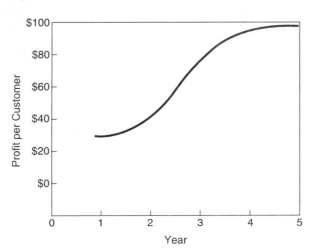

sumer electronics store may have to ask, "What uses do you have in mind for your television receiver aside from watching regular programs? Will you be using it to display digital photographs?" Knowing such information will help the store associate identify which television receiver will satisfy the customer's needs.

After you have identified customer needs, focus on satisfying them rather than doing what is convenient for you or the firm. Assume, for example, the customer says, "I would like to purchase nine reams of copier paper." The sales associate should not respond, "Sorry, the copying paper comes in boxes of ten, so it is not convenient to sell you nine reams." The associate might, however, offer a discount for the purchase of the full ten-ream box if such action fits company policy.

3. *Show care and concern.* During contacts with your customer, show concern for his or her welfare. Ask questions such as the following: "How have you enjoyed the television set you bought here awhile back?" "How are you feeling today?" After asking the question, project a genuine interest in the answer. A strictly business approach to showing care and concern is to follow up on requests. A telephone call or e-mail message to the requester of your service is usually sufficient follow-up. A follow-up is effective because it completes the communication loop between two people.

4. *Communicate a positive attitude.* A positive attitude is conveyed by factors such as appearance, friendly gestures, a warm voice tone, and good telephone communication skills. If a customer seems apologetic about making a heavy demand, respond, "No need to apologize. My job is to please you. I'm here to serve."

5. *Make the buyer feel good.* A fundamental way of building a customer relationship is to make the buyer feel good about himself or herself. Also, make the buyer feel good because he or she has bought from you. Offer compliments about the customer's healthy glow, or a report that specified vendor requirements (for an industrial customer). An effective feel-good line is, "I enjoy doing business with you."

HUMAN RELATIONS SELF-ASSESSMENT EXERCISE 9-1

Would You Buy from You?

One of the most effective ways to assess your effectiveness in handling customers is via the question: "If you were the customer, would you buy from yourself?" You would if you scored well on the following quiz. Answer each question by checking the appropriate blank. If you do not deal with external customers, take this quiz in relation to your handling of internal customers.

	Yes	*No*
1. Is your image one of honest and straightforward sincerity?	____	____
2. Based on your experience with customers over about the past year, *from the buyer's point of view,* would you be classified as reliable?	____	____
3. Could you say your customers obtained special benefits dealing with you that they wouldn't have obtained from others?	____	____
4. Do you think you come off as an expert in the eyes of your customers?	____	____
5. Have you been effective helping to solve customer problems?	____	____
6. Wherever possible, would you say you handled customer complaints to the buyer's satisfaction?	____	____
7. Is *integrity* one of the most important words in your vocabulary?	____	____
8. Apart from your business dealings, do you think customers believe you have their personal welfare and well-being at heart?	____	____
9. Can you honestly say most of your company's customers believe you have their personal welfare and well-being at heart?	____	____
10. Do customers regard you as a good, reliable source of product and industry information?	____	____
11. Has doing business with you contributed positively to most of your customers' profit performance?	____	____
12. Would most of your company's customers continue dealing with you even if a competitor approached them with a price a little bit lower?	____	____
Total number of yes answers	____	____

Your Rating: Multiply the sum of your answers by 5. If you achieved a score of 55 or higher it's a privilege to do business with you; 50 is well above average; and 40 to 45 is mediocre.

SOURCE: Adapted from "Making . . . Serving . . . Keeping . . . Customers," 1992. Reprinted with permission of Dartnell, 4660 N. Ravenswood Ave., Chicago, IL 60640, (800) 621-5463.

6. *Smile at every customer.*   Smiling is a natural relationship builder and can help you bond with your customer. Smile several times during each customer contact, even if your customer is angry with your product or service. Yet guard against smiling constantly or inappropriately, because your smile then becomes meaningless.

7. *Display strong business ethics.*   Ethical violations receive so much publicity that you can impress customers by being conspicuously ethical. Look for ways to show that you are so ethical that you would welcome making your sales tactics public knowledge. Also, treat the customer the same way you would treat a family member or a valued friend.

8. *Be helpful rather than defensive when a customer complains.*   As described earlier, look at a complaint professionally rather than personally. Listen carefully and concentrate on being helpful. The upset customer cares primarily about having the problem resolved and does not care whether you are at fault. Use a statement such as, "I understand this mistake is a major inconvenience. I'll do what I can right now to solve the problem." Remember also that complaints that are taken care of quickly and satisfactorily will often create a more positive impression than mistake-free service.

9. *Be helpful to customers who have the wrong extension.*   When a customer has the wrong telephone extension, avoid transferring the call and possibly losing the customer. Instead, take the customer's telephone number, call the person in your company best equipped to help the customer, and ask that worker to return the customer's call.

10. *Avoid grumbling about your job in earshot of customers.* Complaining about your job in front of customers looks bad for your company and can discourage customers from returning. Furthermore, in one case a federal appeals court ruled that an ophthalmology center had the right to dismiss four nurses who grumbled about working conditions in front of patients.[14]

All of the ten points just made emphasize the importance of practicing good human relations with customers. Good customer service stems naturally from practicing good human relations.

APPRECIATING DIVERSITY AMONG COWORKERS AND CUSTOMERS

The workforce in the United States and Canada is becoming increasingly culturally diverse. We are fast approaching the point whereby the majority of new workers are women, blacks, Hispanics, and immigrants. Only one-third of the 145-million-person workforce is now native-born white males. Another key aspect of diversity is that more disabled people are joining the workforce. Diversity among customers is also increasing, reflecting the mix in society.

Appreciating diversity is generally thought of in terms of welcoming differences among people. Yet diversity expert R. Roosevelt Thomas, Jr., now proposes that diversity should be redefined as a collective of differences *and* similarities.[15] The most important general principle for human relations is that appreciating diversity leads to an appreciation of everyone, whether they are members of a minority or majority group.

Succeeding in a diverse environment requires more than avoiding discriminatory behavior. Instead, success is facilitated by working comfortably with people of different sexes, races, ethnicity, values, sexual orientations, and physical capabilities. The job applicant who exhibits an ability to work effectively in a diverse environment is at a competitive advantage for many jobs.[16] Diversity skills can sometimes be displayed by descriptions of past work and school experiences with diverse people. Speaking a second language is also impressive.

The information already presented for dealing with coworkers and customers can be applied toward building relationships with diverse groups. In addition, it is important to develop an appreciation of cultural diversity in the workplace. Toward this end we will discuss recognizing diversity on the job and describe training for such purposes.

RECOGNIZING CULTURAL DIFFERENCES

Cultural diversity can be better understood if it is recognized that many apparent differences in personality actually arise from culture. For example, both white and black North Americans feel that authority should be challenged. However, Asians and Hispanics tend to respect and obey authority. Another notable difference is that Hispanic culture perceives music, family members, and food as appropriate for the workplace. Americans and Canadians reject these practices and may regard them as unprofessional.

Some forms of discrimination become more explainable, even if still unacceptable, when their cultural origins are recognized. For example, in many Asian countries few women hold executive positions in industry. It is therefore difficult for some Asian workers employed in North America to accept women as their administrative superiors.

The key principle to recognizing cultural differences is to be alert to these differences, and to be sensitive to how they could affect your dealings with people. Recognize that not everybody fits the same stereotype and adjust your assumptions accordingly. A furniture store manager who viewed the world with a *heterosexual bias* made the following mistake: A customer said he wished to return an end table because, after he brought it home, his partner said the table just didn't fit. The store manager responded, "What didn't your wife like about the table?" The customer replied angrily, "My partner is a man, and he said the design is atrocious." The customer then demanded a refund instead of a merchandise exchange.

VALUING CULTURAL DIFFERENCES

Recognizing cultural differences is an excellent starting point in becoming a multicultural worker. More important, however, is to *value* cultural differences. The distinction goes well beyond semantics. If you place a high value on cultural differences, you will perceive people from other cultures to be different but equally good. Gunnar Beeth, the owner of an executive placement firm in Brussels, Belgium, defines a multicultural worker as ". . . someone who is deeply convinced that all cultures are equally good, enjoys learning the rich variety of foreign cultures and mostly likely has been exposed to more than one culture in childhood."[17]

Beeth notes that you cannot motivate anyone, especially someone of another culture, until that person first accepts you. A multilingual sales representative has the ability to explain the advantages of a product in other languages. In contrast, a multicultural sales rep can motivate foreigners to make the purchase. The difference is substantial.[18]

DIVERSITY AWARENESS TRAINING

To help employees relate comfortably to people of different cultures and appreciate diversity, many companies conduct **diversity awareness training.** These programs provide an opportunity for employees to develop the skills necessary to deal effectively with each other and with customers in a diverse environment.

A key component of these programs is to help workers recognize cultural differences, as previously described. Another important part of diversity awareness training is to develop empathy for diverse viewpoints. To help training participants develop empathy, representatives of various groups explain their feelings related to workplace issues. In one segment of such a program, a minority group member was seated in the middle of a circle.[19] The other participants sat at the periphery of the circle. First, the coworkers listened to a Vietnamese woman explain how she felt excluded from the in-group composed of whites and African-Americans in her department. "I feel like you just tolerate me. You do not make me feel that I am somebody important."

The next person to sit in the middle of the circle was Muslim. He complained about people wishing him Merry Christmas. "I would much prefer that my coworkers would stop to think that I do not celebrate Christian holidays. I respect your religion, but it is not my religion."

Human Relations Skill-Building Exercise 9-1 will give you direct experience in diversity awareness training. Being nonconfrontational in nature, the exercise usually leads to harmony and other positive feelings.

SUMMARY

Getting along with coworkers and customers is important for performing your job satisfactorily or better. Methods and tactics that center around taking the initiative to establish good relationships with coworkers include:

1. Develop allies through being civil.

2. Make other people feel important.

HUMAN RELATIONS SKILL-BUILDING EXERCISE 9-2

Developing Emphathy for Differences

Depending on the size and physical layout of the classroom choose one of the following exercises. If the seats are movable and the class is about 25 members or fewer, the class is organized into a large circle. Each person in turn describes in what way he or she has been perceived as different from others. The difference can include such factors as racial, ethnic, physical, religious, disability status, or speaking accent. Any difference can be meaningful. As in the accompanying text, the person explains his or her feelings about being different, including any thoughts of being discriminated against. Other group members then react to the person's perceptions. Finally, the class discusses what they have learned from the empathy-circle exercise.

If the class is bigger than 25 or the seats are stationary, the exercise just described can be conducted by having students come up in front of the class one at a time.

---

3. Maintain honest and open relationships.

4. Be a team player.

5. Avoid backstabbing.

Team player approaches include: sharing credit; a cooperative attitude; information sharing; giving emotional support; following the golden rule; establishing trust and keeping confidences; avoiding cliques; avoiding sabotaging or undermining the group; shared laughter; attending company-sponsored events; and managing the challenge of being the boss's favorite.

Methods and tactics of getting along with coworkers that center around reacting constructively to their behavior include:

1. Follow group standards of conduct.

2. Express interest in the work of others.

3. Use appropriate (nonexaggerated) compliments.

4. Deal effectively with difficult people, including taking problems professionally, using tact and diplomacy, using humor, listening and responding, and reducing nonverbal differences between you two

5. Face maturely the challenge of the office romance.

Job success also requires building good relationships with both internal and external customers. Research supports the widely accepted belief that good customer service is good for business. Representative techniques for building constructive customer relationships include: (1) Establish customer satisfaction goals, (2) understand customer needs and place them first, (3) show care and concern, (4) communicate a positive attitude, (5) make the buyer feel good, (6) smile at every customer, (7) display strong business ethics, (8) be helpful rather than defensive with customer complaints, (9) help customers who have the wrong extension, and (10) avoid grumbling in earshot of customers.

The North American workforce is becoming increasingly culturally diverse. Success on the job is facilitated by working comfortably with people of different sexes, races, religions, ethnicity, values, sexual orientations, and physical capabilities. To work comfortably with such groups, it is important to recognize cultural differences. Being alert to cultural differences enhances understanding. If you place a high value on cultural differences, you will perceive people from other cultures to be different but equally good. Being multicultural is more important than being multilingual when attempting to motivate someone from a different culture. Diversity awareness training helps workers develop the skills necessary to deal effectively with each other and customers in a diverse environment.

Questions and Activities

1. Why study about getting along with coworkers and customers? Isn't common sense good enough to develop smooth working relationships with people?

2. Why is it important to make people feel important?

3. Give an example of a group norm that exists for the class for which you are studying this text.

4. Make up an emotionally supportive statement to give to a coworker who just learned that he or she will be demoted and is upset about the circumstance.

5. Have you noticed any gender differences in the frequency of backstabbing? Explain.

6. How might placing too much emphasis on being a good team player and fitting in with the group hurt a person's chances of becoming an executive?

7. A survey of industrial customers revealed that 90 percent of them prefer the sales representatives who call on them to use a soft sell. How does this finding fit the information in this chapter about customer relationships?

8. In Japan, many middle managers are expected to regularly entertain customers until past 10 P.M. Explain whether you think this is going too far to satisfy customers.

9. What might you do to impress a job interviewer that you have good cultural diversity skills?

10. Ask a person who has achieved job success what he or she thinks are two important ways of getting along with coworkers and customers. Compare notes with classmates.

A HUMAN RELATIONS CASE PROBLEM

"I Think Better Alone"

Jimmy Yang works as a business analyst for an aerospace firm. As an analyst he carries out a variety of tasks related to developing contracts for customers. Among these tasks are keeping track of shipments by vendors, establishing a database of parts used in building a helicopter, and keeping a current record of suppliers. As Yang commented about his job, "It's not easy to explain in a few words what I do because it changes almost weekly. There are hundreds of details to take care of in preparing and maintaining a contract. It's like planning a wedding. Unless you have actually been through it, you couldn't imagine how many different suppliers get involved in launching a wedding.

"I'm learning a lot about the aerospace business. I think if I continue to perform well I'll be eligible for a promotion to supervisor in four years. A great feature of my job is that I spend part of my time talking to people in our company, and part of my time with a computer. I do word processing, spreadsheets, and graphics. Even more interesting, I get to search the Internet for some of the information we need for our contracts. To add to the excitement of my job, I get to talk to some of our suppliers and customers. It's a well-rounded job. I look forward to coming to work each day except for a few minor hassles."

Susan Perez, the program manager (much like a team leader) to whom Jimmy reports, believes strongly in teamwork. According to Perez, "Our company is built on a foundation of teamwork. We believe strongly in collective intelligence, that groups of people can solve problems better than individuals working alone. That's one of the reasons we have cubicles and open work areas. Our employees can exchange ideas freely without having to make appointments to see each other, make telephone calls, or keep sending e-mail messages back and forth to each other."

One day Perez asked Yang how much progress he had made in assembling the database of current suppliers to the company. Perez was concerned that Jimmy's project had fallen behind schedule. "I should have the report within one week," responded Jimmy. "I've been doing the most important work on assembling the database on weekends. And last weekend the office was shut down for routine maintenance on the mainframe."

"Jimmy, why must you do so much of the work on weekends? We expect you to contribute about 5 hours per week of work beyond the standard 40, but that doesn't mean you have to work every weekend."

"My problem," said Jimmy, "is that working in a team during the week slows me down. It's not easy doing precision work when you work in a team. People are always chatting or asking you questions. It's tough concentrating when you need to accomplish something that requires heavy thinking.

"If I walk away from my teammates to go off on my own project, they'll think I'm rude. We spend so much time in team meetings during the week, that it doesn't give me enough time to work on a project like assembling a database. If I had a private office I could get work done much more quickly. I think better alone."

"That's a strange reaction for a person in a company organized around teams. Teams should make work easier for you, not more difficult. How good are your teamwork skills, Jimmy?"

(Continued)

"I think my teamwork skills are plenty good. That's part of my problem. If I didn't go along with the team so much, I would have more time to get my individual work done. Being part of a team means I have to put in extra hours to get my assignments done on time. That's the reason I'm not as far along on assembling the database as you would like."

Questions

1. How can Jimmy Yang resolve his dilemma of wanting to be a good team player yet still get his work done on time?

2. If you were Susan Perez, how would you react to Yang's excuses for falling behind on his project?

3. How realistic is Perez's philosophy of teamwork?

REFERENCES

[1] Dot Yandle, "Incivility: Has It Gone Too Far to Fix?" *Success Workshop* (Supplement to *Pryor Report*), March 1997, p. 1.

[2] Shelia Murray Bethel, *Making a Difference* (New York: G. P. Putnam's Sons, 1989).

[3] Andrew J. DuBrin, "Sex Differences in the Endorsement of Influence Tactics and Political Behavior Tendencies," *Journal of Business and Psychology*, Winter 1989, pp. 1–15.

[4] Several of the items on this list are from "Golden Rule Still Shines," *Teamwork*, sample issue 1997 from Dartnell, Chicago, Ill.; Fernando Bartolome, "Nobody Trusts the Boss Completely—Now What?" *Harvard Business Review*, March-April 1989, pp. 135–142.

[5] Tony Lee, "Competition for Jobs Spawns Backstabbers and a Need for Armour," *The Wall Street Journal*, November 3, 1993, p. B1.

[6] Dru Scott, *Customer Satisfaction: The Other Half of Your Job* (Los Altos, CA: Crisp Publications, 1991), p. 16.

[7] Jane Michaels, "You Gotta Get Along to Get Ahead," *Woman's Day*, April 3, 1984, p. 58.

[8] Kaye Loraine, "Dealing with the Difficult Personality," *Supervision*, April 1989, pp. 6–8.

[9] Sam Deep and Lyle Sussman, *What to Say to Get What You Want* (Reading, MA: Addison-Wesley, 1995).

[10] Rick Kirschner and Rick Brinkman, *Dealing with Difficult People: How to Bring Out the Best in People at Their Worst* (New York: McGraw-Hill, 1994).

[11] Cited in Kathleen Driscoll, "Survival through Satisfaction," Rochester, N.Y., *Democrat and Chronicle/Times-Union*, June 10, 1996, p. 3.

[12]Frederick F. Reicheld and Earl Sasser, Jr., "Zero Defects: Quality Comes to Services," *Harvard Business Review,* September-October 1990, p. 106.

[13]Linda Thornburg, "Companies Benefit from Emphasis on Superior Customer Service," *HRMagazine,* October 1993, pp. 46–49; "Getting Closer to the Customer," *Getting Results,* August 1997, p. 8; "Complaints Are Good for You," *Working Smart,* June 1996, p. 1.

[14]Leah Beth Ward, "Grumbling about Work Could Cost Your Job," *The New York Times* syndicated story, January 13, 1997.

[15]R. Roosevelt Thomas, Jr., *Redefining Diversity* (New York: AMACOM, 1996).

[16]Arnola C. Ownby and Heidi R. Perreault, "Teaching Students to Understand and Value Diversity," *Business Education Forum,* February 1994, p. 27.

[17]Gunnar Beeth, "Multicultural Managers Wanted," *Management Review,* May 1997, p. 17.

[18]Ibid.

[19]Suzanne Elshut and James Little, "The Case for Valuing Diversity," *HRMagazine,* June 1990, pp. 50–51.

ADDITIONAL READING

Cannie, Joan Koob. *Keeping Customers for Life.* New York: AMACOM, 1991.

Caudron, Shari. "Don't Make Texaco's $175 Million Mistake." *Workforce,* March 1997, pp. 58–66.

Jones, Thomas O., and Sasser, Earl, Jr. "Why Satisfied Customers Defect." *Harvard Business Review,* November-December 1995, pp. 88–99.

Nemetz, Patricia L., and Christensen, Sandra L. "The Challenge of Cultural Diversity: Harnessing a Diversity of Views to Understand Multiculturalism." *Academy of Management Review,* April 1996, pp. 434–462.

Pine, B. Joseph II, Peppers, Don, and Rogers, Martha. "Do You Want to Keep Your Customers Forever?" *Harvard Business Review,* March-April 1995, pp. 103–114.

Settoon, Randall P., and Adkins, Cheryl L. "Newcomer Socialization: The Role of Supervisor, Coworkers, Friends, and Family Members." *Journal of Business and Psychology,* Summer 1997, pp. 507–516.

Ury, William. *Getting Past No: Negotiating with Difficult People.* New York: Bantam Books, 1991.

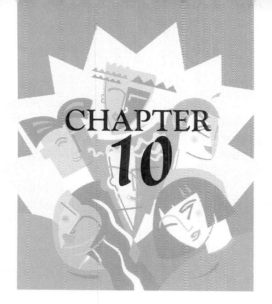

CHAPTER 10

CHOOSING A CAREER AND DEVELOPING A PORTFOLIO CAREER

Learning Objectives

After studying the information and doing the exercises in this chapter, you should be able to:

▼ Make a tentative career choice if you have not already selected a first career

▼ Identify skills that could serve as the basis for your career

▼ Appreciate the complexity of choosing a career

▼ Search for useful information about occupations and careers

▼ Apply the concept of data, people, or things to yourself

▼ Explain the basics of career switching and developing a portfolio career

Vincent Barnard was recently promoted to a supervising teller position in a bank, putting him on track to become a bank manager. Vincent enjoys his work and is proud of his accomplishments. Asked how he chose to launch his career as a teller, Vincent explained: "Four years ago as graduation was fast approaching, I didn't have a clue as to what aspect of business I should enter. One day it struck me that since I was using the Internet for so many other purposes, perhaps it could help me find a career track. After surfing in different directions, I hit upon *America's Job Bank*. Being kind of an adventurer [laughs], I thought I would poke into a table called "Largest Non-Traditional Male Occupations."

"I was surprised to find out that only 10 percent of tellers are male. I figured that if I became a teller, maybe I would stand out because of being a man. Also, I always liked banks because the work they do is so important. Next I followed through by applying to a few banks for a teller position. My job search resulted in one good job offer, and here I am today. I'm glad I put some effort into finding the right career."

Vincent's success in finding a career that is working for him so far, illustrates a major theme of this chapter: For many people, finding the right career requires careful thinking and systematic effort. If you have not already chosen a career, or are thinking of changing careers, this chapter is especially important. If you are content with your career, this chapter can be read with the intention of learning more about that vital part of your life. What a person does for a living is one of the key influences in his or her life. Your career is also a prime source of your self-concept and self-esteem.

The purpose of this chapter is to help you choose a career by describing systematic methods of career selection. For those who have already chosen a career field in general, this chapter may help you narrow down your career choice within your field. For example, a person entering the computer field might choose to emphasize those aspects of computers dealing heavily with people, such as computer sales or information systems.

SELF-KNOWLEDGE AND CHOOSING A CAREER

A **career** is a series of related job experiences that fit into a meaningful pattern. If you have a series of odd jobs all your working life, that is hardly a career. But if each job builds carefully on the previous one, we say you are "building a career." We assume that by making a sound initial choice of occupation, you will be on the first step toward building a real career. Chapters 11 through 14 provide information to help you advance in whatever career you have chosen.

A general strategy for making a sound career choice is to understand first the inner you, including what you have to offer. You then match that information with opportunities in the outside world. The Self-Knowledge Questionnaire presented in Chapter 1 asks many questions that are relevant for making a career choice. Almost any of the information provided by candid answers to those questions could help you make a sound career choice. Several specific illustrations are in order.

Question 1 asks, "How far have I gone in school?" If you answered, "Three years of high school," or "Four years of high school and two years of business school," you will need additional education for many fields. Among them are management, teaching, counseling, or social work.

Question 9 asks, "What aspect of these jobs did I enjoy?" Suppose you answered, "Anytime I was left alone to do some figuring or report writing I was happy. Thinking made me happy." Your answer could mean that you should search for a field in which working with ideas and data is more important than working with people or things. What about investigating laboratory work or financial analysis?

Question 25 asks, "What are the biggest motivational forces in my life?" Suppose you answered, "Doing exciting work, having enough money for myself and my loved ones to live well, and being well respected." An answer of this nature suggests you would be motivated to perform well in an occupation that offered mentally stimulating work, was high paying, and held in high regard by others. Perhaps selling financial services or commercial real estate would fit your interests. Or how about a career as an international art dealer, traveling in your private jet?

Some additional questions useful in clarifying the type of work you would prefer are presented in Human Relations Self-Assessment Exercise 10-1.

THE IMPORTANCE OF SKILLS IN CHOOSING A CAREER

In addition to other aspects of self-understanding, knowing which skills and abilities you possess—and enjoy performing—can be the basis for a successful career. A **skill** is a learned, specific ability such as writing a report, preparing a Web site, or conducting a job interview. A vast number of skills could be exercised in a career, including such skills as selling, calculating currency exchanges, and coaching workers. Identifying your skills is important both in choosing a career and in finding a job. Prospective employers want to know what a job candidate can actually *do*, or what skills he or she possesses.

An enlightening perspective is that your best skill represents your **core competency,** or whatever you do best. But there is more to core competency than what is suggested in your job title.[1] Your core competency is

HUMAN RELATIONS SELF-ASSESSMENT EXERCISE 10-1

Learning More About Yourself

By candidly answering the questions that follow, you may be able to develop some new understanding about your career preferences. Try to write at least 25 words in response to each question, even if your answer is uncertain.

1. What kind of work would make me proud?

_____

_____

2. What would be a horrible way for me to make a living?

_____

_____

3. How important is a high income to me? Why?

_____

_____

4. How do I really feel about what other people think of the kind of work I do?

_____

_____

5. What kind of work would really be fun for me to do?

_____

_____

6. What kind of work would I be willing to do for ten consecutive years?

_____

_____

7. What kind of work would make me feel self-fulfilled?

_____

_____

8. What is my attitude toward doing the same thing every workday?

_____

_____

9. How do I really feel about being held responsible when things go wrong?

_____

_____

the aspect of your job which you perform particularly well. As a collection agent, your core competency might be obtaining partial payments with accounts so long overdue others consider them almost uncollectible. If you have developed a core competency early in your schooling or temporary work experience, making a sound career choice is easier. An adolescent with superior skill in explaining to others how to use electronic devices might have the necessary core competency for a career in technical writing. (A big part of a technical writer's job is preparing operating manuals for equipment.)

Julie Griffin Levitt has developed a useful way of identifying skills[2] as outlined in Human Relations Self-Assessment Exercise 10-2. As you develop several of these skills to an above-average degree, they may become your core competency.

GETTING HELP FROM A CAREER COUNSELOR

In choosing a career or switching careers, a beneficial method of learning more about yourself in relation to the world of work is to obtain help from a professional **career counselor.** A counselor usually relies on a wide variety of tests plus an interview to assist you in making a sound career choice. It is untrue that any single test will tell you what occupation you should enter. Tests are designed to provide useful clues, not to give you definite answers. Nor is it true that a career counselor will tell you what occupation you should enter. Using tests and human judgment, the counselor assists you to become more aware of yourself and the alternatives that might suit your circumstances. This chapter emphasizes choosing a career by yourself. It is recommended, however, that you seek the assistance of a guidance counselor, career counselor, or counseling psychologist.

INTEREST TESTING TO IDENTIFY CAREERS OF INTEREST

Career counseling emphasizes finding a career that suits a person's interests. The most widely used instrument for matching a person's interests with careers is the **Strong Interest Inventory** (**SII**). The output of the SII is a computer-generated report that provides potentially useful information about making career choices.[3]

The Strong asks 325 questions about your preferences (likes, dislikes, or indifferences) concerning occupations, school subjects, activities, amusements, and types of people. Exhibit 10-1 presents a sampling of such questions. A person's answers to these questions are used to compute three sets of scores: (1) general occupational themes, (2) basic interest scales, and (3) occupational scales.

Scores on the Strong Interest Inventory

Each of the six occupational themes is associated with one or more basic interest scales as follows:

R Theme (Realistic): High scores on this theme tend to be rugged, robust, practical individuals who are physically strong and frequently

HUMAN RELATIONS SELF-ASSESSMENT EXERCISE 10-2

Skills Profile

Directions

Review the following skills areas and specific skills. In the space provided, write down each one you believe is a strong skill for you. You can also add a specific skill that was not included in the skill area listed at the left.

Skill Area	*Specific Skills*	*A Strong Skill for Me*
Communication	writing, speaking, knowledge of foreign language, telephone skills, persuasiveness, listening	_____
Creative	originating ideas, thinking up novel solutions	_____
Interpersonal relations	ability to get along well with others, being a team player, diplomacy, conflict resolution, understanding others	_____
Management	ability to lead, organize, plan, motivate others, make decisions, manage time	_____
Manual and mechanical	mechanically inclined, build, operate, repair, assemble, install, drive vehicles	_____
Mathematics	math skills, computers, analyzing data, budgeting, using statistical techniques	_____
Office	keyboarding, filing, business math, bookkeeping, spread sheets, word processing, database management, record keeping	_____
Sales	persuading others, negotiating, promoting, dressing fashionably	_____
Scientific	investigating, researching, compiling, systematizing, diagnosing, evaluating	_____
Service of customers	serving customers, handling complaints, dealing with difficult people	_____
Service of patients	nurturing, diagnosing, treating, guiding, counseling, consoling, dealing with emergencies	_____
Other skill area:	_____	_____

SOURCE: Abridged and adapted from Julie Griffin Levitt, *Your Career: How to Make It Happen,* 2d ed. (Cincinnati, OH: South-Western Publishing Co., 1990), pp. 19–21.

EXHIBIT 10-1

TYPE OF TEST ITEMS FOUND ON THE STRONG INTEREST INVENTORY

1. Actor	L	I	D
2. Aviator	L	I	D
3. Architect	L	I	D
4. Astronomer	L	I	D
5. Athletic director	L	I	D
6. Auctioneer	L	I	D
7. Author of novel	L	I	D
8. Author of scientific book	L	I	D
9. Auto sales representative	L	I	D
10. Auto mechanic	L	I	D

NOTE: In this section of the test, the subject indicates whether he or she would like (L), dislike (D), or be indifferent to (I) working in each occupation.

---

aggressive in outlook. The basic interest scales carrying the realistic theme are: Agriculture, Nature, Adventure Military Activities, and Mechanical Activities.

I Theme (Investigative): High scorers on this theme enjoy science and scientific activities, and are not particularly interested in working with others. They also enjoy solving abstract problems. The basic interest scale carrying the investigative theme are as follows: Science, Mathematics, Medical Science, and Medical Service.

A Theme (Artistic): High scorers on these themes are artistically oriented and like to work in settings where self-expression is welcome. The associated interest scales are: Music/Dramatics, Art, and Writing.

S Theme (Social): High scorers on this theme are sociable, responsible, humanistic, and concerned with the welfare of others. The associated interest scales are: Teaching, Social Service, Athletics, Domestic Arts, and Religious Activities.

E Theme (Enterprising): High scorers on this theme are skillful with words and use this capability to sell, dominate, and lead. The associated interest scales are: Public Speaking, Law/Politics, Merchandising, Sales, and Business Management.

C Theme (Conventional): High scorers on this theme prefer the ordered activities, both verbal and numerical, that characterize office work. They are comfortable following the rules and regulations of a large firm. The associated interest scale is Office Practices.

The Strong Interest Inventory has 119 occupational scales, divided among the six general occupational themes and basic interest scales. For example, the following occupations are among those associated with the conventional theme and the office practices scales: accountant, banker, credit manager, business education teacher, food service manager, nursing home administrator, and secretary.

Interpreting the Strong Profile

With the assistance of a counselor, a person looks for patterns of high and low scores. High scores indicate interests similar to people in occupational areas and occupations, whereas low scores suggest the opposite.

Assume that a person scores very high on the Office Practices Scale, and high on the occupations of banker and credit manager. The same person also scores very low on the Investigative theme, the Medical Service Interest Scale, and the medical technical and respiratory therapist Occupational Scales. We conclude that this person would be happier as an office manager than as an ambulance medic!

Note that interest is not the same as ability. Some people may not have the mental aptitude and skills to do well in the occupations they would enjoy. Interest is but one important factor contributing to successful performance. Being interested in your field makes its biggest contribution to keeping you motivated.

MATCHING YOUR CAREER TO YOUR LIFESTYLE

Another consideration in using self-knowledge to assist in choosing a career is to take into account your lifestyle preferences. Ideally, you should pursue a career that provides you with the right balance among work, leisure, and interaction with people. Some degree of compromise is usually necessary. If your preferred lifestyle is to take two-hour lunch breaks each workday, it would be difficult to attain a high level of responsibility. Executives, public relations specialists, and sales representatives who seem to spend considerable time at lunch are usually conducting business over their meals. They are not taking time out during the workday. If a cornerstone of your lifestyle is to remain in top physical and mental shape, you should probably avoid some of the high-pressure careers, such as ambulance paramedic or securities sales representative. On the other hand, you would want to avoid a career that provided too little challenge.

As just hinted, the term **lifestyle** can refer to many different key aspects of your life. In terms of making a career choice, it is helpful to regard lifestyle as the pattern by which a person invests energy into work and nonwork. Being the proverbial beach bum or ski bum is one lifestyle. So is being the 90-hour-a-week government executive.

Today, an increasing number of people at different stages in their careers are making career choices that improve their chances of leading their preferred lifestyles. The general manager of a plant in a small town

makes a revealing comment about modern lifestyles: "A number of years ago we couldn't get nearly the number of skilled people we needed to work here. The people who had a choice wanted to live in an area near a big city. Now we get loads of unsolicited résumés. It seems that a lot of people want access to camping and fishing. I think they're also worried about crime and pollution in the cities."

The move toward a healthy balance between work and nonwork might also be considered part of the movement toward a higher quality of life. For some people, living in a $1,800-a-month studio apartment in New York or Washington, D.C., represents a high quality of life. Such city dwellers would, of course, have to aspire toward very high-paying occupations in order to support their preferences. How will your preferred lifestyle influence your career decision making?

Another key aspect of matching your career to your lifestyle is to choose a career that enables you to achieve the right balance between work and personal life. People vary widely in what they consider the right balance. Individuals who want to be home at regular hours and on weekends, with very little travel, will usually have to avoid industrial sales or managerial work. On the other hand, individuals who prefer the excitement of breakfast meetings, weekend meetings, and travel might choose the two occupations just mentioned.

Flexible work schedules are a major mechanism for matching preferred lifestyle to career choice. Many people whose preferred lifestyle does not permit full-time work seek opportunities to work part-time. Others, whose preferred lifestyle is to minimize commuting and working outside the home, seek employment as telecommuters. If you choose to work at home, however, your job choices are more limited than a person who is willing to work in a traditional office.

An emerging trend of matching preferred lifestyle to your career takes place at a later point in a person's career. As such, it is a method of modifying, rather than choosing, a career to fit a living pattern. **Downshifters** are workers who choose shorter hours and less-demanding work to allow more time for other activities. To achieve more happiness, these people ask their employers to be even more flexible about work hours and job demands. (A job that is too stressful can interfere with the ability to enjoy leisure.)

Recent studies show that 4 percent of the Baby Boomer segment of the workforce is part of a movement to downshift, and the percent is increasing rapidly. People of other age groups are also joining the movement toward sacrificing some career success to have more time for family and leisure.[4] What is your evaluation of the merits of downshifting? Would you want a shorter, easier job with less pay so that you can upshift in other areas of life?

FINDING OUT ABOUT OCCUPATIONS

Whether or not you have already made a career choice, you should follow a fundamental rule of plotting your career—get the facts. Few people have valid information about careers they wish to pursue. A glaring example of occupational misinformation relates to the legal field. Many young people say, "I would like to be a lawyer. I'm good at convincing people. And I know I could sway a jury." Similarly, "I want to be a paralegal. I have the mind of a detective. I know I could break most of the tough cases given me to research."

In reality, the work of a lawyer or paralegal includes the processing of much nonglamorous information. One example is figuring out how much money a bankrupt bakery owes to 27 different suppliers. Four sources of occupational information are printed and electronic material, computer-assisted career guidance, spoken information, and firsthand experience. Without this information, it is difficult to find a good fit between yourself and career opportunities.

PRINTED AND ELECTRONIC INFORMATION

Most libraries and bookstores are well supplied with information on career opportunities. The most comprehensive source document of occupational information is the *Occupational Outlook Handbook,* published every two years by the U.S. Department of Labor. Each occupation listed is described in terms of (1) nature of the work, (2) places of employment, (3) training, (4) other qualifications and advancement, and (5) employment outlook. Using the *Handbook,* you can find answers to such questions as "What do claims examiners do and how much do they earn?"

The Internet is also a useful source of career information, much of it based on the *Occupational Outlook Quarterly.* Search for *America's Job Bank,*[5] which contains loads of useful information about such topics as job growth, average salaries, and suggestions for conducting a job search.

Searching for the "Bureau of Labor Statistics" will also provide large quantities of information about occupations.

COMPUTER-ASSISTED CAREER GUIDANCE

Several career-guidance information systems have been developed for access by computer. The information contained in these systems is designed to help users plan their careers. Guidance information systems go one step beyond printed information because you can ask questions of (interact with) the computer. For instance, when you are keyed in on a specific occupation, you can ask "What is the promotion outlook?" and "What effect will technology have?"

A widely used career-guidance information system is DISCOVER, available from The American College Testing Program (ACT).[6] Prior knowledge of computers is not required to use DISCOVER or other similar software. The system is intended for use by postsecondary students and by adults seeking a new career direction outside their current employment.

SPEAKING TO PEOPLE

An invaluable supplement to reading about occupations is speaking to people engaged in them. No matter what occupation interests you, search out a person actually employed in that kind of work. Most people welcome the opportunity to talk about themselves and the type of work they do. If you do not know anyone engaged in the career field that interests you, do some digging. A few inquiries will usually lead to a person you can contact. It is best to interview that person in his or her actual work setting to obtain a sense of the working conditions people face in that field.

Remember, however, that many people will probably say that although they are very happy in their work, there are better ways to make a living. Ask your dentist, doctor, lawyer, or plumber about his or her field, and you will likely be told, "Don't believe all those stories about people in this field being wealthy. We work long and hard for our money. And there's always the problem of people not paying their bills. I don't recommend that you enter this field."

Suppose you want to learn about the field of insurance claims adjuster, yet you do not know anyone who knows any person doing this kind of work. Try the cold-canvas method. Telephone one or two insurance companies and ask to speak to a manager in the claims adjusting department. When you reach a person in that department, indicate that you are trying to make a sound career choice and then proceed with your inquiry. The success of this approach is remarkably high. You will probably be granted an interview with an enthusiastic company representative.

FIRSTHAND EXPERIENCE

If you want to explore an occupation in depth, it is important to obtain some firsthand experience in that occupation. Part-time and temporary employment is particularly useful. One man who is a self-employed land-scape consultant first tried out the field by working two summers for an established business. Some schools offer cooperative, or work-study, programs. However modest your cooperative employment, it can provide you with much valuable information. For instance, it is surprisingly helpful to observe whether people engaged in that type of work ever smile or laugh. If not, the work might be intense and dreary. Exhibit 10-2 illustrates an extreme case of how a co-op experience can shape and boost a person's career.

Temporary work in a field you might wish to enter could lead to a job offer. It is standard practice for employers to use part-time and temporary jobs as a way of screening prospective employees. A woman who is now a sales representative for a well-known business corporation presents this anecdote: "I took the most menial clerical position in the marketing department. My supervisor told her boss that I was a good worker—somebody who would give a fair shake to the company. Now I'm making more money and having more fun than I thought possible at my age."

EXHIBIT 10-2

WORTH HER WEIGHT IN OIL

Petroleum engineer Shauna Freeman dismisses her reputation as an oilpatch whiz. Freeman saved her employers $2 million before she graduated from the University of Alberta. "That's what we're supposed to do," said the twenty-three-year-old engineer, who spent five years alternating between college and co-op jobs.

Freeman received international recognition when named North America's Co-Operative Education Student of the Year. Her award places her as the top co-op student among 30,000 from sixty universities.

In talking about her accomplishments, Freeman says, "You're trying to produce as much oil as you can for as little as possible." One time she was given the assignment of planning how to hook up a field of oil wells into a pipeline. Freeman recommended delaying the project until depressed oil prices rose to justify the expense. Another time, Freeman discovered an existing oil deposit was much larger than the original map indicated. Using that information, the energy firm earned an extra $1 million when it sold the property.

Freeman has received high praise from her placement supervisors. One noted, "I gave her the envelope of authority. She took it to the limits. And that's a compliment. We haven't had anybody around here with that kind of enthusiasm in a long time."

Freeman received job offers from the three firms she applied to. She chose to join Chevron's Edmonton office as an oil production engineer. Her new boss said, "She's coming with obviously high credentials. We're expecting good things from her and look forward to her joining the organization."

SOURCE: Adapted from "Top Co-op Student Is Oilpatch Whiz," *The Toronto Star,* March 20, 1993, p. C4.

CHOOSING A GROWTH OCCUPATION

Another important type of occupational information for career selection relates to growth opportunities within the field. An advantageous way of choosing a career is to pursue an occupation that appears to have growth potential, *providing work in that field matches your interests*. Entering a rapidly growing field will not do a person much good if he or she does not enjoy the work, because it will be difficult to perform well in the long run.

Using the growth-occupation strategy, the career seeker searches for a match between his or her capabilities and a growth occupation in a growth field. For example, a person who likes providing support to others and working extensively with computers might choose secretarial work (a growth occupation).

How do you identify growth occupations? One way is to use the sources described in the section about finding career information. Exhibit 10-3 lists growth occupations based on such sources and other career information. The growth-occupation strategy is even more effective when combined with entering a growth field (such as hotel and tourism, and digital information equipment). The payoff from working in a growth field is that career advancement is likely to be more rapid than in a stable or declining field.

EXHIBIT 10-3

FAST-GROWING OCCUPATIONS IN BUSINESS AND RELATED FIELDS

Occupational Title	Total U. S. Job Openings by 2005
Salespeople, retail	4,374,000
General managers and top executives	3,512,000
Secretaries except legal and medical	3,109,000
Marketing and sales worker supervisors	2,673,000
Clerical supervisors and managers	1,600,000
Receptionists and information clerks	1,337,000
Financial managers	950,000
Systems analysts	928,000
Food service and lodging managers	771,000
Computer engineers	872,000
Correctional officers	194,000
Personnel, training, and labor-relations specialists	129,000
Heating, air-conditioning, and refrigeration mechanics	125,000
Artists and commercial artists	117,000
Management analysts	109,000

SOURCE: America's Job Bank, © 1997 (www.ajb.dni.us/almis/info_q19.html); *Occupational Outlook Quarterly*, Spring 1996, U.S. Department of Labor; Bureau of Labor Statistics, Office of Employment Projections, November 1995.

DATA, PEOPLE, OR THINGS

A helpful way of looking at career choices is to characterize jobs according to the amount of time devoted to data (or ideas), people, or things. The *Dictionary of Occupational Titles,* published by the Department of Labor, uses the data, people, or things categories in describing all the occupational titles.

1. *Data* refers to working with facts, information, and ideas made from observations and interpretations. The activities involved in working with data are synthesizing, coordinating, analyzing, compiling, computing, copying, and comparing. Analyzing information by computers, for example, gives a person ample opportunity to work with data.

2. *People* refers to working with human beings, and also to working with animals as if they were human. The activities involved in working with people are mentoring, negotiating, instructing, supervising, diverting, persuading, speaking/signaling, serving, and taking instructions/helping. A customer service representative would have ample opportunity to work with people, as the representative regularly handles customer complaints.

3. *Things* refers to work with inanimate objects such as tools, equipment, and products. The activities involved in working with things are setting up, precision working, operating/controlling, driving/operating, manipulating, tending, feeding/offbearing, and handling. An office equipment repair technician would have ample opportunity to work with things while making service calls.

Most jobs involve a combination of dealing with data, people, and things. It is usually a question of the relative proportion of each dimension. Managers, for example, have high involvement with data and people and low involvement with things. Registered nurses have an average involvement with all three.

Understanding your preferences for working with data, people, and things sharpens a career choice. Job satisfaction is likely to increase when the individual engages in work that fits his or her relative interest in data, people, and things. A person with a balanced preference for all three would probably enjoy a position selling business equipment that also required substantial preparation of sales reports.

 DEVELOPING A PORTFOLIO CAREER
AND CAREER SWITCHING

It is becoming increasingly common for people to either switch the emphasis of activities in their work or switch careers entirely. An example of switching the emphasis of activities would be a salesperson who is working with computers to shift to a new field in which he or she worked primarily with computers and did no selling. People modify their careers for a variety of reasons, all centering around the idea that something is missing in their present one. Here we look at two closely related approaches to changing direction in a career: developing a portfolio career and career switching.

DEVELOPING A PORTFOLIO CAREER

Many people would like to change careers yet not be confined to focusing on one major type of job activity. To accomplish this, a growing number of people are developing a **portfolio career,** in which they use a variety of skills and earn money in several different ways. In addition to a desire to diversify, a portfolio career helps many people cope with the trend toward availability of fewer full-time positions. According to The Bureau of Labor Statistics, 18 percent of the U.S. workforce works part time (35 hours or less per week). To earn the equivalent of a full-time salary, many people are piecing together more than one part-time position. As more part-time positions pay benefits, working for more than one employer becomes more feasible.

According to career advisor Susan Larson, having a portfolio (or collection) of income-generating possibilities makes you more resistant to the effects of losing one job. You spread your risk by earning money in several ways. The career portfolio minimizes risks by accumulating groups of skills that can provide income. If one skill is not in demand, another might be.[7] A stenographer, for example, who also sold real estate might shift to full-time real estate sales if her company discontinued stenography. A common example of a skill portfolio is that of a person with a full-time position who has a part-time position requiring different skills. A department manager within a retail store might install satellite dishes as a part-time activity.

An important part of developing a portfolio career is keeping your occupational skills current. Suppose a person is able to translate documents from Japanese to English and English to Japanese, but is currently not working as a translator. Translation skills fade rapidly, so the person should continue to practice this bilingual skill at home.

CAREER SWITCHING

From the perspective of career specialist Douglas T. Hall, the career of the twenty-first century will be driven more by the person than the organization. The ultimate career goal is psychological success that comes from attaining important goals such as achievement and family happiness. This stands in contrast to the older goal of climbing the corporate pyramid and making lots of money.[8] (Of course, this is still the major career goal for many people.) The new type of career emphasizes doing work that fits your major values in life. Whether in pursuit of psychological success or old-fashioned success, many people find it necessary to switch careers.

A major principle of career switching is to *be thorough.* Go through the same kind of thinking and planning that is recommended for finding a first career. Everything said in this chapter about choosing a first career is also relevant for choosing a later career. The advantage for the career switcher, however, is that the experienced person often has a better understanding of the type of work he or she does not want to do.

A new career should be *built gradually*. Few people are able to leave one career abruptly and step into another. For most people who switch careers successfully, the switch is more of a transition than an abrupt change. A constructive approach would be to take on a few minor assignments in the proposed new field, and then search for full-time work in that field after building skill. An electronics technician, for example, might request to visit customers with sales representatives to facilitate a switch to industrial selling.

A major reason that many employees consider a new career is that they crave more independence. As a consequence, an increasingly popular path for the career switcher is to *move from salaried employment to self-employment*. The prospective self-employed person needs to decide on which particular business to enter. For many people, self-employment means continuing to perform similar work, such as the company cafeteria manager entering the food catering business. Other formerly employed workers go into competition with their former employers, such as a print shop manager opening a print shop of her own. For those who lack specific plans of their own, prepackaged plans can be purchased. A sampling of these is listed in Exhibit 10-4.

Another self-employment possibility is to purchase a franchise, thus lowering the risk of a start-up business. Currently, franchises account for about one-third of retail sales in the United States and Canada. Yet franchises require a substantial financial investment, ranging from about $6,000 to $500,000. Another caution is that some franchise operators may work around 70 hours per week to earn about $12,000 per year.

EIGHT SUGGESTIONS FOR CAREER PREPARATION

Preparing for a career is closely related to choosing a career. To prepare is to be ready to meet the challenges that lie ahead in whatever career you choose. Several of the points below[9] reinforce what you have already studied in this text, or will study in Chapter 12.

1. *Be flexible.* You may have one career field in mind, such as business. Do not overlook the possibilities of applying your education and skills to a rapidly expanding field such as tourism. Also, be flexible about the size of firm you hope to work for. Most of the job growth continues to take place in small and medium-size firms.

2. *Develop interpersonal skills.* Good interpersonal skills, especially communication skills, are a foundation for many careers. Employers seek employees who speak and write well. Most jobs require contact with coworkers and customers, or working as part of a team—meaning that people skills are essential.

EXHIBIT 10-4

A SAMPLING OF OPPORTUNITIES FOR SELF-EMPLOYMENT, AS SUG-GESTED BY ENTREPRENEUR BUSINESS START-UP GUIDES

Computer-Based Businesses
Computer Consulting
Computer Repair Service
Electronic Bulletin Board Service
Laser Printing Recharging & Repair

Financial Services
Check Cashing Service
Financial Aid Services
Financial Broker
Real Estate Investment

Cleaning/Maintenance Businesses
Apartment Preparation Service
Damage Restoration
Garage Detailing Service
Parking Lot Striping & Maintenance

Services to Business
Collection Agency
Language Translation Service
Medical Billing
Mobile Bookkeeping

Personal Services
Private Investigator
Event Planning Service
Image Consulting
Operating a 900 Number

Foodservice Businesses
Coffeehouse
Food Court Restaurants
Mobile Frozen Yogurt
Mobile Restaurant/Sandwich Truck

Wholesale Businesses
Import/Export Business
Liquidated Goods Broker
Wholesale Distribution Business
Marketing a Family Recipe

Retail Businesses
Antique Sales & Restoration
Body Care Boutique
Pet Hotel & Grooming Service
Self-Storage Center

---

3. *Think globally.* Many jobs are becoming international jobs even if they do not involve travel. An increasing amount of business is being conducted with customers and suppliers from other countries. To capitalize on the globalization of business, polish your skills in your second language. (Some people may have to learn a second language for the first time.) It is also important to study the culture associated with your second language.

4. *Develop your computer skills.* Computers have become an integral part of most jobs, including people-oriented jobs such as sales. Have you noticed how many outside-sales representatives work with laptop computers? Lack of good computer skills can be a career retardant.

5. *Get an edge.* Although we may be experiencing boom economic times, employers can still afford to be choosy. Any extra skill or knowledge can help distinguish you from other job applicants. Advanced computer skills, foreign language skills, and another degree are assets for most fields.

6. *Keep learning after you have chosen a field.* With technologies changing so rapidly, training has become a way of life in business and industry. Be prepared to take the initiative to acquire valuable new skills before the company offers you a training program.

7. *Be less concerned about promotions, it is what you know and how you apply it that really counts.* The corporate world today places much less emphasis on promotions than on acquiring skills and applying them well. *Promotion* in the new sense of the word often means getting to work on the most exciting projects and taking turn at being a team leader. Both of these activities can lead to higher compensation even if they do not lead to a change in job title.

8. *Strive for high-quality work.* Most employers assume that workers at all levels will strive to make high-quality goods and provide high-quality service. Many companies expect employees to apply quality principles to their work, so it is important to study books and articles about quality. Apply quality principles such as "Do it right the first time." Also, think of quality as simply being conscientious and terrific at what you do.

SUMMARY

For many people, finding the right career requires careful thinking and systematic effort. What a person does for a living is one of the key influences in his or her life. Your career is also a prime source of your self-concept and self-esteem. A general strategy for making a sound career choice is to understand first the inner you, including what you have to offer.

Knowing which skills and abilities you possess and enjoy performing can be the basis for a successful career. Your best skill is your core competency. Skill areas can be divided into: communication, creative, interpersonal relations, management, manual and mechanical, mathematics, office, sales, scientific, service of customers, and service of patients.

Career counseling, including interest testing, can be helpful in making a good career choice. Ideally, a person should choose a career that meshes with his or her preferred lifestyle. A growing number of people are downshifting their careers to give them more time for leisure.

Gathering valid information about careers is useful in making a good career choice. Four sources to consult are printed and electronic information (such as *America's Job Bank*), computer-assisted career guidance, knowledgeable people, and firsthand experience. The last category covers information gained from visiting places or work or from part-time or temporary employment. Choosing a career in a growth occupation is often advantageous.

A helpful way of looking at occupations is to characterize every job by the proportion of time you devote to working with data, people, or things. It is best to choose an occupation or field that fits your preferences in these three work dimensions.

It is becoming increasingly common for people to either switch the emphasis of activities in their work or switch careers entirely. A portfolio career is one in which a person has a variety of skills that can be used to earn money in different ways. The skill portfolio is particularly useful when a person holds two or more part-time positions.

Career switching is necessary for many reasons including the pursuit of psychological happiness. Switching careers follows many of the same principles as choosing a first career. A new career should be built gradually, often by phasing into the new career part time. To satisfy a desire for independence, many people switch careers from being an employee to self-employment.

At the same time you might be choosing a career, think of preparing for a career. Suggestions along these lines include: Be flexible; develop interpersonal skills; think globally; develop computer skills; get an edge; keep learning; and focus more on skills and knowledge than promotions.

Questions and Activities

1. How do you explain the fact that many students who are studying business still need to choose a career?

2. Now that you have read this chapter, what do you think you would do differently should you be choosing a career or career switching?

3. Associations that represent professional athletes have been asking lately that the owners of sports teams provide career guidance for players. Why would professional athletes need career guidance?

4. Which of the skills listed in Self-Assessment Exercise 10-2 do you think will take the longest to develop? Why?

5. What occupations would you suggest for a person who scored very high on the Enterprising and Conventional themes on the Strong Interest Inventory?

6. What career might a person enter who wants to earn a good living yet limit work to a maximum of 40 hours per week?

7. How might attempting to match your career to your lifestyle block your career progress?

8. In your own words, what really is a "portfolio career"?

9. Which skills do you think would be the most important to develop before entering self-employment?

10. Speak to someone you think has a successful career to find out how that person made his or her career choice. Be ready to discuss your findings in class.

REFERENCES

[1]"Your Personal Core Competency," *Executive Strategies,* February 1996, p. 11.

[2]Julie Griffin Levitt, *Your Career: How to Make It Happen,* 2d ed. (Cincinnati, OH: South-Western College Publishing, 1990), pp. 11–21.

A HUMAN RELATIONS CASE PROBLEM

The Uncertain Career Choice

One year prior to entering college, Allison engaged her family, friends, and high-school guidance counselor in helping her make a good career decision. Allison was asked by her guidance counselor what activities in life she enjoyed the most. Allison's answer to this question provided her a strong clue to a possible career path.

Allison responded thoughtfully, "I've really enjoyed my vacations with my parents. I've always been impressed with the way hotels and cruise ships operate. The people in charge are so polite, well dressed, and well spoken. I would enjoy working with people in the hotel and travel field. I also like the atmosphere of hotels. It's kind of in my blood."

With this initial hunch about a career prospect, Allison next conducted serious research. She investigated programs of study in hotel and tourism. She also telephoned anybody she thought might know of someone working at a professional level in the hotel field.

Allison arranged interviews with two hotel managers and one assistant hotel manager. She also spoke to a friend's brother who had worked as a photographer on a few cruises. Based on these interviews and her own observations, Allison decided to major in hotel and tourism upon entering college.

Three weeks before the first fall semester at college, Allison asked to reserve dinnertime one Friday night for serious conversation. "What's on your mind, Allison," asked her dad.

Allison replied, "Mom and Dad, I'm not so sure I want to go into the hotel and tourism field. I think the work is great, but the sacrifice might be too big."

"What sacrifice?" asked her mother.

"The sacrifice," said Allison, "is that I couldn't lead a normal life. When my friends were off from work, I'd be working. When other people would be on vacation, I would be busier than ever. Another problem is that if you do a good job as a hotel manager, you're moved around from hotel to hotel.

"How could I ever lead a normal social life? How could I ever get married and raise children?"

Allison's dad commented, "Are you telling me that nobody in the hotel field has friends or family?"

"Maybe they have friends," said Allison, "but they must all be working at hotels or restaurants. These people are probably a culture of their own."

Allison's mom replied, "If you feel that strongly, pick another major. Just drop the whole idea. Find a field like office management where you could lead a normal life."

"It's not that simple," responded Allison. "I still want to enter the hotel and tourism field. I know I would love the work. It's just the work schedule that might ruin it.

"I'm going to have to give my career choice a lot more thought."

Questions

1. How serious is the career choice problem facing Allison?

2. In what way is Allison facing a conflict?

(Continued)

3. What advice can you give Allison for deciding whether to pursue a career in hotel and tourism?

HUMAN RELATIONS SKILL-BUILDING ACTIVITY 10-1

The Uncertain Career Seeker

The skill-building involved in the following role play is to either develop skill in thinking through career issues or in being a sympathetic listener.

The previous case serves as background information for this role play. One person plays the role of Allison who visits her guidance counselor to mull over her career choice dilemma. Allison has considerable emotion about making a career choice. Another student plays the role of the guidance counselor who wants to both ask Allison the right questions and give her concrete advice. Run the role play for 10 to 15 minutes.

[3]The description of the Strong Interest Inventory is based on James G. Clawson, John P. Kotter, Victor A. Faux, and Charles C. McArthur, *Self-Assessment and Career Development,* 3d ed. (Upper Saddle River, NJ: Prentice Hall, 1992), pp. 125–135.

[4]Jennifer J. Laabs, "Downshifters: Workers Are Scaling Back. Are You Ready?" *Personnel Journal,* March 1996, pp. 62–76.

[5]http:www.ajb.dni.us/almis/info_q19.html.

[6]*DISCOVER for Colleges and Adults,* The American College Testing Program, updated regularly.

[7]Quoted in Kathleen Driscoll, "Portfolio Career May Be the Way to Reinvent Your Future," Rochester, N.Y., *Democrat and Chronicle,* February 17, 1997, p. 5.

[8]Douglas T. Hall, "Protean Careers of the 21st Century," *Academy of Management Executive,* November 1996, p. 8.

[9]"Seven Tips for Career Preparation," *NBEA Keying In,* November 1993, p. 8; Anne Fisher, "Six Ways to Supercharge Your Career," *Fortune,* January 13, 1997, pp. 46–47.

ADDITIONAL READING

Bolles, Richard N. *The Three Boxes of Life and How to Get Out of Them.* Berkeley, CA: Ten Speed Press, revised regularly.

Bolles, Richard N. *The 1998 What Color Is Your Parachute: A Practical Manual for Job Hunters and Career Changers.* Berkeley, CA: Ten Speed Press, 1998.

Career Confidential, newsletter published by Bureau of Business Practice, Waterford, CN.

Corporate Job Outlook!, newsletter published by Plunkett Research Ltd., Galveston, TX.

Jones, Maggie. "25 Hottest Careers for Women." *Working Women,* July/August 1996, pp. 37–48.

Moreau, Daniel. *Take Charge of Your Career.* Washington D.C.: Kiplinger Books, 1997.

Harris, Jim. *Getting Employees to Fall in Love with Your Company.* New York: AMACOM, 1996.

Rubin, Harriet. *The Princessa: Machiavelli for Women.* New York: Doubleday/Currency, 1997.

CHAPTER 11

CONDUCTING A JOB SEARCH

Learning Objectives

After studying the information and doing the exercises in this chapter, you should be able to:

▼ Improve your chances of finding a suitable job

▼ Target your job search and recognize what qualifications employers in general are seeking

▼ Identify job-finding methods and use the Internet to assist you in your job search

▼ Prepare an effective cover letter, job résumé, and follow-up letter

▼ Identify types of employment tests and physical examinations an applicant is likely to take.

▼ Face the adversity sometimes found in a job search.

Angelica Santorelli was applying for an office supervisor position at a company in Oakland, California. Several company representatives interviewed her, including a person from the human resources department and the manager who would be her boss. Angelica thought to herself, "I'm getting down to the wire. I must deliver a deal breaker. It must be something that will convince this wonderful company that I am

the person for the job. It's obvious there are other candidates for this position. I have to finish strong." Angelica's moment came when the hiring manager asked, "What is your most important character trait?"

"Honesty and integrity," replied Angelica, "and I can give you a good example. Two weeks ago my family and I were traveling to British Vancouver. We stopped at the currency exchange to buy some Canadian money with American money. I laid down $300 on the counter. Before giving me the Canadian money, the clerk wrote down $400 in his register. I said to the man, 'Sir, you have made a mistake in my favor. You wrote down $400. Could you please count my money again?' After counting correctly this time, the clerk thanked me profusely. He said that very few people would be that honest."

The hiring manager said, "Great story Angelica. You proved your point." Four days later Angelica received a job offer which she attributed in part to being able to support her claim of "honesty" with a specific anecdote.

Angelica's story is repeated in different versions everyday. With careful planning and preparation (such as preparing answers to typical interview questions in advance), a job search is more likely to be successful. Job searches are important for several reasons. You may be starting your career; you may be tired of your present job; you may want to boost your career; and you might be laid off or fired. Another reason for conducting a job search is to find a new position within a large company.

The purpose of this chapter is to provide the basic information you need to conduct a successful job search, including sources of job leads, preparation of a cover letter and résumé, and performing well in an interview. This chapter also presents a few fine points to help give you an edge over those who do the minimum necessary to find a suitable position.

TARGETING YOUR JOB SEARCH

A job search begins with a reasonably flexible description of the type of job or jobs you are looking for. Flexibility is called for because, with so many different jobs available, it is difficult to be too specific. A reasonable objective might be something of this nature: "I am searching for a job in the numerical field, with a large employer, located within 30 miles of here. I prefer accounting work. My minimum salary would be $475 per week."

Your chances of finding suitable employment are directly proportional to the number of positions that will satisfy your job objectives. One person with an interest in the literary field might be willing to accept a job only as a newspaper reporter—always a difficult position to find. Another person with the same background is seeking a job as (1) a newspaper reporter, (2) a magazine staff writer, (3) a copywriter in an advertising agency, (4) a communications specialist in a firm, or (5) a copywriter in a public relations firm. The second person has a better chance than the first of finding a job.

Closely tied in with the type of work you are seeking is the type of organization in which you would prefer to work. Unless you have had exposure to different types of organizations, you may have only tentative answers to this question. Questioning people who work at different places can provide you with some useful clues. Further, plant tours open to the public can provide valuable tips about what it is like to work in that particular firm. Visits to stores, restaurants, and government agencies will provide informal information about the general nature of working conditions in those places. As you begin your job search, ask yourself these questions to help you identify the type of organization that *might* be right for you:

- Would I feel more comfortable working in an office with hundreds of other people? Or would I prefer just a handful of coworkers?

- Would I prefer working in a place where people went out of their way to dress in a stylish manner? Or would I prefer an informal place where not so much emphasis was placed on appearance?

- Would I prefer to work in a small town or in a busy metropolitan area?

- How important is access to stores and restaurants?

- Would it be best for me to work where I could rely on public transportation?

- Would I really prefer an easygoing atmosphere or a highly competitive, "rat race" environment?

- How important are the social aspects of work to me? Would I be happy only in a place where I could meet prospective dates and make new friends?

Not every job candidate can afford to be so selective about a prospective employer. The more your skills are in demand, and the more prosperous the times, the more selective a person can be in choosing an employer.

QUALIFICATIONS SOUGHT BY EMPLOYERS

What you are looking for in an employer must be matched against what an employer is looking for in an employee. Job interviewers do not all agree on the qualifications they seek in employees. Nevertheless, a number of traits, characteristics, skills, and accomplishments are important to many employers.[1] Human Relations Self-Assessment Exercise 11-1 summarizes these qualifications in a way that enables you to apply them to yourself as you think about your job search.

JOB-FINDING METHODS

Two cornerstone principles of conducting a job campaign are to (1) use several different methods, and (2) keep trying. These two principles should be applied because most approaches to job finding are inefficient, yet effective. *Inefficient* refers to the fact that a person might have to make over 100 contacts to find just one job. Yet the system is *effective* because it does lead to a desired outcome—finding a suitable position.

Job-finding techniques are divided here into six types: (1) networking, (2) Internet and résumé database services, (3) mail campaign, (4) telesearch, (5) placement offices, employment agencies, and career fairs, and (6) help-wanted ads. Human Relations Skill-Building Exercise 11-1 will help sensitize you to the many ways of finding a suitable position.

NETWORKING (CONTACTS AND REFERRALS)

By far the most effective method of finding a job is through personal contacts. **Networking** is the process of establishing a group of contacts who can help you in your career. Networking is particularly helpful because it taps you into the "insider system" or "internal job market." The internal job market is the large array of jobs that haven't been advertised and are usually filled by word of mouth or through friends and acquaintances of employees.

About 85 percent of job openings are found in the hidden job market. The other 15 percent of jobs are advertised or registered with employment agencies and placement offices. The best way to reach the jobs in the hidden market is by getting someone to recommend you for one. When looking for a job, it is therefore important to tell every potential contact of your job search. The more influential the person the better. Be specific about the type of job you are seeking.

To use networking effectively, it may be necessary to create contacts aside from those you already have. Potential sources of contacts include:

HUMAN RELATIONS SELF-ASSESSMENT EXERCISE 11-1

Qualifications Sought by Employers

Following is a list of qualifications widely sought by prospective employers. After reading each qualification, rate yourself on a 1-to-5 scale on the particular dimension. 1 = very low; 2 = low; 3 = average; 4 = high; 5 = very high.

1.	Appropriate education for the position under consideration, and satisfactory grades	1	2	3	4	5
2.	Relevant work experience	1	2	3	4	5
3.	Communication and other interpersonal skills	1	2	3	4	5
4.	Motivation and energy	1	2	3	4	5
5.	Problem-solving ability (intelligence) and creativity	1	2	3	4	5
6.	Judgment and common sense	1	2	3	4	5
7.	Adaptability to change	1	2	3	4	5
8.	Emotional maturity (acting professionally and responsibly)	1	2	3	4	5
9.	Teamwork (ability and interest in working in a team effort)	1	2	3	4	5
10.	Positive attitude (enthusiasm about work and initiative)	1	2	3	4	5
11.	Customer service orientation	1	2	3	4	5
12.	Computer skills	1	2	3	4	5
13.	Willingness to continue to study and learn about job, company, and industry	1	2	3	4	5
14.	Likability and sense of humor	1	2	3	4	5
15.	Dependability, responsibility, and conscientiousness (including good work habits and time management)	1	2	3	4	5

Interpretation: Consider engaging in some serious self-development, training and education for items that you rated yourself low or very low. If you accurately rated yourself as 4 or 5 on all the dimensions, you are an exceptional job candidate.

Friends

Parents and other family members

Parents of friends

Friends of parents

Work associates

Faculty and staff

HUMAN RELATIONS SKILL-BUILDING EXERCISE 11-1

Creative Job-Finding Techniques

Job seekers often make the mistake of not exploring enough different methods for finding a job. After exploring a few conventional techniques, such as making a trip to the placement office, they sit back and wait for job offers to pour in. A better approach is to search for creative alternatives to finding a job. Think of every possibility, then sort out the workable from the unworkable later on. To accomplish this task, the class will be organized into brainstorming groups. The goal is to specify as large a number of job-finding techniques as possible. Follow the guidelines for brainstorming presented in Chapter 3, Exhibit 3-2.

After each group has assembled and edited its job-finding techniques, group leaders will present their findings to the rest of the class. Groups can then compare their job-finding suggestions.

Former or present employer (if you hold a temporary job)

Athletic team members and coaches

Religious and community groups

Trade and professional associations

Career and job fairs

To capitalize on these contacts, it is helpful to carry business cards. You do not have to be employed to use a business card. Simply place on your card a notation such as, "Alex Catalino, accounting specialist, Dallas, Texas." Also include your address and telephone number. An electronic-mail address on your business card adds flair.

An important caution about networking: Too many people are consuming too much of other people's time to help them with their job searches. Keep your request for assistance brief and pointed. Ask to reciprocate in any way you can. For example, you might prepare a chart or conduct research for a manager who gave you a job lead.

THE INTERNET AND RÉSUMÉ DATABASE SERVICES

The Internet is now a standard part of job hunting. For little or no cost, the job seeker can post a résumé or scroll through hundreds of job opportunities. The Career Mosaic Web site alone receives about 35 million hits per month, from both job seekers and recruiters. Web sites such as Career Mosaic and E-Span are résumé database services because they give employers access to résumés submitted by job hunters. The organizers of E-Span explain to employers that the service provides access to millions of qualified candidates through the World Wide Web, the Internet, and more than ten on-line networks and bulletin boards.

Many position announcements on the Internet require the job seeker to send an electronic résumé (described later in this chapter), while others request one by fax or paper mail. Technical positions such as computer programmer, engineering technician, or accountant are more likely to be found on the Internet than general positions. However, there are thousands of exceptions. Job hunting on the Internet is menu driven, as you will discover if you visit the Web sites listed in Exhibit 11-1.

EXHIBIT 11-1

POPULAR JOB SEARCH WEB SITES

- Monster Board: http://www.monster.com
- E-Span: http://www.espan
- CareerMosaic: http://www.service.com:80/cm
- CareerBuilder: http://www.careerbuilder.com
- CareerPath: http://www.careerpath.com
- CareerWeb: http://www.cweb.com
- JobTrak: http://www.jobtrak.com
- Job Center: http://www.jobcenter.com
- Job World: http://www.job.world.com
- HispanData: http://www.HispanStar* (for employers searching for Hispanic workers, and workers looking to fill such positions)

Job hunting on the Internet can lead to a false sense of security. Using the Internet, a résumé is cast over a wide net, and hundreds of job postings can be explored. As a consequence, the job seeker may think that he or she can sit back and wait for a job offer to come through the e-mail. In reality, the Internet is just one source of leads that should be used in conjunction with other job-finding methods. Remember also that thousands of other job seekers can access the same job openings, and many of the positions listed have already been filled.

UNSOLICITED LETTER CAMPAIGN

A standard and still current method of job-finding is the **unsolicited letter campaign,** or writing directly to a company you would like to work for. The plan is to come up with a master list of firms for whom you would like to work. You make up the list according to the categories most relevant to your situation, such as by industry or geographic location. Your list can be developed through the Internet by using search engines to access such categories as "furniture makers, South Carolina." Business directories in libraries, such as those published by Dun and Bradstreet and Standard and Poor, provide full addresses and names of key people in the firms listed.

When writing the prospective employer, send the letter to a specific individual rather than Dear Sir, Madam, or Ms. The mailing should consist of a cover letter and résumé. Should somebody be interested in your letter, it could get you into the insider system. The person will either contact you directly or refer your letter and résumé to a hiring manager.

TELESEARCH

A related approach to the mail campaign is the **telesearch,** obtaining job leads by making unsolicited phone calls to prospective employers. The list of prospects can be assembled in the same manner as the mail campaign. Begin your inquiry into an organization by contacting the person who would be your boss if you landed the job you really want. A major goal of the telesearch is to establish direct contact with as many of these decision makers as you can.

John Truitt advises *not* to call an executive and ask if there are any openings. Such an inquiry invites a "no" response. Instead, use a brief presentation (about one minute) to attempt to arrange an interview:

> "Mr. Caldone, my name is Jack Paradise. I have three years of experience in your area of business and would like to drop by your office this week to discuss working for you. Would 3 P.M. on Thursday be convenient, or would 3 P.M. on Friday better fit your schedule?"[2]

This kind of approach is brief and direct, yet ends with a "choice of two," making it easier for the prospective employer to agree to an interview. If the person contacted has an opening or is interested in learning more about you, you will probably get the interview or be asked to mail in a résumé. Even if you fail to get an interview, you might be able to obtain a job lead from your contact. Inquire about who the person knows who might be interested in hiring someone with your experience.

The telesearch, like the unsolicited letter campaign, is used to make the prospective employer want to meet you. Use the interview to make him or her want to hire you. Although the prospective employer cannot see you, smile and speak with confidence and enthusiasm. Truitt estimates that approximately 100 telephone calls will be needed to receive about five to ten interviews.

Placement Offices, Employment Agencies, and Career Fairs

Your placement office is a primary avenue for finding a job. Even if you do not find a job through the placement office, you will still gain insight into the job-finding process. If recruiters visit your campus, you can gain experience in being interviewed. Placement offices also provide information about the job-search process.

Employment agencies can also lead you to the right position. Employers use employment agencies to advertise jobs and screen applicants, particularly in large cities. Agencies tend to be more valuable for people with about five to ten years of work experience than for newcomers. Not to be overlooked, however, is that many employment agencies specialize in temporary help. After working for the employer for about nine months, the temporary job might become permanent. A concern expressed about employment agencies is that they sometimes encourage applicants to accept less-than-ideal positions just so the agency can earn a placement fee.

A variation of an employment agency is a *career agent,* who for a fixed fee works on behalf of his or her client (you). The career agent provides job-search and career counseling, and also has links with employers to help clients find positions. If a career agent finds you a position you could not have found for free, the service can be valuable.

Career (or job) fairs function somewhat like a temporary placement office. A large number of employers may visit the fair to recruit employees. At the same time, a large number of applicants register at the fair and present their résumés. In addition to directly conducting a job search, career fairs are also useful for learning about employment trends, skills required in certain positions, or developing your network of career contacts.

Help-Wanted Ads

A thorough job search includes scanning the help-wanted section of classified ads. Although part of the *outsider system,* help-wanted ads are still a standard way of finding a suitable position. Help-wanted ads are found in local and national newspapers as well as in professional and trade magazines. Because so many people respond to ads listing attractive-sounding positions, this method yields relatively few interviews—yet it can lead to finding the one job you are seeking. Four types of want ads are described next:

1.   *Open ads*   disclose considerable information about the position opening, including the name of the employer, phone number, nature of the job and the company's business, and qualifications sought. Starting salary is sometimes mentioned. Consequently, open ads attract the largest number of applicants.

2.   *Blind ads*   conceal the organization in which the advertised position is available, but may contain other important information. The reader is requested to respond by sending a letter and résumé to a post office box or the newspaper. By placing a blind ad, the company does not have to deal with a large number of unqualified callers. Another reason the company uses a blind ad is to maintain secrecy with competitors and employees. One remote disadvantage of responding to a blind ad when currently employed is that the advertiser may be your employer.

3.   *Employment agency ads*   are placed by agencies and list one or more job openings for their employer clients. Agencies tend to advertise their more attractive openings. These positions may be filled quickly, but the agency may encourage the job hunter to examine other possibilities. One of the purposes of want ads placed by employment agencies is to enlarge their pools of qualified candidates.

4.   *Catch ads*   promise unusually high-paying job opportunities without requiring specific job qualifications. Frequently these jobs involve selling difficult-to-sell merchandise, strictly on commission or with a modest weekly draw against commission. Respondents often find that they are required to sell home siding, food supplements, or magazine subscriptions. Furthermore, you might be asked to purchase the merchandise, which you will then attempt to sell to customers. These jobs are best suited for high-risk takers.

Another way of using classified ads to secure a job is to place a position-wanted ad, describing the position you seek and your qualifications. Your ad must be creative and eye-catching because so many people self-advertise. Robert D. Lock cautions that most of the responses to these ads are from employment agencies and career advisers offering to help you conduct a job search.[3] Position-wanted ads are thus a long shot, but could work.

In addition to being aware of the various job-finding methods, it is also important to consider *when* to begin a job search. In general, the bigger the job, the longer the job campaign. Finding a position within 30 days is exceptional, whereas a total time of about six months is typical. You will usually need several months to prepare your résumé and cover letter, pursue all the methods described in this section, and wait to hear from employers.

COVER LETTERS

A résumé or job application form is necessary but not sufficient for conducting an intelligent job campaign. You also need a cover letter to accompany such documents. The cover letter multiplies the effectiveness of the résumé because it enables you to prepare a tailor-made, individual approach to each position you pursue. The most important purpose of the cover letter is to explain why you are applying for the position in question. Simultaneously, you try to convince the prospective employer why you should be considered. Here we look at two effective types of cover letters.

ATTENTION-GETTING COVER LETTER

Most job seekers use the conventional approach of writing a letter attempting to impress the prospective employer with their backgrounds. A more effective approach is to capture the reader's attention with a direct statement of what you might be able to do for the company. Keep this "what I can do for you" strategy paramount in mind at every stage of finding a job. It works wonders in the job interview, as it will in the rest of your career.

After you have stated how you can help the employer, present a one-page summary of your education and the highlights of your work experience. A sample cover letter is presented in Exhibit 11-2. Notice that the opening line is an attention-getter: "Without a good service department, a car dealership is in big trouble." You may not want to write an outrageous or flip cover letter, but it should have enough flair to attract the reader's attention.

Employment specialist Richard H. Beatty recommends a slightly different version of the attention-getting cover letter. He explains that an effective cover letter has five parts: an attention-grabbing introduction, a paragraph selling your value to the employer, a background summary paragraph, a compelling follow-up action statement, and an appreciative close. Beatty recommends mentioning a personal contact as part of the attention-grabber.[4] An example: "Meg Atwood, your computer operations manager, mentioned that you are looking for a talented person to manage your Web site. I would very much like to talk to you about this position."

THE T-FORM COVER LETTER

A novel format for a cover letter is one that systematically outlines how the applicant's qualifications match up against the job requirements posted in the position announcement.[5] The T-form (or column) approach gives the reader a tabular outline of how the applicant's background fits the position description. The T-form cover letter, presented in Exhibit 11-3, is also recommended because it has an attention-getting format.

EXHIBIT 11-2

SAMPLE ATTENTION-GETTING COVER LETTER

27 Buttercup Lane
Little Rock, AR 72203
Phone/Fax (501) 275-5602
RMJ29@aol.com

Date of Letter
Mr. Bart Bertrand
President
South View Dodge
258 Princess Blvd.
Little Rock, AR 72201

Dear Mr. Bertrand:

Without a good service department, a new-car dealership is in big trouble. An efficiency-minded person like myself who loves autos, and likes to help customers, can do wonders for your service department. Give me a chance, and I will help you maintain the high quality of after-sales service demanded by your customers.

The position you advertised in the *Dispatch* is an ideal fit for my background. Shortly, I will be graduating from Pine Valley College with an associate's degree in automotive technology. In addition, I was an automotive mechanics major at Monroe Vocational High.

My job experience includes three years of part-time general work at Manny's Mobil Service, and two years of clerical work at Brandon's Chrysler-Plymouth. Besides this relevant experience, I'm the proud owner of a mint condition 1980 sports coupe I maintain myself.

I'm very stable in this community. A well-paying, secure job where I can make a contribution is important to me.

My enclosed résumé contains additional information about me. When might I have the opportunity to be interviewed?

Sincerely yours,

Rita Mae Jenkins

PREPARING AN EFFECTIVE JOB RÉSUMÉ

The major purpose of a résumé is to help you obtain a job interview, not a job. A résumé is needed both as an outside candidate and often when seeking a transfer within a large firm. Effective résumés are straightforward, factual presentations of a person's experiences, education, skills, and

---
EXHIBIT 11-3

██

THE T-FORM COVER LETTER

Gregory N. Colon
2127 Marketview Avenue
Atlanta, GA 30342
Phone/Fax (404) 441-0761
gnc26@aol.com

Sales Manager
Southeast Supply Corporation
200 Ashford Center North, Suite 650
Atlanta, GA 30338

Dear Sales Manager:

In response to your recent advertisement in the *Atlanta Gazette* for telemarketing sales professionals, please consider the following:

REQUIREMENTS	MY QUALIFICATIONS
Prior sales experience a must	Two years of full-time and part-time selling including retail and magazine subscription renewals
Great communicator	Two different managers praised my communication skills; received an A in two communication skills courses
Self-motivated	Worked well without supervision; considered to be a self-starter
Reliable	Not one sick day in two years; never late with a class assignment

Your opportunity excites me, and I would be proud to represent your company. My résumé is enclosed for your consideration.

Sincerely,

Gregory N. Colon

enclosure

accomplishments. Yet a résumé is much like art. People have different ideas about what constitutes an effective résumé. To add to the confusion, some people spell résumé with the acute accents (résumé is a French word), and some without. A challenge in preparing an effective résumé is to suit many different preferences.

Résumé length illustrates how employers hold different opinions about the best résumé format. A national survey of employers indicated that 24 percent said the résumé should be "no longer than one page"; 42 percent said "no longer than two pages," and 34 percent, "determined by information."[6]

A few general guidelines will be offered here which will help you avoid serious mistakes. An overall perspective to keep in mind is, "If your résumé is not a winner, it's a killer."[7] Done properly, a résumé can lead to an interview with a prospective employer. Done poorly, it will block you from further consideration.

THREE TYPES OF RÉSUMÉS

The three most commonly used résumé formats are the chronological, functional, and targeted. You might consider using one of these types, or a blend of them, based on the information about yourself you are trying to highlight. Whichever format you choose, you must include essential information.

The **chronological résumé** presents your work experience, education, and interests, along with your accomplishments, in reverse chronological order. A chronological résumé is basically the traditional résumé with the addition of accomplishments and achievements. Some people say the chronological résumé is too bland. However, it contains precisely the information that most employers demand, and it is easy to prepare.

The **functional résumé** organizes your skills and accomplishments into the functions or tasks that support the job you are seeking. A section of a functional résumé might read:

SUPERVISION: Organized the activities of five park employees to create a smooth-running recreation program. Trained and supervised four roofing specialists to help produce a successful roofing business.

The functional résumé is useful because it highlights the things you have accomplished and the skills you have developed. In this way, an ordinary work experience might seem more impressive. For instance, the tasks listed above under "supervision" may appear more impressive than listing the jobs "playground supervisor" and "roofing crew chief." One problem with the functional résumé is that it omits the factual information many employers demand.

The **targeted résumé** focuses on a specific job target or position and presents only information about you that supports that target. Using a target format, an applicant for a sales position would list only sales jobs. Under education, the applicant would focus on sales-related courses such as communication skills and marketing. A targeted résumé is helpful in dramatizing your suitability for the position you are seeking. However, this résumé format omits other relevant information about you, and a new résumé must be prepared for each target position.

Whichever résumé format you choose, it is best to place your most salable asset first. If your work experience is limited, place education before work experience. If your skills are more impressive than your education or work experience, list them first.

A general-purpose résumé, following a chronological format, is presented in Exhibit 11-4. This person chose to place work experience before education. Although her résumé is chronological, it also allows room for accomplishments and skills. Many people have achieved good results with this format. However, do not restrict yourself. Investigate other résumé formats, including exploring software that provides the user a résumé outline.

A current development in résumé construction is to prepare one primarily for electronic databases. Many companies store résumés electronically, making it important to prepare one that is suitable for an electronic database. If a job search Web site calls for an electronic résumé, it can be entered into the right place on the Web page. At other times an electronic résumé is printed and mailed to the employer who in turn uses a optical scanner to enter the résumé in the company database. A distinguishing feature of an electronic résumé is that it contains keywords that fit the requirements of a keyword search. The job-seeker should isolate keywords (nouns and adjectives) by placing them right under the individual's name, address, and telephone numbers. Zane K. Quible recommends that keywords should be selected from among the following information.[8]

- Titles of jobs held by applicant

- Names of job-related tasks performed by the applicant

- Industry jargon such as "zero defects," "customer delight," or "just-in-time inventory management." Also acronyms such as JIT for "just in time"

- Special skills or knowledge possessed by the applicant

- Degrees earned

- High school program or college major (for college graduates, delete information about the high school program)

- High schools or colleges attended

- Special awards or honors received

- Nature of interpersonal skills the applicants possesses

Most of this information, of course, should also be included in a conventional printed résumé. Exhibit 11-5 illustrates an electronic résumé.

EXHIBIT 11-4

A GENERAL-PURPOSE RÉSUMÉ

Rita Mae Jenkins
27 Buttercup Lane
Little Rock, AR 72203
Phone/Fax (501) 275-5602
RMJ29@aol.com

Qualification Summary
Experience in administrative support activities for automobile dealership. Education in office management and automotive repairs

Job Objective
Management position in service department of automobile dealership

Job Experience

1998–present
- Senior support specialist, Brandon Chrysler-Plymouth, Little Rock. Responsible for receiving customer payments for auto services; invoice preparation; varied tasks as requested by service manager.
- Set up database that saved space and reduced file-searching time.

1995–1998
Service station attendant, Manny's Mobil Service. Performed variety of light mechanical tasks such as assisting in brake relining, installing exhaust systems, tune-ups, independent responsibility for lubrication and oil changes.
- Increased sales of tires, batteries, and accessories by 18 percent during time periods on duty.

Formal Education

1996–1998
Pine Valley Vocational Technical School, Associate's Degree, automotive technology, May 1998. Studied all phases of auto repair including computerized diagnostics, service department management. Attended school while working about 30 hours per week. Grade Point Average, 3.35.

1992–1996
Harrison Technical High School, Little Rock. Graduated 10th in class of 137. Majored in automotive repair and maintenance. Studied business education topics including bookkeeping, computer utilization, office systems and procedures.

Job-Related Skills
Word processing, spreadsheet analysis, database development, bookkeeping. Able to handle customer complaints and concerns in person or by phone. Can diagnose and repair wide range of automotive problems for domestic and important vehicles. Can converse in Spanish with customers.

Service Activities
Treasurer, Autotech Club at Pine Valley; Vice President Computer Club at Harrison Technical; participant in Big Sister Program in Little Rock.

References
On file with placement office at Pine Valley Vocational Technical. Permissible to contact present or former employer.

EXHIBIT 11-5

ELECTRONIC RESUME

Sara L. Adams
123 Elmwood Terrace
Framingham, MA 01701
(617) 332-1485 FAX (617) 372-4587
SLAdams@hmp.aol

Keywords: Accountant. Bookkeeper. Accounts receivable ledger. Accounts payable ledger. Financial reports. Business Administration. Lotus 1-2-3. Excel. Windows 95. Windows 97. French. Supervision. President's Honor Roll. Superior oral communication skills. Superior written communication skills. Self-starter. Quick learner. Conscientious. Detail oriented. Reliable. Top 5 percent of class. IBM-compatible computers. Lakeville College, Framingham, MA.

Job objective: To work as accountant or bookkeeper for private or public business, with eventual goal of becoming supervisor of bookkeeping or accounting, or office manager.

Education:	Lakeville College, Framingham, MA, 1996–1998 Accounting major. Associate's degree in Business Administration with High Honors. East Framingham High School, National Honor Society, 1992.
Experience:	London's Department Store, Framingham, MA 1992–present. Full time for four years, then part time while attending college. Performed bookkeeping and cashier activities. Maintained accounts receivable and accounts payable ledgers. Prepared variety of financial reports.
Key Accomplishment:	Developed a system of prompt payments which saved employer approximately $55,000 per year.
College Activities and Honors	President of Accounting Club for two years. Team Leader of Student Misconduct Committee. President's Honor Roll, each semester, 1996–1998. Delta Phi Kappa Honorary, 1996–1998.

HOW TO HANDLE THE JOB OBJECTIVE SECTION

On the résumé, a **job objective** is the position you are applying for now or intend to hold in the future. A job objective is also referred to as a *job target* or a *position objective*. Although stating a job objective seems easy, it is a trouble spot for many résumé writers. Early in their careers many people feel compelled to state their long-range career objectives in the job objective section. A 21-year-old might state, "To become president of an international corporation." Certainly this is a worthy objective, but it is better to be more modest at the outset.

Employers will tend to interpret the job objective as a statement of your short-term plans. If you think your long-term objective should be stated, you might divide the section into "immediate objective" and "long-term objective." Current practice is to use the position under consideration as a job objective. Longer-term objectives can then be discussed during the job interview.

Another challenge with the job objective section is that your objective will often have to be tailored to the specific job under consideration. The job objective you have printed on your résumé may not fit exactly the job you are applying for. You might be considering a sales career. You find two good leads, one for selling an industrial product and one for a consumer product. You would want your objective on one résumé to mention industrial sales and on the other, consumer sales.

One approach to this problem is to keep your résumé filed in a word processor. You can then modify the job objective section for a given job lead. Another approach is to omit the job objective section. Your cover letter can describe the link between you and the job under consideration. Notice how the cover letter in Exhibit 11-3 made this link. (The same person, however, did include a job objective on her résumé.)

HOW DO YOU WRITE A RÉSUMÉ WHEN YOUR BACKGROUND DOES NOT FIT THE POSITION?

Job seekers sometimes lack the type of experience expected to qualify them for a position they seek. This lack of direct fit may occur when the applicant is switching fields, or is entering the workforce after a long absence. In both instances it is helpful to emphasize skills and experience that would contribute to success in the job under consideration.

Assume a person with five years of experience as a bookkeeper applies for a sales representative position at an office equipment company. The bookkeeper is advised to make these types of entries on his or her résumé: "Five years of experience in working directly with office equipment including computers, fax machines, and high-speed copiers." "Able to size up equipment needs of accountants and bookkeepers." "Accustomed to negotiating budgets with managers."

Assume a person has 20 years of experience managing a household, but has not worked outside the home. The candidate applies for an assistant manager position in a restaurant. The person should list relevant skills such as "Able to plan and prepare holiday meals and parties for large groups of people." The candidate is also advised to describe his or her volunteer work because such experience may be job-related. For example, "Coordinated church picnic for 250 people, including recruiting and supervising ten workers, and raising the necessary funds."

WHAT ABOUT THE CREATIVE-STYLE RÉSUMÉ?

Since so many résumés are sent to employers, it is difficult to attract an employer's attention. The solution offered to this problem is a creatively prepared résumé. A **creative-style résumé** is one with a novel format and design. Do not confuse this idea with the "created résumé" in which you "create" facts to make a favorable impression. Many employers verify facts presented on a résumé. Evidence of distortions of the truth or lying usually lead to immediate disqualification of the applicant. And résumé misinformation uncovered after the applicant is hired can lead to immediate dismissal.

One creative approach is to print your résumé in the format of a menu. One job seeker went so far as calling his education the "appetizer," his work experience the "entrée," and his hobbies and interests the "dessert." Others try to make their résumés distinctive by printing them on tinted or oversized paper. A current trend is to present yourself in a video instead of using a written résumé. According to one job counselor, this approach is ill-advised for most people, because few people appear impressive in a video.

If done in a way to attract positive attention to yourself, creative-style résumés have merit. The generally accepted approach, however, is for résumés to be conservative. In one study, 93 percent of college recruiters surveyed preferred white or ivory color for the résumé. For the entry-level job applicant, the conservative approach is the safest bet.[9] If you are applying for a position in which creative talent is a primary factor, the creative-style résumé is helpful. A more conventional job requires a more conventional résumé. Human resource specialists often object to oversized résumés because they are difficult to fit into standard files.

HAVING A SUCCESSFUL JOB INTERVIEW

A successful job campaign results in one or more employment interviews. Screening interviews are often conducted by telephone, particularly for customer-service positions requiring telephone skills. More extensive interviews are usually conducted in person. Becoming a skillful interviewee requires practice. You can acquire this practice as you go through the job-finding process. In addition, you can rehearse simulated job interviews with friends and other students. Practice answering the questions posed in Exhibit 11-6. You might also think of several questions you would not like to be asked, and develop answers for them.

EXHIBIT 11.6

QUESTIONS FREQUENTLY ASKED OF JOB CANDIDATES

The following questions are of the same basic type and content encountered in most employment interviews. Practice answering them in front of a friend, camcorder, or mirror.

1. Why did you apply for this job?
2. What are your short-term and long-term goals?
3. What do you expect to be doing five years from now?
4. How much money do you expect to be earning five years from now?
5. What are your strengths? Weaknesses?
6. Tell me about yourself.
7. How would other people describe you?
8. How do you determine or evaluate success?
9. Why did you prepare for the career you did?
10. What makes you think you will be successful in business?
11. Why should we hire you?
12. Describe how well you work under pressure.
13. Why is it taking you so long to find a job?
14. What has been your biggest accomplishment on the job?
15. What do you know about our firm?
16. Here's a sample job problem. How would you handle it?

Videotaping the practice interviews is especially helpful because it provides feedback on how you handled yourself. In watching the replay, pay particular attention to your spoken and nonverbal communication skills. Then make adjustments as needed.

1. *Prepare in advance.* Be familiar with pertinent details about your background, including your employment history. Bring to the interview your social security number, driver's license, résumé, and the names of references. Prepare a statement in your mind of your uniqueness—what differentiates you from other job candidates. Sometimes the uniqueness is not strictly job related, such as being a champion figure skater.

Present yourself favorably but accurately in the interview. Job hunters typically look on the employment interview as a game in which they must outguess the interviewers. A sounder approach is to do your best to present a positive but accurate picture of yourself. The suggestions presented next will help you create a professional impact.

It is important to know some significant facts about your prospective employer. Annual reports, company brochures, and newspaper and magazine articles should provide valuable information. Enter the name of the company in one or more Internet search engines for quick access to information about the employer. A brief conversation with one or two current employees might provide some basic knowledge about the firm.

2. *Dress appropriately.* So much emphasis is placed on dressing well for job interviews that some people overdress. Instead of looking businesslike, they appear to be dressed for a wedding or a funeral. The safest tactic is to wear moderately conservative business attire when applying for most positions. Another important principle is to gear your dress somewhat to the type of prospective employer. If you have a job interview with an employer where sports attire is worn to the office regularly, dress more casually. Recognize also that dress standards have more latitude than in the past.

3. *Focus on important job factors.* Inexperienced job candidates often ask questions about noncontroversial topics such as paid holidays, benefits, and company-sponsored social activities. All these topics may be important to you, but explore them after the basic issue—the nature of the job—has been discussed. In this way you will project a more professional image.

4. *Be prepared for a frank discussion of your strengths and areas for improvement.* Almost every human resources interviewer and many hiring managers will ask you to discuss your strengths and areas for improvement (or weaknesses). Everyone has room for improvement in some areas. To deny them is to appear uninsightful or defensive. However, you may not want to reveal problem areas unrelated to the job, such as recurring nightmares or fear of heights. A mildly evasive approach is to emphasize areas for improvement that could be interpreted as strengths. An example: "I get too impatient with people who do sloppy work."

5. *Do not knock former employers.* To justify looking for a new position, or having left a position in the past, job candidates often make negative statements about former employers. Employer-bashing makes you appear unprofessional. Furthermore, it may suggest that you are likely to find fault with any employer.

6. *Ask a few good questions.* An intelligent interviewee asks a few good questions. An employment specialist for managers said, "The best way to impress somebody on an interview is to ask intelligent questions."[10] Here are a few questions worth considering:

  a. If hired, what kind of work would I actually be doing?

  b. What would I have to accomplish on this job to be considered an outstanding performer?

7. *Let the interviewer introduce the topic of compensation.* Often the interviewer will specify the starting salary and benefits, allowing little room for questioning. If asked what starting salary you anticipate, mention a realistic salary range—one that makes you appear neither desperate or greedy. Careful research, such as reading want ads or checking with the placement office, will help you identify a realistic salary range. If the interviewer does not mention salary, toward the end of the interview ask a question such as, "By the way, what is the starting salary for this position?"

8.   *Smile and exhibit a positive attitude.*   People who smile during job interviews are more likely to receive a job offer.[11] It is also important to express a positive attitude in other ways, such as agreeing with the interviewer and being impressed with facts about the company. If you want the job, toward the conclusion of the interview explain why you see a good fit between your qualifications and those demanded by the job. For example, "The way I see it, this job calls for somebody who is really devoted to improving customer service. That's me. I love to take good care of customers." Smiling also helps you appear relaxed.

9.   *Emphasize how your skills can benefit the employer.*   To repeat, an effective job-getting tactic is to explain to a prospective employer what you think you can do to help the company. Look for opportunities to make **skill-benefit statements,** brief explanations of how your skills can benefit the company.[12] Preparing these skill-benefit statements requires considerable self-examination. Practice is required to make the statements smoothly and confidently without appearing pompous or arrogant. If you were applying for a billing specialist position in a company that you knew was having trouble billing customers correctly, you might make this skill-benefit statement: "Here is how I would apply my skill and experience in setting up billing systems to help develop a billing system with as few bugs as possible: _____."

Another way to show how your skills can benefit the employer is to relate the employer problem to one you successfully resolved in the past. In the billing system example, you might state that your previous employer had a billing problem and then explain how you helped solve the problem.

10.   *Ask for the job and follow through.*   If you want the job in question, be assertive. Make a statement such as, "I'm really interested. What is the next step in the process?" "Is there any other information I could submit that would help you complete your evaluation of me?" Part of asking for the job is to follow through. Mail a follow-up letter within three working days after the interview. Even if you decide not to take the job, a brief thank-you letter is advisable. You may conceivably have contact with that firm in the future. A sample follow-up letter is shown in Exhibit 11-7.

11.   *Recognize that from a legal standpoint, you do not have to answer every question.*   Employment interviewers will sometimes intentionally or unintentionally ask questions that violate employment law. From a legal standpoint, you do not have to answer such a question. However, if you choose not to answer a given question because you think it is illegal, decline tactfully. If you want the job, you need to maintain rapport with the interviewer. Suppose the employer asks, "Do you plan to have a family soon?" (An illegal question.) You might respond, "Might I possibly pass on this question? It is my understanding that I am not supposed to answer questions about plans for having children." Exhibit 11-8 presents some frequently asked questions that violate various state, provincial, and federal employment laws.

EXHIBIT 11-7

Sample Follow-Up Letter

Rita Mae Jenkins
27 Buttercup Lane
Little Rock, AR 72203
Phone/Fax (501) 275-5602
RMJ29@aol.com

Date of Writing Letter

Mr. Bart Bertrand
President
South View Dodge
258 Princess Blvd.
Little Rock, AR 72201

Dear Mr. Bertrand:

Thank you for my recent chance to discuss the assistant service manager position with you and Mr. Ralph Alexander. It was illuminating to see what a busy, successful operation you have.

I was impressed with the amount of responsibility the assistant service manager would have at your dealership. The job sounds exciting and I would like to be part of the growth of the dealership. I realize the work would be hard and the hours would be long, but that's the kind of challenge I want and can handle.

My understanding is that my background is generally favorable for the position, but that you would prefer more direct experience in managing a service operation. Since the car repair and service business is in my blood, I know I will be a fast learner.

You said that about two weeks would be needed to interview additional candidates. Count on me to start work on July 1, should you extend me a job offer.

Sincerely yours,

Rita Mae Jenkins

PSYCHOLOGICAL TESTING AND THE PHYSICAL EXAMINATION

Psychological and physical testing are two more challenges facing job candidates who have made it through the interview. Psychological testing (sometimes referred to as personnel testing) can help both the employer and job candidate find a mutually satisfactory fit. The good fit is most

EXHIBIT 11-8

*TWELVE FREQUENTLY ASKED ILLEGAL QUESTIONS
DURING A JOB INTERVIEW*

Job candidates should be prepared for these questions during interviews, even though asking them is improper and illegal.

1. How many children do you have?

2. How did you get that name?

3. How old are you? (Or, "What year did you graduate from high school?")

4. Where (or what country) do you come from?

5. As a woman, how well do you work with men?

6. How good is your health?

7. How much do you weigh?

8. Are you disabled or handicapped?

9. Are you married or single?

10. Do you own or rent your home?

11. Are you a minority?

12. What are your religious holidays?

SOURCE: Adapted from Knight-Ridder News Service April 21, 1997; "Interviewing Others Well: Your Job Depends on It," *Executive Strategies,* March 1996, p. 1.

likely to be found when the tests are accurate and fair, and the candidate answers them accurately. It is best to take these tests with a positive, relaxed attitude. Being physically and mentally well rested is the best preparation. Specialists who develop the test profiles of successful candidates are not expecting an incredible display of human attributes. Also, psychological tests and the physical exam are but two factors in making hiring decisions.

PSYCHOLOGICAL TESTING

Five types of psychological tests are widely used: achievement, aptitude, personality, interest, and integrity (or honesty) tests. The fifth category is used particularly in the retail and financial services industries.

1. *Achievement tests* sample and measure the applicant's knowledge and skills. They require applicants to demonstrate their competency on job tasks or related subjects. A person applying for a position as a paralegal might be given a test about real estate and matrimonial law. Giving an applicant a sample of work to perform, such as making a sales pitch, is based on the same idea as a paper and pencil achievement test.

2. *Aptitude tests* measure an applicant's capacity or potential for performing satisfactorily on the job, given sufficient training. Mental-ability tests are the best-known variety of aptitude test. They measure ability to solve problems and learn new material. Mental-ability tests measure such specific aptitudes as verbal reasoning, numerical reasoning, and spatial relations (visualizing three dimensions). Scores on mental-ability tests are related to success in most jobs in which problem-solving ability is important. The NFL uses mental-ability testing with prospects to test their ability to learn complicated plays. Quarterbacks (the people who directs the plays on field) are expected to have the highest scores!

3. *Personality tests* measure personal traits and characteristics that could be related to job performance. Among the many personal characteristics measured by these tests are conscientiousness, self-confidence, and emotional maturity. A recent development is to measure emotional intelligence, including such factors as optimism and ability to control impulses. Personality tests have been the subject of heated controversy for many years. Critics are concerned that these tests invade privacy and are too imprecise to be useful. Nevertheless, personality factors have a profound influence on job performance.

4. *Interest tests* measure preferences for engaging in certain activities such as mechanical, numerical, literary, or managerial work. They also measure a person's interest in specific occupations such as accountant, social worker, or sales representative. Interest tests are designed to indicate whether a person would enjoy a particular activity or occupation. They do not attempt, however, to measure a person's aptitude for that activity or occupation. The Strong Interest Inventory described in Chapter 10 is an interest test.

5. *Integrity tests* are of two types: paper-and-pencil and polygraph tests (often referred to as lie-detector tests). Paper-and-pencil integrity (or honesty) tests ask people questions that directly or indirectly measure their tendency to tell the truth. A direct question would be, "Should an employee be disciplined for stealing ten dollars worth of supplies from the company?" (A dishonest person would answer no.) An indirect question would be, "Do you read the editorial page of your newspaper every day?" (Only a dishonest person would answer yes. Almost nobody can claim a perfect record in this regard.)[13] Some integrity tests measure attitudes about theft, safety regulations, company policies, and related topics. Recent research evidence indicates that scores on integrity tests are positively associated with tests of conscientiousness, emotional stability, and agreeableness.[14]

Polygraphs record a person's internal physiological responses, such as heart rate and breathing rate, in response to questions. The level of emotional response to neutral questions is compared to responses to key questions. The federal Employee Polygraph Protection Act of 1988 severely limits the use of the polygraph for preemployment screening. Preemployment polygraphs can still be used by governments and government contractors engaged in national security activities. Applicants who will be working in security positions or those with direct access to drugs can still be administered polygraph tests. The devices also can still be used to investigate employee theft. Refusal to take the test cannot be used as the basis for dismissal.

THE PHYSICAL EXAMINATION AND DRUG TESTING

As part of the employee selection process, you will be required to take a physical examination. From the company's standpoint, this exam is important for two reasons. First, it gives some indication as to the applicant's ability to handle a particular job. A person with a back injury would have difficulty handling a job that required constant sitting. High absenteeism would be the result. Second, the physical exam provides a basis for later comparisons. This lessens the threat of an employee claiming that the job caused a particular injury or disease. According to one survey, firms that use physical exams find a 26 percent reduction in injuries, a 55 percent decrease in workers' compensation (insurance) costs, and a 15 percent increase in employee retention.[15]

The physical examination has increased in importance since the passage of the Americans with Disabilities Act of 1991. An employer cannot deny a disabled individual a job because of increased insurance costs or the high cost of health benefits. However, the employer can deny employment to a disabled person if having the individual in the workplace poses a threat to his or her safety or the safety of others.[16]

Approximately one-half of employers test job applicants for the use of illegal drugs. You may therefore have to submit to drug testing for a job you want.[17] Testing for substance abuse includes urinalysis, blood analysis, observation of eyes, and examination of the skin for punctures. In addition, some employers use personality tests that measure a person's tendencies toward drug use or other counterproductive behavior. As you can imagine, such form of drug testing is unpopular with job candidates.[18]

Although employers have a legal right to screen applicants for illegal drug use, some people are concerned that inaccurate drug testing may unfairly deny employment to worthy candidates. A strong argument in favor of drug testing is that employees who are drug abusers may create such problems as lowered productivity, lost time from work, and misappropriation of funds.[19]

MANAGING THE DOWNSIDE
OF CONDUCTING A JOB SEARCH

For some people, finding a job is an easy task, particularly if they happen to be in a field in which the number of positions available is far greater than the number of job applicants. For many other people, the job search can be a mixed experience: some joy and some frustration. Much rejection can be expected. Few people are wanted by every employer. You have to learn to accept such rejection in stride, remembering that a good deal of personal chemistry is involved in being hired. Suppose the person doing the hiring likes you personally. You then have a much greater chance of being hired for the position than does another individual of comparable merit. If the interviewer dislikes you, the reverse is true.

Rejection and rudeness are frequently encountered in job hunting, which can easily create discouragement. Keep pressure on yourself to avoid slowing down because you are discouraged. Recent research documents the fact that assertive behaviors are associated with success in finding a job, even when the job hunter has average job qualifications.[20] Remember, you have to perform dozens of tasks to find a job. Many of them have already been described, such as preparing a statement of your job objective, a cover letter, and a résumé. You also have to line up your references and take care of every job lead that comes your way. When you do not have a job, almost no sensible lead should be ignored. Each lead processed takes you one step closer to finding a job. And all you are looking for is one job.

Despite the new high-tech approaches to job finding, the entire process is inefficient but effective. Although you may have to make 100 contacts to find a suitable position (inefficiency), you will probably find the position thus making the process effective (it gets the intended results).

SUMMARY

Job search skills may be used at different stages in your career. The job search begins with a reasonably flexible statement of the type of job you are seeking (your job objective). Knowing what type of organization you would prefer to work for will help focus your job search. Qualifications frequently sought by employers are listed in Self-Assessment Exercise 11-1 and should be kept in mind during the job search.

A systematic job search uses many job-finding methods including: networking (contacts and referrals); the Internet and résumé database services; mail campaign; a telephone campaign; placement offices, employment agencies, career fairs; and help-wanted ads. The number of job offerings on the World Wide Web continues to increase.

A cover letter should accompany a résumé and application form. An attention-getting cover letter should explain why you are applying for a particular position and identify your potential contribution to the employer. A T-form cover letter systematically outlines how the applicant's qualifications match up against the job requirements posted in the position announcement. The T-form approach gives the reader a tabular outline of how the applicant's background fits the position description.

The major purpose of a résumé is to help you obtain a job interview. There is no one best way to prepare a résumé. Effective résumés are straightforward, factual presentations of a person's experiences, skills, and accomplishments.

The chronological résumé presents your work experience, education, and interests, along with your accomplishments, in reverse chronological order. The functional résumé organizes your skills and accomplishments into the functions or tasks that support the job you are seeking. The targeted résumé focuses on a specific job target or position, and presents only information that supports the target. A distinguishing feature of an electronic résumé is that it contains keywords that fit the requirements of a keyword search. Keywords should be placed right under the information identifying the individual.

The job objective on your résumé should describe the position you are seeking now or in the short-term future. When your credentials do not fit closely the position description, emphasize on your résumé those skills from other experiences that would help you succeed in the position. Creative-style résumés bring favorable attention to your credentials, but should be used with discretion.

Rehearse being interviewed, and then present yourself favorably but accurately in the interview. Specific interview suggestions include: (1) Prepare in advance; (2) dress appropriately; (3) focus on important job factors; (4) be prepared to discuss your strengths and areas for improvement; (5) do not knock former employers; (6) ask good questions; (7) let the interviewer introduce the topic of compensation; (8) smile and exhibit a positive attitude; (9) emphasize how your skills can benefit the employer; (10) ask for the job and follow through; and (11) recognize that from a legal standpoint you do not have to answer every question.

Psychological testing may be part of the employment process, with five types of test being widely used: achievement, aptitude, personality, interest, and integrity (or honesty) tests. The physical exam, including possible drug testing, is another key step on the way to being hired.

Conducting a job campaign is typically inefficient, but ultimately effective. The process is demanding, with some joys and many frustrations. It is therefore important to keep pressure on yourself to perform the many chores required of a successful job-hunting campaign. Follow up on every lead, and try not to take rejection and rudeness personally.

Questions and Activities

1. During times when there is a shortage of skilled workers, why is it still important to study how to conduct a job campaign?

2. How realistic are the qualifications sought by employers for positions in business and related fields?

3. How might a person's length of job experience influence which job-hunting technique is the most suitable?

4. What can you do today to help you develop a contact that could someday lead to a job?

5. Some job seekers send fax messages instead of postal mail when conducting an unsolicited letter campaign. Identify an advantage and a disadvantage of using fax messages for this purpose.

6. What special challenges do voice-mail systems present for job seekers?

7. Given that people have so many different opinions about what makes for an effective résumé, what kind of résumé should a job seeker prepare?

8. Assuming that an employer would accept a video résumé, would you prepare and send one? Why or why not?

9. Assume you are being interviewed for a position you really want, and the interviewer asks you several questions that could be considered in violation of employment law. How would you respond to his or her questions?

10. Whether you are actually looking for a job now, use the Internet to uncover an opening for a position that appears well suited to your interests. Be ready to discuss with classmates the results you achieved.

A HUMAN RELATIONS CASE PROBLEM

Why Isn't My Résumé Getting Results?

Billy Joe Wentworth was working in the family business as a manufacturing technician while he attended career school. Although he got along well with his family members, Billy Joe wanted to find employment elsewhere so he could build a career on his own. Billy Joe's job objective was a position in industrial sales. He compiled a long list of prospective employers. He developed the list from personal contacts, classified ads in newspapers, and job openings on the Internet. Billy Joe clipped a business card with a brief handwritten noted to each résumé. The note usually said something to the effect, "Job sounds great. Let's schedule an interview at you convenience." The résumé is shown in Exhibit 11-9.

After mailing out 200 résumés, Billy Joe still did not have an interview. He asked his uncle and mentor, the owner of the family business, "Why isn't my résumé getting results?"

Questions

1. What suggestions can you make to Billy Joe for improving his résumé? Or does it require improvement?

2. What is your evaluation of Billy Joe's approach to creating a cover letter?

EXHIBIT 11-9

RÉSUMÉ OF BILLY JOE WENTWORTH

BILLY JOE WENTWORTH
275 Birdwhistle Lane
Cleveland, Ohio 44131
(216) 614-7512 (Please call after 7 PM weekday nights)
Billyjoe@wentworth.com

Objective
Long-range goal is Vice President of sales of major corporation. For now, industrial sales representative paid by salary and commission.

Job Experience
Five years experience in Wentworth industries as manufacturing technician, tool crib attendant, shipper, and floor sweeper. Voted as "employee of the month" twice.

Two years experience in newspaper delivery business. Distributed newspapers door to door, responsible for accounts receivable and development of new business in my territory.

Education
Justin Peabody Career College, business administration major with manufacturing technology minor. Expect degree in June 1999. 2.65 GPA. Took courses in sales management and selling. Received a B+ in professional selling course.

Cleveland Heights High School, business and technology major, 1992–1996. Graduated 45th in class of 125. 82% average.

Skills and Talents
Good knowledge of manufacturing equipment; friends say I'm a born leader; have been offered supervisory position in Wentworth Industries; real go getter.

References
Okay to contact present employer except for my immediate supervisor Jill Baxter with whom I have a personality clash.

REFERENCES

[1]Julie Griffin Levitt, *Your Career: How to Make It Happen* (Cincinnati: South-Western College Publishing, 1990), pp. 129–131; "CEOs Speak Out: What Is Needed to Work in Today's Ever-Changing Business World," *Keying In,* November 1996, pp. 1–2; Brien N. Smith, Carolee Jones, and Judy Lane, "Employers' Perceptions of Work Skills," *Business Education Forum,* April

1997, pp. 11–17; Clifford E. Montgomery, "Organizational Fit Is Key to Job Success," *HRMagazine,* January 1996, pp. 94–96.

[2]John Truitt, "7 Ways to Get a Job . . . Fast," *Business Week Careers,* October 1987, p. 4.

[3]Robert D. Lock, *Job Search: Career Planning Guidebook, Book II* (Pacific Grove, CA: Brooks/Cole, 1988), pp. 34–35.

[4]Richard H. Beatty, *The Perfect Cover Letter* (New York: John Wiley & Sons, 1997).

[5]Based on form used by Garrett Associates, Alexandria, Virginia.

[6]Mary Alice Griffin and Patricia Lynn Anderson, "Résumé Content," *Business Education Forum,* February 1994, p. 11.

[7]Peggy Schmidt, "When to Start Looking for a Job," *Business Week's Guide to Careers,* February 1986, p. 71.

[8]Zane K. Quible, "Job Seeking Process," in *The Changing Dimensions of Business Education* (Reston, VA: National Business Education Association, 1997), p. 176.

[9]R. Neil Dortch, "Résumé Preparation," *Business Education Forum,* April 1994, p. 47.

[10]"Talking with Lynn Bignell about Job Hunting," *Working Smart,* November 1991, p. 7.

[11]Susan Kleinman, "Is Your Attitude Killing Your Career?" *Cosmopolitan,* May 1994, p. 225.

[12]Ellen Forman, "Surviving under the Microscope," *Sun-Sentinel* syndicated story, April 21, 1997; Nancy K. Austin, "The New Job Interview: Beyond the Trick Question," *Working Woman,* March 1996, pp. 23–24.

[13]Paul R. Sackett, Laura R. Burris, and Christine Callahan, "Integrity Testing for Personnel Selection: An Update," *Personnel Psychology,* Autumn 1989, p. 493.

[14]Paul R. Sackett and James E. Wanek, "New Developments in Use of Measures of Honesty, Integrity, Conscientiousness, Dependability, Trustworthiness, and Reliability for Personnel Selection," *Personnel Psychology,* Winter 1996, p. 822.

[15]"Testing Pays Off," *HR Fact Finder,* November 1996, p. 6

[16]Paul M. Mastrangelo, "Do College Students *Still* Prefer Companies without Employment Drug Testing?" *Journal of Business and Psychology,* Spring 1997, p. 325.

[17]"Drug and Literacy Testing Update," *The Fact Finder,* March 1994, p. 2.

[18]Joseph G. Rosse, Richard C. Ringer, and Janice L. Miller, "Personality and Drug Testing: An Exploration of the Perceived Fairness of Alternatives to Urinalysis," *Journal of Business and Psychology,"* Summer 1996, pp. 459–475.

[19]Rob Brookler, "Industry Standards in Workplace Drug Testing," *Personnel Journal,* April 1992, p. 128.

[20]Mark J. Schmitt, Elise L. Amel, and Ann Marie Ryan, "Self-Reported Assertive Job-Seeking Behaviors of Minimally Educated Job Hunters," *Personnel Psychology,* Spring 1993, p. 119.

ADDITIONAL READING

Career Press Editors. *Résumés! Résumés! Résumés!* (2d ed.). Hawthorne, NJ: Career Press, 1995.

Dutton, Gail. "Getting the Right Job: A Matter of What Else You Know." *Management Review,* May 1996, p. 6.

Http://www.careerbuilder.com/

Krilowicz, Thomas J., and Lowery, Christopher M. "Evaluation of Personality Measures for the Selection of Textile Employees." *Journal of Business and Psychology,* Fall 1996, pp. 55–61.

Lorenzen, Elizabeth A. (ed.). *Career Planning and Job Searching in the Information Age.* Binghamton, NY: The Haworth Press, 1996.

McCune, Jenny C. "Good Help Is Hard to Find: A Web-Based Campaign Might Be a Good Place to Start." *Management Review,* June 1997, pp. 30–31.

Solomon, Charlene Marmer. "Testing at Odds with Diversity Efforts?" *Personnel Journal,* April 1996, pp. 131–140.

Stevenson, Ollie. *101 Great Answers to the Toughest Job Search Problems.* Franklin Lakes, NJ: Career Press, 1995.

CHAPTER 12

DEVELOPING GOOD WORK HABITS

Learning Objectives

After studying the information and doing the exercises in this chapter, you should be able to:

▼ Appreciate the importance of good work habits and time management

▼ Decrease any tendencies you might have toward procrastination

▼ Develop attitudes and values that will help you become more productive

▼ Develop skills and techniques that will help you become more productive

▼ Overcome time-wasting practices

An advertising agency vice president was having trouble getting assignments completed. She hired productivity expert Stephanie Winston to get her on track. Winston showed the executive how (and where) to block out periods of private time to accomplish creative work undisturbed. Not only was the vice president's problem solved, but shortly thereafter she was promoted to senior vice president. She attributes the unexpected promotion to the change in her work habits that Winston engineered.[1]

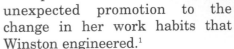

The experience of the advertising agency executive dramatically illustrates how good work habits and time management contribute to success in business. Furthermore, a person is more likely to be fired from a job or flunk out of school because of poor **work habits** rather than poor aptitude. Work habits refer to a person's characteristic approach to work, including such things as organization, priority setting, and handling of paper work and e-mail. Poor work habits also interfere with social life because of such problems as canceled social engagements.

People with good work habits tend to achieve higher career success and have more time to invest in their personal lives. They also enjoy their personal lives more because they are not preoccupied with unfinished tasks. Effective work habits are also beneficial because they eliminate a major stressor—the feeling of having very little or no control over your life. Being in control also leads to a relaxed, confident approach to work.

Good work habits and time management are more important than ever because of today's emphasis on **productivity,** the amount of quality work accomplished in relation to the resources consumed. Good work habits and time management lead to high personal productivity.

The goal of this chapter is to help you become a more productive person who is still flexible. Someone who develops good work habits is not someone who becomes so obsessed with time and so rigid that he or she makes other people feel uncomfortable. Ideally, a person should be well organized yet still flexible.

Information about becoming more productive is organized here into four related categories. One is overcoming procrastination, a problem that plagues almost everybody to some extent. The second is developing attitudes and values that foster productivity. The third category is the lengthiest: developing skills and techniques that lead to personal productivity. The fourth category is overcoming time wasters.

DEALING WITH PROCRASTINATION

The leading cause of poor productivity and career self-sabotage is **procrastination,** delaying a task for an invalid or weak reason. Procrastination is also the major work-habit problem for most workers and students. Human Relations Self-Assessment Exercise 12-1 gives you the opportunity to think about your own tendencies toward procrastination. Unproductive people are the biggest procrastinators, but even productive people have problems with procrastination at times. A business owner who does not

---

HUMAN RELATIONS SELF-ASSESSMENT EXERCISE 12-1

Procrastination Tendencies

Circle yes or no for each item:

1. I usually do my best work under pressure.	Yes	No
2. Before starting a project I go through such rituals as sharpening every pencil, straightening up my desk more than once, and discarding bent paper clips.	Yes	No
3. I crave the excitement of the "last minute rush."	Yes	No
4. I often think that if I delay something, it will go away, or the person who asked for it will forget about it.	Yes	No
5. I extensively research something before taking action, such as obtaining five different estimates before getting the brakes repaired on my car.	Yes	No
6. I have a great deal of difficulty getting started on most projects, even those I enjoy.	Yes	No
7. I keep waiting for the right time to do something, such as getting started on an important report.	Yes	No
8. I often underestimate the time needed to do a project and say to myself, "I can do this quickly, so I'll wait until next week."	Yes	No
9. It is difficult for me to finish most projects or activities.	Yes	No
10. I have several favorite diversions or distractions that I use to keep me from doing something unpleasant.	Yes	No

Total yes responses _____

Scoring: The greater the number of yes responses, the more likely it is that you have a serious procrastination problem. A score of 8, 9, or 10 strongly suggests that your procrastination is lowering your productivity.

ordinarily procrastinate might delay preparing taxes knowing that she was behind in her taxes.

Why People Procrastinate

People procrastinate for many different reasons. One is that we perceive the task to be done (such as quitting a job) as unpleasant. Another reason we procrastinate is that we find the job facing us to be overwhelming, such as painting a house. Another major cause of procrastination is a fear of the consequences of our actions.

One possible negative consequence is a negative evaluation of your work. For example, if you delay preparing a report for your boss or instructor, that person cannot criticize its quality. Bad news is another negative consequence that procrastination can sometimes delay. If you think your personal computer needs a new disk drive, delaying a trip to the computer store means you will not have to hear the diagnosis: "Your disk drive needs replacement. We can do the job for about $300."

Another reason some people procrastinate is that they **fear success.** People sometimes believe that if they succeed at an important task, they will be asked to take on more responsibility in the future. They dread this possibility. Some students have been known to procrastinate completing their degree requirements to avoid taking on the responsibility of a full-time position.

People frequently put off tasks that do not appear to offer a meaningful reward. Suppose you decide that your computer files need a thorough updating, including deleting inactive files. Even if you know this task should be done, the accomplishment of updated files might not be a particularly meaningful reward.

Finally, people often procrastinate as a way of rebelling against being controlled. Procrastination, used in this way, is a means of defying unwarranted authority.[2] Rather than submit to authority, a person might tell himself, "Nobody is going to tell me when I should get a report done. I'll do it when I'm good and ready." Such people might be referred to as "anticontrol freaks."

Techniques for Reducing Procrastination

To overcome, or at least minimize, procrastination we recommend a number of specific tactics. A general approach, however, is simply to be aware that procrastination is a major drain on productivity. Being aware of the problem will remind you to take corrective action in many situations. When your accomplishment level is low, you might ask yourself, "Am I procrastinating on anything of significance?"

Calculate the Cost of Procrastination.   You can reduce procrastination by calculating its cost.[3] One example is that you might lose out on obtaining a high-paying job you really want by not having your résumé and cover letter ready on time. Your cost of procrastination would include the difference in salary between the job you do find and the one you really wanted. Another cost would be the loss of potential job satisfaction.

Counterattack. Forcing yourself to do something overwhelming, frightening, or uncomfortable helps to prove that the task was not as bad as initially perceived.[4] Assume that you have accepted a new position but have not yet resigned from your present one because resigning seems so uncomfortable. Set up a specific time to call your manager, or his or her assistant, to schedule an appointment. Force yourself further to show up for the resignation appointment. After you break the ice with the statement, "I have something important to tell you," the task will be much easier.

Jump-Start Yourself. You can often get momentum going on a project by giving yourself a tiny assignment just to get started. One way to get momentum going on an unpleasant or overwhelming task is to set aside a specific time to work on it. If you have to write a report on a subject you dislike, you might set aside Saturday from 3 P.M. to 4 P.M. as your time to first attack the project. If your procrastination problem is particularly intense, giving yourself even a five-minute task such as starting a new file, might help you gain momentum. After five minutes, decide if you choose to continue for another five minutes. The five-minute chunks will help you focus your energy.

Another way to jump-start yourself is to find a **leading task** to perform. A leading task is an easy warm-up activity. If you were procrastinating about calling back an angry customer, you might first send an e-mail message stating that you are investigating the problem and will telephone shortly.

Peck Away at an Overwhelming Task. Assume that you have a major project to do that does not have to be accomplished in a hurry. A good way of minimizing procrastination is to peck away at the project in 15- to 30-minute bits of time. Bit by bit the project will get down to manageable size and therefore not seem so overwhelming.

A related way of pecking away at an overwhelming task is to subdivide it into smaller units. For instance, you might break down moving into a series of tasks such as filing change-of-address notices, locating a mover, and packaging books. Pecking away can sometimes be achieved by setting aside as little as five minutes to work on a seemingly overwhelming task. When the five minutes are up, either work five more minutes on the task or reschedule the activity for sometime soon.

Motivate Yourself with Rewards and Punishments. Give yourself a pleasant reward soon after you accomplish a task you would ordinarily procrastinate about. You might, for example, jog through the woods after having completed a tough take-home exam. The second part of this tactic is to punish yourself if you have engaged in serious procrastination How about eating only oatmeal for five days?

Make a Commitment to Other People. Put pressure on yourself to get something done on time by making it a commitment to one or more other people. You might announce to coworkers that you are going to get a project of mutual concern completed by a certain date. If you fail to meet this date, you may feel embarrassed. One administrative assistant told his coworkers, "I will get the new coffee system in our office by March 31, or I will buy everybody's coffee for a week."

Express a More Positive Attitude about Your Intentions. Expressing a more positive attitude can often lead to changes in behavior. If you choose words that express a serious intention to complete an activity, you are more likely to follow through than if you choose more uncertain words. Imagine that a coworker says, "I *might* get you the information you need by next Friday." You probably will not be surprised if you do not receive the information by Friday. In contrast, if your coworker says, "I *will . . .* Friday," there is less likelihood the person will procrastinate. Psychologist Linda Sapadin believes that you are less likely to procrastinate if you change you "wish" to "will," your "like to" to "try to," and your "have to" to "want to."[5]

Use Subliminal Messages About Overcoming Procrastination. Software called *Mindset* flashes reinforcing messages across the menu bar on your computer. You can adjust the frequency and duration of the suggestions. The message can flash by subliminally (below the level of conscious awareness) or remain on the screen for a few seconds. The procrastination message is: "My goals are obtainable. I am confident in my abilities. I make and keep deadlines."[6]

DEVELOPING THE PROPER ATTITUDES AND VALUES

Developing good work habits and time-management practices is often a matter of developing proper attitudes toward work and time. For instance, if you think that your job is important and that time is valuable, you will be on your way toward developing good work habits. In this section we describe a group of attitudes and values that can help improve your productivity through better use of time and improved work habits.

BECOME A GOAL-ORIENTED PERSON AND VALUE YOUR TIME

Becoming goal-oriented is perhaps the first step in any serious program of improving work habits and time management. Being committed to a goal propels people toward good use of time. Imagine how efficient most employees would be if they were told, "Here is five days' worth of work facing you. If you get it finished in less than five days, you can have all that time saved to yourself." (One negative side effect, however, is that many employees might sacrifice quality for speed.)

As a consequence of being goal-oriented, successful people believe that their time is valuable. It is therefore difficult to engage them in idle conversation during working hours. As you proceed further into your career, the value of your time will usually increase. A person might choose to invest some discretionary time into career-building activities such as learning about team leadership or marketing on the Internet.

VALUE GOOD ATTENDANCE AND PUNCTUALITY

On the job, in school, or in personal life, good attendance and punctuality are essential for developing a good reputation. Also, you cannot contribute to a team effort unless you are present. Poor attendance and consistent lateness are the most frequent reasons for employee discipline. Furthermore, many managers interpret high absenteeism and lateness as signs of emotional immaturity.

Two important myths about attendance and punctuality should be challenged early in your career. One is that a certain number of sick days are owed an employee. Some employees who have not used up their sick days will find reasons to be sick at the end of the year. Another myth is that absence is preferred to lateness. Some employees believe, for example, that it is more honorable to be absent because of illness than late because of oversleeping. Consequently, the employee who oversleeps calls in sick rather than face the embarrassment of arriving at work late.

VALUE NEATNESS, ORDERLINESS, AND SPEED

Neatness, orderliness, and speed are important contributors to workplace productivity and therefore should be valued. An orderly desk or work area does not inevitably signify an orderly mind. Yet orderliness does help

most people become more productive. Less time is wasted and less energy is expended if you do not have to hunt for missing information. Knowing where information is and what information you have available is a way of being in control of your job. When your job gets out of control, you are probably working at less than peak efficiency. Being neat and orderly helps you achieve good performance. Frequently breaking your concentration for such matters as finding a memo or a computer manual inhibits high performance.

Neatness is linked to working rapidly because clutter and searching for misplaced items consumes time. Employers emphasize speed today to remain competitive in such matters as serving customers promptly and bringing new products and services to the market. Speed is widely considered to be a competitive advantage. In the words of organizational consultant Price Pritchett:

> So you need to operate with a strong sense of urgency. Accelerate in all aspects of your work, even if it means living with a few more ragged edges. Emphasize *action*. Don't bog down in endless preparation trying to get things perfect before you make a move. Sure, high quality is crucial, but it must come quickly. You can't sacrifice speed. Learn to fail fast, fix it, and race on.[7]

The best approach to maintaining a neat work area and to enhance speed is to convince yourself that neatness and speed are valuable. You will then search for ways to be neat and fast, such as putting back a computer manual immediately after use or making phone conversations brief. The underlying principle is that an attitude leads to a change in behavior.

Develop an Ethic of Effectiveness and Quality

An ethic of effectiveness extends from the work ethic, as described in Chapter 2. The **effectiveness ethic** focuses on the need for excellent work and doing work the best way.[8] A person with a strong effectiveness ethic will continuously look for better ways of doing the work. Similarly, the person will routinely challenge the status quo by asking, "What changes can I make to perform my job better?" For the pizza delivery specialist, improved performance might take the form of changing a map to one that indicates streets in more detail. For the insurance claims specialist, a change might mean developing a broader database of auto replacement parts suppliers.

A positive attitude toward quality is part of an effectiveness emphasis because quality focuses on satisfying the needs of both external and internal customers. If your mental set is that of totally satisfying your customer, you will produce work of high quality based on pride. Another important component of quality is painstaking attention to detail to ensure that all work activities are done right the first time.

Work Smarter, Not Harder

People caught up in trying to accomplish a job often wind up working hard, but not in an imaginative way that leads to good results. Much time and energy are thus wasted. If you develop the attitude of seeking to work smarter rather than harder, your productivity and satisfaction will increase. Let's look at an example of the difference between working harder and working smarter.

> A service technician checks his schedule to find that he has 35 service calls lined up for the week. If he takes the service calls in order of the time of their request, he will spend more than five full days crisscrossing his territory to visit customers. Taking the calls by time of request means that he will be working harder. In contrast, if he groups his calls according to proximity to each other, he can cover all customers in three and one-half days. The time savings comes from less travel time, thus allowing him to work smarter.[9]

BECOME SELF-EMPLOYED PSYCHOLOGICALLY

A distinguishing characteristic of many self-employed people is that they care deeply about what they accomplish each day.[10] Most of their job activities directly or indirectly affect their financial health. Additionally, many self-employed people enjoy high job satisfaction because they have chosen work that fits their interests. Because of the factors just mentioned, the self-employed person is compelled to make good use of time. Also, the high level of job satisfaction typical of many self-employed people leads them to enjoy being productive.

If a person working for an employer regards his or her area of responsibility as self-employment, productivity may increase. To help regard employment by others as self-employment, keep this thought in mind Every employee is given some assets to manage to achieve a good return on investment. If you managed the printing and copying center for your company, you would be expected to manage that asset profitably.

APPRECIATE THE IMPORTANCE OF REST AND RELAXATION

A productive attitude to maintain is that overwork can be counterproductive and lead to negative stress and burnout. Proper physical rest contributes to mental alertness and improved ability to cope with frustration. Constant attention to work or study is often inefficient. It is a normal human requirement to take enough rest breaks to allow yourself to approach work or study with a fresh perspective. Each person has to establish the right balance between work and leisure within the bounds of freedom granted by the situation.

Neglecting the normal need for rest and relaxation can lead to **workaholism,** an addiction to work in which not working is an uncomfortable experience. Some types of workaholics are perfectionists who are never satisfied with their work, and therefore find it difficult to leave work behind. In addition, the perfectionistic workaholic may become heavily focused on control leading to rigid behavior. However, some people who work long and hard are classified as achievement-oriented workaholics who thrive on hard work and are usually highly productive.[11]

To help achieve rest and relaxation, some business people take *power naps*. You can train yourself to take these 15-minute naps to give you short bursts of energy and stretch your stamina over a long day. A few minutes' power nap in the late afternoon can keep you going for an overtime assignment. Where to take these naps is left to your imagination, depending on your work situation. Some workers nap in their cars when the temperature is moderate.

 TIME-MANAGEMENT TECHNIQUES

So far we have discussed improving productivity from standpoints of dealing with procrastination and developing the right attitudes and values. Skills and techniques are also important for becoming more productive. Here we describe some well-established methods of work-habit improvement, along with several new ones. For these techniques to enhance productivity, most of them need to be incorporated into and practiced regularly in our daily lives.[12] This is particularly true because many of these techniques are habits, and habits have to be programmed into the brain through repetition.

CLEAN UP AND GET ORGANIZED

An excellent starting point for improving work habits and time management is to clean up the work area and arrange things neatly. Eliminate clutter by throwing out unnecessary paper and deleting computer files that will probably never be used again. The idea is to learn to simplify the work area so that there are fewer distractions and the brain can be more focused. In addition, finding important files becomes easier. Getting organized includes sorting out which tasks need doing, including assignments and projects not yet completed. Getting organized can also mean sorting through the many small paper notes attached to the computer and on the wall.

A major reason a clean-up campaign is needed periodically is that many people have packrat tendencies. It is difficult to throw out tangible items (including paper, souvenir ball pens, and supply catalogues) because possessions give us a sense of security, status, and comfort.[13] A major clean-up principle is, therefore, to discard anything that is no longer valuable. A suggestion worth considering is to throw out at least one item everyday from the office and home. Since new items come into the office and home almost daily, you will always have possessions left.

PLAN YOUR ACTIVITIES

The primary principle of effective time management is **planning:** deciding what you want to accomplish and the actions needed to make it happen. The most elementary—and the most important—planning tool is a list of tasks that need doing. Almost every successful person works from a "to do" list. These lists are similar to the daily goals described in Chapter 2. Before you can compose a useful list, you need to set aside a few moments each day to sort out the tasks at hand. A list used by a working parent is presented in Exhibit 12-1.

Where Do You Put Your Lists?   Many people dislike having small "to do" lists stuck in different places. One reason is that these lists are readily lost among other papers. Many people therefore put lists on desk calendars or printed forms called *planners* which are also available in electronic form as hand-held devices. Planners give you an opportunity to record your activities in intervals as small as 15 minutes. Some planners are part of a system that enables you to link your daily activities to your mission in life. For many people these planners are invaluable, for others they are a burden that leads to overstructuring their lives.

EXHIBIT 12-1

A SAMPLE "TO DO" LIST

From the Desk of Jennifer Bartow

JOB

Make ten calls to prospects for new listings.
Have "For Sale" signs put outside Hanover Blvd. house.
Set up mortgage appointment at 1st Federal for the Calhouns.
Get old file cabinets replaced.
Order new memo pads.
Meet with the Goldsteins at 5 P.M.
Set up time to show house to the Bowens.

HOME

Buy running shoes for Todd.
Buy Jeans for Linda.
Get defroster fixed on freezer.
Write and send out monthly bills.
Clip cat's nails.
Check out problem with septic tank.
Make appt. with dentist to have chipped filling replaced.

FIRST REALTY CORPORATION
Jacksonville, Florida

Another useful approach for organizing your lists is to use a notebook small enough to be portable. The notebook becomes your master list to keep track of work tasks, errands, social engagements, and shopping items. Anything else requiring action might also be recorded—even a reminder to clean up the work area again.

How Do You Set Priorities?   Faced with multiple tasks to do at the same time, it is possible to feel overwhelmed and freeze as a result. The time-tested solution is to establish a priority to each item on the "to do" list. A typical system is to use *A* to signify critical or essential items, *B* to signify important items, and *C* for the least important ones. Although an item might be regarded as a *C* (for example, refilling your stapler), it still has a contribution to make to your productivity and sense of well being. Many people obtain a sense of satisfaction from crossing an item, however trivial, from their list. Furthermore, if you are conscientious, small undone items will interfere with concentration.

How Do You Schedule and Follow Through?   To be effective, a "to do" list must be an action tool. To convert your list into action, prepare a schedule of when you are going to do each of the items on the list. Follow through by doing things according to your schedule, checking them off as you go along.

Get Off to a Good Start

Get off to a good beginning, and you are more likely to have a successful, productive day. Start poorly, and you will be behind most of the day. According to Douglass Merrill, people who get going early tend to be in the right place at the right time more often, thus seeming to be lucky. "When you start early, you are lucky enough to get a good parking spot. You are lucky enough to avoid traffic jams. You are lucky enough to finish your job by the end of the day.[14] To get off to a good start regularly, it is important to start the day with the conscious intention of starting strong.

An effective way of getting off to a good start is to tackle the toughest task first, because most people have their peak energy in the morning. With a major task already completed, you are off to a running start on a busy workday.

Make Good Use of Office Technology

Only in recent years have companies begun to achieve productivity increases from office automation. One reason office automation has not been as successful as hoped is that many office workers do not make extensive use of the technology available. Used properly, most high-tech devices in the office can improve productivity and quality. Among the most productivity-enhancing devices are word processors, e-mail, spreadsheets, computer graphics, fax machines, voice mail, and photocopiers.

How you use these devices is the key to increased productivity. Two examples follow:[15]

- A laptop computer can help you be much more productive during periods of potential downtime. While waiting in someone's office or in an airport or on the plane, you can spend your time answering correspondence.

- A fax machine has many productivity-enhancing applications. One manager frequently visits clients in the late afternoon. If there are important papers she must see before she leaves, she has them faxed to her office at home. Using this method, she saves a trip back to the office, but she can review the work in ten minutes during the evening.

Another approach to using information technology to improve your productivity is to use personal information manager (PIM) software. The purpose of such software is to help you organize your work, following many of the principles of time management. PIM software usually combines the functions of an address book, appointment book, alarm clock, "to do" list, telephone dialer, and note pad. Among such software are *Lotus Organizer, Sharkware Pro,* and *Sidekick.*

CONCENTRATE ON ONE TASK AT A TIME

Effective people have a well-developed capacity to concentrate on the problem or person facing them, however surrounded they are with potential distractions. The best results from concentration are achieved when you are so absorbed in your work that you are aware of virtually nothing else at the moment. As described in Chapter 3, this is the flow experience. Another useful byproduct of concentration is that it reduces absentmindedness. If you really concentrate on what you are doing, the chances diminish that you will forget what you intended to do.

Conscious effort and self-discipline can strengthen concentration skills. An effective way to sharpen your concentration skills is to set aside ten minutes a day and focus on something repetitive, such as your breathing pattern or a small word. This is the same approach that is used in meditation to relieve stress. After practicing concentration in the manner just described, concentrate on an aspect of your work such as preparing a report.

STREAMLINE YOUR WORK AND EMPHASIZE IMPORTANT TASKS

As companies continue to operate with fewer workers than in the past despite good economic times, more nonproductive work must be eliminated. Getting rid of unproductive work is part of *reengineering* in which work processes are radically redesigned and simplified. Every employee is expected to get rid of work that does not contribute to productivity or help customers. Another intent of work streamlining is to get rid of work that does not add value for customers. Here is a sampling of work that typically does not add value:

- E-mail or paper messages that almost nobody reads
- Sending receipts and acknowledgments to people who do not need them
- Writing and mailing reports that nobody reads or needs
- Meetings that do not accomplish work, exchange important information, or improve team spirit
- Checking up frequently on the work of competent people

In general, to streamline or reengineer your work, look for duplication of effort and waste. An example of duplication of effort would be to routinely send people e-mail and fax messages covering the same topic. An example of waste would be to call a meeting for disseminating information that could easily be communicated by e-mail.

Important (value-contributing) tasks are those in which superior performance could have a large payoff. No matter how quickly you took care of making sure that your store paid its bills on time, for example, this effort would not make your store an outstanding success. If, however, you concentrated your efforts on bringing unique and desirable merchandise into the store, this action could greatly affect your business success.

In following the *A-B-C* system, you should devote ample time to the essential tasks. You should not pay more attention than absolutely necessary to the *C* (trivial) items. Many people respond to this suggestion by saying, "I don't think concentrating on important tasks applies to me. My job is so filled with routine, I have no chance to work on the big breakthrough ideas." True, most jobs are filled with routine requirements. What a person can do is spend some time, perhaps even one hour a week, concentrating on tasks of potentially major significance.

TACKLE DISTASTEFUL TASKS FIRST

Another method of increasing productivity is to tackle distasteful tasks first. As explained earlier, a distasteful task often fosters procrastination. By gritting your teeth and directly attacking something unpleasant, you will free yourself to work on the more pleasant. Doing the relatively more enjoyable activities thus becomes a reward for having worked through the less attractive activities. Tackling distasteful tasks first is therefore a method of self-motivation.

The "distasteful first" principle can readily be applied to schoolwork. Tackle first the homework assignment you dislike the most. After the least favorite assignment is completed, you may find it relaxing and rewarding to work on an assignment of greater personal interest. In general, save the best for last and watch your productivity climb.

WORK AT A STEADY PACE

In most jobs, working at a steady clip pays dividends in efficiency. The spurt worker creates many problems for management. Some employees take pride in working rapidly, even when the result is a high error rate. At home, too, a steady pace is better than spurting. A spurt houseworker is one who goes into a flurry of activity every so often. An easier person to live with is someone who does his or her share of housework at an even pace throughout the year.

Another advantage of the steady-pace approach is that you accomplish much more than someone who puts out extra effort just once in a while. The completely steady worker would accomplish just as much the day before a holiday as on a given Monday. That extra hour or so of productivity adds up substantially by the end of the year. Despite the advantages of maintaining a steady pace, some peaks and valleys in your work may be inevitable. Tax accounting firms, for example, have busy seasons.

CREATE SOME QUIET, UNINTERRUPTED TIME

Time-management specialist Merrill Douglass observes that most office workers find their days hectic, fragmented, and frustrating. Incessant interruptions make it difficult to get things done. The constant start-stop-restart pattern lengthens the time needed to get jobs done. Quiet time can reduce the type of productivity drain just described. To achieve quiet time, create an uninterrupted block of time enabling you to concentrate on your work. This could mean turning off the telephone, not accessing your e-mail, and blocking drop-in visitors during certain times of the workday.

Quiet time is used for such essential activities as thinking, planning, getting organized, doing analytical work, writing reports and doing creative tasks. One hour of quiet time might yield as much productive work as four hours of interrupted time.[16]

Quiet time is difficult to find in some jobs, such as those involving customer contact. An agreement has to be worked out with the manager about when and where quiet time can be taken. A buyer for office supplies in an insurance company worked out a sensible quiet-time arrangement. He reports, "I worked out a deal with my manager whereby every Thursday morning from 9 to 12, I could take my work into a vacant office adjacent to the boardroom. We agreed that I could be reached only in an emergency. It wasn't a way to goof off. Each month I had to write my boss a brief report of what I accomplished during my uninterrupted time."

MAKE USE OF BITS OF TIME

A truly productive person makes good use of miscellaneous bits of time, both on and off the job. While waiting in line at a post office, you might update your "to do" list; while waiting for an elevator, you might be able to read a brief report; and if you have finished your day's work ten minutes before quitting time, you can use that time to clean out a file. By the end of the year your productivity will have increased much more than if you had squandered these bits of time.

The craze referred to as "grazing" is a variation of making good use of bits of time. **Grazing** is eating meals on the run to make good use of time ordinarily spent on sitting down for meals. Many ambitious people today nibble at snacks rather than disrupt their work by visiting a restaurant. Grazing does have its disadvantages: You cannot network while grazing; eating while working can be bad for digestion; and it may deprive you of a needed rest break.

STAY IN CONTROL OF PAPERWORK, THE IN-BASKET, AND E-MAIL

Despite the widespread use of electronic messages, the workplace is still overflowing with printed messages, including computer printouts. Paperwork essentially involves taking care of administrative details such as correspondence, expense account forms, and completing surveys. Responding to e-mail messages has created additional administrative details that require handling, even if they are actually *electronic work* rather than paperwork.

Unless you handle paperwork and e-mail efficiently, you may lose control of your job or home life, which could lead to substantial negative stress. Ideally, a small amount of time should be invested in paperwork and routine e-mail every day. Nonprime time (when you are at less-than-peak efficiency but not overly fatigued) is the best time to take care of administrative routine.

The in-basket remains the center of paperwork. For many overwhelmed workers, their entire desk top becomes the in-basket. Four steps are particularly helpful in keeping an in-basket under control: (1) Give some attention to the in-basket everyday. (2) Sort in-basket items into an action file and a reading file. (3) Take care of the action items as soon as possible. (4) Read items in the reading file during bits of time on the job or at home.

 # OVERCOMING TIME WASTERS

Another basic thrust to improved personal productivity is to minimize wasting time. Many of the techniques already described in this chapter help to save time. The tactics and strategies described next, however, are directly aimed at overcoming the problem of wasted time.

MINIMIZE DAYDREAMING

"Taking a field trip" while on the job is a major productivity drain. Daydreaming is triggered when the individual perceives the task to be boring—such as reviewing another person's work for errors. Brain research suggests that younger people are more predisposed to daydreaming than older people. Apparently, older people use neurons better to focus on tasks.[17]

Unresolved personal problems are an important source of daydreaming, thus blocking your productivity. This is especially true because effective time utilization requires good concentration. When you are preoccupied with a personal or business problem, it is difficult to give your full efforts to a task at hand.

The solution is to do something constructive about whatever problem is sapping your ability to concentrate (as discussed in Chapter 4 about wellness and stress.) Sometimes a relatively minor problem, such as driving with an expired operator's license, can impair your work concentration. At other times, a major problem, such as how best to take care of a parent who has suffered a stroke, interferes with work. In either situation, your concentration will suffer until you take appropriate action.

PREPARE A TIME LOG TO EVALUATE YOUR USE OF TIME

An advanced tool for becoming a more efficient time manager is to prepare a time log of how you are currently investing your time. For five full workdays, write down everything you do, including such activities as responding to mail and taking rest breaks. One of the most important outputs of a time log is to uncover time leaks. A **time leak** is anything you are doing or not doing that allows time to get away from you. Among them are spending too much time for lunch by collecting people before finally leaving, and walking to a coworker's cubicle rather than telephoning.

A major time leak for many workers is **schmoozing,** or informal socializing on the job, including small talk and telephone conversations with friends. Schmoozing is useful in relieving tension and increasing job satisfaction, but too much of this activity is a major loss of productive time.

AVOID BEING A COMPUTER GOOF-OFF

We are all aware of the productivity improvements possible when computers are used in the office. An unproductive use of computers, however, is to tinker with them to the exclusion of useful work. Many people have become intrigued with computers to the point of diversion. They become habituated to creating new reports, exquisite graphics, and making endless changes. Some managers spend so much time with computers that they neglect leadership responsibilities, thus lowering their productivity.

In addition to the problems just cited, Internet surfing for purposes not strictly related to the job has become a major productivity drain. Sixty-three percent of the human resources executives who responded to a survey said that employees are putting more time into Net surfing and other diversionary activities.[18] One of the more popular computerized pin-ball games. *Full Tilt! 2,* can be hidden behind a spreadsheet with a single stroke.

The message is straightforward: To plug one more potential productivity drain, avoid becoming a computer goof-off.

Keep Track of Important Names, Places, and Things

How much time have you wasted lately searching for such items as a telephone number you jotted down somewhere, your keys, or an appointment book? A supervisor suddenly realized he had forgotten to show up for a luncheon appointment. He wanted to call and apologize but was unable to locate the person's name and phone number! Standard solutions to overcoming these problems are to keep a wheel file (such as Rolodex) of people's names and companies. It is difficult to misplace such a file. Many managers and professionals store such information in a database or even in a word processing file. Such files are more difficult to misplace than a pocket directory.

Two steps are recommended for remembering where you put things. First, have a parking place for everything. This would include putting your keys and appointment book back in the same place after each use. (This tactic supports the strategy of being neat and orderly to minimize time wasting.) Second, make visual associations. To have something register in your mind at the moment you are doing it, make up a visual association about that act. Thus, you might say, "Here I am putting my résumé in the back section of my canvas bag."

Set a Time Limit for Certain Tasks and Projects

Spending too much time on a task or project wastes time. As a person becomes experienced with certain projects, he or she is able to make accurate estimates of how long a project will take to complete. A paralegal might say, "Getting this will drawn up for the lawyer's approval should take two hours." A good work habit to develop is to estimate how long a job should take and then proceed with strong determination to get that job completed within the estimated time period.

A productive version of this technique is to decide that some low- and medium-priority items are worth only so much of your time. Invest that much time in the project, but no more. Preparing a file on advertisements that come across your desk is one example.

Be Decisive and Finish Things

A subtle way of improving your personal productivity is to be decisive. Move quickly, but not impulsively, through the problem-solving and decision-making steps outlined in Chapter 3 when you are faced with a nonroutine decision. Once you have evaluated the alternatives to the problem, choose and implement one of them. Set a limit to how much time you will invest in arriving at a decision to a problem. Next, set a limit to the amount of time you will spend implementing your solution. If you are in charge of this year's office party committee, you might decide to hold the party at a particular party house. Decide next on approximately how much time you should invest in the project, and stick to your limit.

Another aspect of being decisive is making the decision to finish tasks you have begun. Incomplete projects lower your productivity. Marge Baxter puts it this way: "It's better to complete a few things than to have seventeen things half done."[19] Another point to remember is that nobody gives you credit for an unfinished project.

Now that you have studied various ways to improve your personal productivity, do Human Relations Skill-Building Exercise 12-1.

SUMMARY

People with good work habits tend to be more successful in their careers than poorly organized individuals, and they tend to have more time to spend on personal life. Good work habits are more important than ever because of today's emphasis on productivity and quality.

Procrastination is the leading cause of poor productivity and career self-sabotage. People procrastinate for many reasons including their perception that a task is unpleasant, overwhelming, or may lead to negative consequences. Fear of success can also lead to procrastination. Awareness of procrastination can lead to its control.

Eight other techniques for reducing procrastination are: (1) calculate the cost of procrastination; (2) counterattack the burdensome task; (3) jump-start yourself; (4) peck away at an overwhelming task; (5) motivate yourself with rewards and punishments; (6) make a commitment to other people; (7) express a more positive attitude about your intentions; and (8) use computerized subliminal messages.

Developing good work habits and time-management practices is often a matter of developing proper attitudes toward work and time. Seven such attitudes and values are: (1) become a goal-oriented person and value your time; (2) value good attendance and punctuality; (3) value neatness, orderliness, and speed; (4) develop an ethic of effectiveness and quality; (5) work smarter, not harder; (6) become self-employed psychologically; and (7) appreciate the importance of rest and relaxation.

Twelve skills and techniques to help you become more productive are: (1) clean up and get organized; (2) plan your activities; (3) get off to a good start; (4) make good use of office technology; (5) concentrate on one task at a time; (6) streamline your work and emphasize important tasks; (7) tackle distasteful tasks first; (8) work at a steady pace; (9) create some quiet, uninterrupted time; (10) make use of bits of time; and (11) stay in control of paperwork, the in-basket, and e-mail.

Six suggestions for overcoming time wasting are (1) minimize daydreaming; (2) prepare a time log and evaluate your use of time; (3) avoid being a computer goof-off; (4) keep track of important names, places, and things; (5) set a time limit for certain tasks and projects; and (6) be decisive and finish things.

HUMAN RELATIONS SKILL-BUILDING EXERCISE 12-1

The Personal Productivity Checklist

Class Project

Each class member will use the preceding checklist to identify the two biggest mistakes he or she is making in work habits and time management. The mistakes could apply to work, school, or personal life. In addition to identifying the problem, each student will develop a brief action plan about how to overcome it. For instance, "One of my biggest problems is that I tend to start a lot of projects but finish very few of them. Now that I am aware of this problem, I am going to post a sign over my desk that reads, 'No one will give me credit for things I never completed.' "

Students then present their problems and action plans to the class. After each student has made his or her presentation, a class discussion is held to reach conclusions and interpretations about the problems revealed. For instance, it might be that one or two time management problems are quite frequent.

Especially applicable to me

Overcoming Procrastination

1. Increase awareness of the problem. _____
2. Calculate cost of procrastination. _____
3. Jump-start yourself. _____
4. Peck away at an overwhelming task. _____
5. Motivate yourself with rewards and punishments. _____
6. Make a commitment to other people. _____
7. Express a more positive attitude about your intentions. _____
8. Use subliminal messages about overcoming procrastination. _____

Developing Proper Attitudes and Values

1. Become a goal-oriented person and value your time. _____
2. Value good attendance and punctuality. _____
3. Value neatness, orderliness, and speed. _____
4. Develop an ethic of effectiveness and quality. _____
5. Work smarter, not harder. _____
6. Become self-employed psychologically. _____
7. Appreciate the importance of rest and relaxation. _____

(Continued)

Time Management Techniques

1. Clean up and get organized. _____
2. Plan your activities (including a "to do" list with priority setting). _____
3. Get off to a good start. _____
4. Make good use of office technology. _____
5. Concentrate on one task at a time. _____
6. Streamline your work and emphasize important tasks. _____
7. Tackle distasteful tasks first. _____
8. Work at a steady pace. _____
9. Create some quiet, uninterrupted time. _____
10. Make use of bits of time. _____
11. Stay in control of paperwork, the in-basket, and e-mail. _____

Overcoming Time Wasters

1. Minimize daydreaming. _____
2. Prepare a time log to evaluate your use of time. _____
3. Avoid being a computer goof off. _____
4. Keep track of important names, places, and things. _____
5. Set a time limit for certain tasks and projects. _____
6. Be decisive and finish things. _____

Questions and Activities

1. In recent years, companies that sell desk planners and other time-management devices have experienced all-time peak demands for their products. What factors do you think are creating this boom?

2. What factors about a person's appearance might be accurate indicators of his or her work habits and time management?

3. To what extent do athletes practice good work habits and time management during the game?

4. Some students contend that because they work best when they put things off until the last moment, procrastination probably will not hurt them in their career. What is wrong with their reasoning?

5. It is widely recognized that procrastination is generally unproductive. However, can you give an example of how procrastination has benefited you or somebody you know?

6. Some workers are concerned that if too much work streamlining takes place in the company, some workers will lose their jobs. What is your position?

7. What principle of work habits and time management described in this chapter helps explain that being unusually tidy and well organized will not necessarily make a person successful?

8. Identify five bits of time you could put to better use.

9. Complaints are mounting that e-mail and the Internet can often lower the productivity of workers. What might be the problem?

10. Ask an experienced businessperson how he or she uses the computer to improve his or her work habits and time management. Be prepared to share your findings in class.

REFERENCES

[1]David Palmer, "How America's Most Successful Executives Accomplish So Much in So Little Time," *Executive Focus,* October 1996, p. 23.

[2]Theodore Kurtz, "10 Reasons Why People Procrastinate," *Supervisory Management,* April 1990, pp. 1–2.

[3]Alan Lakein, *How to Gain Control of Your Time and Your Life* (New York: Wyden Books, 1973), pp. 141–151.

[4]"Don't Procrastinate," *Practical Supervision,* January 1989, p. 3.

[5]Linda Sapadin, *It's About Time! The Six Styles of Procrastination and How to Overcome Them* (New York: Viking, 1996).

[6]Michael Maran, "Program Yourself: Software for the Right Side of Your Brain," *Success,* October 1991, p. 58. (Software produced by Visionary Software, Portland, Oregon.)

[7]Price Pritchett, *The Employee Handbook of New Work Habits for a Radically Changing World* (Dallas, TX: Pritchett & Associates, Inc. 1997), p. 11.

[8]"Developing an Effectiveness Ethic," *Getting Results,* July 1996, p. 1.

[9]"Be Efficient—Get Organized," *Working Smart,* March 1994, p. 8.

[10]Raymond P. Rood and Brenda L. Meneley, "Serious Play at Work," *Personnel Journal,* January 1991, p. 90.

[11]Mildred L. Culp, "Working Productively with Workaholics while Minimizing Legal Risks," syndicated column, Passage Media, 1997.

[12]Jolene D. Scriven, "Teaching Time Management," *Business Education Forum,* February 1996, p. 19.

[13]Odette Pollar, "So, You Are Called a Packrat!" *The Pryor Report,* March 1996, p. 9.

A HUMAN RELATIONS CASE PROBLEM

The Busy Office Manager

Mike Powers looked at a clock on the electric range and said to Ruth, his wife: "Oh no, it's 7:25. It's my morning to drop off Jason and Gloria at the child-care center. Jason hasn't finished breakfast, and Gloria is still in her pajamas. Can you get Gloria dressed for me?"

Ruth responded, "OK, I'll help Gloria. But today is your turn to take care of the children. And I have a client presentation at 8:30 this morning. I need to prepare for a few more minutes."

"Forget I asked," said Mike. "I'll take care of it. Once again I'll start my day in a frenzy, late for child care, and just barely making it to work on time."

"Why didn't you get up when the alarm rang the first time?" asked Ruth.

"Don't you remember, we talked until one this morning? It seems like we never get to talk to each other until midnight."

After getting Jason and Gloria settled at the child care center, Mike dashed off to the public accounting firm where he worked as the office manager. After greeting several staff members, Mike turned on his computer to check his e-mail. Ann Gabrielli, one of the partners in the firm, left the following message: "See you today at 11:30 for the review of overhead expenses. Two other partners will be attending."

Mike quickly looked at his desk calendar. According to his calendar, the meeting was one week from today. Mike called Gabrielli immediately, and said, "Ann, my apologies. My schedule says that the meeting is one week from today at 11:30, not today. I'm just not ready with the figures for today's meeting."

"My calendar says the meeting is today," said Gabrielli harshly. I'm ready for the meeting and so are Craig and Gunther (the other partners). This isn't the first time you've gotten your weeks mixed up. The meeting will go on, however poorly you have to perform."

"I'll be there," said Mike. "It's just a question of reviewing some figures that I've already collected."

After putting down the phone, Mike calculated that he had about 2 hours and 40 minutes in which to prepare a preliminary report on reducing overhead. He then glanced at his desk calendar to see what else he had scheduled this morning. The time looked clear except for one entry, "PA/LC."

"What is 'PA/LC'" thought Mike. "I can't imagine what these initials stand for. Wait a minute, now I know. The initials stand for performance appraisal with Lucy Cruthers, our head bookkeeper. I'm not ready for that session. And I can't do it this morning. Mike then sent Cruthers an e-mail message, suggesting that they meet the following week at the same time.

Cruthers answered back immediately. She wrote that she would not be able to meet the following week because that was the first day of her vacation. Mike sent her another note: "I'll get back to you later with another date. I don't have time now to make plans."

Next, Mike informed the department assistant, Lois Chavez, that he had to hurriedly prepare for the 11:30 meeting. Mike asked for her cooperation in keeping visitors away for the rest of the morning.

(Continued)

He then called up the directory on his hard drive to look for the file on overhead expenses he had begun last week. As he scanned through the directory, he found only three files that might be related to the topic: COST, EXPENSES, and TRIM. Mike reasoned that the file must be one of these three.

Mike retrieved the file, COST. It proved to be a summary of furniture expenses for the firm. Upon bringing EXPENSES up on the screen, Mike found that it was his expense account report for a business trip he took seven months ago. TRIM was found to be a list of cost estimates for lawn-care services.

Agitated, and beginning to sweat profusely, Mike asked Chavez to help him. "I'm stuck," he pleaded. "I need to find my file for the overhead expense analysis I was doing for the partners. Do you recall what I named this file? Did I give it to you on disk?"

"Let me see if I can help," said Chavez. "We'll search your directory together." Chavez scanned about 100 files. "What a clutter," she sighed. "You ought to clean out your files sometime soon. Here's a possibility, PTR."

"I doubt it," said Mike. " 'PTR' stands for partner. I'm looking for a file about overhead expenses."

"But you are preparing the file for the partners, aren't you?"

Lois proved to be right. The PTR file contained the information Mike sought. Within 30 minutes he completed the spreadsheet analysis he needed. He then prepared a brief memo on the word processor, explaining his findings. With 20 minutes left before the presentation, Mike asked Lucy if she could run off three copies in a hurry. Lucy explained that the department's photocopying machine was not operating. She said she would ask to use the photocopier in another department.

"Bring them into my meeting with the partners as soon as you can," said Mike. "I've run out of time."

On the way to the meeting, Mike exhaled a few times and consciously relaxed his muscles to overcome the tension accumulated from preparing the report under so much pressure. Mike performed reasonably well during the meeting. The partners accepted his analysis of overhead expenses and said they would study his findings further. As the meeting broke up at 12:30, the senior partner commented to Mike, "If you had gotten your weeks straight, I think you could have presented your analysis in more depth. Your report was useful, but I know you are capable of doing a more sophisticated analysis."

After returning from lunch, Mike reviewed his daily planner again. He noticed a Post-it™ note attached to the light on his desk. The entry on the slip of paper said, "Racquetball, monday night with Ziggy."

"Not again," Mike said to himself in a groan of agony. "Tonight I have to get Jason and Gloria to bed. Ruth has a makeup class scheduled for her course in Japanese. I'll have to call Ziggy now. I hope he's in his office."

Mike left an URGENT message on Ziggy's e-mail, offering his apologies. He thought to himself, "I hope Ziggy won't be too annoyed. This is the second time this year I've had to reschedule a match at the last moment."

Mike returned from lunch at 2:00 P.M. He decided to finish the report on overhead he had prepared for the partners. By 4:00 P.M. Mike was ready to begin the tasks outlined on his daily planner. At that point Lois Chavez walked into Mike's office and announced: "There's a representative here from Account Temps. She said she was in

(Continued)

the building, so she decided to drop in and talk about their temporary employment services."

"Might as well let her in," said Mike. "We will be hiring some temporary book-keepers soon. Account Temps has a good reputation. It's getting too late to do much today anyway."

Mike made it to the child-care center by 5:45 and packed Jason and Gloria into the family minivan. Gloria, the oldest child, asked if the family could eat at Hardee's this evening. Mike said, "OK, but I'll have to stop at an ATM first. I don't have enough cash on hand to eat out. We'll stop at the ATM then stop by the house and see if Mom wants to eat out tonight before class."

Mike and the children arrived home at 6:15 and asked Ruth if she would like to have a family dinner at Hardee's this evening.

"I have about one hour to spare before class," said Ruth. "Why not? By the way, how was your day?"

"My day?" asked Mike with a sigh. "I just fell one day farther behind schedule. I'll have to do some paperwork after the children are asleep. Maybe we can watch the late night news together this evening. We should both be free by then."

Questions

1. What time-management mistakes does Mike appear to be making?

2. What does Mike appear to be doing right from the standpoint of managing time?

3. What suggestions can you offer Mike to help him get his schedule more under control?

HUMAN RELATIONS SKILL-BUILDING EXERCISE 12-2

Helping a Busy Office Manager

The preceding case presents background information for this role play. One person plays the role of Mike Powers, who has decided to meet with a time-management counselor to discuss his problems. Mike feels that if he doesn't get help soon, he will be doing serious damage to his career, and perhaps his marriage.

Another person plays the role of a time-management counselor who will listen to Mike and attempt to understand the root of his problem. The counselor will then make some recommendations. This particular counselor has a reputation for being a good listener, yet is known to give dogmatic recommendations.

[14]Merrill Douglass, "Timely Time Tips: Ideas to Help You Manage Your Time," *Executive Management Forum,* September 1989, p. 4.

[15]"Save Time By Doing Two Things at Once," *Working Smart,* October 1991, p. 5.

[16]Douglas, "Timely Time Tips," p. 4.

[17]Paul Chance, "The Wondering Mind of Youth," *Psychology Today,* December 1988, p. 22.

[18]Brenda Park Sundoo, "This Employee May Be Loafing: Can You Tell? Should You Care?" *Personnel Journal,* December 1996, p. 56.

[19]Quoted in Beth Brophy and Diane Cole, "10 Timely Tips," *USA Weekend,* October 25–27, 1985, p. 22.

 ## ADDITIONAL READING

Denton, D. Keith. "Process Mapping Trims Cycle Time." *HRMagazine,* February 1995, pp. 56–61.

Fletcher, Jerry L. *Patterns of High Performance: Discovering the Ways People Work Best.* San Francisco, CA: Berrett-Koehler Publishers, 1995.

Hemphill, Barbara. *Training the Office Tiger: The Complete Guide to Getting Organized at Work.* Washington, D.C.: The Kiplinger Washington Editors, Inc., 1996.

Kanigel, Robert. *The One Best Way: Frederick Winslow Taylor and the Enigma of Efficiency.* New York: Viking, 1997.

Majchrzak, Ann, and Wang, Qianewi. "Breaking the Functional Mind-Set in Process Organizations." *Harvard Business Review,* September-October 1996, pp. 92–99.

Mayer, Jeffrey J. *Winning the Fight Between You and Your Desk.* New York: Harper-Collins, 1994.

Oldham, Greg R., and Cummings, Anne. "Can Personal Stereos Improve Productivity?" *HRMagazine,* April 1996, pp. 95–99.

CHAPTER 13

GETTING AHEAD IN YOUR CAREER

Learning Objectives

After studying the information and doing the exercises in this chapter, you should be able to:

▼ Explain the new model of career-advancement in organizations

▼ Select several strategies and tactics for getting ahead in your career by taking control of your own behavior

▼ Select several strategies and tactics for advancing your career by exerting control over your environment

▼ Recognize how to deal with the challenge of hidden barriers to career advancement

*C*hances are Prospect Associates Ltd., a consulting firm, won't ever offer Drew Melton a corner office and his pick of the company art collection. He started out as a copy-machine operator three years ago, and that's exactly where he is today. Yet Melton is not in a dead-end job. Two weeks after he was hired by Prospect Associates, Melton went to its president, Laura Henderson, and told her how he could run document production better and faster. Henderson gave him the opportunity to run the operation his way.

"They're listening to my ideas, and that's why I'm making changes and contributing to the company," says Melton. Today he runs his own photocopy operation, dispensing advice to Prospect's harried consultants who rely on his painstaking attention to detail to give their proposals a professional look.

The company president and Melton agree that he has advanced, although he has not climbed a corporate ladder. He has increased his contribution to the company by sharpening his skills and expanding the scope of his job. His salary has increased by more than 40 percent; he's respected by the company's professional staff; and there's no pressure on him to move up.[1]

Drew Melton's story is an example of how people are advancing their careers today using a blend of traditional tactics (such as displaying initiative) and modern tactics (growing within the job). In this chapter we focus on strategies, tactics, and attitudes that will help you achieve promotion or hold on to a position you enjoy. The same approaches will enable you to achieve **career portability,** the ability to move from one employer to another when necessary.

We have divided the vast information about career advancement into four sections. The first section describes the new model, or concept, of career advancement. The second section deals with approaches to managing or taking control of your own behavior to advance or retain a good position. The third section deals with approaches to exerting control over your environment to improve your chances for success. A brief section is also included on dealing with hidden barriers to career advancement.

THE NEW MODEL OF CAREER ADVANCEMENT

Career advancement has acquired a shift in emphasis in recent years to accommodate the new organization structures. The major shift has been less emphasis on vertical mobility, or moving up the ladder, to more emphasis on lateral growth, or advancing by learning more. Drew Melton's experience in expanding his position in the photocopy room illustrates the new model of career advancement. Here we look briefly at the key components of the new model of career advancement.

1. *More emphasis on horizontal growth.* As just mentioned, the major shift in career advancement has been toward more emphasis on learning new skills and acquiring new knowledge in a position at the same organizational level. Many companies even give pay raises to employees who learn new job-related skills. Despite the emphasis on horizontal growth, many workers still aspire to climb the organizational ladder. Also, many companies offer promotion to a higher-level position as a reward for good performance.

2. *More emphasis on temporary leadership assignments.* In the traditional model of career advancement, an individual would strive to be promoted to a management or leadership position. The person would then hold on to that position unless demoted or fired. Today, many leadership positions are temporary, such as working as the head of a project to launch a new product. After the product is launched, the person might return to a group member (individual contributor) position. Or a person might be assigned as a committee head because of his or her expertise. After the committee has completed its work, the person returns to a nonleadership position.

3. *Climbing the ladder of self-fulfillment.* For an increasing number of people, doing work that contributes to self-fulfillment is more important than a focus on promotion or earnings growth. To advance in your career would be to find work that provides more self-fulfillment. Individual preferences determine what type of work is self-fulfilling. For one person, learning more about information technology might be self-fulfilling. For another, helping career beginners grow and develop might satisfy the need for self-fulfillment.

4. *Continuous learning.* According to career expert Douglas T. Hall, careers for the 21st century will consist of a series of short learning stages. *Career age,* or how long a person has been engaged in a type of work, will become more important than chronological age.[2] At one point in your career you might need to rapidly learn how to conduct research on the Internet. At another stage, you might need to learn rapidly how to organize a trade show.

5. *Being promoted as much for learn-how as know-how.* Hall also predicts that in the 21st century, demand in the labor market will shift from those with know-how (present skills) to those with learn-how (learning capability).[3] A track record of being able to learn will give people the portability mentioned at the start of this chapter. Being able to learn rapidly makes continuous learning possible. The reason that learn-how is so important is that organizations face such rapid technological change.

The new model of career advancement is compatible with a modern definition of success. **Career success** as used here means attaining the twin goals of organizational rewards and personal satisfaction. Organizational rewards include such experiences as occupying a high-ranking position, more money, challenging assignments, and the opportunity for new learning. Personal satisfaction refers to enjoying what you are doing. If your employer highly values your contribution and your job satisfaction is high, you are experiencing career success. However, success in general also includes accomplishment and satisfaction in personal life.

 ## TAKING CONTROL OF YOURSELF

The unifying theme to the strategies, tactics, and attitudes described in this section is that you must attempt to control your own behavior. You can advance your career by harnessing the forces under your control. Such a perspective is important because more than at any time in the past, individuals have the primary responsibility for managing their own careers. In the tough language of career counselor William Morin:

> Surely you no longer believe that unconditional loyalty, or even doing a good job, guarantees employment. You've probably even memorized the new mantra: "My career is my responsibility." . . . Truth is, it's way past time to embrace the fact that you are really in charge of your career.[4]

The following section concentrates on getting ahead by trying to control your external environment in some small way. Do not be concerned about overlap between the general categories of controlling yourself versus controlling the environment. Instead, be concerned about the meaning and application of the strategies and tactics. Recognize also that the information throughout this chapter will help you take responsibility for managing your career.

Develop Outstanding Interpersonal Skills

Getting ahead in business-related fields is exceedingly difficult unless you can relate effectively to other people. Workers are bypassed for promotion generally because someone thinks they cannot effectively be responsible for the work of others. Workers are more likely to be terminated for poor interpersonal skills than for poor technical skills.

Effective interpersonal or human relations skills refer to many specific practices. It is particularly important to understand and cope with a wide variety of personality types. Chapters 6 through 9 of this book focus on important interpersonal skills such as communication, resolving conflict, being assertive, and listening to customers. Interpersonal skills also include other topics in this book, such as being self-confident and exerting leadership (Chapter 14).

Develop Expertise

A starting point in getting ahead is to develop a useful job skill. This tactic is obvious if you are working as a specialist, such as an insurance underwriter. Being skilled at the task performed by the group is also a requirement for being promoted to a supervisory position. After being promoted to a supervisor or another managerial job, expertise is still important for further advancement. It helps a manager's reputation to be skilled in such things as memo writing, computer applications, preparing a budget, and interviewing job candidates. Another important skill is **troubleshooting,** the knack for pinpointing and analyzing snags in work flow as they arise.

PERFORM WELL ON ALL YOUR ASSIGNMENTS

Common sense and research support the idea that you have to perform well on your present assignment in order to move ahead.[5] Good job performance is the bedrock of a person's career. In rare instances a person is promoted on the basis of favoritism alone. In all other situations an employee must have received a favorable performance appraisal to be promoted. Before an employee is promoted, the prospective new boss asks, "How well did this person perform for you?"

CREATE GOOD FIRST IMPRESSIONS

Every time you interact with a new person inside or outside your company, you create a first impression. Fair or not, these first impressions have a big impact on your career. If your first impression is favorable, you will often be invited back by an internal or external customer. Your first impression also creates a halo that may influence perceptions about the quality of your work in the future. If your first impression is negative, you will have to work extra hard to be perceived as competent later on.

Looking successful contributes to a positive first impression. Your clothing, your desk and office, and your speech should project the image of a successful, but not necessarily flamboyant, person. Your standard of dress should be appropriate to your particular career stage and work environment. Appropriate dress for an inventory specialist is not the same as for an outside salesperson dealing with industrial customers. Appearing physically fit is also part of the success image.

Projecting a sense of control is another key factor contributing to a positive first impression. Show that you are in control of yourself and the environment. Avoid letting your body language betray you—nonverbal messages are sent by fidgeting or rubbing your face. Make your gestures project self-assurance and purpose.[6] A verbal method of appearing in control is to make a positive assertion such as, "This is a demanding assignment and I welcome the challenge."

Another reason first impressions are important is that, according to one theory of leadership, the leader of a group quickly sizes up new group members. Those who create a favorable impression become part of the ingroup and are therefore given more favorable assignments and kept informed more regularly. Group members who do not create a favorable initial impression become part of the outgroup, and are treated much less favorably.[7]

MAKE AN ACCURATE SELF-ANALYSIS

To effectively plan your career and to advance in it, you need an accurate picture of your strengths, areas for improvement, and preferences. The exercises in Chapters 1 and 2, combined with the job-finding material called for in Chapter 11, will provide much of the information needed for self-evaluation. In addition, listen attentively to feedback you receive from growth groups, superiors, and coworkers.

Here is an example of how this strategy might be used. Jimmy, an engineering technician, carefully fills out the Self-Knowledge Questionnaire. He notices that his self-evaluation is weakest in the area of dealing with people. Jimmy then requests a conference with his boss to discuss his development in this area. The verdict comes back, "Much improvement needed. You tend to be too abrupt with people, and you finish people's sentences for them." Jimmy then requests an assignment that emphasizes dealing with people. His boss is generous enough to allow Jimmy to risk a few mistakes to improve his human relations skills. While on this new assignment Jimmy concentrates on not being too abrupt with people. In addition, he plans some community activities that give him a chance to practice human relations skills, such as being toastmaster or assuming a leadership position in a technical society.

DOCUMENT YOUR ACCOMPLISHMENTS

Keeping an accurate record of your job accomplishments can be valuable when you are being considered for promotion, transfer, or assignment to a team or project. Documenting your accomplishments can also be used to verify new learning. In addition, a record of accomplishments is useful when your performance is being evaluated. You can show your manager what you have done for the company lately. Here are two examples of documented accomplishments from different types of jobs:

1. A bank teller suggested one side door be modified to accommodate customers in wheelchairs. Number of physically disabled customers jumped 324 percent in two years.

2. A maintenance supervisor decreased fuel costs in office by 27 percent in one year by installing ceiling fans.

After documenting your accomplishments, it pays to advertise. Let key people know in a tasteful way of your tangible accomplishments. You might request an opportunity to make a presentation to your boss to review the status of one of your successful projects, or use e-mail for the same purpose if it would be presumptuous for you to request a special meeting to discuss your accomplishments.

BE CONVENTIONAL IN YOUR BEHAVIOR

Although this book does not emphasize conformity to conventional norms of behavior, they are of value in getting ahead. More precisely, by flaunting tradition you could hurt your career. Areas in which conventional behavior is expected by most employers include good attendance and punctuality, careful grooming, courtesy to superiors, appropriate amount of smiling, good posture, adherence to company safety rules, and obeying authority. Employees who insist on being nonconformists in these areas do so at considerable risk to their career advancement. The chairman of the board of the world's largest manufacturer of photographic supplies once commented: "The biggest problem with young people today is that they spend so much time fighting the system. After about five years of fighting the system, some of them finally came around and are ready to work with the firm rather than against it. Those are the people we need." In what way do you fight the system?

TAKE A CREATIVE APPROACH TO YOUR JOB

As emphasized in Chapter 3, being creative helps you get ahead in business. Your ideas must be backed up with concrete plans for their implementation. If you are associated with an innovative idea, and that idea pays dividends, your career might receive a big boost. For maximum benefit to your career, make innovative suggestions in areas that are likely to make money or save money. Here are several examples of suggestions along these lines:

- A worker at a law firm suggested that a promising new area of practice would be to challenge English-only company policies. As a result of her suggestion, the firm profitably entered this new area of litigation.

- A worker at a publisher with a large mail-order business suggested the company produce books with a smaller trim size. The yearly savings in mailing and shipping costs were enormous.

KEEP GROWING THROUGH CONTINUOUS LEARNING AND SELF-DEVELOPMENT

Given that continuous learning is part of the new model of career advancement, engaging in regular learning will help a person advance. Continuous learning can take many forms including formal schooling, attending training programs and seminars, and self-study. It is particularly important to engage in new learning in areas of interest to the company, such as developing proficiency in a second language if the company has customers and employees in other countries. Many companies support continuous learning, making it easier for you to implement the tactic of growth through continuous learning. An example follows:

Johnsonville Foods, the Wisconsin sausage maker, encourages employees to attend any company-sponsored training class regardless of its direct applicability to their current jobs. Management at Johnsonville believes that all learning is valuable, whether it can be used at work or at home, now or in the future. The company also encourages every employee to spend one day a year with another employee to learn more about the company.[8]

Self-development can include any type of learning, but often emphasizes personal improvement and skill development. Improving your work habits or team leadership skills would be job-relevant examples of self-development.

An important perspective on continuous learning and self-development is that it can take the form of gradual improvements that result in substantial changes. Such continuous improvement follows the Japanese philosophy of **kaizen,** the relentless quest for a better way and higher-quality work. *Kaizen* keeps you stretching to perform the same activities better than you did yesterday.

Observe Proper Etiquette

Proper etiquette is important for career advancement because such behavior is considered part of acting professionally. **Business etiquette** is a special code of behavior required in work situations. Both etiquette and manners refer to behaving in an acceptable and refined way. Figuring out what constitutes proper etiquette and business manners requires investigation. One approach is to use successful people as models of behavior and sources of information. Another approach is to consult a current book about business etiquette, such as the *Complete Business Etiquette Handbook.* Many of the suggestions offered in these books follow common sense, but many others are far from obvious.

The basic rules of etiquette are to make the other person feel comfortable in your presence, be considerate, and strive not to embarrass anyone. Also, be cordial to all, remembering that everyone deserves our respect.[9] Specific guidelines for practicing etiquette stem from these basic rules. Exhibit 13-1 presents examples of good business etiquette and manners.

Take Sensible Risks

An element of risk taking is necessary to advance very far in your career. Almost all successful people have taken at least one moderate risk in their careers. These risks include starting a new business with mostly borrowed money, joining a fledgling firm, or submitting a ground-breaking idea to management. Terrie M. Williams, the founder of a public relations firm, believes that risk taking is the most essential ingredient in advancing a career. Not risking anything can mean risking even more, including inhibiting your career. Williams offers this explanation:

> When I'm approaching an important meeting, I sometimes find myself thinking, "I'm scared. I don't know if I can carry this off." Whenever I feel that way, I make a conscious effort to remind myself that being scared is

EXHIBIT 13-1

BUSINESS ETIQUETTE AND MANNERS

Below are 14 specific suggestions about business etiquette and manners that should be considered in the context of a specific job situation. For example, "respect the chain of command" is not so relevant in a small, informal company where everyone is on a first-name basis.

1. *Be polite to people in person.* Say "good morning" and "good evening" to work associates at all job levels. Smile frequently. Offer to bring coffee or another beverage for a coworker if you are going outside to get some for yourself.

2. *Write polite letters.* An important occasion for practicing good etiquette is the writing of business and personal letters. Include the person's job title in the inside address, spell the person's name correctly. Use supportive rather than harsh statements. (For example, say "It would be helpful if you could" rather than "you must.") Avoid right margin justification because it is much harsher than indented lines.

3. *Practice good table manners.* Avoid smacking your lips or sucking your fingers. If someone else is paying the bill do not order the most expensive item on the menu (such as a $150 bottle of Dom Pérignon champagne). Offer to cut bread for the other person, and do not look at the check if the other person is paying.

4. *Names should be remembered.* It is good manners and good etiquette to remember the names of work associates, even if you see them only occasionally. If you forget the name of a person, it is better to admit this rather than guessing and coming up with the wrong name. Just say, "I apologize, but I have forgotten your name. Tell me once more, and I will not forget your name again."

5. *Males and females should receive equal treatment.* Amenities extended to females by males in a social setting are minimized in business settings today. During a meeting, a male is not expected to hold a chair or a door for a woman, nor does he jump to walk on the outside when the two of them are walking down the street. Many women resent being treated differently from males with respect to minor social customs. In general, common courtesies should be extended by both sexes to one another.

6. *Shouting is out.* Emotional control is an important way of impressing superiors. Following the same principle, shouting in most work situations is said to detract from your image.

7. *The host or hostess pays the bill.* An area of considerable confusion about etiquette surrounds business lunches and who should pay the check—the man or the woman. The rule of etiquette is that the person who extends the invitation pays the bill. (Do you think this rule should be extended to social life?)

8. *Introduce the higher-ranking person to the lower-ranking person.* Your boss's name will be mentioned before a coworker's; you introduce the older person to the younger person; and a client is introduced first to coworkers.

(Continued)

9. *Address superiors and visitors in their preferred way.*   As the modern business world has become more informal, a natural tendency has developed to address people at all levels by their first names. It is safer to first address people by a title and their last names and then wait for them to correct you if they desire.

10. *Respect the chain of command.*   Organizations value the **chain of command,** the official statement of who reports to whom. It is therefore inadvisable for you to initiate contact with your boss's boss without your boss's permission.

11. *Make appointments with high-ranking people rather than dropping in.* Related to the above principle, it is taboo in most firms for lower-ranking employees to casually drop in to the office of an executive.

12. *When another person is opening a door to exit a room or building, do not jump in ahead of him or her.*   In recent years, many people have developed the curious habit of quickly jumping in past another person (moving in the opposite direction) who is exiting. Not only is this practice rude, it can lead to an uncomfortable collision.

13. *Be courteous about the copy machine.*   If you are using the copier machine for a large run and someone approaches the machine wanting to copy one or two pages, allow that person to interrupt. When two people arrive at the copier machine simultaneously, the person with the smaller job goes first. Refill the machine with paper and reset the machine to "1 copy."

14. *Be sensitive to cross-cultural differences in etiquette.*   When dealing with people from different cultures, regularly investigate possible major differences in etiquette. For example, using the index finger to point is considered rude in most Asian and Eastern countries. The American sign for okay (thumb and index finger forming a circle) is considered a vulgarity in most other countries.

Caution: Although all the above points could have some bearing on the image you project, violation of any one of them would not necessarily have a negative impact on your career. It is the overall image you project that counts the most. Therefore, the general principle of being considerate of work associates is much more important than any one act of etiquette or manners.

SOURCE: Based on information from George Mazzei, *The New Office Etiquette* (New York: Simon & Schuster, 1983); Annette Vincent and Melanie Meche, "It's Time to Teach Business Etiquette," *Business Education Forum,* October 1993, pp. 39–41; "Business Etiquette: Teaching Students the Unwritten Rules," *Keying In,* January 1996, pp. 1–2; "Meeting and Greeting," *Keying In,* January 1996, p. 3.

good. It means I'm embarking on something new and different, and I can only go to the next level.[10]

Learn to Manage Adversity

Some adversity is almost inevitable in an ambitious person's career. It is difficult to get through a career without at least once being laid off, fired, demoted, transferred to an undesirable assignment, or making a bad investment. Company mergers and takeovers also contribute to adversity because so many people are laid off in the process or assigned to lesser jobs.

Personal resilience—the capacity to bounce back from setback—is necessary to overcome adversity. A general-purpose way of handling adversity is to first get emotional support from a friend or family member, and then solve the problem systematically. You follow the decision-making steps described in Chapter 3. Laura, a computer sales representative, explains how she managed adversity:

> Three years ago I hit a low point in my life. The company I worked for was involved in a scandal about paying kickbacks to a few school and city administrators in exchange for several major contracts. I wasn't directly involved in offering the kickbacks, but I was the sales representative on one of the unethically handled accounts. As you can imagine, I got tarred with the same brush.
>
> At about the same time, my boyfriend was arrested for illegal stock trading. In a two-week period, I faced unemployment and the necessity to either help my boyfriend through his turmoil, or leave him. At first I thought the world was caving in on me. I cried on the shoulder of my girl-friend and my mother. After those conversations, I realized I was still a good person. I admit I should have been more perceptive about the wrong-doings of my firm and my boyfriend. Yet *I* had done nothing wrong.
>
> I had the self-confidence to face the world in a positive way. I told prospective employers that they could check out my story. I didn't offer kickbacks to anyone. My only error on the job was having had too much trust in my employer. Based on my good sales record, I did find a comparable job. I also decided to help my boyfriend through his rough times. So what if a few people thought I was too forgiving? I have enough confidence in myself to stick with my own inclinations.

Two other points about managing adversity are particularly relevant here. First, attempt not to be bitter and cynical about your problem. Bitterness and cynicism can freeze a person into inaction. Second, look to minimize the self-doubt that grows from a mental script called the *fear narrative*. According to Kenneth Ruge this is a narrative in which you tell yourself that if you try again, something terrible will happen. "The word *can't* becomes the operative word and you become its prisoner." The best anticote is to create an opposite narrative whereby you think, "How can I use my imagination and creativity to move beyond this *can't* to achieve my goals?"[11]

EXERTING CONTROL OVER THE OUTSIDE WORLD

In this section we emphasize approaches that require you to exert some control over the outside environment. If you do not control it, at least you can try to juggle it to your advantage. For example, "find a mentor" suggests that you search out a friendly and supportive person in your field who can help you advance in your career.

DEVELOP A FLEXIBLE CAREER PATH

Planning your career inevitably involves some form of goal setting. If your goals are laid out systematically to lead to your ultimate career goal, you have established a **career path**, a sequence of positions necessary to achieve a goal.

Here we describe two types of career paths. One type emphasizes climbing up the ladder in a traditional organization. The other emphasizes the horizontal movements that fit better the new model of career advancement. Human Relations Self-Assessment Exercise 13-1 will help you identify an ideal job for yourself.

The Traditional Career Path

A traditional career path is based on the assumption that a person will occupy a series of positions, each at a higher level of responsibility than the

---

HUMAN RELATIONS SELF-ASSESSMENT EXERCISE 13-1

Discovering Your Ideal Job

To develop insights into your ideal job, do the following:

1. Take a blank sheet of paper or computer file. On the top, write, "What I enjoy about my career." Underneath, record what you consider to be the most enjoyable aspects of a present or past job (full-time, part-time, or temporary). If your work experience is limited, think of a good job familiar to you.

2. On a second sheet of paper or another computer file, record the title, "My career standards." Below, list all the standards or values you have for your career. Include factors such as who you would like to work with, how much money you would like to earn, and the type of people you want to serve. To get started, complete the statement, "In my ideal career, I will . . . (earn, produce, create, etc.)." Strive for at least ten statements.

3. Now add the statements made in the first list to the second by converting them to statements relating to an ideal job. To illustrate, if a statement from the first list was "opportunity to help people," modify it to read, "In my ideal career, I will have the opportunity to help people."

   When you have completed the above, delete the word "standards" from the top of your page, and substitute the word "goals." Set priorities for statements by assigning a rank of 1 to the most important item, 2 the next important, and so on.

4. On a new sheet of paper or the next page on the computer file, key the new heading, "My career goals." List items 1 through 10 on your list. Later, after you have accomplished these ten goals, you can work on the others on your list.

   Make a photocopy of your list and place it where you will see it regularly— in your daily planner, on top of your desk, or on your kitchen bulletin board. From this point forward, take actions that will help you achieve these goals. Make them happen. If you enjoy helping others, take the initiative to help a work associate as soon as convenient.

   When you accomplish each item on your list—such as helping others solve problems—you should be moving toward creating a job that you love. An ideal job is the starting point for an ideal career.

SOURCE: Adapted from Stuart Kamen, "Do What You Love," *Success Workshop*™, vol. 1, no. 1, 1994.

previous one. A person thus climbs the organizational ladder or hierarchy. If a career path is laid out in one firm, it must be related to the present and future demands of that firm. If you aspire toward a high-level manufacturing position, you would need to know the future of manufacturing in that company. Many U.S. and Canadian firms, for example, plan to conduct more of their manufacturing in the Pacific Rim or Mexico. If you were really determined, you might study the appropriate language and ready yourself for a global position.

While sketching out a career path you should list your personal goals. They should mesh with your work plans to help avoid major conflicts in your life. Some lifestyles, for example, are incompatible with some career paths. You might find it difficult to develop a stable home life (spouse, children, friends, community activities, garden) if you aspired toward holding field positions within the Central Intelligence Agency.

Your career path is a living document and may need to be modified as your circumstances change. Keep in mind changes in your company and industry. If becoming a branch manager is an important step in your career path, check to see if your company or industry still has branch managers. The changing preferences of your family can also influence your career path. A family that wanted to stay put may now be willing to relocate, which could open up new possibilities on your career path.

Contingency ("what if?") plans should also be incorporated into a well-designed career path. For instance, "If I don't become an agency supervisor by age 35, I will seek employment in the private sector." Or, "If I am not promoted within two years, I will enroll in a business school program."

Lisa Irving, an ambitious 20-year-old, formulated the following career path prior to receiving an associate's degree in business administration. Lisa's career goals are high, but she has established contingency plans. Presented as an example, not an ideal model, is Lisa's career plan path:

WORK

1. Purchasing trainee for two years

2. Assistant purchasing agent for three years

3. Purchasing agent for five years (will join Purchasing Managers Association)

4. Purchasing supervisor for five years

5. Purchasing manager for six years

6. Manager, materials handling for five years

7. Vice president, procurement, until retirement

PERSONAL LIFE

1. Rent own apartment after one year of working

2. Attend college evenings until receive B.S. in business administration

3. Marriage by age 27 (plan only one marriage)

4. One child by age 30

5. Live in private home with husband and child by age 33

6. Volunteer work for Down's syndrome children.

7. Travel to India before age 50.

CONTINGENCY PLANS

1. Will seek new employment by stage 3 if not promoted to purchasing agent.

2. If not promoted to vice president by stage 6, will consider opening small retail business.

3. If I encounter sex discrimination at any stage, will look for employment with firm that has large government contracts (where discrimination is much less likely).

4. If I develop stress disorder at any point, will seek nonsupervisory position in purchasing field.

Career paths can also be laid out graphically, as shown in Figure 13-1. One benefit of a career path laid out in chart form is that it gives a clear perception of climbing steps toward your target position. As each position is attained, the corresponding step can be shaded in color or cross-hatched.

Most of the goals just mentioned include a time element, which is crucial to sound career management. Your long-range goal might be clearly established in your mind (such as owner and operator of a health spa). At the same time you must establish short-range (get any kind of job in health spa) and intermediate-range (manager of a health spa by age 30) goals.

Figure 13-1   A Career Path

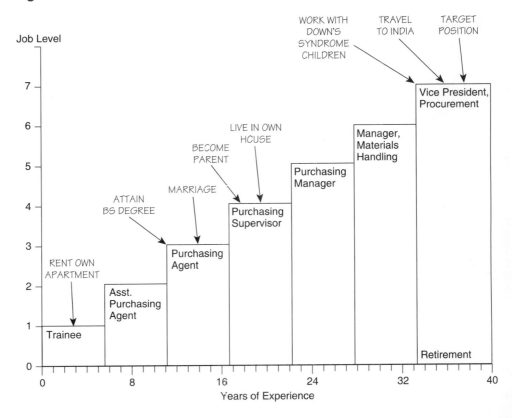

Goals set too far in the future that are not supported with more immediate goals may lose their motivational value.

The career path under discussion features a steady progression of promotions, yet a reasonable number of years in each position. Such planning is realistic because promotions often take a long time to achieve.

The Horizontal Career Path

A current analysis of career paths concludes that it is the norm for organizations to have no fixed career paths. Instead of plotting a series of moves over a long time period, many individuals can only make predictions about one or two years into the future.[12] A significant feature of the horizontal career path is that people are more likely to advance by moving sideways than moving up. Or, at least, people who get ahead will spend a considerable part of their career working in different positions at or near the same level. In addition, they may occasionally move to a lower-level position to gain valuable experience. With a horizontal career path, the major reward is no longer promotion but the opportunity to gain more experience and increase job skills.

A horizontal career path, as well as a traditional (or vertical) career path, does not necessarily mean the person stays with the same firm. For example, a worker might spend three years in one company as an electronics technician, three years in another as a sales representative, and then three years as a customer service specialist in a third company. All three positions would be approximately at the same level. The third company then promotes the individual to a much-deserved position as the marketing team leader. Following is a horizontal career path for Michael Wang, a career school graduate who did attempt to make long-range predictions about his career.

CAREER	PERSONAL LIFE
1. Electronics technician at office equipment company for three years	1. Rent own apartment after one year of working
2. Computer repair technician for three years for computer company	2. Attend seminars to upgrade marketing and computer knowledge
3. Customer service representative for two years.	3. Study Spanish with goal of becoming bilingual
4. Sales support specialist at computer company for three years	4. Purchase condo
5. Marketing research specialist for two years	5. Marriage by age 29
6. Outside sales representative for photocopying machine company for four years	6. Start raising family by age 31

7. Sales manager in small office equipment company for five years

8. Owner of electronic equipment servicing company for rest of career

7. Run for county legislature by age 34

8. Spend one month in Taiwan visiting relatives by age 36

9. Begin investment program for children's education

CONTINGENCY PLANS

1. If cannot obtain experience as market research analyst, customerservice rep, or sales rep, will continue to develop as electronic technician

2. If cannot find employment as sales manager, will attempt to become supervisor of electronic technicians

3. If do not raise sufficient funds for starting own business, will continue in corporate job until retirement

1. Will purchase double or triple house if purchasing condo is not feasible

2. If cannot raise funds for running for office, will do volunteer work for youths

3. If not married by age 29, will continue to search for life partner beyond that age

Figure 13-2 presents a horizontal career path. After having studied the two types of career paths, do Human Relations Skill-Building Exercise 13-1.

HAVE AN ACTION PLAN TO REACH YOUR GOALS

As described in Chapter 2, a useful goal is backed up by a logical plan for its attainment. A recommended practice is to supplement your career path

Figure 13-2   A Horizontal Career Path

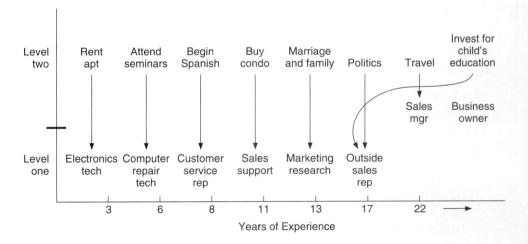

HUMAN RELATIONS SKILL-BUILDING EXERCISE 13-1

Career Pathing

1. Each class member will develop a tentative career path, perhaps as an outside assignment. About six volunteers will then share their paths with the rest of the class. Feedback of any type will be welcomed. Class members studying the career paths of others should keep in mind such issues as:

    a. How logical does it appear?

    b. Is this something the person really wants or is it simply an exercise in putting down on paper what the ambitious person is supposed to want?

    c. How well do the individual's work plans mesh with personal plans?

2. Each class member will interview an experienced working person outside of class about his or her career path. Most of the people interviewed will have already completed a portion of their path. They will therefore have less flexibility (and perhaps less idealism) than people just getting started in their careers. The conclusions reached about these interviews will make a fruitful class discussion. Among the issues raised might be:

    a. How familiar were these people with the idea of a career path?

    b. How willing were they to talk about themselves?

    c. Were many actual "paths" discovered, or did a series of jobs simply come about by luck or "fate"?

---

with a description of your action plans. Lisa Irving, the woman who wants to succeed in the purchasing field, might include an action plan of this nature:

> To become manager of materials handling, I will need to: (1) perform in an outstanding manner as purchasing manager by such means as coordinating the billing system with the sales department, (2) engage in continuous self-study about the entire materials-handling field (3) be active in the local purchasing association group, and (4) make sure that top management is aware of my talent and ambition.

Action plans can be drawn up in minute detail. As with any other aspect of career planning, however, avoid becoming too rigid in your thinking. Career paths and career plans are only tentative. A different path to your goal might fall right in your lap. Ten years from now, for instance, Lisa might receive a telephone call from an executive employment agency. The caller might say, "My client has engaged me to find a materials manager who is competent. Your name was given to us. Could you possibly meet me for lunch to discuss this exciting career opportunity?"

PRACTICE NETWORKING

Developing a network of contacts was recommended in Chapter 11 as a method of finding a job. Currently the most popular career-advancement tactic, networking has several purposes. The contacts you establish can help you find a better position, offer you a new position, become a customer, become a valuable supplier, or help you solve difficult problems. People in your network can also offer you emotional support during periods of adversity.

A recommended approach to networking is to keep a list of at least 25 people whom you contact at least once a month. The contact can be as extensive as a luncheon meeting or as brief as an e-mail message. The starting point in networking is to obtain an ample supply of business cards. You then give a card to any person you meet who might be able to help you now or in the future. While first developing your network, be inclusive. Sandy Vilas says, "Remember the 3-foot rule—anyone within three feet of you is someone you can network with."[12] Later as your network develops, you can strive to include a greater number of influential and successful people.

People in your network can include relatives; people you meet while traveling, vacationing, or attending trade shows; and classmates. A substantial amount of social networking also takes place over computer networks, specifically in the form of community groups (such as astrology buffs) on the Internet. The people in these groups can become valuable business contacts. Community activities and religious organizations can also be a source of contacts. Golf is still considered the number-one sport for networking because of the high-level contacts the sports generate. In recent years, the number of business women who have learned golf for networking purposes has increased substantially.

Exhibit 13-2 illustrates networking among people who are already advanced in their careers. Some of their practices can be incorporated at earlier stages in your career.

ACHIEVE BROAD EXPERIENCE

Most people who land high-ranking positions are people of broad experience. Therefore, a widely accepted strategy for advancing in responsibility is to strengthen your credentials by broadening your experience. Workers who follow the new model of career advancement, as illustrated by the horizontal career path, are automatically achieving broad experience. It is best to achieve breadth early in your career because it is easier to transfer when an individual's compensation is not too high. (As explained earlier, the company practice of *broadbanding* makes it easier for workers to move from one position to another.)

Broadening can come about by performing a variety of jobs, or sometimes by performing essentially the same job in different organizations. You can also achieve breadth by working on committees and special assignments.

PRACTICE SELF-NOMINATION

A more general strategy for achieving breadth is to practice self-nomination. Have the courage and assertiveness to ask for a promotion or a transfer. Your manager may not believe that you are actually seeking

---

EXHIBIT 13-2

"DIGITAL DAMES" MEET TO EXCHANGE VITAL INFORMATION

Mary Furlong is the president of Third Age Media, a small but growing on-line company. She needs to learn how to sail soon because it's the preferred leisure activity of potential investors in her company. Another woman says she needs to learn golf for the same reason. She asks, "Anyone want to spend some time at the driving range this weekend?" Hands shoot up, e-mail addresses are exchanged, and plans are made. The hope is that these connections will lead to deals being cut. Such is the purpose of Digital Dames, an informal group of women CEOs trying to succeed in the fast-moving world of Silicon Valley.

The group was formed in 1996 by Christine Comaford, CEO of PlanetU. She deliberately set out to start an old girl's network—something she believed was vital for women computer executives. The Digital Dames now meet about every six weeks, moving from house to house, varying the cuisine but never the format—great food, even better desserts, and a circle of chairs.

The group uses a standard format. Everyone sits down and introduces herself and explains what she needs at the moment, whether it's advice or people to join her board of directors, employees, or money. Cheers go up when Tara Lemmey of Narrowline in San Francisco announces that her company was launched the week before. "And what do you need?" prompts Anu Shukla, CEO of Rubric Inc. in San Francisco

One of the Digital Dames said you could never have a similar group of male computer CEOs: "Never. They wouldn't share their ideas and their weaknesses and their fears. We share our problems. Whereas men tend to gloat and tell you about their victories. Besides, they wouldn't bring food, they would all bring beer." [Do you think this woman is being sexist?]

SOURCE: Adapted from Elizabeth Weise, "Women Computer CEOs Building Network: 'Digital Dames' Meet to Exchange Vital Information," Associated Press story, September 2, 1997.

---

more responsibility. An effective method of convincing him or her is to volunteer yourself for specific job openings or for challenging assignments. A boss may need convincing, because many more people will be seeking advancement than are actually willing to handle more responsibility.

BE VISIBLE

A big career booster for many people is to call favorable attention to themselves and their accomplishments. Ways of gaining visibility include: performing well on committee assignments, winning a suggestion award, performing well in a company-sponsored athletic event, getting an article published in a trade magazine, getting your name in the firm's newspaper, or distinguishing yourself in a community activity. Once you achieve visibility, you have a better chance of being noticed by an important person in the firm.

FIND A MENTOR

Most successful career people have had one or more mentors during their career. A **mentor** is a more experienced person who guides, teaches, and coaches another individual. In years past, mentors were almost always higher-ranking people. Today mentors can be peers and even lower-ranking individuals. A lower-ranking individual, for example, can educate you on how other parts of the organization work—something you may need to know to advance.[14]

Mentorship is an important development process in many occupations: master-apprentice, physician-intern, teacher-student, and executive-junior executive. An emotional tie exists between the less-experienced person (the protégé) and the mentor. The mentor serves as a positive model and a trusted friend. Bob, a 30-year old sales manager, describes how finding a mentor helped him in his career:

> My career had its first big boost when I was noticed by Walt Brainbridge, our regional manager. He personally complimented me for my showing in a sales contest. From that point on he would ask to see me when he visited our office. He gave me lots of encouragement and told me what a good future I had with the firm. Without asking for credit, Walt was the one who assigned me to some of the best accounts. He set me up to succeed. He taught me a lot of good tricks, including how to fight the feeling of being rejected. I don't think I would have advanced nearly as far as I have today without Walt.

MANAGE LUCK

Few people do well in their careers without a good break along the way. Lucky events include your company suddenly expanding and therefore needing people to promote into key jobs; your boss quitting on short notice and you being asked to take over his or her job; or the business field in which you are working suddenly experiencing a boom, similar to the plastics recycling business today.

To be lucky, you first have to clarify what you want. Otherwise, you may not recognize an opportunity when it comes your way. Assume you know that you want to become an officer in your trade association. Consequently, you will seize the opportunity when you hear that the group is looking for a new treasurer.

The strategy is not to simply wait for luck to come you way. In the words of Ray Kroc, founder of McDonald's: "Luck is a dividend of sweat. The more you sweat, the luckier you get."[15] Manage luck to some extent by recognizing opportunities and taking advantage of them. The unlucky person is often the individual who, out of timidity, lets a good opportunity slip by. A good way of capitalizing on luck is to be ready to take advantage of opportunities when they come along. If you maintain a record of excellent work performance, and you strive to complete your program of studies, you will position yourself to take advantage of opportunities.

BALANCE YOUR LIFE

Balancing your life among the competing demands of work, social life, and personal interests can help you advance your career. As mentioned several places in this book, having balance gives you additional energy and vitality which will help you in your career. Without balance, a career person runs the risk of burnout and feeling that work is not worthwhile. Stephen Covey, the popular guru about leadership and family living, offers this perspective:

> Always being the last to leave the office does not make you an indispensable employee. In fact, those who work long hours for extended periods are prone to burnout. The trick is to have your priorities clear, honor your commitments and keep a balance in life.[16]

Now that you have studied many methods for advancing your career, do Human Relations Skill-Building Exercise 13-2 to help you analyze the strategies and tactics you might choose to fit your personality and work situation.

DEALING WITH HIDDEN BARRIERS TO ADVANCEMENT

Concern exists that many white women as well as people of color of both sexes are held back from high-level promotions by a glass ceiling. A **glass ceiling** is an invisible but difficult-to-penetrate barrier to promotion based on subtle attitudes and prejudices. Fewer than 10 percent of senior executives in business are women, although women hold about 43 percent of managerial jobs in the United States.[17] White women, women of color,

---

HUMAN RELATIONS SKILL-BUILDING EXERCISE 13-2

Selecting a Suitable Career-Advancement Strategy

As with most suggestions for self-improvement some of the suggestions in this chapter will have more relevance for you than will others. Among the factors influencing which strategy is best suited to you are your personality, the stage of your career, and the place you work.

Each class member will write down the two strategies described in this chapter that he or she will most probably put into action (or is already using), and provide a brief explanation of why this strategy is particularly relevant. Once these analyses are completed, each person will share his or her answers with the rest of the class.

It will be interesting to note if any strategy or tactic for getting ahead is mentioned by virtually all class members.

and men of color face few barriers to advancement for one or two promotions. Women appear to be making a breakthrough at middle-management levels. Yet after that point, with many notable exceptions, their promotional opportunities are often limited.

An analysis of several factors contributing to the glass ceiling points to possible solutions to the problem employers can pursue. A dominant factor is tradition. Men often promote men, and white people often promote white people, because they are familiar with them. Another reason for the glass ceiling is a lack of acceptance of women and minorities in key positions by top-level managers.[18] The acceptance problem is higher in heavy industry than in service firms and consumer-oriented firms such as Levi Strauss, PepsiCo, and General Foods.

One strategy for overcoming the glass ceiling is to be patient. Barriers are lifting gradually in some companies and rapidly in others. As the workforce continues to be more diverse, additional promotional opportunities are open to women and minorities. Within five years from now the glass ceiling may be shattered, particularly as women and minorities gain middle-management experience. In one survey, 82 percent of male CEOs said that lack of general management/line experience (such as being a plant manager) prevents women from advancing to top executive positions.[19]

Individuals who have strong evidence that they are discrimination victims can lodge a formal complaint with the company, and then with an outside agency. Filing discrimination charges is more effective if a person is denied a first promotion. It is more difficult to prove discrimination took place when a person is not offered an executive position. The reason is that executives are chosen by difficult-to-pin-down factors such as broad thinking ability and personal appeal.

Another strategy for overcoming barriers to advancement is to enthusiastically apply all the other approaches described in this chapter. For example, today, African-Americans are using networking more extensively to help them land key positions in industry. A glass ceiling may exist for most people, but not for every woman and every member of selected minority groups. An outstanding performer who is also perceived as having superior leadership characteristics will often break through barriers to advancement.

 SUMMARY

Career advancement has acquired a shift in emphasis in recent years to accommodate the new organization structures. The major shift has been less emphasis on vertical mobility to more emphasis on lateral growth, or advancing by learning more. The new model also shows more emphasis on temporary leadership assignments, more self-fulfillment, continuous learning, and being promoted for the ability to learn.

One set of strategies and tactics for getting ahead can be classified as taking control of your own behavior. Included are the following:

1. Develop outstanding interpersonal skills.
2. Develop expertise.

3. Perform well on all your assignments.

4. Create good first impressions.

5. Make an accurate self-analysis.

6. Document your accomplishments.

7. Be conventional in your behavior.

8. Take a creative approach to your job.

9. Keep growing through continuous learning and self-development.

10. Observe proper etiquette.

11. Take sensible risks.

12. Learn to manage adversity.

13. Do work you are passionate about.

14. Be a good corporate citizen.

Another set of strategies and tactics for career advancement center around taking control of your environment, or at least adapting it to your advantage. Included are the following:

1. Develop a flexible career path (including the traditional and lateral types).

2. Have an action plan to reach your goals.

3. Practice networking.

4. Achieve broad experience.

5. Practice self-nomination.

6. Be visible.

7. Find a mentor.

8. Manage luck.

9. Balance your life.

For some people, another part of managing their careers is dealing with hidden barriers to advancement. These barriers take the form of a glass ceiling, an invisible but difficult-to-penetrate barrier to promotion based on subtle attitudes and prejudices. Diligently applying career-advancement strategies and tactics, including outstanding performance, can help overcome these barriers.

Questions and Activities

1. Explain in your own words, the new model of career advancement in organizations.

2. What are some of the organizational rewards that a successful person can hope to attain?

3. Why was career planning less complex 20 years ago?

4. Why not simply do a good job and forget about all the other strategies and tactics described in this chapter?

5. People seeking jobs early in their careers often comment that employers are looking for specialists, not generalists. Which career-advancement tactic does this comment support?

6. Identify several jobs for which observing good business etiquette would be particularly important.

7. Why is "doing what you love" closely linked to intrinsic motivation?

8. Describe an incident in which you or somebody you know was a good corporate citizen.

9. Identify several tactics you would be willing to use to become more visible in a large company.

10. Use the Internet to search for a good career-advancement suggestion. Be prepared to share your findings in class.

REFERENCES

[1]Adapted from Donna Fenn, "Best Career Advancement: Bottoms Up." *Inc. Magazine Archives, www.inc.com/incmagazine/archives/07930581.html.*

[2]Douglas T. Hall, "Protean Careers of the 21st Century," *Academy of Management Executive,* November 1996, p. 9.

[3]Ibid., p. 10.

[4]William Morin, "You Are Absolutely, Positively on Your Own," *Fortune,* December 9, 1996, p. 222.

[5]Joseph A. Raelin, "First-Job Effects on Career Development," *Personnel Administrator,* August 1983, pp. 71–76; Julie Griffin Levitt, *Your Career: How to Make It Happen,* 2d ed. (Cincinnati, OH: South-Western Publishing, 1990), p. 294.

[6]Robert P. Vecchio, "Are You In or OUT with Your Boss?" *Business Horizons,* 1987, pp. 76–78; Randall P. Settoon, Nathan Bennett, and Robert C. Liden, "Social Exchange in Organizations: Perceived Organizational Support, Leader-Member Exchange, and Employee Reciprocity," *Journal of Applied Psychology,* June 1996, pp. 219–227.

[7]Jim Harris, *Getting Employees to Fall in Love with Your Company* (New York: AMACOM, 1996), p. 87.

[8]"Business Etiquette: Teaching Students the Unwritten Rules," *Keying In,* January 1996, p. 2.

[9]"When the Knot in Your Stomach Is a *Good* Thing," *Executive Strategies,* July 1996, p. 5.

A HUMAN RELATIONS CASE PROBLEM

Career Development at Sears Credit

Several years ago the credit card division of Sears went through a major reorganization. Among the changes were closing 50 small units, expanding nine others, and accepting third-party credit cards in competition with the Sears Charge Card. A voluntary retirement program was also implemented. These sweeping changes had a big impact on the careers of Sears Credit's associates. Sears launched a career development program to create a better fit between associates' skills and workloads, and the reengineered company.

New Career Strategies
The reorganization of Sears Credit, including shrinking the workforce from 13,000 to 10,000 employees, had many career implications:

- Virtually all jobs were newly created or significantly redefined.

- Established career paths were no longer available to follow.

- Many outsiders had to be hired to bring critical skills to the organization.

- Many associates needed to be developed to fill future positions.

The top-level managers at Sears Credit and the human resource professionals decided that it wanted the company to have open communication about career opportunities, the developmental (improvement) needs of individuals, and new staffing procedures. The group also concluded that Sears Credit needed to help its associates and managers develop a new perspective on their careers. The old mindset was that "the company will take care of me." A proactive attitude was now required that redefined success in terms of what's important to the individual rather than how fast you get promoted.

Sears Credit redefined responsibility for career development. Associates would have to take on new responsibility for managing their careers, and their managers would need to act as coaches in supporting the career development of associates. Another need identified was for the associates to create career goals that included more than promotions. Another requirement was that goals had to be linked to the needs of the business and the direction of the changing organization.

Planning the Project

The manager of training and development at Sears Credit and a career development consultant headed a team to plan the career development project. The team received excellent support from top management including the fact that Jane Thomson, the executive vice president of credit, was a leading champion of career development.

A key element of the process was defining the skills and competencies needed for success within the restructured jobs. The competencies fell into five major categories: business knowledge and contribution to financial results; leadership; customer focus; individual effectiveness; and associate development.

(Continued)

The team developed a manager/peer assessment and self-assessment inventories. In this way the associates could contribute to identifying growth areas for themselves. All salaried associates participated in a two-day workshop, "Managing Your Career Within Sears Credit." The workshop incorporated new modes of career development, self-assessment activities, company information, and a process for career-development planning. Managers attended an additional workshop, "Managing Career Development." The workshop provided training in coaching skills, and advice on how the managers could manage their own careers.

One of the most important components of the career-development system was a new compensation program. The director of human resources spearheaded a change to a broadbanding compensation program that rewards development moves previously not entitled to a promotional increased because they were lateral moves. (A broadbanding system allows a person to carry the same salary from one job to another rather than having a fixed salary range for each position.)

Early Results

Six months after launching the career-development program, the team in charge conducted a survey about reactions to the program. It was found that most associates were taking responsibility for their own career management. In fact, 93 percent reported they had specific career goals and plans to reach those goals. They also reported that they were more aware and realistic about their interests, strengths, and developmental needs. Also, they were more knowledgeable about the competencies needed for different levels of responsibility and compensation bands.

Approximately 80 percent of associates have had career discussions with their managers. A majority of these associates recorded their goals into the database to communicate them to human resources for staffing decisions.

Questions

1. What evidence will Sears Credit need to determine if their career-development program is a true success?

2. What principles and techniques of career development described in this chapter are illustrated in the case just presented?

3. Make a suggestion to improve the career-development program at Sears Credit.

HUMAN RELATIONS SELF-ASSESSMENT EXERCISE 11-2

The Career-Development Inventory

Career-development activities inevitably include answering some penetrating questions about yourself. Following are 12 representative questions to be found on career-development inventories. You may need several hours to do a competent job answering these questions. After individuals have answered these questions by themselves, it may be profitable to hold a class discussion about the relevance of the spe-

(Continued)

cific questions. A strongly recommended procedure is for you to date your completed inventory and put it away for safekeeping. Examine your answers in several years to see (1) how well you are doing in advancing your career and (2) how much you have changed.

Keep the following information in mind in answering this inventory: People are generous in their self-evaluations when they answer career-development inventories. So you might want to discuss some of your answers with somebody else who knows you well.

1. How would you describe yourself as a person?

2. What are you best at doing? Worst?

3. What are your two biggest strengths or assets?

4. What are the two traits, characteristics, or behaviors of yours that need the most improvement?

5. What are your two biggest accomplishments?

6. Write your obituary as you would like it to appear.

7. What would be the ideal job for you?

8. Why aren't you richer and more famous?

9. What career advice can you give yourself?

10. Describe the two peak experiences in your life.

11. What are your five most important values (the things in life most important to you)?

12. What goals in life are you trying to achieve?

[10]"The Bounce-Back Factor: Regain Lost Confidence and Charge Ahead," *Executive Strategies,* June 1997, p. 6.

[11]Philip M. Podaskoff, Michael Ahearne, and Scott B. MacKenzie, "Organizational Citizenship Behavior and the Quantity and Quality of Work Group Performance," *Journal of Applied Psychology,* April 1997, pp. 262–270.

[12]Maury Peiperl and Yehuda Baruch, "Back to Square Zero: The Post-Corporate Career," *Organizational Dynamics,* Spring 1997, p. 7.

[13]Quoted in "Network Your Way Up," *Working Smart,* February 1997, p. 4.

[14]Marshall Loeb, "The New Mentoring," *Fortune,* November 27, 1995, p. 213.

[15]Quoted in "The Secret to Being Lucky," *Success Workshop* (Supplement to *Pryor Report*), March 1996, p. 1.

[16]Stephen Covey, "How to Succeed in Today's Workplace," *USA Weekend,* August 29–31, 1997, pp. 4–5.

[17]Stephen Barr, "Up Against the Glass," *Management Review,* September 1996, p. 13.

[18]Rose Mary Wentling, "Breaking Down Barriers to Women's Success," *HRMagazine,* May 1995, pp. 81–83.

[19]Barr, "Up Against the Glass," p. 17.

 ## ADDITIONAL READING

Ashford, Susan J., and Black, J. Steward. "Proactivity During Organizational Entry: The Role of the Desire for Control." *Journal of Applied Psychology,* April 1996, pp. 199–214.

Barkley, Nella. *The Crystal-Barkley Guide to Taking Charge of Your Career.* New York: Workman, 1995.

Baumann, Barbara; Duncan, John; Forrer, Stephen E.; and Leibowitz, Zandy. "Amoco Primes the Talent Pump." *Personnel Journal,* February 1996, pp. 79–84.

Bell, Chip R. *Managers as Mentors: Building Partnerships for Learning.* San Francisco: Berrett-Koehler, 1996.

Bolles, Richard Nelson. *The 1999 What Color Is Your Parachute?* Berkeley, CA: Ten Speed Press, 1999.

Bridges, William. *Job Shift.* Reading, MA: Addison-Wesley Publishing, 1995.

Jacobs, Deborah L. "When Your Boss Is the Barrier." *Working Woman,* June 1995, pp. 51–52.

Mapes, James P. *Quantum Leap Thinking: An Owner's Guide to the Mind.* Beverly Hills, CA: Dove Books, 1996.

DEVELOPING SELF-CONFIDENCE AND BECOMING A LEADER

Learning Objectives

After studying the information and doing the exercises in this chapter, you should be able to:

▼ Develop a strategy for increasing your self-confidence if you think it is desirable to do so

▼ Understand the relationship of self-confidence to leadership

▼ Identify a number of personal traits and characteristics of effective leaders

▼ Identify a number of behaviors of effective leaders

▼ Map out a tentative program for developing your leadership potential and skills

*K*atrina Makowski worked for several years as a member of the central support staff in a large law firm. One afternoon, office manager George Dixon entered Katrina's work area. With a warm smile, he said, "Congratulations Katrina. On behalf of the rest of the managers in our firm, we are asking you to become the first team leader for support services." Katrina said she would be thrilled to accept the appointment, yet asked, "Why me? I'm not the most experienced support specialist in the group." George replied, "Don't be unnecessarily modest. We have seen you handle many tough situations quite well. You're always on top of everything, so in control. We want somebody self-confident to be the first team leader for support services."

The situation surrounding Katrina's promotion illustrates the importance of personal qualities, such as take-charge ability and self-confidence, for leadership. If your efforts at developing career thrust are successful, you will eventually become a leader. Rising to leadership can happen when people come to respect your opinion and personal characteristics, and thus are influenced by you. Another way of becoming a leader is to be appointed to a formal position, such as supervisor or team leader, in which it is natural to exert leadership. Your greatest opportunity for exerting leadership, however, will come about from a combination of these methods of influence. As a result, an individual with appealing personal characteristics who is placed in a position of authority will find it relatively easy to exert leadership.

Our study of leadership will first focus on self-confidence because of its close relationship to leadership. We then focus on the characteristics of leaders, their actions and attitudes, followed by an overview of how to develop your leadership potential.

THE IMPORTANCE OF SELF-CONFIDENCE AND SELF-EFFICACY

Self-confidence is necessary for leadership because it helps assure group members that things are under control. Assume you are a manager in a company that is rumored to be facing bankruptcy. At a meeting you attend, the president sobs, "I'm sorry, I'm just no good in a crisis. I don't know what's going to happen to the company. I don't think I can get us out of this mess. Maybe one of you would like to try your hand at turning around a troubled company."

In this situation, company employees would feel insecure. Many would be so preoccupied with finding new employment that they couldn't concentrate on their work. You would want the president to behave in a confident, assured manner. Yet if the president were too arrogant about things, if he or she dismissed the problem too lightly, you might not feel secure, either.

In other leadership situations as well, the leader who functions best is self-confident enough to reassure others and to appear in control. But if the leader is so self-confident that he or she will not admit errors, listen to criticism, or ask for advice, that too creates a problem. Being too self-confident can also lead the person to ignore potential problems, thinking that "I can handle whatever comes my way." Human Relations Self-Assessment Exercise 14-1 provides some insight into your level of self-confidence.

An appropriate amount of self-confidence is also important because it contributes to self-efficacy. Various studies have shown that people with a high sense of self-efficacy tend to have good job performance. They also set relatively high goals for themselves.[1] Self-efficacy is thus related to self-confidence, but is tied more directly into performing a task. A straightforward implication of self-efficacy is that people who think they can perform well on a task do better than those who think they will do poorly.

An encouraging note is that self-efficacy can be boosted through training. In an experiment, 66 unemployed people participated in a self-efficacy workshop. The group included bookkeepers, clerks, teachers, skilled mechanics, and technicians. The workshop featured watching video clips of successfully performing job-search behaviors, followed by encouragement from the trainer and peers. In contrast to unemployed people who did not attend the workshop, the people who were trained in self-efficacy became more involved in job searches.[2] Being involved in job searches included telephoning about a job and obtaining an interview.

Self-efficacy contributes to leadership effectiveness because a leader with high self-efficacy will usually believe that a task is doable. As a result, the leader can inspire others to carry out a difficult mission such as correcting a serious customer problem.

DEVELOPING SELF-CONFIDENCE

Self-confidence is generally achieved by succeeding in a variety of situations. A confident sales representative may not be generally self-confident unless he or she also achieves success in activities such as forming good personal relationships, navigating complex software, writing a letter, learning a second language, and displaying athletic skills.

Although this general approach to self-confidence building makes sense, it does not work for everyone. Some people who seem to succeed at everything still have lingering self-doubt. Low self-confidence is so deeply ingrained in this type of personality that success in later life is not sufficient to change things. Following are some specific strategies and tactics

HUMAN RELATIONS SELF-ASSESSMENT EXERCISE 14-1

How Self-Confident Are You?

Indicate the extent to which you agree with each of the following statements. Use a 1-to-5 scale: (1) disagree strongly; (2) disagree; (3) neutral; (4) agree; (5) agree strongly.

	DS	D	N	A	AS
1. I frequently say to people, "I'm not sure."	5	4	3	2	1
2. I perform well in most situations in life.	1	2	3	4	5
3. I willingly offer advice to others.	1	2	3	4	5
4. Before making even a minor decision I usually consult with several people.	5	4	3	2	1
5. I am generally willing to attempt new activities for which I have very little related skill or experience.	1	2	3	4	5
6. Speaking in front of the class or other group is a frightening experience for me.	5	4	3	2	1
7. I sweat a lot when people challenge me or put me on the spot.	5	4	3	2	1
8. I feel comfortable attending a social event by myself.	1	2	3	4	5
9. I'm much more of a winner than a loser.	1	2	3	4	5
10. I am cautious about making any substantial change in my life.	5	4	3	2	1

Total score: _____

Scoring and interpretation: Calculate your total score by adding the numbers circled. A tentative interpretation of the scoring is as follows:

45–50   Very high self-confidence with perhaps a tendency toward arrogance
38–44   A high, desirable level of self-confidence
30–37   Moderate, or average, self-confidence
10–29   Self-confidence needs strengthening

for building and elevating self-confidence. They will generally work unless the person has deep-rooted feelings of inferiority. The tactics and strategies are arranged approximately in the order in which they should be tried to achieve best results.

TAKE AN INVENTORY OF PERSONAL ASSETS AND ACCOMPLISHMENTS

Many people suffer from low self-confidence because they do not appreciate their own good points. Therefore, a starting point in increasing your self-confidence is to take an inventory of personal assets and accomplishments. This same activity was offered in Chapter 1 as a method of developing self-esteem. Personal assets should be related to characteristics and behaviors, rather than tangible assets such as an inheritance. Accomplishments can be anything significant in which you played a key role in achieving the results. Try not to be modest in preparing your list of assets and accomplishments. You are looking for any confidence booster you can find.

Two lists prepared by different people will suffice to give you an idea of the kinds of assets and accomplishments that might be included.

LILLIAN

Good listener; most people like me; good handwriting; good posture; inquisitive mind; good at solving problems; good sense of humor; patient with people who make mistakes; better-than-average appearance. Organized successful fund drive which raised $30,000 for church; graduated tenth in high-school class of 500; achieved first place in industrial bowling league; daughter has an excellent career.

ANGELO

Good mechanical skills; work well under pressure; good dancer; friendly with strangers; strong as an ox; good cook; can laugh at my own mistakes; great-looking guy; humble and modest. Made award-winning suggestion that saved company $25,000; scored winning goal in college basketball tournament; dragged child out of burning building.

The value of these asset lists is that they add to your self-appreciation Most people who lay out their good points on paper come away from the activity with at least a temporary boost in self-confidence. The temporary boost, combined with a few success experiences, may lead to a long-term gain in self-confidence.

An important supplement to listing your own assets is hearing the opinion of others on your good points. This tactic has to be used sparingly, however, and mainly with people who are personal-growth-minded. A good icebreaker is to tell your source of feedback that you have to prepare a list of your assets for a human relations exercise (the one you are reading about right now). Since that person knows of your work on your capabilities, you hope that he or she can spare a few minutes for this important exercise.

For many people, positive feedback from others does more for building self-confidence than does feedback from yourself. The reason is that self-esteem depends to a large extent on what we think others think about us Consequently, if other people—whose judgment you trust—think highly of you, your self-image will be positive.

DEVELOP A SOLID KNOWLEDGE BASE

A bedrock for projecting self-confidence is to develop a base of knowledge that enables you to provide sensible alternative solutions to problems

Intuition is very important, but working from a base of facts helps you project a confident image. Formal education is an obvious and important source of information for your knowledge base. Day-by-day absorption of information directly and indirectly related to your career is equally important. A major purpose of formal education is to get you in the right frame of mind to continue your quest for knowledge.

In your quest for developing a solid knowledge base to project self-confidence, be sensitive to abusing this technique. If you bombard people with quotes, facts, and figures, you are likely to be perceived as an annoying know-it-all.

USE POSITIVE SELF-TALK

A basic method of building self-confidence is to engage in **positive self-talk,** saying positive things about yourself to yourself. As explained by Jay T. Knippen and Thad B. Green, the first step in using positive self-talk is to objectively state the incident that is casting doubt about self-worth.[3] The key word here is *objectively*. Terry, who is fearful of poorly executing a report-writing assignment, might say, "I've been asked to write a report for the company, and I'm not a good writer."

The next step is to objectively interpret what the incident *does not* mean. Terry might say, "Not being a skilled writer doesn't mean that I can't figure out a way to write a good report, or that I'm an ineffective employee."

Next, the person should objectively state what the incident *does* mean. In doing this, the person should avoid put-down labels such as "incompetent," "stupid," "dumb," "jerk," or "airhead." All these terms are forms of negative self-talk. Terry should state what the incident does mean: "I have a problem with one small aspect of this job, preparing professional-level reports. This means I need to improve my report-writing skill."

The fourth step is to objectively account for the cause of the incident. Terry would say, "I'm really worried about writing a good report because I have very little experience in writing along these lines."

The fifth step is to identify some positive ways to prevent the incident from happening again. Terry might say, "I'll get out my textbook on business communications and review the chapter on report-writing," or "I'll enroll in a course or seminar on business report-writing."

The final step is to use positive self-talk. Terry imagines his boss saying, "This report is really good. I'm proud of my decision to select you to prepare this important report."

Positive self-talk builds self-confidence and self-esteem because it programs the mind with positive messages. Making frequent positive messages or affirmations about the self creates a more confident person. An example would be, "I know I can learn this new equipment rapidly enough to increase my productivity within five days." If you do make a mistake, your positive self-talk might be, "It's taken me more time than usual to learn how to use this new equipment. I know I'll have the problem licked in a few days."

Positive self-talk contributes to self-confidence in another important way. According to Douglas Bloch, a writer and lecturer, teaching children to think positively about themselves by practicing positive self-talk helps develop adult personalities capable of meeting life's challenges.[4]

AVOID NEGATIVE SELF-TALK

As mentioned above, you should minimize negative statements about yourself to bolster self-confidence. A lack of self-confidence is reflected in statements such as, "I may be stupid but . . . ," "Nobody asked my opinion," "I know I'm usually wrong, but . . . ," "I know I don't have as much education as some people, but . . ." Self-effacing statements like these serve to reinforce low self-confidence.

It is also important not to attribute to yourself negative, irreversible traits such as "idiotic," "ugly," "dull," "loser," and "hopeless." Instead, look upon your weak points as areas for possible self-improvement. Negative self-labeling can do long-term damage to your self-confidence. If a person stops that practice today, his or her self-confidence may begin to increase.

USE POSITIVE VISUAL IMAGERY

Assume you have a situation in mind in which you would like to appear confident and in control. An example would be a meeting with a major customer who has told you over the telephone that he is considering switching suppliers. Your intuitive reaction is that if you cannot handle his concerns without fumbling or appearing desperate, you will lose the account. An important technique is this situation is **positive visual imagery,** or picturing a positive outcome in your mind. To apply this technique in this situation, imagine yourself engaging in a convincing argument about why your customer should retain your company as the primary supplier. Imagine yourself talking in positive terms about the good service your company offers and how you can rectify any problems.

Visualize yourself listening patiently to your customer's concerns and then talking confidently about how your company can handle these concerns. As you rehearse this moment of truth, create a mental picture of you and the customer shaking hands over the fact that the account is still yours.

Positive visual imagery helps you appear self-confident because your mental rehearsal of the situation has helped you prepare for battle. If imagery works for you once, you will be even more effective in subsequent uses of the technique.

STRIVE FOR PEAK PERFORMANCE

A key strategy for projecting self-confidence is to display **peak performance.** The term refers to much more than attempting to do your best. To achieve peak performance you must be totally focused on what you are doing. When you are in the state of peak performance, you are mentally calm and physically at ease. Intense concentration is required to achieve this state. You are so focused on the task at hand that you are not distracted by extraneous events or thoughts.

The mental state achieved during peak performance is akin to a person's sense of deep concentration when immersed in a sport or hobby. On days tennis players perform way above their usual game, they typically comment: "The ball looked so large today, I could read the label as I hit it." On the job, focus and concentration allows the person to sense and respond to relevant information coming both from within the mind and from outside stimuli. When you are at your peak, you impress others by responding intelligently to their input.

Psychologist Charles Garfield says it is easy to detect those who have achieved or will achieve peak performance. Based on his study of more than 1,500 successful people, he concludes that peak performers have a mission in their work and lives. They have something they deeply care about to which they are fully committed.[5] Turning in peak performance helps you develop superior self-confidence, which projects through to others.

Sports psychologist James E. Loehr refers to peak performance as the ideal performance state. A person who achieves this state is able to attain exceptionally high performance while facing heavy pressure. A complex training program is required to attain the ideal performance state. The program includes identifying the right themes and keeping them alive on a daily basis. A person begins by identifying four areas for improvement, such as (1) insecurity, (2) defensiveness, (3) rigidity, and (4) pessimism. The person then converts these four weaknesses into strengths and make them important life themes: (1) confidence, (2) openness, (3) flexibility, and (4) optimism. Anything a person does that reinforces one of these themes during a given day is entered in a log. For example, a person might make an optimistic comment to her manager about sales for the week. Tracking these themes brings them to life and allows for peak performance, or the ideal performance state.[6]

BOUNCE BACK FROM SETBACKS AND EMBARRASSMENTS

An effective self-confidence builder is to convince yourself that you can conquer adversity such as setbacks and embarrassments, thus being resilient. The vast majority of successful leaders have dealt successfully with at least one significant setback in their careers, such as being fired or demoted. In contrast, crumbling after a setback or series of setbacks will usually lower self-confidence. Two major suggestions for bouncing back from setbacks and embarrassments are present next.

Get Past the Emotional Turmoil.   Adversity has enormous emotional consequences. The emotional impact of severe job adversity can rival the loss of a personal relationship. The stress from adversity leads to a cycle of adversity followed by stress, followed by more adversity. A starting point in dealing with the emotional aspects of adversity is to *accept the reality of your problem.* Admit that your problems are real and that you are hurting inside. A second step is *not to take the setback personally.* Remember that setbacks are inevitable so long as you are taking some risks in your career. Not personalizing setbacks helps reduce some of the emotional sting.

If possible, *do not panic*. Recognize that you are in difficult circumstances under which many others panic. Convince yourself to remain calm enough to deal with the severe problem or crisis. Also, *get help from your support network*. Getting emotional support from family members and friends helps overcome the emotional turmoil associated with adversity.

Find a Creative Solution to Your Problem.   An inescapable part of planning a comeback is to solve your problem. You often need to search for creative solutions, using the problem-solving and decision-making steps described in Chapter 3. Suppose a person faced the adversity of not having enough money for educational expenses. The person might search through standard alternatives such as applying for financial aid, looking for more lucrative part-time work, and borrowing from family members. Several students have solved their problem more creatively by asking strangers to lend them money as intermediate-term investments. An option the investors have is to receive a payback based on the future earnings of the students.

LEADERSHIP AND BEING A LEADER

So far we have emphasized the importance of developing self-confidence so that you are able to provide leadership to others. **Leadership** is the process of bringing about positive changes and influencing others to achieve organizational goals. Self-confidence makes a contribution to leadership because people tend to be influenced by a person of high—but not unreasonable—self-confidence. The keywords in understanding leadership are *change* and *influence*. A leader often challenges the status quo and brings about improvements. A leader also influences people to do things, such as achieve higher performance, they would not do in his or her absence.

Effective leadership at the top of organizations is necessary for their prosperity, and even survival.[7] Effective leadership is also important throughout the organization, particularly in working with entry-level workers. Good supervision is needed to help employees deal with customer problems, carry out their usual tasks, and maintain high quality. The most rapidly growing form of leadership in the workplace is the team leader.

A **team leader** is a person who facilitates and guides the efforts of a small group which is given some authority to govern itself. Many firms use work teams instead of traditional departments to accomplish work. For example, a work team might take care of various aspects of issuing an insurance policy. Instead of having power over the group, the team leader works with teammates to help them achieve their goals.

Before studying the personal qualities and behaviors of effective leaders, do Human Relations Self-Assessment Exercise 14-2. The exercise will help you understand how ready you are to assume a leadership role. Taking the quiz will also give you insight into the type of thinking characteristic of leaders.

HUMAN RELATIONS SELF-ASSESSMENT EXERCISE 14-2

Readiness for the Leadership Role

Instructions

Indicate the extent to which you agree with each of the following statements. Use a 1-to-5 scale: (1) disagree strongly; (2) disagree; (3) neutral; (4) agree; (5) agree strongly. If you do not have leadership experience, imagine how you might react to the questions if you were a leader.

1. It is enjoyable having people count on me for ideas and suggestions.	1 2 3 4 5
2. It would be accurate to say that I have inspired other people.	1 2 3 4 5
3. It's a good practice to ask people provocative questions about their work.	1 2 3 4 5
4. It's easy for me to compliment others.	1 2 3 4 5
5. I like to cheer up people even when my own spirits are down.	1 2 3 4 5
6. What my team accomplishes is more important than my personal glory.	1 2 3 4 5
7. Many people imitate my ideas.	1 2 3 4 5
8. Building team spirit is important to me.	1 2 3 4 5
9. I would enjoy coaching other members of the team.	1 2 3 4 5
10. It is important to me to recognize others for their accomplishments.	1 2 3 4 5
11. I would enjoy entertaining visitors to my firm even if it interfered with my completing a report.	1 2 3 4 5
12. It would be fun for me to represent my team at gatherings outside our department.	1 2 3 4 5
13. The problems of my teammates are my problems too.	1 2 3 4 5
14. Resolving conflict is an activity I enjoy.	1 2 3 4 5
15. I would cooperate with another unit in the organization even if I disagreed with the position taken by its members.	1 2 3 4 5
16. I am an idea generator on the job.	1 2 3 4 5
17. It's fun for me to bargain whenever I have the opportunity.	1 2 3 4 5
18. Team members listen to me when I speak.	1 2 3 4 5
19. People have asked to me to assume the leadership of an activity several times in my life.	1 2 3 4 5
20. I've always been a convincing person.	1 2 3 4 5

Total score: _____

(Continued)

Scoring and Interpretation: Calculate your total score by adding the numbers circled. A tentative interpretation of the scoring is as follows:

- 90–100   High readiness for the leadership role
- 60–89   Moderate readiness for the leadership role
- 40–59   Some uneasiness with the leadership role
- 39 or less   Low readiness for carrying out the leadership role

If you are already a successful leader and you scored low on this questionnaire, ignore your score. If you scored surprisingly low and you are not yet a leader, or are currently performing poorly as a leader, study the statements carefully. Consider changing your attitude or your behavior so that you can legitimately answer more of the statements 4 or 5. Studying the rest of this chapter will give you additional insights into the leader's role that may be helpful in your development as a leader.

TRAITS AND CHARACTERISTICS OF EFFECTIVE LEADERS

A major thrust to understanding leaders and leadership is to recognize that effective leaders have the "right stuff." In other words, certain inner qualities contribute to leadership effectiveness in a wide variety of situations. **Effectiveness** in this situation means that the leader helps the group accomplish its objectives without neglecting satisfaction and morale. The characteristics that contribute to effectiveness depend somewhat on the situation. A supervisor in a meat-packing plant and one in a medical office will need different sets of personal characteristics. The situation includes such factors as the people being supervised, the job being performed, the company, and the cultural background of employees. In the next several pages, we describe some of the more important traits and characteristics of leaders. Many of these traits and characteristics are capable of development and refinement.

HUMAN RELATIONS SKILLS

An effective leader must work well with people. Working well with people does not necessarily mean a leader is particularly easygoing. It means that a leader relates to people in such a way as to capture their trust and cooperation. A leadership researcher observed that human relations skills involve:

- Accepting responsibility for your own ideas and feelings

- Being open to your own and other's sentiments

- Experimenting with new ideas and feelings

- Helping others accept, be open to, and experiment with their own ideas and attitudes[8]

- Being a warm person and projecting warmth, thus establishing better rapport with group members

It is difficult, of course, to limit what constitutes "human relations" skills because it can encompass so many different behaviors.

TRUSTWORTHINESS

Group members consistently believe that leaders must display honesty, integrity, and credibility. Leaders themselves believe that honesty and integrity make a difference in their effectiveness. Researchers and observers also share these views. Warren G. Bennis, a leadership authority, interviewed more than 100 corporate leaders and 50 private-sector leaders during a 13-year period. One of the common threads he found was the capacity of leaders to generate and sustain trust. He observed a consistency among what leaders think, feel, and do. Bennis said it drives people crazy when bosses don't walk their talk.[9] How would you feel if you worked for a boss you couldn't trust?

Trust can be eroded in ways other than inconsistency and dishonesty. Bennis believes that the large disparity between the pay of top executive and that of lower-ranking workers damages trust. He contends that when CEOs of large corporations make 187 times the pay of average workers, it creates an "us versus them" mentality within the workforce rather than promoting teamwork.[10]

The importance of honesty also emerged in a study by the Center for Creative Leadership. Research showed that managers who became executive leaders are likely to espouse the following formula: "I will do exactly what I say I will do when I say I will do it. If I change my mind, I will tell you in advance so you will not be harmed by my actions."[11]

INSIGHT INTO PEOPLE AND SITUATIONS

Good insight helps you develop human relations skills. **Insight** is a depth of understanding that requires considerable intuition and common sense. Insight into people and situations involving people is an essential leadership characteristic. A leader with good insight is able to make better work assignments and do a better job of training and developing group members.

An example of an insightful leader would be one who looks at the expression on subordinates' faces to see if they really understand a new procedure. If not, the leader would provide more explanation. An example of poor insight would be to hold a departmental meeting late in the afternoon before a major religious or national holiday. Why try to capture employees' attention when they are thinking about something else? An emergency meeting, however, would be an exception to this principle of poor insight.

SENSITIVITY TO PEOPLE AND EMPATHY

Having insight leads to **sensitivity**—taking people's needs and feelings into account when dealing with them. Sensitivity also implies that the leader minimizes hurting the feelings of people and frustrating their needs. Being sensitive to people is therefore needed for leadership effectiveness.

Insensitivity to others prevents many up-and-coming managers from realizing their full potential. In a study of executive leadership, psychologists compared "derailed" executives with those who had progressed to senior management positions. The leading category of fatal flaws was insensitivity to others, characterized by an abrasive, intimidating, bullying style.[11]

Achieving sensitivity to others requires **empathy,** the ability to place yourself in the other person's shoes. To empathize with another person you don't have to agree, but you do have to understand. As a team leader you might ask a team member to work late one Thursday The team member says, "That's my night to play bingo. Working is out of the question." You can understand how important bingo is to that person, and express your understanding. Nevertheless, you emphasize the importance of the project.

STRONG WORK MOTIVATION AND HIGH ENERGY

Leadership positions tend to be both physically and mentally demanding. A successful leader must be willing to work hard and long to achieve success. Many leaders appear to be driven by a need for self-fulfillment. Another fundamental reason strong work motivation is required for effectiveness is that a person has to be willing to accept the heavy responsibility that being a supervisor entails. As one department manager said, "Whoever thought being a manager would mean that I would have to fire a single parent who has three children to feed and clothe?"

PROBLEM-SOLVING ABILITY AND OPENNESS TO EXPERIENCE

A current theory of leadership supports the view that effective leaders have good problem-solving ability. According to **cognitive resource theory,** the major source of the plans, decisions, and strategies that guide the group's actions are the leader's intellectual abilities.[12] Effective leaders anticipate problems before they occur and diligently stay with them until they are solved. By so doing, a leader demonstrates creative problem solving.

Practical intelligence is usually the most important type of problem-solving ability on the job. The president of a large company makes this comment about intelligence and leadership success:

> Sometimes less than a top IQ is an advantage because that person doesn't see all the problems. He or she sees the big problem and gets on and gets it solved. But the extremely bright person can see so many problems that he or she never gets around to any of them.[13]

Closely related to cognitive skills is the personality characteristic of **openness to experience,** a positive orientation toward learning. People who have considerable openness to experience have well-developed intellects. Traits commonly associated with this dimension of the intellect include being imaginative, cultured, curious, original, broad-minded, intelligent, and artistically sensitive.

Ability to Perform the Group Task

The closer a leader is to the actual work of the group, the more skilled he or she must be with technical details. For example, the supervisor of internal auditing should be skilled at auditing. Being skilled in the actual work of the group can also be referred to as **technical competence.**

One widely held belief—that once you are a top-level leader you can leave technical details behind—is greatly exaggerated. Most successful people are still quite knowledgeable about the details of the field in which they found success. A recently appointed top executive of a major architectural and engineering firm had this to say about his new position: "I'm not going to be doing any design work on the boards and that's been true for a long time. But having a design sensibility is something you bring to the job every day, both in dealing with clients and in trying to help the people in the office do their work."[14]

Charisma

An important quality for leaders at all levels is **charisma,** a type of charm and magnetism that inspires others. Not every leader has to be charismatic, yet to be an effective leader you need some degree of this personality quality. A leader's charisma is determined by the subjective perception of him or her by other people. It is therefore impossible for even the most effective leaders to inspire and motivate everyone. Even popular business leaders are disliked by some of their employees. Charisma encompasses many traits and characteristics. Here we focus on vision, enthusiasm and excitement, and humor.

Vision. Top-level leaders need a visual image of where the organization is headed and how it can get there. The person with vision can help the organization or group establish a vision. The progress of the organization is dependent on the executive having a vision, or optimistic version of the future. Effective leaders project ideas and images that excite people and, therefore, inspire employees to do their best. Leadership positions of lesser responsibility also call for some vision. Each work group in a progressive company might be expected to form its own vision, such as "We will become the best accounts receivable group in the entire auto replacement parts industry."

Enthusiasm and Excitement. A psychoanalyst and Harvard Business School professor observes that leaders get excited about their work. Because of their contagious excitement, they stimulate group members.[15] Workers respond positively to enthusiasm, especially because enthusiasm may be perceived as a reward for good performance. Enthusiasm is also effective because it helps build good relationships with group members. Spoken expressions of enthusiasm include such statements as "great job,"

and "I love it." The leader can express enthusiasm nonverbally through gestures, nonsexual touching, and so forth.

Sense of Humor.   Humor is a component of charisma and a contributor to leadership effectiveness. Humor helps leaders influence people by reducing tension, relieving boredom, and defusing anger. The most effective form of humor by a leader is tied to the leadership situation. It is much less effective for the leader to tell rehearsed jokes. A key advantage of a witty, work-related comment is that it indicates mental alertness. A canned joke is much more likely to fall flat.

A sales manager was conducting a meeting about declining sales. He opened the meeting by saying, "Ladies and gentlemen, just yesterday I completed a computerized analysis of our declining sales. According to my spreadsheet analysis, if we continue our current trend, by the year 2004 we will have sales of negative $2,750,000. No company can support those figures. We've got to reverse the trend." The manager's humor helped dramatize the importance of reversing the sales decline.

HUMAN RELATIONS SKILL-BUILDING EXERCISE 14-1

A Sense of Humor on the Job

One person plays the role of a manager who has scheduled a staff meeting. The manager's task is to inform employees that the seventh competent worker in the last year has just resigned. You want to make effective use of humor to relieve some of the tension and worry. Make a couple of humorous introductory comments. Five other people should play the roles of the remaining staff members. Make effective use of humor yourself in response to the manager's comments.

The Entrepreneurial Spirit

An entrepreneurial leader assumes the risk of starting an innovative business. We ordinarily think of an entrepreneur as being self-employed because the person is a business owner. Yet the same entrepreneurial spirit can be applied as an employee. (This is much like the work habit technique of being self-employed psychologically.) A group leader with an entrepreneurial spirit would search for new activities for the group. The head of a manufacturing unit might say to the group, "Let's ask top management if we can take a shot at making this part that we now buy from a supplier."

The entrepreneurial spirit can also be expressed by reading trade publications and newspapers to keep up with what is happening in the industry. Talking with customers or others in the organization to keep aware of changing needs and requirements shows a spark of entrepreneurial thinking. The leader with an entrepreneurial spirit also visits other firms, attends professional meetings, and participates in educational programs. All the activities just mentioned help the leader think of new activities for the group.

BEHAVIORS AND SKILLS OF EFFECTIVE LEADERS

The personal traits, skills, and characteristics just discussed help create the potential for effective leadership. A leader also has to *do* things that influence group members to achieve good performance. The behaviors or skills of leaders described next contribute to productivity and morale in most situations.

Practice Strong Ethics

Being trustworthy facilitates a leader practicing strong (or good) **ethics,** the study of moral obligation, or separating right from wrong. Ethics deals with doing the right thing by employees, customers, the environment, and the law.[16] Practicing good ethics contributes to effective leadership for several reasons. Workers are more likely to trust an ethical than an unethical leader, which helps the leader gain the support of the group. Good ethics serves as a positive model for group members, thus strengthening the organization. Also, ethical leaders help group members avoid common ethical pitfalls in the workplace. Many of these unethical practices, as listed next, can lead to lawsuits against the company:

- Lying or misrepresenting facts

- Blaming others for your mistakes

- Divulging personal or confidential information to others in the company to promote yourself

- Permitting or failing to report violations of legal requirements

- Protecting substandard performers from proper discipline

- Condoning or failing to report theft or misuse of company property

- Suppressing grievances and complaints

- Covering up accidents and failing to report health and safety hazards

- Ignoring or violating higher management's commitments to employees

- Taking credit for the ideas of others.[17]

To simply a complex issue, an effective leader practices the Golden Rule—*Do unto others as you would have others do unto you.* Similarly, Steven Covey encourages leaders to follow natural principles such as doing only good things.[18] He urges corporate executives, for example, to establish only those goals that will benefit people.

Develop Partnerships with People

Leadership is now regarded as a long-term relationship, or partnership, between leaders and group members. According to Peter Block, in a **partnership** the leader and group members are connected in such a way that the power between them is approximately balanced. To form a partnership, the leader has to allow the group members to share in decision making. Four conditions are necessary to form a true partnership between the leader and group members:

1. *Exchange of purpose.* The leader and team member should work together to build a vision.

2. *A right to say no.* In a partnership, each side has the right to say no without fear of being punished.

3. *Joint accountability.* Each person takes responsibility for the success and failure of the group.

4. *Absolute honesty.* In a partnership, not telling the truth to each other is an act of betrayal. When group members recognize that they have power, they are more likely to tell the truth because they feel less vulnerable to punishment.[19]

Help Group Members Reach Goals and Achieve Satisfaction

Effective leaders help group members in their efforts to achieve goals.[20] In a sense, they smooth out the path to reaching goals. One important way to do this is to provide the necessary resources to group members. An important aspect of a leader's job is to ensure that subordinates have the proper tools, equipment, and human resources to accomplish their objectives.

Another way of helping group members achieve goals is to reduce frustrating barriers to getting work accomplished. A leader who helps group members cut through minor rules and regulations would be engaging in such behavior. In a factory, a supervisory leader has a responsibility to replace faulty equipment, make sure unsafe conditions are corrected, and see that troublesome employees are either rehabilitated or replaced.

Another important general set of actions characteristic of an effective leader is looking out for the satisfaction of the group. Small things sometimes mean a lot in terms of personal satisfaction. One office manager fought for better coffee facilities for her subordinates. Her thoughtfulness contributed immensely to job satisfaction among them.

Giving group members emotional support is another effective way of improving worker satisfaction. An emotionally supportive leader would engage in activities such as listening to group members' problems and offering them encouragement and praise. Again, basic human relations skills contribute to leadership effectiveness.

MAKE EXPECTATIONS KNOWN

People function better when they know what they have to do to achieve work goals. Each person needs to know what is expected of him or her to make a contribution to the mission of the department. The leader provides answers to such questions as "What am I as an individual supposed to do to help the company build this ocean liner?" or "What can I do to help get this budget completed today?"

SET HIGH EXPECTATIONS

In addition to making expectations clear, it is important for leaders to set high expectations for group members. If you as a leader expect others to succeed, they are likely to live up to your expectations. This mysterious phenomenon has been labeled the **Pygmalion effect.** According to Greek mythology, Pygmalion was a sculptor and king of Cyprus who carved an ivory statue of a maiden and fell in love with the statue. The statue was soon brought to life in response to his prayer.

The point of the Pygmalion effect is that the leader can elevate performance by the simple method of expecting others to perform well. The manager's high expectations become a self-fulfilling prophecy. Why high expectations lead to high performance could be linked to self-confidence. As the leader expresses faith in the group members' abilities to perform well, they become more confident of their skills.

GIVE FREQUENT FEEDBACK ON PERFORMANCE

Effective leaders inform employees how they can improve and praise them for things done right. Less-effective leaders, in contrast, often avoid confrontation and give limited positive feedback. An exception is that some ineffective leaders become involved in many confrontations—they are masters at reprimanding people!

MANAGE A CRISIS EFFECTIVELY

When a crisis strikes, that's the time to have an effective leader around. When things are running very smoothly, you may not always notice whether your leader is present. Effectively managing a crisis means giving reassurance to the group that things will soon be under control, specifying the alternative paths for getting out of the crisis, and choosing one of the paths.

CULTIVATE A STRONG CUSTOMER ORIENTATION

Effective leaders are strongly interested in satisfying the needs of customers, clients, or constituents. Such an orientation helps inspire employees to satisfy customers—a necessity for company survival. A customer-oriented leader asks questions such as, "How would what you are proposing better satisfy our customers?" or "What have you done lately to keep our customers happy?"

ASK THE RIGHT QUESTIONS

As in the example just presented, leaders do not need to know all the answers. Instead, a major contribution can be to ask the right questions. Although being knowledgeable about the group task is important, there are many times when asking group members penetrating questions is more important. In today's complex and rapidly changing business environment, the collective intelligence of group members is needed to solve problems.[21] Asking questions, rather than giving answers, is the natural method of helping group members become better problem solvers. Here are sample questions a leader might ask group members to help them meet their challenges:

- What are you going to do differently to reduce by 50 percent the time it takes to fill a customer order?

- Top management is thinking of getting rid of our group and subcontracting the work we do to outside vendors. What do you propose we do to make us more valuable to the company?

- Can you figure out why the competition is outperforming us?

DEVELOPING YOUR LEADERSHIP POTENTIAL

How to improve your potential for becoming a leader is a topic without limits. Almost anything you do to improve your individual effectiveness will have some impact on your ability to lead others. If you strengthen your self-confidence, improve your memory for names, study this book carefully, read studies about leadership, or improve your physical fitness, you stand a good chance of improving your leadership potential. Five general strategies might be kept in mind if you are seeking to improve your leadership potential:

1. *General education and specific training.*   Almost any program of career training or education can be considered a program of leadership development. Courses in human relations, management, or applied psychology have obvious relevance for someone currently occupying or aspiring toward a leadership position. Many of today's leaders in profit and nonprofit organizations hold formal degrees in business. Specific training programs will also help you improve your leadership potential. Among them might be skill development programs in interviewing, employee selection, listening, assertiveness training, budgeting, planning, improving work habits, resolving conflict, and communication skills. After acquiring knowledge through study, you then put the knowledge into practice as a leader.

2. *Leadership development programs.*   A focused way of improving your leadership potential is to attend development programs designed specifically to improve your ability to lead others and develop self-confidence. A popular type of leadership development program called *outdoor training* places people in a challenging outdoor environment for a weekend or up to ten days. Participants are required to accomplish physical feats such as climbing a mountain, white water canoeing, building a wall, or swinging between trees on a rope.[22]

Participants in these outdoor programs learn such important leadership skills and attitudes as teamwork, trusting others, and a confidence in their ability to accomplish the seemingly impossible. Exhibit 14-1 presents details about the type of leadership training under discussion.

3. *Leadership experience.*   No program of leadership improvement can be a substitute for leadership experience. Because leadership effectiveness depends somewhat on the situation, a sound approach is to attempt to gain leadership experience in different settings. A person who wants to become an executive is well advised to gain supervisory experience in at least two different organizational functions (such as customer service and finance).

First-level supervisory jobs are an invaluable starting point for developing your leadership potential. It takes considerable skill to manage a fast-food restaurant effectively or to direct a public playground during the summer. A supervisor frequently faces a situation in which subordinates are poorly trained, poorly paid, and not well motivated to achieve company objectives.

4. *Modeling effective leaders.*   Are you committed to improving your leadership skill and potential? If so, carefully observe a capable leader in action and incorporate some of his or her approaches into your own behavior. You may not be able to or want to become that person's clone, but you can model (imitate) what the person does. For instance, most inexperienced leaders have a difficult time confronting others with bad news. Observe a good confronter handle the situation, and try that person's approach the next time you have some unfavorable news to deliver to another person.

EXHIBIT 14-1

ELECTRONIC COMPANY STAFF AT OUTWARD BOUND

The top executive at TCI West, Inc., an electronics firm, wanted key personnel to develop into a smooth team. He chose Outward Bound training because he hoped to break down communication barriers and put all participants on equal footing. The first TCI representatives were sent to a course on orienteering in the Nevada desert. Among these people were top managers, marketing directors, and five manager trainees. The group learned rappeling, rock climbing, and first aid. They hiked through hot desert days and awakened to temperatures of 5°F (–15°C). They cooked meals, pitched tents, rationed water, and taught each other outdoor techniques.

Another TCI group participated in an Outward Bound river program. One exercise that incorporates team building, leadership, and communication skills required participants to intentionally flip a raft over in deep water. Next, they had to return it to the upright position and then help each other back into the raft.

Developing trust is another critical aspect of Outward Bound. Participants must trust the commands that are shouted from the person leading the raft through swirling rapids. They must trust the lead person's sense of direction while hiking through the desert. Most of all, they must trust the person belaying the rappel that will save them from serious injury or death in case of a fall. (A *belay* is a mountain-climbing hold to secure the rope.)

Among the lessons learned are that getting help from others is not always a sign of weakness, that it's all right not to be perfect, and that most fears can be put in proper perspective.

SOURCE: Based on facts in Sally Howe, "TCI West Trains Outdoors," *Personnel Journal,* June 1991, pp. 58–59.

5. *Self-development of leadership characteristics and behavior.* Our final recommendation for enhancing your leadership potential is to study the leadership characteristics and behaviors described in this chapter. As a starting point, identify several attributes you think you could strengthen within yourself given some self-determination. For example, you might decide that with effort you could improve your enthusiasm. You might also believe that you could be more emotionally supportive of others. It is also helpful to obtain feedback from reliable sources about which traits and behaviors you particularly need to develop.

SUMMARY

Before most people can exert leadership, they need to develop an appropriate amount of self-confidence. Self-confidence is necessary for leadership because it helps assure group members that things are under control. A leader who is too self-confident, however, may not admit to errors, listen to criticism, or ask for advice. Also, you may appear insecure if you are too self-confident.

A general principle of boosting your self-confidence is to experience success (goal accomplishment) in a variety of situations. As you achieve one set of goals, you establish slightly more difficult goals, thus entering a success cycle. The specific strategies for building self-confidence described here are:

1. Take an inventory of personal assets and accomplishments.
2. Develop a solid knowledge base.
3. Use positive self-talk.
4. Avoid negative self-talk.
5. Use positive visual imagery.
6. Strive for peak performance.
7. Bounce back from setbacks and embarrassments.

Leadership is the process of bringing about positive changes and influencing others to achieve organizational goals. Effective leadership is needed at the top of organizations, but supervisors and team leaders also need to provide effective leadership. Effective leaders have the "right stuff." Certain traits and characteristics contribute to leadership effectiveness in many situations. Among them are: human relations skills; trustworthiness; insight into people and situations; sensitivity to people and empathy; strong work motivation and high energy; problem-solving ability and openness to experience; ability to perform the group task; charisma (including vision, enthusiasm and excitement, and a sense of humor); and an entrepreneurial spirit.

Behaviors and skills of an effective leader (one who maintains high productivity and morale) include the following:

1. Practice strong ethics.
2. Develop partnerships with people (emphasize power sharing).
3. Help group members reach goals and achieve satisfaction.
4. Make expectations known.
5. Set high expectations.
6. Give frequent feedback on performance.
7. Manage a crisis effectively.
8. Cultivate a strong customer orientation.
9. Ask the right questions.

Many activities in life can in some way contribute to the development of a person's leadership potential. Five recommended strategies for improving your leadership potential or leadership skills are: (1) general education and specific training, (2) participation in leadership-development programs, (3) acquisition of leadership experience, (4) modeling experienced leaders, and (5) self-development of leadership characteristics and behavior.

Questions and Activities

1. When you meet another person, on what basis do you conclude that he or she is self-confident?

2. What is the difference between "trying your hardest" and achieving peak performance?

3. What positive self-talk can you use after you have failed on a major assignment?

4. Which work habits and time-management practices (see Chapter 12) are well suited to helping a person achieve peak performance?

5. Several companies in the telecommunications field aggressively "steal" employees from other companies who are not looking for a job. What is your evaluation of the ethics of such a practice?

6. Several studies have shown that about one-half of workers are cynical about the ethics and integrity of business leaders. What can business leaders do to regain the trust of employees?

7. Provide an example of something a leader motivated or inspired you to do that you would not have done without his or her presence.

8. Why is the "ability to perform the group task" essential for a team leader?

9. Create a vision for a past or present employer, or for any other company of your choosing.

10. How might your current program of study contribute to your development as a leader?

REFERENCES

[1]Marilyn E. Gist and Terence R. Mitchell, "Self-Efficacy A Theoretical Analysis of Its Determinants and Malleability," *Academy of Management Review,* April 1992, pp. 183–211.

[2]Dov Eden and Arie Aviram, "Self-Efficacy Training to Speed Reemployment: Helping People to Help Themselves," *Journal of Applied Psychology,* June 1993, pp. 352–360.

[3]Jay T. Knippen and Thad B. Green, "Building Self-Confidence," *Supervisory Management,* August 1989, pp. 22–27.

A HUMAN RELATIONS CASE PROBLEM

"How Can I Inspire My Team?"

Pierre Binet considered himself fortunate to be chosen as team leader for one of the newly formed work teams at Madison Casualty Inc. The purpose of the new teams was to improve customer service. Each team now had the authority to issue policies and settle claims—within limits—for particular geographic regions. Before this organization into teams, separate departments existed for sales administration, underwriting, and claims. Although Madison Casualty was profitable, the company received too many criticisms of poor service. Many complaints were made by external customers that claims took too long to settle. Company sales representatives complained that the underwriting procedures for issuing policies were too lengthy.

One of Binet's early steps was to call frequent team meetings to discuss how service was going to be improved. He emphasized to the group that Madison Casualty had moved into the modern era and that the teams were empowered to look for ways to improve efficiency. Binet also emphasized that each team member had more responsibility than under the previous organizational structure. Each team member would be doing some sales administration, some underwriting, and some claims work.

Molly Goldwin, a team member, commented during one of Binet's meetings: "Just think of it, three jobs in one and being paid just the same as before."

At the same meeting, another team member asked, "What's so special about calling us a team? I had a nice job in the underwriting department before these teams were formed. I enjoyed the work. Now my job is more confusing."

"The company decided this was the way to go. Trust me, everything will work out fine in the end. Just go along with the team idea for now."

Four months after the work teams were formed, his boss, Nancy Wong, met with Binet to discuss progress. Wong told Binet, "Your team isn't making as much progress as I would like. Policies aren't being issued any faster. Customer complaints about slow claims settlements are at the same level as before we converted to teams. The other teams are making more progress. Does your team have a problem?"

"We might have a problem," said Binet. "Everyone comes to work just as in the days before teams. They do most of their work alone, but get together when needed. It just seems to be business as usual. So far, the idea of being a high-producing team hasn't caught on."

"Are you being an effective team leader?" asked Wong.

"I think I am," said Binet. "I do everything I'm supposed to. I hold meetings. I take care of the paperwork and answer e-mail, I try to settle problems."

"I'll be back with you in three months to discuss the progress of your team. I want to see some improved results in terms of better customer service."

Questions

1. How can Binet be a more effective team leader?

2. What can Binet do to inspire his team?

3. How would you analyze this case in terms of motivation? (Review Chapter 2.)

HUMAN RELATIONS SKILL-BUILDING EXERCISE 14-2

Inspiring the Team

One student plays the role of Pierre Binet who calls a meeting designed to inspire the team toward new heights of productivity and customer service. Be dramatic. Use whatever inspirational approaches you think might work. Five other students play the role of team members, none of whom were expecting an inspirational meeting. If Binet inspires you, act accordingly. If he fails to inspire you, demonstrate your lack of inspiration.

[4]Douglas Bloch, *Positive Self-Talk for Children* (New York: Bantam, 1993).

[5]Work cited in Michael Rozek, "Can You Spot a Peak Performer?" *Personnel Journal,* June 1991, p. 77.

[6]James E. Loehr, *Stress for Success* (New York: Evans, 1997).

[7]Genevieve Capowski, "Anatomy of a Leader: Where Are the Leaders of Tomorrow?" *Management Review,* March 1994, pp. 10–17.

[8]Jay Hall, "What Makes a Manager Good, Bad, or Average?" *Psychology Today,* August 1976, p. 53.

[9]Cited in Julie Cohen Mason, "Leading the Way into the 21st Century," *Management Review,* October 1992, p. 19.

[10]Richard M. Hodgetts, "A Conversation with Warren Bennis on Leadership in the Midst of Downsizing," *Organizational Dynamics,* Summer 1996, p. 75.

[11]Morgan W. McCall, Jr., and Michael M. Lombardo, *Off the Track: Why and How Successful Leaders Get Derailed,* technical report no. 21 (Greensboro, NC: Center for Creative Leadership, 1983), p. 11.

[12]Robert P. Vecchio, "Theoretical and Empirical Examination of Cognitive Resource Theory," *Journal of Applied Psychology,* April 1990, p. 141.

[13]Quoted in Priscilla Petty, "If You've Been in Your Job Long, You Need to Freshen Up on Ambition," Gannett News Service syndicated column, September 30, 1986.

[14]"Architectural Firm Picks New President," *The New York Times,* May 21, 1981, p. D2.

[15]Abraham Zaleznik, *The Managerial Mystique: Restoring Leadership in Business* (New York: Harper & Row, 1989).

[16]"Ethics—Business Educators Teach Students To . . . Do the Right Thing!" *Keying In,* January 1997, p. 1.

[17]Robert B. Maddux and Dorothy Maddux, *Ethics in Business: A Guide for Managers* (Los Altos, CA: Crisp Publications, 1994).

[18]George W. Fotis, "Interactive Personal Ethics," *Management Review,* December 1996, p. 46; "Covey Proposes Principle-Based Leadership," *Management Review,* September 1995, pp. 20–21.

[19]Peter Block, *Stewardship: Choosing Service over Self-Interest* (San Francisco: Berrett-Koehler Publishers, 1993), pp. 27–32.

[20]Robert T. Keller, "A Test of the Path-Goal Theory of Leadership with Need for Clarity as a Moderator in Research and Development Organizations," *Journal of Applied Psychology,* April 1989, pp. 208–212.

[21]Ronald A. Heifetz and Donald L. Laurie, "The Work of Leadership," *Harvard Business Review,* January-February 1997, p. 124.

[22]Jennifer J. Laabs, "Team Training Goes Outdoors," *Personnel Journal,* June 1991, p. 59.

ADDITIONAL READING

Bower, Marvin. *The Will to Lead: Running a Business with a Network of Leaders.* Boston, MA: Harvard Business School Press, 1997.

Conger, Jay A. "Personal Growth Training: Snake Oil or Pathway to Leadership?" *Organizational Dynamics,* Summer 1993, pp. 19–30.

Covey, Stephen R. *First Things First.* (New York: Simon & Schuster, 1994).

DuBrin, Andrew J. *Personal Magnetism: Discover Your Own Charisma and Learn to Charm, Inspire, and Influence Others.* New York: AMACOM, 1997.

Gardner, Howard. *Leading Minds: An Anatomy of Leadership.* New York: Basic Books, 1995.

Losoncy, Lewis E. *The Motivating Team Leader.* Delray Beach, FL: St. Lucie Press, 1995.

McLean, J. S., and Weitzel, William. *Leadership: Magic, Myth, or Method?* New York: AMACOM, 1992.

Rosener, Judy B. America's *Competitive Secret: Women Managers.* New York: Oxford University Press, 1997.

Smith, Gregory P. *The New Leader: Bringing Creativity and Innovation to the Workplace.* Delray Beach, FL: St. Lucie Press, 1996.

15

MANAGING YOUR PERSONAL FINANCES

Learning Objectives

After studying the information and doing the exercises in this chapter, you should be able to:

▼ Do a better job of managing your personal finances

▼ Establish a tentative financial plan for yourself and your family

▼ Pinpoint basic investment principles

▼ Identify several major forms of investments

▼ Develop a plan for managing your creditworthiness

▼ Give yourself a yearly financial checkup

Anne Scheiber retired in 1944, after a 23-year career as an auditor for the Internal Revenue Service. When she died in 1995, at age 101, she donated $22 million to Yeshiva University to support scholarships for Jewish female students. While working at the tax agency, Scheiber never earned more than $4,000 a year and never received a promotion, despite having a law degree. While working at the IRS, Scheiber invested

her $5,000 in savings in the stock market. Scheiber's tax returns show her annual dividends increased over the years from $900 in 1936 to more than $750,000 in recent years. Scheiber lived frugally in the same apartment in New York City and never even changed the furniture.[1]

You may not want to live the lifestyle of the woman just described, but her story illustrates an important point. With good personal financial management, even people with modest incomes can amass a large amount of money. It is also important to manage personal finances in such a way that money becomes a source of satisfaction rather than a major worry. Financial problems can lead to other problems. Poor concentration stemming from financial worries may lead to low job performance. Many relationship problems stem from conflict about finances. Worry about money can also drain energy that could be used to advance your career or enrich your personal life.

The purpose of this chapter is to present information that should enable you to start on the road to financial comfort and escape financial discomfort. Our approach is to cover the basics of personal financial planning, investment principles, choosing investments, managing and preventing debt, giving yourself a yearly financial checkup, and retiring rich.

 YOUR PERSONAL FINANCIAL PLAN

A highly recommended starting point in improving your present financial condition and enhancing your future is to develop a personal financial plan. Two key elements of a personal financial plan are financial goals and a budget. The spending plan, or budget, helps you set aside the money for investments that you need to accomplish your goals. The subject of how to invest the money your investment plan provides is described at later points in this chapter.

EXHIBIT 15-1

FINANCIAL GOAL SETTING

Goal	Target Date	Years to Goal	Dollars Needed
1. Pay off credit cards	June 2001	1½	$4,275
2. Pay for son's college	September 2018	18	$130,000
3. Down payment on home	June 2005	4½	$20,000

ESTABLISHING FINANCIAL GOALS

Personal finances is yet another area in which goal setting generally improves performance. A common approach to financial goal setting is to specify amounts of money you would like to earn at certain points in time. An individual might set yearly financial goals, adjusted for inflation. Another might set goals for five-year intervals. Another common financial goal is to obtain enough money to cover a specific expense, such as making a down payment on a new car. These goals should include a target date, such as shown in Exhibit 15-1. An important supplement to establishing these goals is an investment table which specifies the amount of money needed to achieve the goal (see Table 15-1). Financial goals are sometimes expressed in terms of the allocation of money. Among these goals would be:

- Putting pay raises into savings or reducing debt

- Participating in an automatic savings or retirement plan whereby a financial institution deducts money from each paycheck

- Investing 10 percent of each net paycheck into a mutual fund

Financial goals are sometimes more motivational when they point to the lifestyle you hope to achieve with specific amounts of money. In this way money becomes the means to the ends that bring satisfaction and happiness. Here are two examples of financial goals expressed in terms of what money can accomplish:

- By 2003 I want to earn enough money to have my own apartment and car, and buy nice gifts for my family and relatives.

- By 2030, I want to earn enough money to have paid for my house, own a vacation home near a lake, and take a winter vacation each year.

TABLE 15-1

MONTHLY SAVINGS NEEDED TO REACH GOAL
(5% AFTER-TAX RATE OF RETURN)

	Dollar Goals				
Years	$5,000	$10,000	$20,000	$50,000	$100,000
2	198	395	791	1,977	3,954
4	94	188	376	939	1,878
6	59	119	238	594	1,189
8	42	85	169	423	846
10	32	64	128	321	641
20	12	24	48	121	242
30	6	12	24	60	120

NOTE: This chart assumes that deposits are made at the beginning of each month, and interest is compounded monthly.

DEVELOPING A BUDGET (SPENDING PLAN)

When most people hear the word *budget,* they think of a low-priced item or miserly spending habits. Their perception is only partially correct. A **budget** is a plan for spending money to improve your chances of using your money wisely and not spending more than your net income. Exhibit 15-2 presents advice from a financial advisor that will help you understand the key role a budget plays in managing personal finances. Most of the topics she covers are presented in more detail later in this chapter. Reading this advice will give you the right mental set for ensuring your financial future. Developing a budget can be divided into a series of logical steps. Exhibit 15-3 presents a worksheet helpful for carrying out the plan.

Step 1: *Establishing goals.*   It is important to decide what you or your family really need and want. If you are establishing a family budget, it is best to involve the entire family. For the sake of simplicity, we will assume here that the reader is preparing an individual budget. Individual budgets can be combined to form the family budget. Goal setting should be done for the short, intermediate, and long term. A short-term goal might be "replace hot water heater this February." A long-term goal might be "accumulate enough money for a recreational vehicle within ten years."

Step 2: *Estimating income.*   People whose entire income is derived from salary can readily estimate their income. Commissions, bonuses, and investment income are more variable. So is income from part-time work, inheritance, and prizes.

Step 3. *Estimating expenses.*   The best way to estimate expenses is to keep close track of what you are actually spending now. After listing all

---

EXHIBIT 15-2

FINANCIAL TIPS FOR GENERATION XERS

Ginger Applegarth, finance correspondent for *The Today Show,* and president, Applegarth Advisory Group, was asked, "In the third millennium, Generation X will inherit an economically uncertain world. To young people just starting out in their adult lives, what realistic advice would you offer for saving, investing, and generally preparing prudently for their financial future under uncertain circumstances?"

Applegarth: "The no. 1 thing is to make a budget and see how you are spending. You are creating lifetime spending and saving habits, so a little self-discipline now will reap benefits in the long run. Start out with a zero-based budget, meaning that instead of taking current expenses and subtracting what you can, start with zero and add expenses one by one, until you reach your limit.

"Make saving a weekly habit and have funds taken out of your paychecks or checking account. If you have credit cards, use them only if you pay off the balance each month. Review your expenses each week and plan for the coming week. If you are eligible for a retirement plan, join it!

"Become a smart investor. Read personal finance magazines, talk with friends and start to develop a relationship with a financial adviser. Make sure you have the right kind of insurance. Especially for Xers, disability and renter's insurance are important."

SOURCE: Reprinted with permission from "Tips for Generation Xers, Young Families and Boomers," *USAA Magazine,* Oct/Nov 1996, p. 13.

---

your expenses, perhaps for two weeks, break the expenses down into meaningful categories such as those shown in Exhibit 15-3. Modify the specific items to suit your particular spending patterns. For instance, computer supplies and on-line service might be such a big item in your spending plan that it deserves a separate category. It is possible that an expense you have now will soon decrease (such as paying off a loan) or increase (such as joining a health club).

Try to plan for large expenses so that they are spaced at intervals over several years. If you plan to purchase a car one year, plan to remodel your kitchen another. If you buy an overcoat one season, you might have to delay buying a suit until the next year.

Use your records and recollections to help you decide whether to continue your present pattern of spending or to make changes. For instance, estimating your expenses might reveal that you are spending far too much on gas for the car. An antidote might be to consolidate errand-running trips or make some trips by foot or bicycle.

For most people a monthly budget makes the most sense because so many expenses are once-a-month items. Included here are rent, mortgage payments, car payments, and credit-card payments.

Step 4: *Comparing expenses and income.* Add the figures in your spending plan. Now compare the total with your estimate of income for the

EXHIBIT 15-3

YOUR SPENDING PLAN

Monthly Expenses

Fixed:

Mortgage or rent   _____

Property insurance   _____

Health insurance   _____

Auto insurance   _____

Other insurance   _____

Educational expenses   _____

Child support
  payments   _____

Taxes:

  Federal   _____

  State or provincial   _____

  Social security   _____

  Local   _____

  Property   _____

Installment loans
  (auto and others)   _____

Set aside for
  emergencies   _____

Variable:

Food   _____

Household supplies   _____

Home maintenance
  and repairs   _____

Medical and dental   _____

Telephone   _____

Clothing   _____

Hair care and cosmetics   _____

Transportation   _____

Car maintenance   _____

Travel and vacation   _____

Clubs/organizations   _____

Hobbies   _____

Other   _____

Total expenses   _____

Monthly Income

Salary   _____

Tips   _____

Bonuses & commissions   _____

Interest & dividends   _____

Insurance benefits   _____

Child support received   _____

Other   _____

Total income   _____

Summary:

Total income   _____

Less total expenses   _____

Balance for savings
  and investment   _____

planning period. If the two figures balance, at least you are in neutral financial condition. If your income exceeds your estimate of expenses, you have made a profit. You may decide to satisfy more of your immediate wants, set aside more money for future goals, or put the balance into savings or investment.

Remember that the true profit from your labor is the difference between your net income and your total expenses. Set-asides are considered an expense, since you will inevitably use up that money to meet future goals or pay for seasonal expenses. Without a miscellaneous category, many budgets will project a profit that never materializes. Any household budget has some miscellaneous or unpredictable items each month. After working with your budget several months, you should be able to make an accurate estimate of miscellaneous expenses.

If your income is below your estimated expenses, you will have to embark on a cost-cutting campaign in your household. If you brainstorm the problem by yourself or with friends, you will come up with dozens of valid expense-reducing suggestions.

Step 5: *Carrying out the spending plan.* After you have done your best job of putting your spending plan on paper, try it out for one, two, or three months. See how close it comes to reality. Keep accurate records to find out where your money is being spent. It is helpful to make a notation of expenditures at the end of every day. Did you forget about that $23 you spent on party snacks Sunday afternoon? It is a good idea to keep all financial records together. You may find it helpful to set aside a desk drawer, a large box, or other convenient place to put your record book, bills, receipts, and other financial papers. Converting paper records into computerized files is strongly recommended for maintaining a spending plan.

Step 6: *Evaluating the plan.* Compare what you spent with what you planned to spend for three consecutive months. If your spending was quite different from your plan, find out why. If your plan did not provide for your needs, it must be revised. You simply cannot live with a spending plan that allows for no food the last four days of the month. If the plan fitted your needs but you had trouble sticking to it, the solution to your problem may be to practice more self-discipline.

A budget usually needs reworking until it fits your needs. Each succeeding budget should work better. As circumstances change, your budget will need revision. A spending plan or budget is a changing, living document that serves as a guide to the proper management of your personal finances.

BASIC INVESTMENT PRINCIPLES

After you have developed a spending plan that results in money left over for savings and investment, you can begin investing. To start developing an investment strategy, or refining your present one, consider the nine investment principles presented next. They are based on the collected wisdom of many financial planners and financially successful people.

1. *Spend less money than you earn.*   The key to lifelong financial security and peace of mind is to spend less money than you earn. By so doing you will avoid the stresses of being in debt and worrying about money. A widely accepted rule of thumb is to set aside 10 percent of your net income for savings and investments. For many people struggling to make ends meet, the 10-percent rule is unrealistic. These people may choose to implement the 10-percent rule later in their careers. A growing practice is to have savings and investments deducted automatically from your paycheck or bank account. The automatic plans ensures that you will set aside each month for investments.

2. *Invest early and steadily to capitalize upon the benefits of compounding.*   Investments made early in life grow substantially more than those made later. You will slowly and steadily accumulate wealth if you begin investing early in life and continue to invest regularly. Let's look at a straightforward example. Assume you invest $1,000 at the start of each year for five years. It earns 8 percent a year and the earnings are compounded. You would have $6,123 at the end of five years. If you invested $1,000 at the start of each year for 25 years, you would have $79,252; at the end of 40 years you would have $290,917. To achieve these full results you would have to make tax-free investments (described in the section about retiring rich).

3. *Keep reinvesting dividends.*   As implied in the second principle, dividends and interest payments must be reinvested to fully benefit from early and regular investments. Here is an illustration based on stock dividends. Assume a person had invested $5,000 in a representative group of common stocks, 30 years ago. The amount accumulated *with* reinvesting dividends is 4 times as great as that *without* reinvesting. The person who did not reinvest the dividends would have accumulated approximately $60,000, while the person who reinvested the dividends would have stocks worth approximately $240,000.

4. *Diversify your investments (use asset allocation).*   A bedrock principle of successful investing is to diversify your investments. This approach is often referred to as *asset allocation* because you allocate your assets to different types of investments. Money is typically apportioned among stocks, bonds, short-term instruments like money-market funds and real estate (including home ownership). A starting point is to accumulate enough money in cash or its equivalent to tide you over for three months in case you are without employment. Readily accessible money is referred to as a *liquid* investment. Your specific allocation of assets (or putting your eggs in many baskets) will depend on your tolerance for risk and your time frame. At the conclusion of the section on choosing your investments, we will describe several different investment allocations.

5. *Maintain a disciplined, long-term approach.*   If you have an investment plan suited to your needs, stick with it over time. The patient, long-term investor is likely to achieve substantial success. Investors who make investments based on hunches and hot tips, and sell in panic when the value of their investments drop, generally achieve poorer returns. Investing regularly often lowers the average cost of your investment purchases. (This technique is referred to as *dollar-cost averaging,* and is described later.)

6. *Practice contrary investing.* If your purpose in making investments is to become wealthy, follow the principle of **contrary investing**—buy investments when the demand for them is very low and sell when the demand is very high. When others are discouraged about purchasing real estate and there are very few buyers around, invest heavily in real estate. When others are excited about real estate investing, sell quickly before prices fall again. In the words of the late billionaire J. Paul Getty, "Buy when everybody else is selling, and hold until everyone else is buying." This is not merely a catchy slogan. It is the very essence of successful investing."[2]

7. *Be willing to accept some risk.* An unreasonable fear of risk is a major investment mistake. Small investors are frequently so afraid of losing their principal that they go to extremes in seeking safe investments. An investment executive explains: "If you put your money into something that *guarantees* you'll get your principal back, there's a good chance inflation will hurt that principal's buying power."[3]

8. *Invest globally as well as domestically.* Diversifying your investments among different countries is another contributor to financial success. Financial advisers regularly suggest international stocks and bonds as a diversification possibility. Overseas markets may offer investors values more promising than those provided domestically. One way to invest internationally is to purchase mutual funds geared to this purpose. Another approach is to purchase American Depository Receipts (ADRs). These are stocks in foreign companies that sell on American stock exchanges in U.S. dollars, which makes it easier for domestic investors to buy and sell foreign stocks.

Be aware, however, that overseas investments have two substantial risks. The value of the overseas currency may go down rapidly, thus lowering your return should you sell your stocks or bonds. Another problem is that a politically unstable government can create havoc in the investment markets. One example is that a government might take over a private company and declare its stocks and bonds invalid.

9. *Pay off debt.* One of the best investment principles of all is the most straightforward. Paying off debt gives you an outstanding return on investment. A common scenario is a person paying about 18 percent on credit card debt, while earning 4 percent from an investment. Paying off the 18 percent debt with money from savings would thus yield a 14 percent profit. (We are excluding home equity loans from consideration because they carry tax-deductible interest.) Another way of looking at the cost of debt is this: You have to earn 13.9 percent a year on your money before taxes to pay off a 10 percent, 4-year loan on a new car.

Another major strategy for paying off debt is to work toward reducing a home mortgage. Making extra payments on a mortgage substantially reduces the time it takes to pay off the mortgage. Suppose a person has a $100,000 mortgage at 8 percent for 30 years. By increasing the mortgage payment just 4 percent each year, the loan will be retired in 15 years, and would save $82,845 in interest. At the same time, the additional payments build equity in your house thus increasing your net worth. A minor concern is that as you pay down the interest on the mortgage, your tax deduction dwindles.

CHOOSING YOUR INVESTMENTS

After understanding some basic principles of investing, you are ready to make choices among different investments. We describe investments here because they are an integral part of managing your personal finances. Investments can be categorized into two basic types: lending money or owning assets. Lending money is referred to as a *debt investment,* while owning an asset is an *equity investment.* For example, when you purchase a corporate bond you are lending money that will pay a fixed rate of return. When you purchase stocks you become an owner of an asset. Our discussion of choosing investments includes their relative risks, relative returns, different types, and selecting the right mix.

TYPES OF INVESTMENT RISKS

As illustrated in Exhibit 15-4, investments vary in the risk of losing the money you invested. Yet not even so-called *safe* investments are without

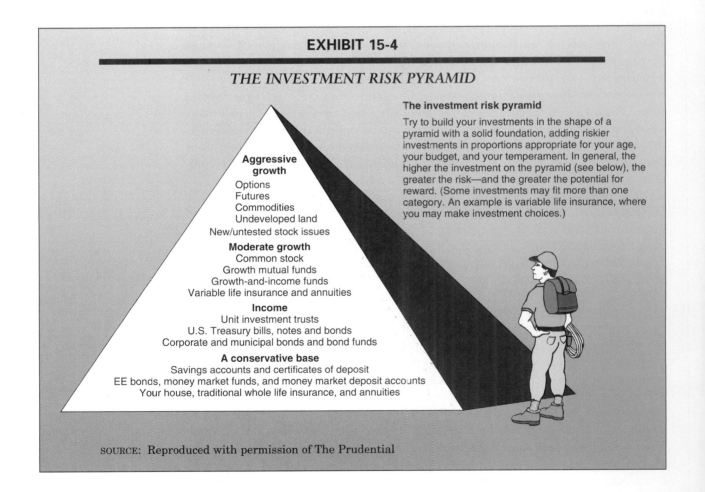

EXHIBIT 15-4

THE INVESTMENT RISK PYRAMID

Aggressive growth
Options
Futures
Commodities
Undeveloped land
New/untested stock issues

Moderate growth
Common stock
Growth mutual funds
Growth-and-income funds
Variable life insurance and annuities

Income
Unit investment trusts
U.S. Treasury bills, notes and bonds
Corporate and municipal bonds and bond funds

A conservative base
Savings accounts and certificates of deposit
EE bonds, money market funds, and money market deposit accounts
Your house, traditional whole life insurance, and annuities

The investment risk pyramid

Try to build your investments in the shape of a pyramid with a solid foundation, adding riskier investments in proportions appropriate for your age, your budget, and your temperament. In general, the higher the investment on the pyramid (see below), the greater the risk—and the greater the potential for reward. (Some investments may fit more than one category. An example is variable life insurance, where you may make investment choices.)

SOURCE: Reproduced with permission of The Prudential

risk. A sophisticated way of understanding risk is to recognize that there are four types.[4] *Investment risk* is the possibility of losing rather than gaining money (the conventional meaning of risk). People with extreme fears of investment risk might put their money in government-insured savings account or in a safe-deposit box.

Market risk means that the market for your type of investment can go up or down at any time. The market for stocks might go up, while you are heavily invested in bonds. Or you might be heavily invested in gold, and the market for gold plummets, but yields of bank certificates of deposit climb upward. People who fear market risk usually believe strongly in diversification.

Inflation risk is the risk that the cost of living will increase faster than the return on your investment. Assume that you have invested a $10,000 inheritance in a money market fund paying an average of 3.75 percent per year. At the same time, inflation proceeds at an average of 4.75 percent per year. Your $10,000 nest egg is losing purchasing power at the rate of 1 percent per year. The person concerned about inflation risk would do well to invest in stocks, bonds, and most money-market investments because they typically have yields that outpace inflation.

Adequacy risk is the risk of not having accumulated enough money to reach your financial goals. One person might plan to retire from corporate life at age 50 so that she can start a business of her own. She forecasts that she will need a lump sum of $250,000 to achieve her goal. In the meantime she suffers from adequacy risk because her investments are growing slowly. She may have to take some big investment risks, such as purchasing large amounts of stocks in start-up companies.

A major principle related to risk taking in investments is to decide how much and what kind of risk you can tolerate. One person might not be able to tolerate watching the values of his or her mutual funds fluctuate from month to month. Another person might not be able to tolerate the risk of missing out on big profits in the stock market by putting money in a savings bank. And a third person might not want to contend with the risk of having too little money for retirement. Understanding how much and what kind of risk you can tolerate will then help you map the best investment strategy for yourself.

DIFFERENT TYPES OF INVESTMENTS

Dozens of different savings plans and investments are available. They include everyday methods of savings as well as exotic investments such as buying into a lottery that gives the winners the rights to own an interactive television station. Here we summarize a variety of popular investments ranging from the most conservative to the more speculative

1. *Passbook savings accounts.* With a passbook (or day-to-day) savings account the user can deposit or withdraw money as often as he or she wishes. This type of account pays slightly more than a regular checking account. Most sophisticated investors make little use of this type of savings account. Passbook savings accounts appeal to those who prefer the most traditional way of depositing money in a bank. Also, funds can be drawn immediately without any penalty.

2. *Certificates of deposit.* Banks and savings and loan associations offering certificates of deposit (CDs) require that you deposit a reasonably large sum of money for a specified time period. The time period can be anywhere from several months to ten years. CDs come in denominations such as $500, $5,000, and $10,000, paying a rate of return in excess of the rate of inflation.

If you have a considerable amount of cash and are not worried about having your money tied up for a fairly long time period, CDs are ideal. If you close one of these accounts before its due date, the amount of penalty lowers the interest rate to approximately that of an interest-bearing checking account.

3. *Money-market funds.* Many people who formerly kept their money in banks have shifted their money to these high-yielding but uninsured funds. Paying well above the inflation rate, many money-market funds can be used almost like checking accounts. Usually you need to invest an initial $2,500 in these funds. An important feature is that you have easy access to your money. Most funds allow you to write checks for amounts of $500 or more. The funds themselves charge a small, almost unnoticed, management fee. They invest your money in high-yield, short-term investments such as loans to the federal government or to top-quality business corporations.

4. *U.S. Treasury securities.* The U.S. government offers five types of secure investments to the public: treasury bills, treasury notes, treasury bonds, U.S. Savings Bonds, and Treasury inflation-protection bonds (TIPs). Treasury bills are offered in denominations of $10,000 or more and mature in 12 months or less. Treasury notes are sold in denominations of $1,000 or more and mature in two to ten years. Treasury bonds have maturity dates of ten or more years and pay high interest rates. United States savings bonds are the best-known government security and are often purchased out of patriotism. Such bonds are guaranteed to double their purchase price after 17 years.

TIPs pay a fixed interest rate twice a year, as determined by a Treasury auction. An additional adjustment is made to reflect the rate of inflation during the semiannual period. Even if the inflation rate goes down, TIPs will still pay at maturity the original issuance price of the bond. Treasury inflation-protection bonds are issued in minimum denominations of $1,000, and usually have ten-year maturities.

5. *Corporate bonds.* Large corporations sell bonds to the public to raise money to further invest in their business. Many of these bonds are 20- to 30-year loans. They pay a fixed rate of return, such as 8 or 10 percent. If you want to cash in your bond early, you may not be able to sell it for the original value, especially if interest rates rise. You would thus take a loss. You can, however, purchase a bond for less than its face value. You might be able to buy a $1,000 bond for $920, collect interest on it, and eventually redeem it for its face value. Trading bonds—buying and selling them for speculation—is a risky activity that should be reserved for knowledgeable investors.

Junk bonds are bonds offering a high yield because they are rated as having a high risk. One reason could be that the firm offering them is facing financial trouble. Junk bonds are best suited to big investors, but some mutual funds invest in them, making them accessible to smaller investors.

6. *Municipal bonds.* Similar in design to corporate bonds, municipal bonds are issued by governments of cities, states, and U.S. territories. "Munis" have strong appeal to many investors because of their tax-free status. Interest income from most municipal bonds is not taxed at the federal, and in many cases, state and local levels. Residents of the state in which a municipal bond is issued are also exempt from paying state income tax on the interest. Because of their tax-exempt status, munis pay lower interest rates than comparable taxable bonds. The higher your tax bracket, the more appealing a municipal bond. The formula to determine the tax-equivalent yields (what interest a taxable bond would have to pay to bring the same return) is:

$$\frac{\text{tax-free yield}}{(1 - \text{tax rate})} = \text{tax-equivalent yield}$$

If the tax-free yield of a muni is 5%, a taxable bond would have to pay 7.81%, assuming you are fortunate enough to be in the 36% federal income tax bracket. Here is the basic math: 5%/(1 – .36) = 5%/.64 = 7.81%. If you also figure in state or provincial tax exemption, the tax-equivalent yield would be even higher.

7. *Common stocks.* Every reader of this book has heard of the stock market, a place where you can purchase shares of public corporations. On a given business day it is not unusual for over 400 million shares of stocks to be bought and sold on the American and Canadian stock exchanges. Common stocks are actually shares of ownership in the corporations issuing them. Stocks pay dividends, but the hope of most investors is that the stock will rise in value. The majority of buying and selling of stocks today is done by institutions rather than by small investors. These institutions include pension funds, banks, and mutual funds (described later).

Stock prices rise and fall over such tangible factors as the price of oil and fluctuations in interest rates. During the last several years, stock prices often dropped when business news was good. Investors feared that good times would lead to inflation, thus driving up interest rates. In turn, bonds would be a more attractive investment than stocks. Yet good news in general, such as progress in peace talks, elevates stock prices. To cope with these price fluctuations, investors are advised to use dollar-cost averaging. Using **dollar-cost averaging,** you invest the same amount of money in a stock or mutual fund at regular intervals over a long period of time. This eliminates the need for the difficult task of trying to time the highs and lows. Since you are investing a constant amount, you buy less when the price is high and more when the price is low. Over a long period of time,

TABLE 15-2

HOW DOLLAR-COST AVERAGING WORKS

Month	Investment	Share Price	Shares Purchased
1	$200	$20	10
2	200	18	11.1
3	200	16	12.5
4	200	18	11.1
5	200	20	10
	$1000		54.7

NOTE: Your average cost per share is $18.28 (the total invested divided by the number of shares purchased). This figure is lower than if you had invested $1,000 in the first month at $20.

you pay a satisfactory price for your stock or mutual fund. Table 15-2 illustrates dollar-cost averaging.

8. *Mutual funds.* Since most people lack the time, energy, and knowledge to manage their own stock portfolios, mutual funds are increasingly relied on. The concept of mutual funds is straightforward. For a modest management fee, a small group of professional money managers invest your money, along with that of thousands of other people, into a broad group of common stocks. Numerous mutual funds exist to suit many different purposes and risk-taking attitudes. You can find mutual funds that invest in conservative, low-risk stocks or flashy, high-risk stocks. The latter tend to have a larger payoff if the company succeeds. Some funds specialize in particular industries such as telecommunications or energy. Mutual funding is no longer restricted to stocks. Some mutual funds invest only in corporate bonds, government securities, or municipal bonds.

Another type of mutual fund invests in neither stocks nor bonds, but in other mutual funds. Called *fund of funds,* they offer an unusually diversified mix of investments. A fund of funds might invest in 50 mutual funds, and each mutual fund in the portfolio invests in about 75 stocks and bonds. The owner of the fund of funds therefore has investments in 3,750 stocks and bonds. Owning a fund of funds simplifies your life as an investor, but it can lead to paying expenses for the fund of funds and all the other mutual funds involved.[5]

9. *Gold.* Gold has long been considered a sound long-term investment despite declining prices in recent years. In January 1980, gold sold for $875 an ounce, and in early 1998 it sold for $292. For many years hoarding gold coins or bars was considered an intelligent hedge against inflation and global unrest. Gold still has its fans who think it is a solid investment in an unstable world. Even when the price of gold is rising, it still has two key disadvantages. Gold has to be stored safely and it pays no dividends or interest.

10. *Real estate.* A natural starting point in making money in real estate is to purchase a single-family dwelling, maintain it carefully, and live in it for many years. Temporary downturns in the housing market should not deter the patient investor. In the long run, most homes increase in value faster than inflation. Homeowners receive many tax benefits, such as income tax deductions on mortgage interest, and interest paid for home equity loans (loans using your house as collateral). Real estate taxes are fully tax-deductible. Furthermore, a homeowner who is at least 55 and who has lived in his or her house for three of the last five years pays no income tax on the first $125,000 of profit.

An investment that is really a form of business ownership is income property—real estate that you rent to tenants. The activities required of a landlord include collecting rent, resolving conflicts among tenants, and maintenance—fixing broken water pipes, painting rooms, etc. The highest returns from income property are derived from rehabilitating dilapidated property—if the owner does most of the physical work. Many people who own income property receive almost no operating profit from their work and investment in the early years. However, in the long run the property increases in value. Also, because the mortgage payments remain stable and rents keep increasing, monthly profits gradually appear.

An indirect way to invest in real estate is through a real estate investment trust, or **REIT**, a pooling of many people's money to invest in real estate or mortgages. These investment devices were created by Congress in 1960 to allow individuals to invest in real estate. REITs must distribute at least 95 percent of taxable income to shareholders but avoid corporate taxes.[6] REITs invest in properties such as apartment buildings, office buildings, shopping malls, and even real estate companies. The value of REITs as investments rises and falls with the overall real estate market.

11. *Coins, antiques, paintings, and other collectibles.* An enjoyable way of investing is to purchase coins and objects of art that you think will escalate in value. Almost anything could become a collectible, including stamps, old advertising items, or even today's touch-tone telephone. You have to be both patient and lucky to cash in on collectibles. You should have a sound, diversified investment program before you invest your money in collectibles. If you are looking for an expensive hobby that might pay off financially, however, collectibles are ideal. Here are a few examples of collectibles that would have proved to be a good investment for their owners:[7]

- *The Amazing Spiderman,* Marvel Comic Group, mint condition worth $15,000 in 1995; worth S.12 in 1963.
- Mickey Mantle Rookie Card, Topps, in excellent condition, worth $18,000 in 1995; worth $.01 in 1952. (That's right, one cent!)
- Ford Model T, Touring, 4 cylinder, excellent condition, worth $15,000 in 1995; worth $8,000 in 1970.

- Ford Edsel, 1957, convertible in excellent condition, worth $50,000 in 1997; cost about $1,600 in 1957.

12. *Life insurance as an investment.*   An investment plan should include life insurance for two reasons. First, the proceeds from life insurance protect dependents against the complete loss of income from the deceased provider. Second, most forms of life insurance accumulate cash, thus making the insurance a profitable investment. The one exception is term life insurance, which is much like insurance on a house or car.

To figure out how much life insurance is necessary, calculate what would be required to support your family members until they can take care of themselves without your income. Take into account all assets in addition to life insurance. If you are single, consider the financial help you are providing loved ones.

CHOOSING THE RIGHT MIX OF INVESTMENTS

A major investment decision is how to allocate your investments among short-term interest-bearing accounts (including cash), stocks, and bonds. The best answer depends on such factors as your career stage, age, and tolerance for risk. In general, younger people are in a better position to take investment risks than those nearing retirement.

In selecting the right mix of investments, choose among three diversification strategies. A *capital preservation* strategy is for people who value holding on to their invested capital. A *moderate* strategy is a compromise between risk and growth potential. The *wealth-building* strategy is a long-range perspective combined with a toleration for risk. These three investment strategies are the basis for the broad guidelines presented in Exhibit 15-5.

RELATIVE RETURNS OF STOCKS AND BONDS

Another key factor in choosing among investments is their relative returns in the past. The past may not guarantee future performance, but it serves as a reliable predictor. Since 1926, U.S. common stocks have returned about 11 percent annually, and corporate bonds about 5 percent. Intermediate government bonds have paid about 5 percent, and three-month treasury bills about 4 percent. Yet some stocks are poor investments despite generally good returns.

Throughout the 1980s and early 1990s, investment yields improved over the long-term historical pattern. In the 1980s the annual return averaged about 18 percent for stocks, 12 percent for corporate bonds, and 9 percent for treasury bills. In the 1990s stocks and bonds yielded similar returns, while treasury bills averaged 4.5 percent as interest rates fell. Highlights of this information are summarized in Table 15-3. In evaluating the rates of returns

EXHIBIT 15-5

SELECTING THE RIGHT MIX OF INVESTMENTS

Capital Preservation Portfolio

For those with a shorter-term horizon, a substantial amount of personal debt, or low-risk tolerance, this portfolio seeks current income and capital preservation with modest growth potential to offset inflation.

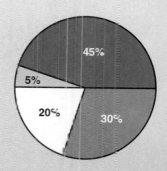

Moderate Portfolio

For those who do not have a high tolerance for risk, but still want reasonable growth potential for their investments, this portfolio seeks both income and capital appreciation.

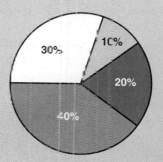

Wealth-Building (Aggressive) Portfolio

For long-range investors who are willing to assume more risk, a growth-oriented portfolio heavily weighted toward stocks is recommended.

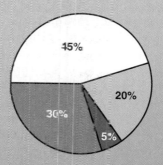

Short-term debt and cash   Domestic stocks   International stocks   Bonds

SOURCE: "Beware of Falling Money Market Rates," *Merrill Lynch & Co., Global Research and Economics Group,* February 1996, p. 5; "What Is Asset Allocation and What Does It Mean to You?" *USAA Magazine,* April 1995, pp. 20–22.

TABLE 15-3	
INVESTMENT PERFORMANCE COMPARISON, 1980s–1998	
Common stocks	19%
Corporate bonds	11%
Long-term government bonds	8%
Treasury bills	7%
Inflation	4%

on stocks and bonds, recognize that the inflation rate for the last ten years has been 3.9 percent.

The rates of return just reported prompt financial specialists to urge every investor to include a minimum of 50 percent common stocks in his or her investment portfolio. Yet some investors resist such advice because they are upset by the fluctuations of the stock market. Instead, they invest in various types of bonds and save cash.

The attractive return on investment from stocks over the years is forthcoming only to those who invest in a portfolio of stocks or mutual funds that match or exceed average returns. A person could easily invest in stocks that become worthless or have substantially below-average returns. Mutual funds, which invest in a portfolio of stocks, are less likely to be poor investments. An even safer bet is index funds. These funds invest in the stocks composing popular indices such as the Dow Jones Industrials or Standard and Poors 500 stocks. The returns from bonds and other debt instruments are much more reliable than those from stocks.

Another caution is that investing in stocks, and in bonds with taxable returns, can be expensive to continue. For example, you must pay income taxes on their returns annually, even if you did not cash in the stocks or bonds. Some people wind up selling off portions of their portfolio, or borrowing money, just to pay taxes on a profit that only exists on paper.

 MANAGING AND PREVENTING DEBT

Debt is inevitable for most people. Few people are wealthy enough, or have sufficient self-discipline, to avoid debt entirely. Major purchases such as a house, cooperative apartment, postsecondary education, or automobile usually require borrowing. Dealing with debt is therefore an important component of managing your personal finances. Here we describe three major aspects of managing and preventing debt: credit management, getting out of debt, and staying out of debt.

MANAGING CREDIT WISELY

Credit management is a problem for many people of all career stages. The number of people filing for bankruptcy in the United States has been climbing steadily, with over 1 million people filing for bankruptcy annually. Borrowing money, of course, is not inherently evil. Imagine what would happen to the banking industry and the economy if nobody borrowed money. Some borrowing in your early career is desirable because without a credit record it is difficult to obtain automobile loans and home mortgages. Good credit is also important because prospective landlords and employers carefully consider an applicant's creditworthiness. Consider the following guidelines for the wise use of credit.[8]

1. Recognize the difference between good debt and bad debt. Good debt finances something that will benefit you in the future, such as a house, education, or self-development. Bad debt typically finances something that you consume almost immediately or that provides little real benefit. Borrowing for a trip to a gambling casino, including money for betting, might fall into this category.

2. Prepare a monthly spending plan as outlined previously to determine how much debt (if any) you can afford to assume. As a general rule, limit your total borrowing to 15 to 20 percent of monthly take-home pay, not including a house mortgage payment.

3. Instead of filling your wallet or handbag with many credit cards, stick to one major credit card and perhaps your favorite department store's charge card. At the same time, avoid lending your credit card to friends. Cards on loan to friends can be lost, stolen, or misused. When you own multiple credit cards, there is more temptation to lend one.

4. Before accepting any new extension of credit, review your budget to see if you can handle it easily. You will have less need for a credit extension if you wait two weeks before making purchases that seem desirable at the time. After the two-week cooling-off period, many of the purchases will seem unimportant.

5. A homeowner with substantial equity accumulated should consider a home equity loan for financing a major purchase, such as an automobile or educational expenses. The interest on home equity loans is fully tax-deductible.

6. Make monthly payments on your debts large enough to reduce the principal on your credit cards and other loans. Otherwise, you may be paying almost all interest and making small progress toward paying off the loan.

7. Even as you are paying off debts, set aside some savings each month. Attempt to increase your savings as little as $15 per month. Within two years you will be saving a substantial amount of money.

8. If you are unable to pay your bills, talk to your creditors immediately. Explain your situation and let them know you plan to somehow meet your debt obligations. Agree to a payment schedule you can meet. Never ignore bills.

9. Choose personal bankruptcy only as a last desperate option. A bankruptcy filing will remain on your credit record for seven to ten years. Creditors may look upon you as a bad risk even 11 years after filing bankruptcy. Future employers may be leery of hiring a person who was such a poor money manager. Of even greater significance, bankruptcy may result in a substantial blow to your self-esteem.

Working Your Way Out of Debt

Working your way out of debt is a major component of debt management. Heavy debt that forces you to postpone savings and investments can also create adverse amounts of stress. You must therefore assertively attack your debts to improve your general well-being. How do you know if you are too far in debt? Human Relations Self-Assessment Exercise 15-1 provides an answer.[9]

A recommended strategy of reducing debt is to **concentrate on one bill at a time.** According to this technique, you first pay off your smallest debt with a variable payment and then concentrate on your next-smallest variable-payment debt. You keep concentrating on one bill at a time until the last debt is eliminated. The technique is illustrated and described in Exhibit 15-6.

A financial specialist might rightfully contend that some loans are uneconomic to discharge more quickly than required. The interest rate you pay on such loans might be less than the return you would earn by investing your extra payments elsewhere, such as in growth stocks. Although this is true from a financial standpoint, the biggest return on your investment from a mental health standpoint is getting out of debt.

A more conventional approach to reducing debt is to apply any money available for debt repayment to the loan bearing the highest interest. Ordinarily this would be credit-card debt or unsecured loans. (The latter are lent by finance companies and often carry charges up to 24 percent.) By paying off loans carrying the highest interest, you pay less in debt. Another debt-reduction tactic is to pay more than the minimum on all loans that allow for variable payment. If you pay only the minimum demanded by most credit-card issuers, it might take 12 years to pay off the balance. In the interim, you would pay far more in interest than the purchase price of the goods and services being bought on time. A specific example:

> Paying the minimum on a credit-card balance of $1,100 with a 18.5% interest will take 12½ years to pay off and cost $2,480.94 in interest. If you pay more than the $10 minimum each month, you can reduce the pay-back period to 6 years and the interest paid to $637.37.[10]

HUMAN RELATIONS SELF-ASSESSMENT EXERCISE 15-1

Are You Too Far in Debt?

1. Is an increasing percentage of your income being spent to pay debts?

2. Do you use credit to buy many of the things you bought in the past for cash?

3. Are you paying bills with money targeted for something else?

4. Have you taken out loans to consolidate your debts, or asked for extensions on existing loans to reduce monthly payments?

5. Does your checkbook balance get lower by the month?

6. Do you pay the minimum amount due on your charge accounts each month?

7. Do you get repeated dunning notices (letters demanding payments) from your creditors?

8. Are you threatened with repossession of your car or cancellation of your credit cards or with other legal action?

9. Have you been drawing on your savings to pay regular bills that you used to pay out of your paycheck?

10. Do you depend on extra income, such as overtime and part-time work, to get to the end of the month?

11. Do you take out new installment loans before old ones are paid off?

12. Is your total savings less than three months' take-home pay?

13. Is your total installment credit (not counting mortgage) more than 20 percent of your take-home pay?

14. Do you become horrorstruck when you look at your credit card bills?

If your answer is yes to two or more of the above questions, financial counselors would advise you to declare war on some of your debts.

Interest payments can also be reduced by switching to a credit-card with lower interest. You pay off the old credit-card debt by borrowing money from the new credit card. Begin payments the first month to avoid incurring extra interest charges.

If you are having problems getting out of debt despite using the tactics just described, the problem could be that you are spending too much. To remedy the situation you can either earn more income or reduce discretionary spending. Look for even minor savings. Many people, for example, are surprised to learn how much they are spending on soft drinks. Purchasing store-brand soft drinks in bulk, or drinking water instead of soft-drinks, can result in more money for debt reduction.

EXHIBIT 15-6

HEATH AND JUDY CONCENTRATE ON ONE BILL AT A TIME

After 17 years of marriage, Heath and Judy had acquired an upsetting level of debt. Part of their problem was the debt they had accumulated in the process of acquiring two, two-family houses that they used as income property. At the urging of a financial counselor, Heath and Judy scrutinized both their debts and their spending habits. Their debt picture looked like this:

Type of Loan	Approximate Balance on Loan	Monthly Payment
Auto	$2,850	$215
Home improvement	1,975	149
Visa	1,828	85
MasterCard	1,859	95
Furnaces for income properties	2,562	185
Tuition	800	90
Orthodontist	750	75
	$12,624	$894

An indebtedness of $12,624 may not seem extreme. Nevertheless, in terms of their living expenses, including the support of three children, $894 a month of debts was creating stress for Heath and Judy. The couple might have tried the traditional debt-reduction program of spreading out their monthly debt-reduction fund over all their bills. In so doing, they would have tried to make approximately equal payments to all creditors. Instead, Heath and Judy chose to reduce their debts by concentrating first on the variable-payment debt with the smallest balance. In other words, they concentrated first on the debt that they were capable of eliminating first.

Following this strategy, Heath and Judy began their debt-reduction program by first working down the Visa debt. Each month they would put as much money as they could spare into their Visa payment, even though they had previously paid only $85 monthly for that particular bill. The couple kept making minimum payments to MasterCard until their Visa balance was reduced to zero. Then came big progress when they were able to make two double payments. (The general principle is to eliminate, one by one, each of the loans for which variable—rather than fixed—payments are possible. In addition, take on new debts for emergency purposes only.)

The above case history indicates that an effective program of debt reduction involves both financial and emotional issues. Getting rid of debts one by one provides an important emotional boost to the debtor. As the debts are peeled off, tension is reduced. The one-debt-at-a-time strategy is also tied in with goal theory. You experience a feeling of accomplishment as each debt is eliminated. Simultaneously, you are motivated to tackle the next variable debt.

STAYING OUT OF DEBT

Some people believe we are on the way to a cashless society. They contend that electronic transfer of funds, credit cards, and **debit cards** (ones that instantly transfer money from your bank account to the account of a merchant) will eliminate the need for cash. High technology may soon make the cashless society a reality. In the meantime, do not dismiss the value of cash in helping you recover from sloppy financial habits.

No one who bought things for cash only ever went bankrupt. Cash also refers to money orders and checks drawn against funds that you legitimately have on hand. If you buy only things that you can actually pay for at the moment of purchase, you may suffer some hardships. It is no fun riding the bus or walking until you save enough money to have another transmission put in your car. It would be agonizing if you needed dental treatment but had to wait until payday to have a broken tooth repaired. On balance, these are small miseries to endure in comparison with the misery of being overburdened with debt. For many people, preoccupation with debt interferes with work concentration and sleep.

Staying out of debt is often difficult because the debtor has deep-rooted problems that prompt him or her to use credit. Among these problems are:

- Perceiving material objects as a way of gaining status

- Purchasing goods and services to relieve depression

- Incurring heavy charges to get even with a spouse or family member

- Believing that the world owes him or her a higher standard of living

Having problems of this nature may require both debt counseling and personal counseling. Unless the person understands his or her emotional problems surrounding borrowing money, the cycle of going into debt then struggling to get out of debt will continue.

PREPARING AN ANNUAL NET WORTH REPORT

A potentially uplifting strategy of managing your finances is to chart your yearly financial status. You can accomplish this by annually evaluating your **net worth**, the difference between your assets and liabilities. It is best to include mostly **liquid assets**—those that can be converted into cash relatively quickly. An exception is to include the equity in your house. (Equity is the net price you could receive for a house minus the mortgage balance, real estate commissions, and closing costs.)

Personal annual reports for two years are presented in Exhibit 15-7. The person who prepared both reports was in financial difficulty when the first report was prepared. Notice the progress this individual has made over the four-year period. In the first year, his liquid assets aside from his home equity and car resale value totaled $1,184. Including house and car, his assets were $32,784. Thanks in part to both self-discipline and modest inflation, his assets jumped to $44,195 four years later. Without the house equity and car resale value, his liquid assets were $4,395.

The liability picture is even more impressive. In the first year, the man had outstanding debts of $15,910. Four years later, his debts had shrunk to $4,058. His liability position had improved an enviable $11,852. Over the same period his asset picture had improved $11,411. Adding both improvements together, we are able to give the individual a financial improvement score of $23,263 for the four-year period. Recognize, however, that the $10,000 growth in house equity was a major contributing factor to his financial improvement.

Personal computer software is available to help you prepare a yearly financial statement, along with monthly budgeting, check writing, check reconciliation and so forth. One such program is Quicken. It can memorize recurring transactions such as monthly mortgage payments and phone bills. Instead of recreating the same check each month, you simply recall

EXHIBIT 15-7

A PERSONAL ANNUAL REPORT

Assets	December 31, Year 1	December 31, Year 4
House equity (based on market value)	$28,000	$38,000
Cash in checking account	141	392
Cash on hand	75	315
Savings account	118	792
Mutual fund	—	896
Car resale value	3,600	1,800
Jewelry resale value	850	2,000
	$32,784	$44,195

Liabilities		
Auto payments	$3,500	—
Visa	1,215	$350
MasterCard	2,150	1400
American Express	850	80
Sears charge	1550	1128
Home improvement loan	3,975	—
Loan from uncle	895	—
Property tax due	850	350
School tax due	650	350
Plumber	275	400
	$15,910	$4,058

the memorized transaction, enter in the new amount if it has changed, and print the check.

HOW TO RETIRE RICH

If you start investing early in your career, you can retire rich even without earning an astronomical salary or winning a lottery. The basic idea is to start a systematic savings and investment plan set aside for retirement only. The dividends and interest paid on these investments are not taxed until retirement, and they keep compounding. As a result, you wind up with an extraordinary amount of money at the end of your career. Details about several of these retirement investment plans are presented next.

Whichever retirement plan you enter, remember to follow the key investment principle of asset allocation. Your retirement funds should be divided among stocks, bonds, short-term notes and cash, and perhaps real estate. In addition to these personal investments, many workers receive retirement income from social security, company pension plans or 401(k) plans, and individual retirement accounts. Financial planners often recommend that people will need about 75 percent of their pre-retirement incomes to live comfortably during retirement. The following paragraphs describe several of the most popular retirement programs.

SOCIAL SECURITY BENEFITS

Both Canada and the United States offer social security income to its citizens who qualify in terms of employment experience. The U.S. government makes available a Personal Earnings and Benefit Statement that estimates how much retirement income a person can anticipate at ages 62, 65, or older. In addition, the statement estimates survivor and disability benefits. Social security pays approximately the minimum wage to individuals who were middle-class wage earners. For example, a person who earned $50,000 in salary in the year before retirement, would receive $13,944 annually (1997 estimate). The payment would be adjusted for inflation periodically. These payments are reduced if the individual earns active (not investment) income of more that $32,000 per year. No person who wanted to retire rich would rely on social security payments exclusively.

EMPLOYEE PENSIONS AND 401(K) PLANS

Many employers in both the private and public sector offer pensions to long-term employees. Some of these pensions pay around 60 percent of the employee's salary at the time of retirement, in addition to medical insurance. However, not everybody stays with one employer for many years, and some companies go bankrupt or misuse pension funds, thus putting your retirement pay at risk. A modern development in company-related retirement programs is 401(k) plans in which the employer and employee both contribute. However, the employee essentially owns the money in the plan and can move it from one employer to another.

Your 401(k) plan can be invested in stocks, bonds, and many other types of investments. Each plan sets a limit on the percentage of your current salary that you can contribute to the plan. The IRS also sets limits, which were $9,500 in 1997. Some employers contribute 50 cents or more for every dollar you contribute. Providing you stay with the employer for a specified period of time, such as three to five years, you can keep the matching contribution. A 401(k) plan held for many years goes a long way toward paying for most people's retirement.

INDIVIDUAL RETIREMENT ACCOUNTS (IRAs) AND SIMPLIFIED EMPLOYEE PLANS (SEPs)

Retirement accounts held by individuals, rather than offered by employers, can be used to invest in most of the types of savings and investments described earlier. Both IRAs and SEPs are popular because they offer generous tax savings. IRAs became even more valuable in 1998. Based on the Tax Payer Relief Act of 1997, there are now many more options for purchasing IRAs.

An **IRA** is a supplemental retirement account, fully funded by the individual, that qualifies for certain tax advantages. Anyone, including government employees with earned income, may open an IRA. Single workers may contribute up to $2,000 per year. One-paycheck couples may invest up to $2,250 annually. Two-paycheck couples may contribute up to $4,000 a year if both work and each earns at least $2,000. Distributions from your IRA may begin as early as age 59½, but must begin by 70½. Early withdrawal incurs a 10 percent penalty plus payment of taxes on the amount withdrawn.

IRA contributions are tax deductible only at moderate income levels. Dividends and interest from an IRA are not taxed as long as they are not withdrawn. When you begin withdrawals, IRA distributions are taxed as ordinary income.

SEPs are retirement plans for individuals who are self-employed or for those who earn part of their income from self-employment. (Keogh plans are virtually the same as SEPs except for a complicated tax-reporting system.) SEPs and IRAs follow many of the same rules, with several exceptions. First, to qualify you must earn some self-employment income. Second, you can invest up to 15 percent of your self-employment income in a SEP, up to a maximum of $30,000. An individual can hold an IRA and a SEP.

The dramatic financial returns from an IRA or SEP are shown in Table 15-4, which assumes that a person invested $2,000 each year. Much of the

TABLE 15-4

HOW IRAS CAN GROW

Years of Contribution	Rate of Return		
	8%	10%	12%
5	$ 11,733	$ 12,210	$ 12,705
10	$ 12,973	$ 31,875	S 35,097
15	$ 54,304	$ 63,544	$ 74,559
20	$ 91,524	S114,550	$144,104
25	$146,212	$196,694	$266,667
30	$226,566	$328,998	$482,554
35	$344,634	$542,048	S863,326

NOTE: This chart assumes a $2,000 yearly contribution at year end, compound interest, and no tax payments.

growth in funds is attributable to compound interest, and no withdrawals on which to pay taxes.

SUMMARY

An important part of managing your personal life is to manage your personal finances in such a way that money is not a major source of worry and concern in your life. Financial problems often lead to marital problems, for example.

Setting financial goals is an important starting point in managing your personal finances. Such goals can be expressed in dollars, the type of things you would like to accomplish with money, or the type of lifestyle you would like to lead.

A vital aspect of financial management is to establish a spending plan or budget, which can be divided into six steps: (1) establishing goals, (2) estimating income, (3) estimating expenses, (4) comparing expenses and income, (5) carrying out the spending plan, and (6) evaluating the plan.

An effective spending plan allows room for investing. Basic investment principles include:

1. Spend less money than you earn.

2. Invest early and steadily to capitalize on the benefits of compounding.

3. Keep reinvesting dividends.

4. Diversify your investments (use asset allocation).

5. Maintain a disciplined, long-term approach.

6. Practice contrary investing.

7. Be willing to accept some risk.

8. Invest globally as well as domestically.

9. Pay off debt.

The two basic types of investments are lending money (debt) or owning assets (equity). All investments carry some risk, which can be divided into four types: investment risk, market risk, inflation risk, and adequacy risk (will the investment cover anticipated future expenses). Investments with the highest investment risk also carry the highest potential rewards. Over time, stocks have yielded much higher returns than bonds.

Among the many ways of investing or saving money are the following: passbook savings accounts; certificates of deposit; money-market funds; U.S. Treasury securities; corporate bonds; municipal bonds; common stocks; mutual funds; gold; real estate; coins, antiques, paintings, and other collectibles; and whole-life insurance.

A major investment decision is how to allocate your investments among short-term interest-bearing accounts, stocks, and bonds. To select the right mix, choose among three diversification (or allocation) strategies: capital preservation, moderate (or compromise), and wealth building. Common stocks pay higher rates of return than corporate or government bonds. However, the return on a given stock or mutual fund is less predictable than bonds held to maturity. Yearly taxes must be paid on profits from stocks and corporate bonds.

Dealing with debt is an important component of managing personal finances. To use credit wisely, recognize the difference between good debt and bad debt. Limit your total borrowing to 15 to 20 percent of monthly take-home pay, not including a house mortgage payment. Using credit cards wisely includes such factors as restricting their use, selectively using a home equity loan, and making more than the minimum monthly payments on loans.

One way of working your way out of debt is to concentrate on one bill at a time—try to pay off first your variable payment with the smallest balance. To stay out of debt, pay for goods and services with cash or check and therefore stop borrowing money.

We recommend giving yourself a yearly financial checkup by preparing a list of your liquid assets and liabilities. Progress is measured in terms of the difference between assets and liabilities. The bigger the positive difference, the better your financial health.

People who start a retirement savings or investment program early in their careers may accumulate large sums of money by retirement. Asset allocation is a major strategy for accumulating retirement funds. Social security benefits contributed modestly to retirement. Employee pensions and 401(k) plans (a portable self-directed pension) are major contributors to funding retirement. In addition, consider an individual retirement account (IRA) or simplified employee plan (SEP).

Question and Activities

1. What types of human relations problems might people avoid by carefully managing their finances?

2. How can clipping coupons for redemption at supermarkets fit into personal financial planning?

3. Assume that after preparing a budget, you conclude that your expenses must be reduced by 10 percent. What cuts would you make?

4. It has often been observed that the majority of people who file for bankruptcy have well above-average incomes. How can this be?

5. Why does preparing a budget sometimes help people reduce their worry about money?

6. How can a person resolve the conflict between investing money for the long range and buying things he or she wants right now?

7. Why is saving money in a safe deposit box, or in a home safe, considered to be very poor money management?

8. What relevance would this chapter have for a full-time student?

9. If you think you will live at least 100 years, how will this affect your investment strategy?

10. Talk to a retired person and inquire what, if anything, he or she would do differently to plan financially for retirement. Be prepared to discuss your findings in class.

REFERENCES

[1]"IRS Auditor Gives School $22 Million Surprise Gift," Associated Press Story, December 4, 1995.

[2]Quoted in "The $3 Billion Man Shares His Secret," *Invest,* September 1993, p. 10.

[3]"The Four Most Common Mistakes Investors Make and How to Avoid Them," *USAA Financial Spectrum,* January 1990, pp. 1–2.

[4]"Making Smart Allocation Choices," *The Participant* (quarterly news for TIAA-Creff participants), November 1993, p. 3.

[5]Jeffrey M. Laderman, "A Bunch of Funds Rolled into One," *Business Week,* September 29, 1997, p. 97.

[6]"The New Word of Real Estate," *Business Week,* September 22, 1997, p. 80.

[7]Doug Bartholomew, "Buy Collectibles for Love, Not Wealth," *Stages,* Winter 1997, p. 21; David Lawder, "New Edsel Flair 40 Years after Flop," *Chicago Tribune,* Section 12, p. 24, September 28, 1997.

A HUMAN RELATIONS CASE PROBLEM

The Problem Budget

The spending plan presented below was submitted by Greg Walters, a 28-year-old man with a good job. He says that owning a home and entertaining his friends are important parts of his lifestyle. Yet he also contends, "I'm committing slow-motion financial suicide. Each month I go further into debt. Right now I don't see a good way out unless I give up a lot of things that are important to me. You've got to have fun in life, don't you?"

Review Greg's budget and make some specific recommendations to him for improving his financial health. Also, what flaws do you find in his logic?

SPENDING PLAN FOR GREG WALTERS

Monthly Expenses

Fixed:

Mortgage or rent	$775
Property insurance	45
Health insurance	35
Auto insurance	45
Other insurance	35
Educational expenses	100
Child support payments	
Taxes:	
Federal	750
State or provincial	210
Social security	210
Local	
Property	175
Installment loans (auto and others)	300
Set aside for emergencies	0

Variable:

Food & beverage	250
Household supplies	40
Home maintenance and repairs	65
Medical and dental	40
Telephone	55
Clothing	110
Hair care and cosmetics	45
Transportation	75
Car maintenance	100
Travel and vacation	225
Clubs/organizations	145
Hobbies	35
Cable TV	35
Online service	25
Total expenses	$3925

Monthly Income

Salary	$3800
Tips	
Bonuses & commissions	
Interest & dividends	
Insurance benefits	
Child support received	
Other	
Total income	$3800

Summary:

Total income	$3800
Less total expenses	3925
Balance for savings and investment	(125)

FINANCIAL SKILL-BUILDING EXERCISE 15-1

The True Return on a Municipal Bond

A person is in the 28 percent federal income tax bracket and decides to purchase municipal bonds that yield 6 percent. What would the taxable yield have to be on a corporate bond to be equivalent to the 6 percent tax-free yield?

[8]"Taking Control of Debt," *Aide Magazine,* December 1993, pp. 17–28; "Credit Card Pitfalls: How to Help Your College Student Avoid the Credit Trap," *USAA Magazine,* Aug/Sept 1996, pp. 27–29.

[9]"Debt-Danger Signal Quiz," *Aide Magazine,* December 1992, p. 26; Jane Bryant Quinn, "More People Facing Personal Credit Crisis," syndicated column, September 10, 1991.

[10]Patricia Amend, "Paying Down Debt,' *Fidelity Focus,* Fall 1996, p. 14.

ADDITIONAL READING

"The Best Mutual Funds." *Business Week,* February 3, 1997, pp. 62–109. (See also the comparable article for the current year.)

Eisenberg, Richard. *Money Book of Personal Finance.* New York: Warner Books, 1996.

Heady, Christy. *The Complete Idiot's Guide to Making Money on Wall Street* Indianapolis, IN: Alpha Books, 1994.

Kobliner, Beth. *Get a Financial Life: Personal Finance in Your Twenties and Thirties.* New York: Simon & Schuster, 1996.

Loeb, Marshall. *Marshall Loeb's Lifetime Financial Strategies.* New York: Little Brown, 1996.

"The World's Best Investments." *Business Week,* June 17, 1996, pp. 98–129.

"Securing Your Future: A Self-Help Guide." *Business Week,* July 21, 1997, pp. 62–66. (See also *Business Week's Annual Retirement Guide* for the current year.)

Tobias, Andrew. *My Vast Fortune: The Money Adventures of a Quixotic Capitalist.* New York: Random House, 1997.

www.americanexpress.com/advisors.

CHAPTER 16

FINDING HAPPINESS AND ENHANCING YOUR PERSONAL LIFE

Learning Objectives

After studying the information and doing the exercises in this chapter, you should be able to:

▼ Explain how happiness is contingent on keeping the various spheres of life in balance

▼ Specify factors that contribute to personal happiness

▼ Describe a plan for meeting a romantic partner

▼ Explain how partners can meet the challenge of being a dual-income couple

▼ Choose among techniques for keeping a relationship of yours vibrant

At age 55, marketing manager Ken Biltmore lost his job as part of a corporate downsizing. A marketing assistant in his department said to Biltmore, "I'm so sorry to hear what happened to you. You're probably too far along in your career to find a comparable-paying position. And you're too young to retire. Your life must be in turmoil now."

"No, my life is not in turmoil now, only my career. I have a wonderful family, friends, and I do meaningful and exciting volunteer work. I also have good investments. I plan to enjoy life while I patiently look for a new position. But thanks for your concern."

As the marketing manager's situation illustrates, having a rewarding personal life can help a person absorb a career setback. A satisfying and rewarding personal life also contributes to a satisfying and rewarding career. If your personal life is miserable, you will have difficulty concentrating on your work. Of course, a vibrant personal life is also an important end in itself.

In this final chapter, we look at some of the major issues involved in leading an enriched personal life: the components of happiness, finding a partner, managing a dual-income partnership, and keeping a relationship vibrant. In addition, we offer a number of concrete suggestions that may help some people enhance their personal lives.

ACHIEVING HAPPINESS

When asked what is the most important thing in life, most people respond, "happiness." Research and opinion on the topic indicate that people can take concrete steps to achieve happiness. Planning for happiness is possible because it appears to be somewhat under people's control. Unhappiness, in contrast, seems to be more predetermined by genes. Sadness tends to run in families.[1] Our approach to the unlimited topic of understanding how to achieve happiness involves a model of happiness, a listing of keys to happiness, and the five principles of psychological functioning.

THE SPHERES OF LIFE AND HAPPINESS

A practical way of understanding happiness is that it is a byproduct of having the various components of life working in harmony and synchrony. To understand this approach, visualize about six gears with teeth, spinning in unison. As long as all gears are moving properly (and no teeth are broken), a state of equilibrium and fluid motion is achieved. Similarly, imagine that life has six major components. The exact components will differ among people. For most people, the components would be approximately as follows:

1. Work and career
2. Interpersonal life including loved ones and romantic life
3. Physical and mental health
4. Financial health
5. Interests and pastimes, including reading, surfing the Internet, and sports
6. A spiritual life or belief system including religion, science, or astrology

When a person has ample satisfactions in all six spheres, he or she achieves happiness. However, when a deficiency occurs in any of these six factors, the person's spheres are no longer in harmony, and dissatisfaction, or unhappiness, occurs. Yet sometimes if a person is having problems in one sphere (such as the marketing manager described above), satisfaction in the other spheres can compensate temporarily for a deficiency in one. For the long range, a state of happiness is dependent on all six spheres working in harmony. In short, the theme of this book surfaces again: Work and personal life are mutually supportive. Figure 16-1 presents the spheres-of-life model of happiness.

Figure 16-1   The Spheres of Life Model of Happiness

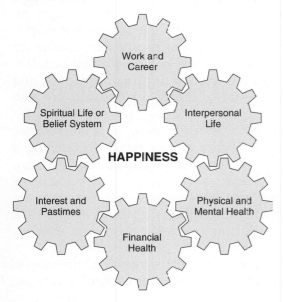

People vary as to how much importance they attach to each sphere of life. A person with intense career ambitions, for example, might place less weight on the interests sphere than would a more leisure-oriented person. However, if any of these spheres are grossly deficient, total happiness will not be forthcoming. Another source of variation is that the importance people attach to each sphere may vary according to the stage of life. A full-time student, for example, might need just enough money to avoid worrying about finances. However, after about ten years of full-time career experience, a person's expenses might peak. The person would then attach more importance to the financial sphere.

THE KEYS TO HAPPINESS

Many people, including psychologists and other human relations specialists, have conducted research and made observations about the ingredients of happiness. If you are aware of these contributors to happiness, you might be able to enhance your happiness. The spheres-of-life model of happiness also furnishes direction for the person seeking happiness: Strive for acceptable levels of achievement in all six spheres. Here we summarize and synthesize a wide range of research and opinion on the keys to happiness.[2]

1. *Give high priority to the pursuit of happiness.*   Having the intention, or goal, of being happy will enhance your chances of being happy. A key principle is to discover what makes you happy and make the time to pursue those activities. Spending time doing what you enjoy contributes directly to happiness.

2. *Experience love and friendship, and find a life partner.*   A happy person is one who is successful in personal relationships and who exchanges care and concern with loved ones. Happy people are able to love and be loved. Hugging people you like, or being hugged by them, is an important part of having enjoyable personal relationships. Married adults, in general, are happier than unmarried, and the results are similar for men and women.[3] Despite the consistency of this finding, it must be interpreted cautiously. It takes a satisfying marriage to bring happiness, and unmarried partners who have a long-term, caring relationship are also likely to be happy.

3. *Develop a sense of self-esteem.*   Self-love must precede love for others. High self-esteem enables one to love and be loved. Developing a good self-image leads to the self-esteem required for loving relationships. A feeling of self-worth is important because it helps prevent being overwhelmed by criticism. An important part of developing self-esteem is not wanting financial success more than other things. Insecure people seek society's approval in the form of purchasing consumer goods and accumulating investments.[4]

4. *Work hard at what you enjoy and achieve the flow experience.*   Love may be the most important contributor to happiness, with staying involved in work you enjoy coming in second. To achieve happiness, it is necessary to find a career that fits your most intense interests. In addition, it helps to achieve regularly the flow experience mentioned in Chapters 2 and 12. Happiness stemming from flow is powerful because it is not dependent on favorable external circumstances such as recognition or love. The happiness that follows from flow is created by the individual.

Hard work contributes to happiness in another important way. A fundamental secret of happiness is accomplishing things and savoring what you have accomplished. A contributor to unhappiness is comparing your successes, or lack of them, to those of other people. To be happy you must be happy with what *you* achieve.

5. *Appreciate the joys of day-to-day living.* Another key to happiness is the ability to live in the present without undue worrying about the future or dwelling on past mistakes. Be on guard against becoming so preoccupied with planning your life that you neglect to enjoy the happiness of the moment. The essence of being a happy person is to savor what you have right now.

6. *Be fair, kind, helpful, and trusting of others.* The Golden Rule is a true contributor to happiness. It is also important to practice charity and forgiveness. Helping others brings personal happiness. Knowing that you are able to make a contribution to the welfare of others gives you a continuing sense of satisfaction and happiness. Related to fairness and kindness is trusting others. Happy people have open, warm, and friendly attitudes.

7. *Have recreational fun in your life.* A happy life is characterized by fun, zest, joy, and delight. When you create time for fun (in addition to the fun in many kinds of work), you add an important element to your personal happiness. However, if you devote too much time to play, you will lose on the fun of work accomplishments. In choosing fun activities, avoid overplanning. Because novelty contributes to happiness, be ready to pursue an unexpected opportunity or to try something different.

8. *Learn to cope with grief, disappointment, setbacks, and stress.* To be happy you must learn how to face problems that occur in life without being overwhelmed or running away. It is also important to persevere in attempting to overcome problems, rather than to whine or engage in self-pity. Once you have had to cope with problems, you will be more able to appreciate the day-to-day joys of life.

9. *Live with what you cannot change.* Psychologist Martin Seligman says that attempting to change conditions unlikely to change sets us up for feeling depressed about failing. Weight loss is a prime example. Nineteen out of twenty people regain the weight they lost. It is therefore better to worry less about weight loss and concentrate on staying in good physical condition by engaging in moderate exercise. Good conditioning contributes much more to health than does achieving a weight standard set primarily to achieve an aesthetic standard.[5] You can then concentrate on being happy about your good physical condition instead of being unhappy about your weight.

10. *Energize yourself through physical fitness.* Engage in regular physical activity, such as dancing or sports, that makes you aerobically fit. Whether it is the endorphins released by exercise, or just the relaxed muscles, physical fitness fosters happiness.

11. *Develop a philosophy or system of belief.*   Another key contributor to happiness is to believe in something besides yourself. Happy people have some system of belief—whether it be religion, philosophy, or science—which comforts them and gives them a reason for being.

THE FIVE PRINCIPLES OF PSYCHOLOGICAL FUNCTIONING

According to Richard Carlson, the best way to achieve inner serenity (or happiness) is to follow the five principles of psychological functioning.[6] These principles act as guides toward achieving a feeling of inner happiness. The first is *thinking,* which creates the psychological experience of life. Feelings come about only after you thought about something or somebody. If you think of another person as attractive, it will lead to a warm feeling toward that person. People who learn to direct their thinking in positive directions, will contribute to their own happiness. Remember that you produce your own thoughts.

The second principle is *moods,* meaning that the positive or negative content of your thinking fluctuates from moment to moment and day to day. Practice ignoring your low (bad) moods rather than analyzing them, and you will see how quickly they vanish. Developing this skill will contribute substantially to healthy psychological functioning. The third principle is *separate psychological realities.* Because each person thinks in a unique way, everyone lives is a separate psychological reality. Accept the idea that others think differently than you, and you will have much more compassion and fewer quarrels. As a result you will be happier. Also, if you accept the principle of separate realities, you will waste less time attempting to change people. At the same time, others will like you more, thus contributing to your happiness.

The fourth principle of psychological functioning is *feelings.* Combined with emotions, feelings are a built-in feedback mechanism that tell us how we are doing psychologically. If your feelings turn negative suddenly, you know that your thinking is dysfunctional. It is then time to make a mental readjustment. If you feel discontented, for example, it is necessary to clear the head and start thinking positively. As a consequence, you will experience contentment and happiness. A key point is that the person will maintain a sense of well-being as long as he or she does not focus on personal concerns.

The fifth principle is *the present moment.* Learning to pay attention to the present moment and to your feelings, enables people to live at peak efficiency, without the distraction of negative thinking. Much like the flow experience, the present moment is where people find happiness and inner peace. Carlson advises, "The only way to experience genuine and lasting contentment, satisfaction, and happiness is to learn to live your life in the present moment."[7] (This supports happiness key number 5.)

Now that you have studied attitudes and activities that contribute to happiness, you are invited to do Human Relations Skill-Building Exercise 16-1. It is designed to bring about a state of happiness.

HUMAN RELATIONS SKILL-BUILDING EXERCISE 16-1

Achieving Happiness

The following exercises will help you develop attitudes that contribute mightily to happiness.

1. **Start the day off right.**   Begin each day with five minutes of positive thought and visualization. Commit to this for one week. When and how do you plan to fit this into your schedule?

_____

_____

_____

2. **Make a list of five virtues you believe in.**   Examples would include patience, compassion, and helping the less fortunate.

_____

_____

_____

_____

3. **Each week, for the next five weeks, incorporate a different virtue into your life.**   On a simple index card, write this week's virtue in bold letters, such as "helping the less fortunate." Post the card in a prominent place. After you have completed one incident of helping the less fortunate, describe in about 10 to 25 words, what you did. Also record the date and time.

_____

_____

_____

4. **Look for good things about new acquaintances.**   List three students, customers, or coworkers you have just met. List three *positive* qualities about each.

_____

_____

_____

_____

(Continued)

5. **List the *positive* qualities of fellow students or coworkers you dislike or have trouble working with.** Remember, keep looking for the good.

_____

_____

_____

_____

6. **Think of school assignments, or job task you *dislike*, and write down the *merits* of these tasks.** Identify the benefits they bring you.

_____

_____

_____

_____

7. **Look at problems as opportunities.** What challenges are you now facing? In what way might you view them which would inspire and motivate you?

_____

_____

_____

_____

SOURCE: Adapted from Stu Kamen, "Turn Negatives into Positives," *Pryor Report Success Workshop,* May 1995, pp. 1–2.

A PLANNED APPROACH TO FINDING A RELATIONSHIP

How many people have you heard complain about a poor social life because of circumstances beyond their control? Such complaints take various forms: "The women in this school are all unappreciative," "The men at my school don't really respect women," "There's absolutely nobody to meet at work," or "This is the worst town for meeting people."

Some of the people expressing these attitudes are systematic when it comes to handling business or technology problems. Under those circumstances they use the problem-solving method. But when it comes to their social lives, they rely heavily on fate or chance.

The approach recommended here is to use your problem-solving skills to improve your personal life. Whatever the problem, try to attack it in a

logical, step-by-step manner. We are not ruling out the influence of emotion and feeling in personal life. We are simply stating that personal life is too important to be left to fate alone. With good fortune you might form a relationship with a stranger you meet at a rapid-oil-change-and-lubrication center. Unfortunately, such good fortune is infrequent.

Too many people leave finding a new relationship to chance or to a few relatively ineffective alternatives. Too many unattached adults lament, "Either you go to a bar or you sit at home." In reality, both men and women can find dates in dozens of constructive ways. It is a matter of identifying some of these alternatives and trying out a few that fit your personality and preferences. See Exhibit 16-1 for more details.

An important consideration in searching for a relationship is to recognize when you experiencing **quest fatigue.** It is the feeling of demoralization and disappointment which takes place when all your efforts at finding a date or mate fail.[8] When quest fatigue sets in, give yourself some time off from the search. Enjoy your activities without a partner, and revitalize yourself before resuming the quest.

The steps to take after making contact with someone are not clear-cut. Some people recommend that you have at least two telephone conversations before arranging a meeting. This advice is particularly applicable when you have not seen the person, as when meeting through an ad or introduction service. It is generally recommended that the first date be informal, such as meeting for coffee and dessert, or a glass of wine. According to Susan Page, who runs singles workshops, during the first date screen for compatibility of what you are looking for in a relationship. Initial physical attraction is

EXHIBIT 16-1

IN SEARCH OF A DATE?

Every relationship begins with one person meeting another. In order to find one good relationship, you may need to date more than a dozen people. Next is a sampling of potentially effective methods for making a social contact.

Highly Recommended

1. Participate in an activity that you do well and enjoy. For example, if you are a good frisbee player, use frisbee playing as a vehicle for meeting people.

2. Get involved in your work or another activity not logically related to dating. People of the opposite sex* naturally gravitate toward a busy, serious-minded person. Besides, the workplace has now become the number one, natural meeting place for singles.

3. Take courses in which the male-female ratio is in your favor, such as automotive technology for women and cooking for men.

4. Ask your friends for introductions and describe the type of person you are trying to meet—but don't be too restrictive.

5. Get involved in a community or political activity in which many single people participate. A good example is to become a political-party worker.

6. For men, join almost any formal singles group such as "Eastside Singles." The membership of these clubs is overwhelmingly female.

7. For women, join a national guard reserve unit. The membership of these units is overwhelmingly male.

8. Take advantage of every social invitation to a party, picnic, breakfast, or brunch. Social occasions are natural meeting places.

9. Place a personal ad in a local newspaper or magazine, stating the qualifications you are seeking in a companion and how you can be reached. Personal ads have achieved such popularity that several national magazines now accept them. Personal ads are frequently integrated with voice mail. (You leave a voice message for the person who placed the ad.) Under many systems, your personal ad consists of a voice message to which people respond.

10. A rapidly growing number of people are meeting through chat rooms on the Internet (*cyberdating*). Chat rooms can be selected according to interests, including movie fans, gays and lesbians, and astrology believers. After exchanging a series of e-mail messages or IMs (instant messages) the two people arrange for an in-person meeting. Many of the people you meet might live in a far-away location. Another problem is that many chat room participants badly misrepresent themselves, and a few have proved to be deranged criminals.

11. Join special-promotion singles groups such as indoor tennis for singles or a singles ski weekend.

(Continued)

At Least Worth a Try

1. While networking for career purposes, also prospect for social companions.

2. Join an introduction (dating) service, particularly one that has an established membership. Introduction services are usually best for those seeking to meet people over age 30.

3. Shop at supermarkets from 11 P.M. to 2 A.M. You will frequently find other single people shopping at that time.

4. Spend a lot of time in laundromats.

5. Strike up a conversation while waiting in line for tickets at the movies or concerts.

6. Congregate, or float around, in large gatherings such as rallies for causes, registration for courses, or orientation programs.

7. Organize a singles party, and require each person invited to bring along an unattached person of the opposite sex—no regular couples allowed.

8. Find valid reasons for visiting other departments at your place of work. Chance meetings at photocopying machines, for example, have allegedly spawned thousands of romances.

*Although these suggestions are primarily geared toward meeting people of the opposite sex, the same principles will generally apply to meeting people and making friends of the same sex.

important, but also look for clues to the type of relationship the person is seeking. Talk about your own general opinions and desires in a relationship and see how your prospective relationship responds.[9]

WHY PEOPLE ARE ATTRACTED TO ONE ANOTHER

As part of enriching social life, it is helpful to understand why people are attracted to each other. Understanding these forces may help in choosing a compatible person for a long-term relationship. Three different psychological explanations of why people develop a strong attraction to each other are balance theory, exchange theory, and the need for intimacy. Attraction can also be attributed to chemical or hormonal reasons. All four of these explanations, to be described next, can apply in a given situation.

BALANCE THEORY OF ATTRACTION

According to **balance theory,** people prefer relationships that are consistent, or balanced. If we are very similar to another person, it makes sense (it is consistent or balanced) to like that person. We are also attracted to similar people because they reinforce our opinions and values. It is usually reassuring and rewarding to discover that another person agrees with you or has similar values.[10]

Balance theory explains why we are eager to stay in a relationship with some people, but it does not explain why opposites often attract each other. People sometimes get along best with those who possess complementary characteristics. A talkative and domineering person may prefer a partner who enjoys listening. The explanation is that a dominant person needs someone to dominate and therefore might be favorably disposed toward submissive people.

Social Exchange Theory of Attraction

A long-standing explanation of why two people become a couple is **social exchange theory,** the idea that human relationships are based mainly on self-interest. This research shows that people measure their social, physical, and other assets against a potential partner's. The closer the match, the more likely they are to develop a long-term relationship.

Exchange theory has been able to predict the permanence of a relationship based on the way each partner feels he or she stacks up against the other. One study of 537 dating men and women found that partners who thought they were getting far more in exchange for what they were giving felt guilty and insecure. In comparison, those who believed they gave more than they got were angry.

The giving was mostly psychological. It included such things as being more physically attractive than the partner, kinder, or more flexible. The greater the imbalance, the more likely the couple was to split up; the more equitable the partners believed the exchange to be, the more likely they were to remain partners. One explanation of these findings is that the feeling of being taken advantage of corrodes a relationship. It is also disturbing to feel that you are taking advantage of your partner.[11]

Need for Intimacy

For some, the balance and exchange theories of mutual attraction are too mechanical and logical. Psychologist David McClelland proposes instead that love is an experience seated in the nonrational part of the brain (the right side). People who believe that they are in love have a strong **need for intimacy.** This craving for intimacy is revealed in the thoughts of people in love who are asked to make up stories about fictitious situations. Their stories reveal a preoccupation with harmony, responsibility, and commitment, and a preference for a relationship that includes warmth and intimacy.

McClelland and his associates say that these themes show up repeatedly in many guises in the stories told by people who say they are in love. The same stories are told by people in situations where love feelings run high, such as just having seen a romantic movie.[12]

The concept of love is part of the need for intimacy, as well as a key part of understanding personal relationships. Every reader has an idea of what love means to him or her. Harry Stack Sullivan, the famous psychiatrist, developed a particularly useful description of love, as follows:

> When the satisfaction or the security of another person becomes as significant to one as is one's own satisfaction or security, then the state of love exists. So far as I know, under no other circumstance is a state of love present, regardless of the popular usage of the word.

A BIOCHEMICAL EXPLANATION OF ATTRACTIVENESS

Another explanation of why certain people are attracted to one another is based on chemicals and specifically hormones. According to this theory, our hormones direct us to sense or screen potential mates. After the initial biochemical attraction, our conscious, psychological preferences—like does he enjoy action movies and golfing—come into play. The interests and lifestyle preferences of the potential mate carry more weight after the initial attraction. While the biochemical factors are at work, the brain is processing the external clues people use to measure sex appeal. Among these personality factors are appearance, clothing, makeup, scent, body language, and voice.[13]

A more specific explanation of attraction between people is based on the presence of pheromones. These are chemical substances released by a person (or animal) to influence the behavior of another member of the same species. A person who emits high doses of pheromones will therefore attract more partners. Conversely, we are physically attracted to people with high doses of pheromones. After the initial physical attraction, however, other more rational factors (e.g., Is this person employed?) enter into the picture. Several companies sell cologne that allegedly contains pheromones, thus making it easier for your to attract Prince or Princess Charming. Because these "attractant" substances are considered cosmetics, and not drugs, they are free from government regulation. Buyer beware.

THE IMPORTANCE OF CHOOSING A PARTNER CAREFULLY

Having a plan for meeting a partner and understanding why people are attracted to each other should be regarded as helpful information for making the right choice. A principal problem in many poor relationships is that the couple used faulty judgment in choosing each other. Of course, it is difficult to be objective when choosing a partner. Your needs at the time may cloud your judgment. Many people have made drastic mistakes in choosing a spouse because they were lonely and depressed when they met the person they married. Being on the rebound from a relationship that went bad makes you particularly vulnerable.

The problem of mate selection is indeed complicated. Do you marry for love, companionship, infatuation, or all three? It has been pointed out that the success rate of the arranged marriages still practiced in a few countries is about as good as that of nonarranged marriages. Since most people have only a limited amount of time to invest in finding the ideal mate, they are content to marry a good fit.

An in-depth study of 300 happy marriages provides a practical clue about mate selection. The most frequently mentioned reason for an enduring and happy marriage was having a generally positive attitude toward each other.[14] If you view your partner as your best friend and like him or her "as a person," you will probably be happy together. As obvious as it sounds, choose only a life partner whom you genuinely like. Some people deviate from this guideline by placing too much emphasis on infatuation.

A unique approach to mate selection would be to ask your family and close friends what they thought of your potential for happiness with your prospective mate. Recent research supports the wisdom of this approach. Tara K. McDonald and Michael Ross studied 74 college students who had been dating approximately six months. The couples were asked how serious they thought they were, how satisfied they were in the relationship, and how in love they were. The researchers also asked the couples' roommates and parents the same questions.

Follow-ups were conducted at 6 months and 12 months to see which couples were still together, and who made the most accurate predictions. The couples themselves were much more optimistic about the prospects for the relationship. Parents were more accurate than the couples in predicting the length of the relationship. The roommates, however, made the most accurate predictions.[15]

The message here is to recognize that when you are contemplating choosing a life partner, you are facing one of life's major decisions. Put all of your creative resources into making a sound decision.

 WORKING OUT ISSUES WITHIN RELATIONSHIPS

People emotionally involved with each other often find themselves in conflict over a variety of issues, especially when they are emotionally dependent upon each other. Without conflict, relationships would be artificial. A study on male-female conflict was conducted among 600 people involved for different periods of time in a variety of relationships such as dating and marriage.[16]

The study found that both men and women were deeply upset by unfaithfulness and physical or verbal abuse. However, distinct differences were found between men and women in other behaviors that disturbed them. Sexual activity was one major area of difference. Women complained men were too sexually aggressive, while men complained that women too often declined sexual activity. A summary of the major areas of male-female conflict found in the study is presented in Exhibit 16-2.

Human relations specialists have formulated some ground rules for resolving the types of conflicts between partners listed in Exhibit 16-2.[17] These rules supplement the techniques for conflict resolution presented in Chapter 9.

EXHIBIT 16-2

COMMON CONFLICTS BETWEEN MEN AND WOMEN

Men Dislike Women Who Are:	*Women Dislike Men Who Are:*
Unfaithful	Sexually aggressive
Abusive	Unfaithful
Self-centered	Abusive
Condescending	Condescending
Sexually withholding	Emotionally constricted
Neglectful	Insulting about their appearance
Moody	Open admirers of another woman's appearance
Self-absorbed with appearance	Inconsiderate
Big spenders on clothes	Do not help much cleaning up the home
Overly concerned about how their face and hair look	

SOURCE: Table prepared from data in David M. Buss, "Conflict Between the Sexes: Strategic Interference and the Evocation of Anger and Upset," *Journal of Personality and Social Psychology,* May 1989, pp. 735–47.

1. *Listen carefully and give feedback.* Many conflicts intensify because the people involved never stop to listen carefully to what the other side is trying to say. After listening to your partner's point of view, express your feelings about the issue. Expressing your feelings leads to more understanding than expressing your judgments. It is preferable to say, "I feel left out when you visit your mother" than to say "You're insensitive to my needs. Look at the way you visit your mother all the time."

To help improve understanding, provide mutual feedback. Although you may disagree with your partner, communicate your understanding: "From your point of view it's frivolous of me to spend so much money on bowling. You would prefer that I invest money in home improvements."

2. *Define the real problem.* What your partner or you grumble about at first may not be the real issue in the conflict. It will require mutual understanding combined with careful listening and sympathy to uncover the real problem. A man might be verbally attacking a woman's dress when he really means that she has gained more weight than he would like. Or a woman might verbally attack a man's beer drinking when her real complaint is that he should be out in the yard raking leaves instead of sitting inside playing video games.

3. *Avoid opening old wounds.* When two people who are emotionally involved become embroiled in a conflict, there is a natural tendency to bring old wounds into the argument. The two of you might be in conflict over finances, and one of you might say, "And I remember the weekend you were in Boston. You never called me." An effective response here would be, "I'm sorry I did not take the time to telephone you, but it doesn't have anything to do with our problem today. Let's talk about the Boston problem later."

4. *Don't hit below the belt.* The expression "below the belt" refers to something that is unfair. Some issues are just plain unfair to bring up in a marital dispute. When you are intimate with another person, you are bound to know one or two vulnerable areas. Here are two below-the-belt comments:

> "You're lucky I married you. What other woman would have married a man who was so much of a loser that he had to declare bankruptcy."

> "Don't complain so much about being mistreated. Remember, when I married you, you were down on your luck and had no place to live."

Is anyone really as cruel as the preceding quotes would suggest? Yes, in the heat of a tiff between partners, many cruel, harsh things are said. If two people want to live harmoniously after the conflict, they should avoid below-the-belt comments.

5. *Be prepared to compromise.* For many issues compromise is possible. The compromise you reach should represent a willingness to meet the other person halfway, not just a temporary concession. On some issues the only compromise can be letting the other person have his or her way now, and waiting to have your turn later. Among such issues that cannot be split down the middle are whether to have children, whether to live in an apartment or a house, whether to go to Miami or London for a vacation, or whether to run a kosher or nonkosher household. Several of these issues should be settled before marriage or living together, since no real compromise on the basic issue is possible in these instances.

6. *Minimize an accusatory tone.* You lessen the accusatory tone when you make "I" statements instead of "you" statements. The door to dialogue is opened when you make a statement such as, "I felt really disappointed when you did not call me to ask about how my promotion interview went." You shut off dialogue when you say, "You don't care about my happiness. You didn't even call to ask about how my promotion interview went."

7. *Be willing to go the extra mile.* To keep a relationship vibrant, there are times when one side will have to make a major concession to the other. If your relationship is solid, in the long run these extra miles will balance out. A middle-aged woman suggested to her spouse that this year, instead of taking their annual vacation trip, the money be invested in her cosmetic surgery. At first the husband bristled, thinking that she was being too self-centered. After thinking through the problem, the man realized that she had a valid point. He agreed to the surgery and the result was an added closeness between the couple. Such closeness between partners after resolving conflict is a frequent occurrence.

8. *Be alert to gender differences in communication style.* As described in Chapter 6, men and women tend to have differences in communication style. One example is that men are more likely to focus on objects and things, and thus will gloss over feelings. In contrast, women are more likely to focus on interpersonal relationships and are eager to communicate feelings. If a couple does face these forms of stereotyped behavior, it is helpful not to devalue the other side for simply acting in a gender-appropriate way. In dealing with the differences just described, the man should not be angry with the woman for focusing too much on feelings and wanting open communication. And the woman should not be angry with the man for being somewhat tightlipped about feelings. Instead, the partners should accept these gender differences and not expect major changes in communication style.

MEETING THE CHALLENGES OF BEING A TWO-INCOME COUPLE

The number of couples in which both partners have full-time jobs has now reached 80 percent, as estimated by the U.S. Bureau of Labor Statistics. Two critical factors influencing this steady growth are women's career aspirations and the need for two incomes to meet living expenses. It is a challenge to run a two-income household in a way that will enhance the couple's personal life. In Chapter 7 we presented information about using organizational support systems to help reduce work-family conflicts. Following are suggestions that couples themselves can implement to increase the chances of a two-income household running more smoothly.

1. *Establish priorities and manage time carefully.* A major contributor to the success of a dual-career relationship is careful time management. Each partner must establish priorities, such as ranking quality time together ahead of adding a community activity to the schedule. Or both partners might inform their employer of a certain date they would be taking as a vacation day to celebrate their wedding anniversary.

2. *Deal with feelings of competitiveness.* Feelings of competitiveness between husband and wife about each other's career often exist even when both have a modern outlook. Competitive feelings are all the more likely to surface when both parties are engaged in approximately the same kind of work. One man became infuriated with his wife when she was offered a promotion before he was. They had both entered the same big company at the same time in almost identical jobs. In contrast, the working couple with traditional views is unlikely to have a problem when the husband outdistances his wife in career advancement.

The familiar remedy of discussing problems before they get out of hand is offered again here. One partner might confess to the other, "Everybody is making such a fuss over you since you won that suggestion award. It makes me feel somewhat left out and unimportant." A sympathetic spouse might reply, "I can understand your feelings. But don't take all this fuss too seriously. It doesn't take away from my feelings for you. Besides, two months from now maybe people will be making a fuss over you for something."

3. *Share big decisions equally.*   A distinguishing characteristic of today's two-income families is that both partners share equally in making important decisions about the domestic side of life. Under such an arrangement, neither has exclusive decision-making prerogatives in any particular area. He may make a decision without consulting her over some minor matter (such as the selection of a plant for the living room). She may make the decision the next time a plant is to be selected for inside the house. But on major decisions—such as relocating to another town, starting a family, or investing in the stock market or real estate—husband and wife collaborate.

4. *Divide the household tasks equitably.*   Many women who work outside the home rightfully complain that they are responsible for too much of the housework and household errands. As indicated by the research of Francine Deutsch, no more 20 percent of dual-income couples share domestic work equally, with women doing most of the work. In her study of married couples with infants, the men doing the most housework were typically those whose wives earned comparable incomes. Also, the wives requested such involvement in the housework.[18]

When household chores are divided unequally, conflict in the home is probable. The recommended solution is for the working couple to divide household tasks in some equitable manner. Equity could mean that tasks are divided according to preference or the amount of effort required. In one family, the husband might enjoy food shopping while the wife enjoys cleaning. Assignments could be made accordingly. Each couple should negotiate for themselves what constitutes an equitable division of household tasks. To participate equitable in household chores and child-rearing, one or both partners might have to reduce the amount of time invested in the career. (Do you recall the term *downshifting?*)

5. *Take turns being inconvenienced.*   In a very traditional family, the woman assumes the responsibility for managing inconvenient household tasks even if she, too, has a job outside the home. The underlying assumption may be that her work is less important than his work. For more modern couples, a more equitable solution is to take turns being inconvenienced. If Sue has to go to work late one day to be around for the plumber, Ted can go to work late when the dog has to be taken to the veterinarian. A working couple with children will frequently have to miss work because of a child's illness or accident, parent-teacher conferences, or school plays.

6. *Develop adequate systems for child care.*   Any working couple with a young child or children will attest to the challenge of adequately balancing work and child demands. Imagine this scenario: Your spouse has already left for work, and you discover that your four-year-old child has a fever of 102°. The child-care center will not accept a sick child, nor will your neighbor who helps out occasionally. She fears contaminating her children. The logical solution is to stay home from work, but you have a crucial work meeting scheduled for 11 A.M.

One solution to dilemmas of this nature, and less serious problems, is to have a diverse support system. Make arrangements with at least three people, including relatives, who could help you out in an emergency.

Retired people, for example, often welcome the challenge of helping out in an emergency.

7. *Share parenting roles.* A dual-career family functions best when both parents take an active interest in child-rearing. Mother and father have to regard spending extensive amounts of time with their child or children as an appropriate activity for their sex. A survey of 330 men and women who were part of a dual-career couple suggests that both partners are heavily involved in child-rearing. Nevertheless, women seem to be more concerned that they are not spending enough quality time with their children.[19]

8. *Decide who pays for what.* Unfortunately, the problem of negotiating who pays for what arises for many two-income families. Many couples find that the additional expenses of a working couple prevent them from getting ahead financially. Child-care expenses are often involved; restaurant meals become more frequent; and a second car is usually a necessity outside of large metropolitan areas.

Thirty couples were surveyed to find out which method of sharing expenses works best. The "big pool" arrangement led to the most satisfaction. Under this arrangement, the couple pools its money into a joint account for household expenses and savings. Each partner receives personal spending money out of the common pot, or from additional income such as second jobs. Most of the satisfied couples used a joint account with one partner taking responsibility for bill paying. Another approach is for the couples to maintain separate accounts, and divide bills based on how much each partner earns. A third approach is for one partner to hand over a paycheck to the other, who has complete charge of bill-paying, budgeting, savings, and investments. The person who hands over the paycheck would need to trust his or her partner completely.[20]

KEEPING YOUR RELATIONSHIP VIBRANT

One of the major challenges in personal life is to keep a relationship with a partner vibrant. For many people, relationships that begin with enthusiasm, rapport, and compatibility end in a dull routine and splitting up. Human Relations Self-Assessment Exercise 16-1 pinpoints some of the symptoms of a relationship gone bad. Here we describe major factors in achieving a mutually rewarding long-term relationship.

KEEP ROMANTIC LOVE IN PROPER PERSPECTIVE

A speaker told an audience that you can tell you are infatuated with your partner if your heart begins pounding at a chance meeting with him or her. An 80-year-old in the audience responded, "I know just what you mean. The Mrs. and I have been married for 55 years, and that's exactly how I feel whenever I run into her downtown." This happy husband is an exception; although infatuation or romantic love is vital in getting a rela-

HUMAN RELATIONS SELF-ASSESSMENT EXERCISE 16-2

Early Warning Signs of a Relationship in Trouble

You know your relationship is in trouble, and in need of revitalization, when several or more of the indicators below are present. The term "partner" refers to a spouse, boyfriend, girlfriend, or significant other.

- You observe that you partner has terrible table manners.

- You perceive that your partner is not as attractive or cute as you thought previously.

- The sound your partner makes with his or her teeth annoys you.

- Your conversation is confined to routine matters such as "Did you put gas in the car?" or "Why are you 15 minutes late?"

- A significant change in routine takes place, such as the partner calling every other day instead of at least once a day.

- You rarely plan ahead for social occasions, such as parties, dinner, or movies, but decide to go out at the last moment—such as making plans for Saturday night at 4 P.M. that day.

- You spend progressively less time together.

- You nitpick each other frequently, and all your partner's quirks begin to bother you.

- You touch each other less and less, including holding hands while walking or driving the car.

- Your fights are more frequent and last longer.

- Small tokens of affection, such as sending love notes, almost disappear.

- You rarely mention your partner favorably to a third party.

- You notice frequent criticisms including back-handed compliments such as, "You look nice today for a person with so little taste in clothing."

- Jumping into binding commitments with little planning, such as having a baby, moving, or buying a house. (Quite often partners think that such major joint activities will save a sinking relationship.)

- You look for an opportunity to spend time with your friends rather than with your partner.

- You rarely look forward to spending time alone with your partner.

- Neither partner ever says, "I love you" any longer.

SOURCE: Several of the signs were collected from relationship experts by Elaine Gross, "Love On the Edge," Gannett News Service Story, March 12, 1996, and from "The Relationship Quiz" used by Worldwide Marriage Encounter (undated).

tionship started, it usually cools down within several years. When infatuation declines, instead of being disappointed, the couple should realize that the relationship has grown more mature and lasting.

A relationship counselor observes that as full of rapture and delight as the first phase of a relationship is, it is essentially a trick of nature designed to bring us together. Nature knows that without the illusion of perfection, we might not choose each other. After the emotional bond is secure, nature lifts the veil.[21] To avoid discouragement and disillusionment, it is important to keep romantic love in proper perspective. It helps launch a relationship, but does not have to be kept at its initial high intensity for a relationship to endure. However, the spark should not be *extinguished*.

STRIVE FOR INTIMACY, PASSION, AND COMMITMENT

True love requires intimacy, passion, and commitment, according to psychologist Robert Sternberg.[22] While a relationship can manage to survive with only one or two of these qualities, the fullest love requires all three. Passion is the quickest to develop, and the quickest to fade. Intimacy, a feeling of emotional closeness, develops more slowly. One requirement for intimacy is that the person has established his or her own identity. Commitment develops most slowly. However, in the current era, commitment is highly sought after by both men and women. In addition, a recent value shift is that more men strive for intimacy now than was previously the case. Monogamy is becoming the rule rather than the exception for an increasing number of couples of all ages—to which sex psychologist Ruth Westheimer says, "To think that being with one partner is now in fashion again is music to my ears."[23]

Intimacy between partners becomes more important as successful relationships mature. Both partners find it increasingly important to understand each others' wants and needs, to listen to and support each other, and to share values. Although passion peaks in the early phases of a relationship, it still matters to a long-term successful relationship. Happily married people usually regard their mates as physically attractive.

While a strong commitment is essential to a long-term relationship, it is not sufficient. Without passion and intimacy, commitment tends to be hollow.

HOLD COMMUNICATION SESSIONS

Good communication is vital for creating and maintaining a loving relationship. Therefore, one way to keep a relationship alive is to hold formal communication sessions in which you tell each other almost anything on your mind. The topics can be both positive and negative. A man may want to tell his partner of something she did that he appreciated very much. Or a woman may want to talk about the way her partner offended her in public. Or a couple may want to discuss concerns about finances, a child, in-law relations, or anything else.

One of many reasons that communication sessions are important is that many couples have different perceptions about what is good and bad in their relationship. The communication sessions help clear up misperceptions. A study of 119 couples conducted by James Deal revealed that partners with more similar perceptions of their marriage and family life were more satisfied with their relationship.[24]

A vital aspect of these sessions is that both facts and feelings are expressed. The statement "I am really afraid we are drifting apart" communicates much more than "You and I haven't been talking too much lately." The role play at the end of this chapter explores the type of communication that can keep a relationship thriving.

Communication sessions are also important because they can sometimes revive a failing relationship. This is true because communication breakdowns often lead to failed relationships. Typically, in the early stages of a relationship, the couple is keenly attuned to each other's thoughts and feelings. The partners look for small verbal and nonverbal signals of contentment and discontent in each other.

After the relationship seems secure, couples often replace the intense monitoring of the early stages with a nonrevealing style of communication. For example, the man and woman may mechanically say to each other, "How was your day?" or "Love ya." This shorthand style of communication obstructs the sending and receiving of messages that could indicate the relationship is in trouble. Introducing communication sessions can make it possible for the couple to deal with subtle problems in the relationship.

Brief communication sessions are particularly needed when a couple travels together because so many relationships take a turn for the worse while traveling. Many couples, for example, are surprised by the conflict that emerges during their honeymoon. One of the problems is that such continuous contact with another person requires considerable adjustment. While driving in a car or seated next to each other in an airplane for a long period of time, the other person's eccentricities become more evident. Have you ever heard of a couple fighting over the *correct way* to fold a road map?

Judi Willard, a psychotherapist, notes that on a trip, couples may bring along emotional baggage they are not even aware of. "The baggage could be unresolved feelings about family or siblings. And while issues may stay hidden at home where there are distractions, it's difficult to camouflage them when you and your companion are traveling together."[25] Should bickering begin, it can be effective to hold a brief communication session over such an issue as why the two differ so strongly about whether they should stay at a hotel versus a motel.

Strive for Novelty in Your Relationship

An unfortunate aspect of many relationships is that they drift toward a routine. A married couple might go to the same place for vacation, meeting the same family and friends for years on end. A man dating a woman might call her every night at the same time. Or a couple's sex life may turn into a routine. Many people have suggested that you try pleasant surprises to keep your relationship vibrant and fun. Make up a list of your own, but here are a few ideas to jog your thinking:

Ask your mate out for dinner on a *Monday* evening.

Write your partner a poem instead of sending a commercial greeting card.

Take up a new activity together in which you are both beginners (such as country dancing or scuba diving) and learn with each other.

MAINTAIN A NONPOSSESSIVE RELATIONSHIP

A **nonpossessive relationship** is one in which both partners maintain separate identities and strive for personal fulfillment, yet are still committed to each other. Such a relationship is based on interdependent love—love involving commitment with self-expression and personal growth.[26] A nonpossessive relationship does not mean that the partners have sexual relationships with other people.

A nonpossessive relationship is helpful because some people find the traditional form of marriage stifling. For example, many married people feel compelled to give up a hobby or interest because the partner does not share the interest. In a nonpossessive relationship, the couple can take many separate paths and pursue different interests and have friends of their own. Unfortunately, if couples pursue nonpossessive relationships too far, they wind up drifting away from each other. The reason is that happy partners spend considerable time with each other enjoying shared activities. Each couple must find the right balance between maintaining separate identities yet spending sufficient time together to remain close.

MAINTAIN A DIFFERENTIATION OF SELF

Closely related to having a nonpossessive relationship is for each partner to achieve a reasonable degree of autonomy by maintaining a **differentiation of self.** The term refers to an individual who is secure and not desperate for signals of approval and affection from others. If you have a differentiation of self, you are not so subject to social pressures from your partner and other family members. Another key characteristic of a person with high differentiation of the self is that he or she is not highly judgmental and not obsessed with his or her place in the family hierarchy.[27] As a consequence, the person is not so demanding and can appreciate the reality that he or she does not dominate the partner's life. The person with self-differentiation can comfortably say, "I'm happy that you going out to dinner with your coworkers. I'll use that time this evening for learning more about digital photography."

This sense of autonomy and laid-back nature makes the person easier to live with, thus avoiding some of the conflict over affection and control that take place in many relationships. In turn, the relationship has a chance to remain more vibrant. A mildly detached person is easier to live with; however, the same caution about nonpossessive relationships is in order. If your differentiation of self and detachment are too pronounced, you will not participate in the closeness required of a vibrant relationship.

To further develop your sensitivity to keeping a relationship vibrant, do Human Relations Skill-Building Exercise 16-2.

 # SUMMARY

A satisfying and rewarding personal life can help a person absorb a career setback, and also contributes to a satisfying and rewarding career. Planning for happiness is somewhat under a person's control. A practical way of understanding happiness is that it is a byproduct of having the spheres of life working in harmony and synchrony. For most people these spheres would be: work and career; interpersonal life, including romance; physical and mental health; financial health; interests and pastimes; and spiritual life or belief system.

Contributors or keys to happiness include the following: (1) giving priority to happiness, (2) love and friendship, (3) self-esteem, (4) working hard at things enjoyed, (5) appreciation of the joys of day-to-day living, (6) fairness, kindness, helpfulness, and trust, (7) recreational fun, (8) coping with

---

HUMAN RELATIONS SKILL-BUILDING EXERCISE 16-2

Keeping Your Relationship Vibrant

The role-playing exercise described here will help you experience the type of communication and interaction required for keeping a relationship vibrant. As with any other role play, visualize yourself in the role briefly described. Try to develop the feel and the flavor of the person depicted.

The man in this relationship is becoming concerned that his wife does not enthusiastically participate in activities involving his family. He prefers that he and his wife spend their Sunday afternoons with his parents and other relatives. He thinks they are all loads of fun and cannot imagine why his wife is beginning to drag her heels about spending time with them. Twice in the last month she has come up with excuses for not going along with him to visit his folks on Sunday.

The woman in this relationship still loves her husband but thinks his preference for Sunday afternoons with his folks is unreasonable. She thinks that it is time for her to pursue her own interests on Sunday afternoons. She plans to confront her husband about the situation this evening.

Two people act out this role play for about 15 to 20 minutes. Other members of the class can act as observers. Among the observation points will be: (1) How well did the couple get to the key issues? (2) How much feeling was expressed? (3) Do they appear headed toward a resolution of this problem?

grief, disappointment, setbacks, and stress, (9) living with what you cannot change, (10) energizing yourself through physical fitness and (11) developing a philosophy or system of belief.

According to Richard Carlson, the best way to achieve inner serenity (or happiness) is to follow the five principles of psychological functioning. First is thinking which brings about feelings. Second is moods, including the idea that you can ignore bad moods. Third is separate psychological realities, meaning that each person thinks in a unique way. Fourth is feelings, which can be turned from negative to positive. Fifth is the present moment, which is where people find happiness and inner peace.

A good social life begins with finding people you want to date. Such an important activity in life should not be left to chance or fate alone. Instead, use a planned approach that includes exploring many sensible alternatives. However, when you experience quest fatigue, back off and enjoy activities without a partner.

Understanding why people are attracted to one another helps in choosing a compatible partner. The balance theory of attraction contends that people prefer relationships that are consistent or balanced, and therefore they are comfortable with people similar to themselves. According to social exchange theory, people seek relationships in which there is an even match of personal assets. A third explanation is that people are attracted to each other because their need for intimacy prompts then to fall in love. A fourth explanation of attraction is based on biochemistry, suggesting that our hormones direct us to sense or screen potential mates. After the initial biochemical attraction, our conscious, psychological preferences come into play.

Whatever the basis for attraction, a partner must be chosen carefully to help prevent a split based on a poor fit. One suggestion would be to ask your family and close friends what they thought of your potential for happiness with your prospective mate.

To keep an intimate relationship healthy, you should resolve issues as they arise. Suggestions for accomplishing this include: Listen carefully and give feedback; define the real problem; avoid opening old wounds; don't hit below the belt; be prepared to compromise; minimize an accusatory tone; be willing to go the extra mile; and be alert to gender differences in communication.

Two-income couples are subject to unique pressures. To sustain a good relationship, a two-income (or dual-career) couple should consider these approaches: (1) Establish priorities and manage time carefully; (2) deal with feelings of competitiveness; (3) share big decisions equally, (4) divide the household tasks equitably; (5) take turns being inconvenienced; (6) develop adequate systems for child care; (7) share parenting roles; and (8) decide who pays for what.

Keeping a relationship vibrant is a major challenge. Among the approaches proposed to meet this goal are: (1) Keep romantic love in perspective; (2) strive for intimacy, passion, and commitment; (3) hold communication sessions, including while traveling; (4) strive for novelty in your relationship; (5) maintain a nonpossessive relationship and (6) maintain a differentiation of self.

Questions and Activities

1. After reading the information in this chapter, do you believe that a person can learn how to be happy?

2. What are some of the skills involved in being happy?

3. How do your "spheres of life" compare with those in Figure 16-1?

4. Identify several positive, and at least one negative, consequence of being happy.

5. In this chapter you were told that the office has become the most frequent place for meeting a mate. In Chapter 9 you were cautioned about the hazards of an office romance. How do you integrate these two opinions?

6. What is your reaction to the practice of having a third party conduct a background investigation of a prospective mate? Also, should the prospective mate be informed of the investigation after it is completed?

7. How well do the balance and exchange theories of attraction explain the formation of friendships that do not involve romance?

8. What information in the previous 15 chapters would be particularly helpful in keeping a relationship vibrant?

9. When one person in a dual-income family loses a job, should that person be responsible for all the household chores? Explain your reasoning.

10. Find a couple that has been together for 30 years or more. Find out what they perceive to be the secret of their successful relationship. Share your findings with class members.

REFERENCES

[1]Diane Swanbrow, "The Paradox of Happiness," *Psychology Today,* July/August 1989, p. 38.

[2]The major sources of information for this list are: Mihaly Csikzentmihalyi, "Finding Flow," *Psychology Today,* July/August 1997, pp. 46–48, 70–71; Swanbrow, "The Paradox of Happiness"; Martin Seligman, *What You Can Change and What You Can't* (New York: Knopf, 1994); Maury M. Breecher, "C'mon Smile!" *Los Angeles Times,* October 3, 1982.

[3]David Meyers, *The Pursuit of Happiness* (New York: Morrow, 1997).

[4]Based on research of Tim Kasser, department of psychology, the University of Rochester, 1994.

[5]Martin Seligman, "Don't Diet, Be Happy," *USA Weekend,* February 4–6, 1994, p. 12.

A HUMAN RELATIONS CASE PROBLEM

Can this Relationship Be Saved?

Lenny Trent and Tammy McGuire were both telemarketers at the Northland Group, a company that provides marketing services and marketing research for other companies. Lenny began employment with the company six months before Tammy. Both were assigned to a one-year project of selling new accounts for the world's fourth largest long-distance telephone company. Given that Lenny had a six-month start on Tammy, he was asked to assist in her training. Lenny's involvement in the training consisted of one day of coaching Tammy on techniques for getting prospects interested in switching long-distance service.

The moment Lenny first shook hands with Tammy to greet her as a new employee, he could feel a touch of electricity surge through his body. At the same time, Tammy thought to herself, "Here's the man I've been looking for." By the end of the first hour of training, Lenny was thinking about when he might be able to ask Tammy out socially. He thought to himself, "I had better wait a week. It's unprofessional to hit on somebody who I'm training."

Three days later, Lenny ran into Tammy at the bagel and sandwich shop across the street from the office. Feeling nervous and eager at the same time, Lenny said, "Tammy, after you've picked up your order, could we walk back to the office together? I have something I want to ask you."

"That would be very nice," replied Tammy.

During their walk back to the office, Lenny extended a dinner invitation to Tammy for the upcoming Saturday night. Such was the beginning of an intense, fun-filled relationship. For six months, Lenny and Tammy saw each other about five times per week. They went to restaurants, movies, concerts, and the theater, and cooked dinner at each other's apartments. Sundays were often spent biking, picnicking, and watching television or reading the newspaper together during the evening. The couple also spent a week-long vacation together as the guest of Tammy's parents at their summer cottage.

After returning home from the cottage on a Sunday night, they said goodnight and returned to their respective apartments. Lenny was assigned to a branch office on Monday, so the two did not see each other at work that day. Around eight o'clock that night Lenny telephoned Tammy, and asked, "How about my popping by to say hello? It seems strange not being together."

Tammy replied, "Maybe not tonight. We did see each other a lot last week."

"What is that supposed to mean?" said Lenny with an angry tone.

"I simply meant that I am tired, and that maybe a couple of days without seeing each other would do us some good. A little space can sometimes breathe life into a relationship."

"Breathe life into a relationship?" Lenny asked sternly. I thought our relationship had plenty of life. Have it your way." He then hung up the telephone.

The couple passed each other in the office on Tuesday. Tammy said, "Why not give me a call tonight Len? The office isn't such a good place to chat." Lenny did call, and the couple got together at Tammy's apartment. After an hour of routine conversation, Tammy said, "Len, I'd like you to go home now. I have to get an early start tomorrow, and I'm too tired to talk."

(Continued)

"Okay, have it your way," said Lenny as he briskly walked out of Tammy's apartment.

The next morning Tammy wrote Lenny an e-mail message suggesting they have lunch together at the bagel shop where they met. Lenny answered affirmatively, and the couple met for lunch. Both felt awkward and groped for something of substance to talk about. Lenny then said, "Hey, let's go to dinner Saturday and maybe watch a video at my place after we eat." Tammy accepted the invitation.

During dinner, Lenny asked, "What's bugging you Tammy. You act like I'm a stranger? Did I do something wrong?"

"Nothing in particular," replied Tammy, "but I wish you wouldn't talk with food in your mouth."

"And what are your elbows doing on the table? And why is the nail polish chipped on half your fingers, Ms. Perfect?"

Back at Lenny's apartment, Lenny asked if Tammy would like a beer. "No thanks," said Tammy, "I don't need to drink beer to have a good time."

"Maybe it isn't beer, but you do need something to chill out a little. You really have a hostile side that's seeping out of you like soap out of a sponge. Let me start the video."

Lenny popped the video into the VCR, and the couple sat back to look at the television screen. "Hold on," said Tammy, "I'm not going to sit here and watch a R-rated violence-and-sex film with you. I'm not in the mood."

"Oh aren't you the prude? If you had told me you wanted to watch a Walt Disney movie, I would have rented one. That's been typical of you since I've known you. You never tell me in advance if you don't like something. Instead, you just nag latter. It's hard to know what will please you."

"Lenny, you're a wonderful guy, but you have terrible taste in so many things. Sometimes I wonder if we're a good fit culturally."

"I agree with you about terrible taste, especially in women," retorted Lenny.

"You really are in a miserable mood to night. Forget the video, and take me home. Maybe we can talk about our relationship some other time. It's obvious we're both not happy with each other right now."

Questions

1. How well are Lenny and Tammy dealing with the problems in their relationship?

2. What can the couple do to invigorate their relationship?

3. What are the prospects of Lenny and Tammy being happily married to each other?

[6]Richard Carlson, *You Can Be Happy No Matter What: Five Principles Your Therapist Never Told You,* revised edition (Novato, CA: New World Library, 1997).

[7]Ibid, p. 71

[8]Howard Halpern, "Single or Married People Share Same Joys and Problems," syndicated column, November 12, 1988.

[9]Quoted in Gary Soulsman, "Looking for Love in All the Right Places," *The Wilmington News Journal,* syndicated story, May 4, 1991.

[10]Dodge Fernald, *Psychology* (Upper Saddle River, NJ: Prentice Hall, 1997), p. 564.

[11]Daniel Goleman, "Making a Science of Why We Love Isn't Easy," *The New York Times,* syndicated story, July 23, 1986.

[12]Ibid.

[13]Pam Janis, "The Science of Sex," *USA Weekend,* March 29–31, 1996, pp. 16–17; Theresa Crenshaw, *Guide to the Ingredients in Our Sex Soup* (New York: Putnam, 1996).

[14]Jeannette Lauer and Robert Lauer, "Marriages Made to Last," *Psychology Today,* June 1985, p. 24.

[15]"Psychologists Explore Why Relationships Last," *American Psychological Association Monitor,* October 1997, p. 9.

[16]David M. Buss, "Conflict Between the Sexes: Strategic Interference and the Evocation of Anger and Upset," *Journal of Personality and Social Psychology,* May 1989, pp. 735–747.

[17]Ann Ellson, *Human Relations* (Englewood Cliffs, NJ: Prentice Hall, 1973), p. 211; Lori Gordon, *Love Knots* (New York: Dell, 1990); John Gray, *Men Are From Mars, Women Are from Venus* (New York: HarperCollins, 1992).

[18]Research summarized in "Psychologist Francine Deutsch Studies Who Washes the Pants in the Family," www.mtholyoke.edu/offices/comm/csj/960308/deutsch.html

[19]Jack L. Simonetti, Nick Nykodym, and Janet M. Goralske, "Family Ties: A Guide for HR Managers," *Personnel,* January 1998, p. 39.

[20]Gwen Schoen, "Money and Marriage," *The Sacramento Bee,* May 14, 1995. See also, www.sacbee.com/money/timemoney/marriage.html.

[21]Harville Hendrix, "Love and Marriage," *Family Circle,* syndicated story, March 17, 1990.

[22]Robert J. Sternberg, *The Triangle of Love: Intimacy, Passion, and Commitment* (New York: Basic Books, 1988).

[23]Quoted in Elizabeth Mehren, "Love! Intimacy! Passion! New Books Say Even (Gasp!) Married Folks Can Have It All," *Los Angeles Times,* syndicated story, February 5, 1994.

[24]Research reported in "Listen and Improve Relations," *The Pryor Report,* May 1994, p. 12.

[25]Mary Fuller, "A Fork in the Road," Gannett News Service story, September 2, 1997.

[26]Francesca M. Cancian, *Love in America: Gender and Self-Development* (Cambridge, England: Cambridge University Press, 1987).

[27]Peter D. Kramer, *Should You Leave?* (New York: Morrow, 1997).

ADDITIONAL READING

Alper, G. *The Singles Scene: A Psychoanalytic Study of the Breakdown of Intimacy.* San Francisco: International Scholars Publications, 1994.

Atkins, Dale, and Powell, Meris (Eds.). *From the Heart: Men and Women Write Their Private Thoughts About Their Married Lives.* New York: Henry Holt and Company, 1994.

Botting, Douglas and Kate. *Sex Appeal: Who Has It, and How to Get It.* New York: St. Martin's Press, 1996.

Brown, H. Jackson, Jr. *Life's Little Instruction Book.* Nashville, TN: Rutledge Hill Press, 1991.

Csikzentmihalyi, Mihaly. *Finding Flow.* New York: Basic Books/HarperCollins, 1997.

Deep, Sam, and Sussman, Lyle. *Yes, You Can! 1,200 Inspiring Ideas for Work, Home, and Happiness.* Reading, MA: Addison-Wesley, 1996.

Keesling, Barbara. *Talk Sexy to the One You Love.* New York: HarperCollins, 1996.

Magid, Rene Y., with Codkind, Melissa M. *Work and Personal Life: Managing the Issues.* Menlo Park, CA: Crisp Publications, 1995.

Wallerstein, Judith. *The Good Marriage: How and Why Love Lasts.* Boston, MA: Houghton Mifflin, 1995.

GLOSSARY

Achievement need   The need to accomplish something difficult, to win over others.

Action plan   A description of how a person is going to reach a goal.

Active listener   A person who listens intensely, with the goal of empathizing with the speaker.

Addiction   A compulsion to use substances or engage in activities that lead to psychological dependence and withdrawal symptoms when use is discontinued.

Aggressive   Acting in an overbearing, pushy, obnoxious, and sometimes hostile manner.

Anger   A feeling of extreme hostility, indignation, or exasperation.

Assertive   To state clearly what you want or how you feel in a given situation without being abusive, abrasive, or obnoxious.

Assertiveness training (AT)   A self-improvement program that teaches people to express their feelings and act with an appropriate degree of openness and assertiveness.

Backstabbing   An attempt to discredit by underhanded means such as innuendo, accusation, or the like.

Balance theory   An explanation of attraction stating that people prefer relationships that are consistent or balanced.

Behavior   The tangible acts or decisions of people, including both their actions and words.

Behavior modification (mod)   A system of motivating people that emphasizes rewarding them for doing the right things and punishing them for doing the wrong things.

Body image   Your perception of your body.

Brainstorming   A technique by which group members think of multiple solutions to a problem.

Brainwriting (or solo brainstorming)   Arriving at creative ideas by jotting them down yourself.

Budget   A plan for spending money to improve your chances of using your money wisely and not spending more than your net income.

Burnout   A condition of emotional, mental, and physical exhaustion along with cynicism in response to long-term job stressors.

Business etiquette   A special code of behavior required in work settings.

Cannabis   A class of drugs derived from the hemp plant that generally produce a state of mild euphoria.

Career   A series of related job experiences that fit into a meaningful pattern.

Career counselor   A specialist whose professional role is to provide counseling and guidance to individuals about their careers.

Career path   A sequence of positions necessary to achieve a goal.

Career portability   The ability to move from one employer to another when necessary.

Career success   Attaining the twin goals of organizational rewards and personal satisfaction.

Carpal tunnel syndrome   A condition that occurs when repetitive flexing and extension of the wrist causes the tendons to swell, thus trapping and pinching the median nerve.

Chain of command   In an organization, the official statement of who reports to whom.

Charisma   A type of charm and magnetism that inspires others.

Chronological résumé   A job résumé that presents work experience, education, and interests, along with accomplishments, in reverse chronological order.

Cognitive resource theory   An explanation of leadership stating that the major source of the plans, decisions, and strategies that guide the group's actions are the leader's intellectual abilities.

Cognitive restructuring   A way of dealing with conflict in which you mentally convert negative aspects into positive ones by looking for the positive elements in a situation.

Communication   The sending and receiving of messages.

Communication (or information) overload   A condition in which the individual is confronted with so much information to process that he or she becomes overwhelmed and therefore does a poor job of processing information.

Competence   As part of wellness, the presence of both job skills and social skills, including the ability to solve problems and control anger.

Compulsiveness   A tendency to pay excessive attention to detail and to be neat.

Concentrate on one bill at a time   A technique of debt reduction by which you pay off your smallest debt with a variable payment and then concentrate successively on your next smallest debts.

Conflict   A condition that exists when two sets of demands, goals, or motives are incompatible.

Confrontation and problem solving   A method of identifying the true source of conflict and resolving it systematically.

Contrary investing   The principle of buying investments when the demand for them is very low, and selling when the demand is very high.

Core competency   With respect to a person, whatever he or she does best.

Creative-style résumé   A job résumé with a novel format and design.

Creativity   The ability to develop good ideas that can be put into practice.

Debit card   A bank card that instantly transfers money from your bank account to the account of a merchant.

Decision making   Choosing one alternative from the various alternative solutions that can be pursued.

Decoding   The process of the receiver interpreting the message and translating it into meaningful information.

Defensive communication   The tendency to receive messages in such a way that our self-esteem is protected.

Denial   The suppression of information by the person who finds it to be uncomfortable.

Depressant   A drug that slows down vital body processes.

Depression   A widespread emotional disorder in which the person has such difficulties as sadness, changes in appetite, sleeping difficulties, and a decrease in activities, interests, and energy.

Developmental opportunity   A positive way of stating that a person has a weakness (or a need for improvement).

Differentiation of self   An individual who is secure and not desperate for signals of approval and affection from others.

Disarm the opposition   A method of conflict resolution in which you disarm the criticizer by agreeing with a valid criticism directed toward you.

Diversity awareness training (or **Valuing differences training**)   A program that provides an opportunity for employees to develop the skills necessary to deal effectively with each other and with customers in a diverse environment.

Dollar-cost averaging   An investment technique in which you spend the same amount of money to purchase shares in a stock or mutual fund at regular intervals over a long period of time.

Dopamine   A neurotransmitter that is associated with pleasure and elation. (A neurotransmitter is a molecule that transports messages from one neuron in the brain to another over a synapse.)

Downshifter   A worker who chooses shorter hours and less demanding work to allow more time for other activities.

Downsizing (or **rightsizing**)   A method of reducing the number of employees to save money and improve efficiency.

Effectiveness   In relation to leadership, helping group members accomplish their objectives without neglecting satisfaction and morale.

Effectiveness ethic   A focus on the need for excellent work and doing work the best way.

Emotional intelligence   Qualities such as understanding your feelings, empathy for others, and the regulation of emotion to enhance living.

Empathy   Understanding another person's point of view, or placing yourself in another's shoes.

Encoding   The process of organizing ideas into a series of symbols, such as words and gestures, designed to communicate with the receiver.

Ethics   The study of moral obligation or separating right from wrong.

Expectancy theory of motivation   An explanation of motivation stating that people will be motivated if they believe that their efforts will lead to desired outcomes.

External locus of control   A belief that external forces control your fate.

Fear of success   The belief that if you succeed at an important task, you will be asked to take on more responsibility in the future.

Feedback   Information that tells you how well you have performed and helps you make corrections where indicated.

Feeling-type individuals   People who have a need to conform and attempt to adapt to the wishes of others.

Fight-or-flight response   The body's battle against a stressor that helps you deal with emergencies.

Flow experience   Total absorption in your work.

Forced-association technique   The process of individuals or groups solving a problem by making associations between the properties of two objects.

Frustration   A blocking of need or motive satisfaction, or blocking of a need, wish, or desire.

Functional résumé   A job résumé that organizes your skills and accomplishments into the functions or tasks that support the job you are seeking.

Galeta effect Improving your performance through raising your own expectations.

Glass ceiling An invisible but difficult-to-penetrate barrier to promotion based on subtle attitudes and prejudices.

Goal An event, circumstance, object, condition, or purpose for which a person strives. Also, a conscious intention to do something.

Grazing Popular term for eating meals on the run to make use of time ordinarily spent sitting down for meals.

Group norms The unwritten set of expectations for group members—what people ought to do.

Hallucinogens A class of drugs that in small doses produce visual effects similar to hallucinations.

Human relations The art of using systematic knowledge about human behavior to improve personal, job, and career effectiveness.

Information (or **communication**) **overload** A condition in which the individual is confronted with so much information to process that he or she becomes overwhelmed and therefore does a poor job of processing information.

Insight A depth of understanding that requires considerable intuition and common sense.

Internal locus of control A belief that you are the primary cause of events happening to yourself.

Interpersonal Anything relating to the interactions between and among people.

Intrinsic motivation A situation in which a person finds joy, excitement, and intense involvement in the work at hand.

Intuition A method of arriving at a conclusion by a quick judgment or "gut feel."

Intuitive-type individuals People who prefer an overall perspective, or the big picture.

IRA (**individual retirement account**) A supplemental retirement account, fully funded by the individual, that qualifies for certain tax advantages.

Job objective The position you are applying for now or a job you intend to hold in the future.

Kaizen The relentless quest for a better way of working and higher-quality work.

Karoshi The Japanese term for death through overwork.

Lateral move Transferring to a job at the same level and approximate salary as your present one.

Lateral thinking Thought process whereby an individual seeks out many alternative solutions to a problem. Lateral thinking is creative and broad-based, as opposed to *vertical thinking*, which zeros in on a single best solution.

Leadership The process of bringing about positive changes and influencing others to achieve organizational goals.

Leading task An easy, warm-up activity that helps you get started on a project that you might otherwise procrastinate doing.

Lifestyle A person's typical approach to living, including moral attitudes, clothing preferences, and ways of spending money.

Liquid assets Assets that can be converted into cash relatively quickly.

Maslow's need hierarchy A widely accepted theory of motivation emphasizing that people strive to fulfill needs. These needs are arranged in a hierarchy of importance—physiological, safety, belongingness, esteem, and self-actualization. People tend to strive for need satisfaction at one level only after satisfaction has been achieved at the previous one.

Mentor A more experienced person who guides, teaches, and coaches another individual.

Micromanagement The close monitoring of most aspects of group member activities by the manager.

Mirroring   A form of nonverbal communication in which one person subtly imitates another, such as following the other person's breathing pattern.

Motive   An inner drive that moves a person to do something.

Narcotic   A drug that dulls the senses, facilitates sleep, and is addictive with long-term use.

Need   An internal striving or urge to do something. (Or a deficit within an individual that creates a craving for its satisfaction.)

Need for intimacy   An explanation of love centering on the idea that people crave intimacy.

Negative affectivity   A tendency to experience aversive (intensely disliked) emotional states.

Negotiation and bargaining   Conferring with another person to resolve a problem.

Networking   The process of establishing a group of contacts who can help you in your career.

Net worth   The difference between your assets and liabilities.

Neurobiological disorders   A quirk in the chemistry or anatomy of the brain that creates a disability.

Noise   An unwanted interference that can distort or block a message.

Nonassertive   A passive type of behavior in which people let things happen to them without letting their feelings be known.

Nonpossessive relationship   A relationship in which both people maintain separate identities and strive for personal fulfillment.

Nonverbal communication   Sending messages other than by direct use of words, such as in writing and speaking with gestures.

Nonverbal feedback   The signs other than words that indicate whether or not the sender's message has been delivered.

Openness to experience   A positive orientation toward learning.

Organizational culture   The values and beliefs of the firm that guide people's actions.

Paradigm   A model, framework, viewpoint, or perspective.

Paraphrase   In listening, to repeat in your own words what the sender says, feels, and means.

Participative leader   A person in charge who shares power and decision making with the group.

Partnership   In leadership, when the leader and group members are connected in such a way the power between them is approximately balanced.

Peak performance   The mental state necessary for achieving maximum results from minimum effort.

Peer evaluations   A system in which coworkers contribute to an evaluation of a group member's job performance.

Perfectionism   A pattern of behavior in which the individual strives to accomplish almost unattainable standards of flawless work.

Performance standard   A statement of what constitutes acceptable performance.

Personality clash   An antagonistic relationship between two people based on differences in personal attributes, preferences, interests, values, and styles.

Planning   Deciding what needs to be accomplished and the actions needed to make it happen.

Portfolio career   A career in which people use a variety of skills to earn money in several different ways.

Positive mental attitude   A strong belief that things will work in your favor.

Positive reinforcement   Rewarding somebody for doing something right.

Positive self-talk   Saying positive things about yourself to yourself to build self-confidence.

Positive visual imagery   Picturing a positive outcome in your mind.

Private self   The actual person that you may be.

Problem   A gap between what exists and what you want to exist.

Procrastination   Putting off a task for no valid reason.

Productivity   The amount of quality work accomplished in relation to the resources consumed.

Psychological hardiness   Describes an individual who tends to profit from stressful situations instead of developing negative symptoms.

Psychotherapy   A method of overcoming emotional problems through discussion with a mental health professional.

Public self   What the person is communicating about himself or herself, and what others actually perceive about the person.

Pygmalion effect   The mysterious phenomenon that occurs when group members succeed because their leader expects them to (i.e., a group tends to live up to the leader's expectations).

Quest fatigue   The demoralization and disappointment which takes place when all your efforts at finding a date or mate fail.

Realistic goal   One that represents the right amount of challenge for the person pursuing the goal.

REIT (real estate investment trust)   A pooling of many people's money to invest in real estate or mortgages.

Relaxation response   A bodily reaction in which the person experiences a slower respiration and heart rate, lowered blood pressure, and lowered metabolism.

Resilience   The ability to withstand pressure and emerge stronger for it.

Role ambiguity   A condition in which a job holder receives confusing or poorly defined expectations.

Role conflict   The state that occurs when a person has to choose between two competing demands or expectations.

Role confusion   Uncertainty about the role you are carrying out. For example, socializing with your boss may create fuzzy demarcation lines at work.

Role overload   A burdensome workload that can lead to stress.

Role underload   Having too little to do can sometimes create stress similar to having too much to do (role overload).

Schmoozing   Informal socializing on the job.

Self   A person's total being or individuality.

Self-concept   The way a person thinks about himself or herself in an overall sense.

Self-defeating behavior   A behavior pattern in which the person intentionally or unintentionally engages in activities or harbors attitudes that work against his or her best interests.

Self-determining work   Work that allows the person performing the task some choice in initiating and regulating his or her own actions.

Self-discipline   The ability to work systematically and progressively toward a goal until it is achieved.

Self-disclosure   The process of revealing your inner self to others.

Self-efficacy   Confidence in your ability to carry out a specific task in contrast to generalized self-confidence.

Self-esteem   Appreciating self-worth and importance, being accountable for your own behavior, and acting responsibly toward others.

Self-respect   How you think and feel about yourself.

Self-understanding   Knowledge about yourself, particularly with respect to mental and emotional aspects.

Sensation-type individuals   People who prefer routine and order.

Sensitivity   Taking people's needs and feelings into account when dealing with them.

SEP (simplified employee pension)   Retirement plans for individuals who are self-employed or for those who earn part of their income from self-employment.

Sexual harassment   Unwanted sexually oriented behavior in the workplace that results in discomfort and/or interference with the job.

Skill   A learned, specific ability to perform a task competently, such as writing a report.

Skill-benefit statement   A brief explanation of how your skills can benefit the company.

Social exchange theory   The idea that human relationships are based mainly on self-interest; therefore, people measure their social, physical, and other assets against a potential partner's.

Stimulants   A class of drugs that produce feelings of optimism and high energy.

Stress   An internal reaction to any force that threatens to disturb a person's equilibrium.

Stressor   The external or internal force that brings about the stress.

Strong Interest Inventory (SII)   The most widely used instrument for matching a person's interests with careers.

Style   A person's characteristic way of doing things.

Substance dependence   A compulsion to use substances or engage in activities that lead to psychological dependence and withdrawal symptoms when use is discontinued.

Success   Used in this book to mean attaining the twin goals of organizational rewards and personal satisfaction.

Summarization   The act of pulling together, condensing, and thereby clarifying the main points the other person communicates.

Support system   A group of people a person can rely on for encouragement and comfort.

Targeted résumé   A job résumé that focuses on a specific job target or position and presents only information about you that supports the target.

Team leader   A person who facilitates and guides the efforts of a small group which is given some authority to govern itself.

Team player   A person who emphasizes group accomplishment and cooperation rather than individual achievement and not helping others.

Technical competence   In leadership, being skilled in the actual work of the group.

Technostress   A stress reaction caused by an inability to cope with computer technologies in a constructive manner.

Telecommuter   An employee who works at home full-time or part-time, and sends output electronically to a central office.

Telesearch   Obtaining job leads by making unsolicited phone calls to prospective employers.

Thinking-type individuals   People who rely on reason and intellect to deal with problems.

Time leak   Anything you are doing or not doing that allows time to get away from you.

Traditional mental set   A fixed way of thinking about objects and activities.

Troubleshooting   The knack for pinpointing and analyzing snags in work flow as they arise.

Type A Behavior   A demanding, impatient, and overstriving pattern of behavior also characterized by free-floating hostility.

Unsolicited-letter campaign A job search method in which the job seeker sends letters to prospective employers without knowing if a job opening exists.

Vertical thinking An analytical, logical thought process whereby an individual is seeking a single best solution to a problem. Narrower than *lateral thinking* because it results in fewer solutions.

Visualization As a stress-management technique, picturing yourself doing something you would like to do. In general, a method of imagining yourself behaving in a particular way to achieve that behavior.

Wellness A formalized approach to preventive health care.

Win-win The belief that, after conflict has been resolved, both sides should gain something of value.

Workaholism An addiction to work in which not working is an uncomfortable experience.

Work ethic A firm belief in the dignity and value of work.

Work habits A person's characteristic approach to work, including such things as organization, priority setting, and handling of paper work and e-mail.

Worst-case scenario The dreadful alternative in a decision-making situation.

INDEX